Never in Anger

Jean L. Briggs   ***Never in Anger***

Portrait of an Eskimo Family

Harvard University Press, Cambridge, Massachusetts, and London, England

© Copyright 1970 by the President and Fellows of Harvard College
All rights reserved

Sixth Printing, 1976

Library of Congress Catalog Card Number 75-105368

ISBN 0-674-60825-9 (cloth)
ISBN 0-674-60828-3 (paper)

Certain portions of the Introduction and Chapters I,
II, and VI of this book appear in *Women in the Field;
Anthropological Experiences*, edited by Peggy Golde, pp.
19–44, Copyright © 1970 by Aldine Publishing Company.

Manufactured in the United States of America

*For Dorothy, Doris, and Alfred
who taught me how rewarding a
picture puzzle world can be*

*for Ben and Sol who put up
with the scattered pieces*

*and for Cora who inspired this
particular solution*

Acknowledgments

This book is based on fieldwork conducted between June 1963 and March 1965 with the financial support of the Wenner-Gren Foundation, the National Institute of Mental Health (Predoctoral Research Fellowship No. 5 Fl MH-20, 701-02 BEH with Research Grant Attachment No. MH-07951-01), and the Northern Co-ordination and Research Centre of the Department of Northern Affairs and National Resources of the Canadian Government (now the Northern Science Research Group of the Department of Indian Affairs and Northern Development). I am indebted to the latter not only for financial support during the first six months of the field period but also for logistic support throughout the whole term, which facilitated my work considerably.

I owe many things to many people. In the period when the research project was being formulated I sought and received advice from a number of individuals acquainted with the North, or with the problems involved in fieldwork in isolated areas. To the following I am particularly grateful: Asen Balikci, Jameson Bond, Norman Chance, Father Pierre Henry, Diamond Jenness, Graham Rowley, Eleanor Shore, Richard Slobodin, and Doug Wilkinson. The solution of most of the practical problems that plagued me before departure I owe to B. F. Shapiro of the Northern Co-ordination and Research Centre, an administrator who markedly increased my admiration for administrators. At the outset, I was and am most indebted to Victor Valentine, then Chief of the Northern Co-ordination and Research Centre, for permitting me to go to live in the remote Chantrey Inlet area in spite of his misgivings, and to Graham Rowley and Richard Slobodin for injecting a reassuring note of confidence into the venture. The back issues of the *London Times* and the package of toffee contributed by Mr. Rowley served me well for many months.

While I was in the Arctic my way was smoothed by many of the white residents and transient scholars I encountered. The Northern Service Officers in Cambridge Bay, David O'Brien in 1963 and Peter Green in 1965, were especially generous with hospitality, advice, and assistance, material and otherwise. Among the others whose friendliness I remember very kindly, I must mention particularly David Damas and Anthony Williamson, who gave me much useful counsel and good cheer; Elizabeth O'Brien, to whom I owe an elegant Christmas dinner of an orange and a boiled chicken leg; Don Hamilton, the pilot who ferried me back and forth and fixed my tape recorder, and his wife, who gave me a haircut which made it possible for me to return to civilization; the fishing guides "Pooch," "Bud," "Barney," and "Jim," who contributed a hundred pounds of ambrosia in the form of vegetables and eggs to my fishy larder; two Royal Canadian Mounted Police officers named "Frank" and "Bill," who provided me with a different sort of ambrosia: English conversation; and finally, Fred Ross, who, when I passed through Cambridge Bay on my way home, let me eat my fill of $4.00 meals at his restaurant for a week—free.

In my travels to and from the Arctic, Charles Hobart at the University of Alberta and Otto Schaefer at the Camsell Hospital in Edmonton were particularly kind, and in San Francisco I incurred lasting debts to Norman and Martha Rabkin, to Charles and Jean Lave, and to Benjamin, Lois, and Janice Paul, who nursed me through a lengthy illness, at no small inconvenience to themselves.

To the residents of Gjoa Haven, both Eskimo and white, I am indebted for more kindnesses than I have room to describe. Fathers Georges Lorson and André Goussaert, and Brother Jérôme Vermeersch, and the schoolteachers, William and Elizabeth Eades, were always ready with hospitality while I was in Gjoa Haven, and while I was at Back River the services they performed for me, the errands they ran for me, alleviated my isolation considerably. Among the many Eskimos who helped me in Gjoa Haven, Aqnayaq and Walter Porter were particularly generous with time and information. The friendship and support of the Anglican missionary and his wife, who appear in the book as Nakliguhuktuq and Ikayuqtuq, were invaluable, as will be evident, I am sure, to a reader of the book. Without their help my fieldwork would have been far less productive; in fact, my continued existence at Back River would have been next to impossible.

My greatest debt is of course to the Utkuhikhalingmiut with whom I stayed, especially the members of the family who adopted me and about whom this book is written. I am sorry that they would not understand or like many of the things I have written about them; I hope, nevertheless, that what I have said will help to further the image of Eskimos as "genuine people" (their word for themselves), rather than "stone age men" or "happy children."

To Cora DuBois I am indebted in many ways. Her advice before I left for the field sobered me, and her letters while I was in the field cheered me. As my thesis advisor, she painstakingly supervised the creation of this book (né thesis) from the original formulation of the idea to the final semicolon.

At various stages and to various degrees the book has also been molded by advice and encouragement (and occasionally tactful discouragement) from the following friends, colleagues, and professors: Christopher Boehm, George Dalton, David Damas, Minnie Freeman, Richard Katz, Elliott Leyton, Alfred Ludwig, Robert Paine, Benjamin Paul, Carol Ryser, Alice Salzman, Miles Shore, Victoria Steinitz, Barbara Stromsted, Beatrice Whiting, John Whiting, and Anthony Williamson.

My notes were mined for relevant data and the results were typed by a number of diligent assistants: Jane Adcock, Ellen Bate, Susan Berson, Patricia DuBrock, Susan Falb, Ellen Glass, Bonnie Gray, Helen Hetherington, Constance Hunter, Judith Kateman, Patricia Knight, Beth Rothschild, Alice Salzman, Sigemund Snyder, and Anne Wilson. Without their work the book would have been a shadow of itself. I was shepherded through the intricacies of punctuation by Barbara Stromsted and through the mysteries of logical organization by Alice Salzman. Winnifred Martin not only succeeded in producing flawless copy out of chaos in the shortest possible time, but also paid me the high compliment of reading what she typed. Dorothy Vanier and Shirley Fraize patiently retyped and re-retyped every time I changed my mind. And I thank my brother, William Briggs, for his craftsmanly way with maps, diagrams, and charts.

On the principle that the last item is the most visible, I have saved for the end my gratitude to Robert Paine and Robert Stebbins, both of the Memorial University of Newfoundland, who at some cost made available the time necessary to complete the book. Without their kindness there would be no book.

Jean L. Briggs

St. John's, Newfoundland
September 1969

Contents

Spelling and Pronunciation Note

The spelling used here is based on an attempt at phonemic analysis of the Utkuhikhalingmiut dialect, but for several reasons it is not completely consistent. First, the phonemic analysis is still incomplete. Moreover, for the sake of simplicity I have removed the glottal stop throughout, and in several instances in order to make familiar words recognizable I have anglicized spellings to bring them partially (though still not completely) into line with established usage. Thus, I have spelled *iklu* (snowhouse) as "iglu," *qaplunaaq* (white man) as "kapluna," and *Nattilingmiut* or *Nattilik* (the name of the Eskimo group that traditionally inhabited the Gjoa Haven area) as "Netsilingmiut" or "Netsilik." Finally, in the case of certain names of English origin (Raigili, Rosi, Saarak, Peeterosi, Goti) that have not been completely incorporated into Utkuhikhalingmiut phonemic patterns, I have retained English phonemes to represent Utkuhikhalingmiut attempts to pronounce the foreign words.

With regard to pronunciation the following guidelines are offered. These are intended only to facilitate pronunciation of words occurring in the text; they do not constitute a technical linguistic analysis.

Vowels

a: as in *father*

ai: like the *i* in *like*

i: Like the *ee* in *keel,* except that before and after *q* and *r* it is pronounced like the *e* in *bed*

u: like the *oo* in *pool,* except that before and after *q* and *r* it is pronounced like the *o* in *pole* or like the *au* in *Paul*

Consonants

h: as in English, except that following *k* or *q* it is sometimes pronounced like English *s* or *sh,* and following *p* like English *s* (thus Utkuhik*h*alingmiut is pronounced Utku-hik*sh*alingmiut and tip*h*i is tip*s*i) *hl:*   is a voiceless *l*, which has no English equivalent; it is formed by placing the tongue in the position for pronouncing *l* and exhaling

j: is usually pronounced like the English *r* (thus u*jj*iq and hu*j*uu*j*aq are pronounced u*rr*iq and hu*r*uuraq)

k: as in English, except that before *l* it is pronounced almost like English *g* (thus i*k*liq is pronounced i*g*liq)

ll: something like English *dl* (thus A*ll*aq is pronounced A*dl*aq)

ng: as in *sing*, never as in *hunger*

p: as in English, except that preceding *l* it is almost *b* (thus qa*p*lunaaq or ka*p*luna is pronounced qa*b*lunaaq or ka*b*luna)

q: like French *kr* or *rk*

r: like the French *r* (except in proper names of English derivation, such as *R*aigili, *R*osi, and Saa*r*ak, where it is pronounced like the English *r*)

tt: like the English *ch* (thus Inu*tt*iaq is pronounced Inu*ch*iaq)

People

These households are also shown in chart form in Appendix III. The household numbers here correspond to those shown on the charts. All names are pseudonyms. Ages are approximate, as the Utku do not keep track of birthdays.

Household I

Piuvkaq: Elder half-brother of Pala (Household II), probably more than seventy years old, the oldest man in Chantrey Inlet. He died during my first winter at Back River.

Huluraq: Piuvkaq's elderly wife, perhaps in her sixties. She died a few days before her husband.

Maata: Piuvkaq's only child by birth, a woman in her mid-twenties, twice widowed. After the death of her parents she moved away from Chantrey Inlet with her children and remarried.

Pamiuq: Piuvkaq's adopted son (really his grandson, the son of a deceased adopted daughter of Piuvkaq), about fourteen years old. He moved away with Maata.

Qijuk: Maata's daughter by her first marriage, about five years old.

Rosi: Maata's daughter by her second marriage, about three years old.

Household II

Pala: Younger half-brother of Piuvkaq (Household I), perhaps in his mid-fifties or older; father-in-law and uncle (father's brother) of Inuttiaq (Household III).

Mannik: a young man of about twenty-five; Pala's eldest son and Inuttiaq's best friend.

Amaaqtuq: Pala's third daughter, about seventeen years old.

Ukpik: Pala's youngest son, about fourteen years old and away at boarding school during the first of the two winters I spent with the Utku.

Akla: Pala's youngest daughter, about ten years old.

Household III

Inuttiaq: a man of about forty; the Anglican lay leader of the Utku; son-in-law and nephew (brother's son) of Pala (Household II); husband of Allaq; my Eskimo father.

Allaq: a woman in her mid-thirties; Inuttiaq's wife and Pala's eldest child; my Eskimo mother.

Kamik: Inuttiaq's eldest daughter, about fourteen years old and away at school during both of the winters I spent at Back River.

Raigili: Inuttiaq's second daughter, about six years old.

Saarak: Inuttiaq's third daughter, about three years old.

Qayaq: Inuttiaq's infant daughter, born while I was at Back River.

Yiini: This is the Utku pronunciation of my Christian name, Jean. I was Inuttiaq's adopted daughter but I am, I think, about the same age as my mother, Allaq.

Household IV

Ipuituq: a young man in his mid-twenties, married to Pala's (Household II) second daughter, Amaruq. He is half-brother to Qavvik (Household VI).

Amaruq: Pala's second daughter, a woman in her mid-thirties; Ipuituq's wife.

Mitqut: Amaruq's daughter by a previous marriage; about thirteen years old and away at boarding school during my second winter at Back River.

(Ipuituq and Amaruq also had a daughter, who was born and died while I was at Back River. She is mentioned only once in the book.)

Household V

Nilak: like Inuttiaq (Household III), a man of about forty; a fairly distant relative of Pala (Household II) and Inuttiaq (refer to Chart I in Appendix III); husband of Niqi.

Niqi: Nilak's wife, a woman of about forty, with apparently sub-
normal intelligence.

Tiguaq: Nilak's adopted daughter (really his deceased brother's
daughter), about seventeen years old.

Household VI

Qavvik: a man probably in his mid-fifties like Pala (Household
II); a Garry Lake (Hanningajuq) Eskimo who married an
Utku woman and almost always camps with the Utku,
though his wife is now dead.

Putuguk: Qavvik's adopted son (really the son of Pala); a young
man in his early twenties; husband of Kanayuq.

Kanayuq: a girl of about eighteen; Putuguk's wife, and a niece
(brother's daughter) of Nilak's (Household V).

(Qanak: a son born to Putuguk and Kanayuq while I was at Back
River. He is mentioned only once in the book, and not by
name.)

Household VII

Kuuttiq: a man in his mid-twenties who was born an Utku but
who has lived most of his adult life in Gjoa Haven. He is
married to an Utku woman, the daughter of Pukiq (Household VIII); they camped with the Utku during my first winter
at Back River.

(Uyaraq: a woman in her early twenties; wife of Kuuttiq and
daughter of Pukiq (Household VIII). She is not mentioned
in the book.)

(Kuuttiq and Uyaraq have two small children: Niaquq, a girl of
about four and Nainnuaq, an infant boy, who are not mentioned in the book.)

Household VIII

Uyuqpa: a Netsilik Eskimo, a man, probably about fifty, who is
married to a Hanningajuq woman and who camped with the
Utku during my first winter in Chantrey Inlet.

Pukiq: wife of Uyuqpa, an elderly Hanningajuq woman, probably in her sixties. By a previous marriage she is the mother of Uyaraq (Household VII), of Ipuituq (Household IV), and of Tutaq (see below under Others).

Itqiliq: Uyuqpa's son by a previous marriage; a boy of about eighteen, considered, like his father and brothers, to be a Netsilik Eskimo.

(Qingak: another son of Uyuqpa by his previous marriage; a boy of about fourteen. He is not mentioned in the book.)

Ukhuk: Uyuqpa's youngest son by his previous marriage; a boy of about eleven.

Others Mentioned in the Book

Nattiq: Nilak's brother, who lives in Gjoa Haven.

Uunai: wife of Nattiq.

Tiriaq: a boy of perhaps seventeen who was away at boarding school during my first winter at Back River; an orphaned nephew (brother's son) of Nilak (Household V). When home from school he usually lived either with Qavvik (Household VI) in Chantrey Inlet (because he is brother to the wife of Qavvik's adopted son, Putuguk), or with his uncle Nattiq in Gjoa Haven.

Tutaq: an unmarried man of about twenty; the youngest son of Pukiq (Household VIII). He lived sometimes with his mother's husband, Uyuqpa; sometimes with his sister's husband, Kuuttiq (Household VII); and sometimes with his brother, Ipuituq (Household IV).

Nakliguhuktuq: the Eskimo Anglican missionary in Gjoa Haven who oversees the religious life of the Utku; a man probably in his early forties. He and his wife sponsored my introduction to the Utku community and arranged for my adoption.

Ikayuqtuq: Nakliguhuktuq's wife, a woman in her mid-thirties.

Note: Of these people, the only ones who spoke any English were the school children: Pamiuq (Household I); Ukpik (Household II); Kamik (Household III); Itqiliq, Qingak, and Ukhuk (Household VIII); Tiriaq and Tutaq, the two unattached young men; and Ikayuqtuq, wife of Nakliguhuktuq. Only Ikayuqtuq spoke it well and easily. However, everyone over the age of six and under the age of fifty or so, with the exception of Niqi (Household V), was literate in Eskimo syllabics.

Never in Anger

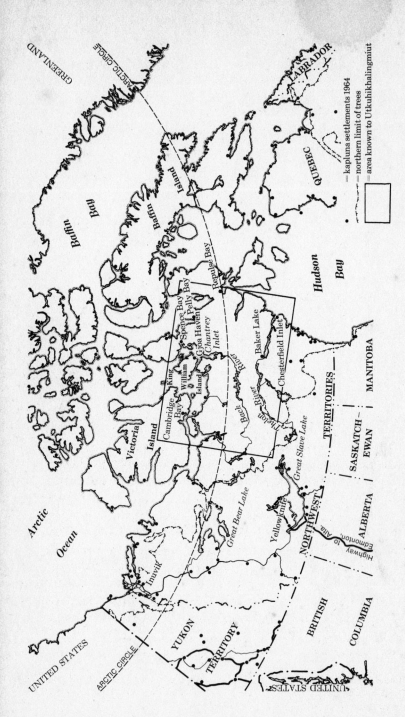

Map I: The Canadian Arctic

Introduction

I. The Study

In the summer of 1963 I went to the Canadian Northwest Territories to make a seventeen-month anthropological field study of the small group of Eskimos who live at the mouth of the Back River, northwest of Hudson Bay. These twenty to thirty-five Eskimos, who call themselves Utkuhikhalingmiut,[1] are the sole inhabitants of an area 35,000 or more miles square. The nearest other people are 150 miles north in Gjoa Haven, a small mission-and-trading settlement of perhaps one hundred Eskimos and four to five kaplunas.[2]

The Utku usually camp near the foot of Chantrey Inlet, the sound seventy-five miles long and nearly a third as wide, into which Back River empties. It takes one and a half to two weeks to make the round trip from Chantrey Inlet to Gjoa Haven by sled

1. Hereafter Utkuhikhalingmiut will be abbreviated to Utku.
2. Qaplunaaq is the Canadian Eskimo name for white man; this is often anglicized to kabloona (here kapluna) in Canadian Arctic literature.

in winter; in summer the trip is impossible altogether, because the open water of Simpson Strait lies between the inlet and King William Island, where Gjoa Haven is. Most Utku men make the sled trip two to three times each winter to trade fox skins for the kapluna goods they see as necessary to their way of life: weapons, clothing, bedding, and cooking equipment, tools and tents, tea, tobacco, flour, and a holiday smattering of more frivolous items. But on the whole, the Utku live quite self-sufficiently in their remote river country.

Contact between the Utku and the outside world has been slight until recently. Brief glimpses of three British and American exploring expeditions,[3] whose members spoke at most a few words of Eskimo, and a visit of a few days with the Greenlandic explorer and ethnographer Knud Rasmussen in 1923 comprise the total of their early encounters with white men. Rasmussen (1931) calculated on the basis of Utku reports that the first guns and modern tools were introduced to the Utku about 1908 by an Eskimo trader from the Baker Lake area to the south; since that time the Utku have traded with increasing frequency, first at Baker Lake and at other posts on the Hudson Bay coast, later at Perry River, and most recently in Gjoa Haven. But it was only after the disappearance of the caribou in 1958 that cloth and canvas largely replaced caribou as materials for clothing and tents. Similarly, it is only in this last decade or so that contacts with kaplunas themselves—missionaries, government personnel, and most recently sports fishermen—have become an expected part, however small, of Utku life.

Anthropologically, too, the Utku have been very little studied. Rasmussen's short visit in 1923 was made with the purpose of collecting ethnographic data; and in 1962 a French ethnographer named Jean Malaurie made a trip of a few days to Chantrey Inlet. But prior to my own trip no long-term studies of the Utku had been made.

I chose this unusually isolated group as a subject of study because I was interested in the social relationships of shamans. I had been assured that the Utku were pagans, and I hoped that in this place, presumably so far from missionary influence, I

3. Back in 1833 (1836); Anderson in 1855 (Rasmussen 1931:468); Schwatka in 1879 (Gilder 1881).

could still find practicing shamans. As it turned out, I was mistaken. The Utku encountered both Catholic and Anglican varieties of Christianity about thirty years ago, and they are now very devout Anglicans; their shamans are all, in their view, either in hell or in hiding. But I did not discover this until long after my arrival in Chantrey Inlet.

When I did finally ascertain that no information on shamanism would be forthcoming, I was of course compelled to find some other aspect of life to study. The choice of subject was determined in part by factors beyond my control, especially by my limited knowledge of the language and by the Utkus' reticence and, during a certain period of my stay, by their resistance to my presence. Because of the language barrier, during the first year of my stay at Back River I was confined very largely to recording those aspects of life that were tangible and visible. After some months I began to follow ordinary conversations and to feel that there was some likelihood of my understanding the answer if I ventured to ask a question. But at about that time a serious misunderstanding arose between the Utku and me. I lost my temper (very mildly as we ourselves would view it) at some kapluna fishermen who visited the inlet during the summer and who broke one of the Eskimo canoes. This incident brought to a head a long-standing uneasiness on the part of the Eskimos concerning my un-Eskimo volatility; and as a result of my unseemly and frightening wrath at the fishermen I was ostracized, very subtly, for about three months.

During this period there was simply no use in asking questions. At best, Utku consider questions boorish and silly; nevertheless, they will sometimes politely attempt to answer them. During this period of tension, however, they did not. Moreover, my intense resentment at the unpleasant situation resulted in a spectacular decline in my own linguistic prowess. I could not remember even the simplest words, which had become second nature to me.

The tensions were eventually resolved. My vocabulary unfroze, and people once more submitted with gracious cheerfulness to my impertinent inquiries. But even with the best of rapport there were subjects that met with great resistance. Historical matters in particular were difficult to discuss, as they were tainted with paganism. Not only could I get no information on shamanism, I could not even obtain the genealogical data necessary for a proper social structural analysis of the group. Perhaps this was because of the very un-Anglican marriage practices that would have been unearthed in the recent, pre-Christian generations. The Utku have heard that it is "bad" to talk about the old days because "in those days people were very confused."

The upshot of this situation was that the aspect of Utku life most accessible for study, and the one most salient in terms of my personal experience, was the patterning of emotional expression: the ways in which feelings, both affectionate and hostile, are channeled and communicated, and the ways in which people attempt to direct and control the improper expression of such feelings in themselves and in others. Emotional control is highly valued among Eskimos; indeed, the maintenance of equanimity under trying circumstances is *the* essential sign of maturity, of adulthood. The handling of emotion is thus a problem that is of great importance also to the Utku themselves.

I was in a particularly good position to observe this emotional patterning both because I was a focus for emotional tension and because I lived with a family as their adopted daughter, sharing their iglu during the winter and pitching my tent next to theirs in summer.

In this book I shall describe Utku emotional patterning in the context of their life as I saw and lived it during my seventeen months in Chantrey Inlet. Instead of attempting to make a formal structural or psychological analysis (for which I lack the requisite systematic data) I shall draw a series of vignettes of individual Utku interacting with members of their family and with their neighbors. I feel that this approach will make maximum use of the research situation: the smallness of the group studied, the intimacy of my living arrangements, and the resulting richness of the behavioral data obtained.

I hope this behavioral description will also supplement previous literature on Eskimos. A great deal, both professional and popular, has been written about Eskimos; few peoples so fascinate the outside world. Much of this literature, however, consists of generalizations about Eskimo life, based partly on the writer's necessarily limited observations and partly on Eskimo informants' reports of what Eskimos do, or ought to do. As in all cultures, there are often discrepancies between what people say about themselves on the one hand and their observed behavior on the other. The two kinds of data provide quite different perspectives on a culture and complement each other.

We do catch vivid glimpses of Eskimo individuals in a number of works, anthropological and otherwise. A partial list includes Brower (1942), Ingstad (1954), Marshall (1933), Mowat (1952, 1959), Poncins (1941), Wilkinson (1956), Jenness (1922, 1928), Lantis (1960), Stefansson (1951), Metayer (1966), Washburne (1940), and almost all the Eskimo publications of Rasmussen and Freuchen. Lantis' book contains short life histories of several Southwest Alaskan Eskimos, and the Eskimo autobiographies edited by Washburne and Metayer are particularly rich in detail concerning the everyday lives of Eskimo individuals. These three books, as well as those of Marshall, Rasmussen, and Freuchen, are especially valuable in that they provide insight into the Eskimos' own view of their behavior. Gubser (1965) does not show us individuals as such, but his book, too, gives excellent data on Eskimo views regarding interpersonal relationships, since his generalizations are based both on observation of Eskimo behavior and on Eskimo statements concerning the meaning of that behavior. None of these authors, however, is concerned primarily with emotional behavior. Moreover, to date no attempt, as far as I know, has been made to analyze the terms in which Eskimos speak about their relationships with one another. Thus, both in its focus and in its use of Eskimo terminology I believe my report may constitute a contribution. I believe, too, that my experience as a "daughter" in an Eskimo family may cast new light on old generalizations concerning relationships between Eskimo men and women. Gubser, Jenness, and Wilkinson were all adopted as "sons"; Freuchen and Rasmussen had Eskimo wives; but to my knowledge the only other account written by one who played a feminine role in an Eskimo family is the autobiography of Anauta (Washburne 1940).

The behavioral data that I utilize in my description of Utku emotional patterns are of several kinds. In the first place, I present observations made by Utku themselves, both on their personal feelings and on the feelings of others in various situations. Because Utku do not label emotions exactly as we do, I insert in the text, whenever possible, the base of the Utku term for the feeling that is described, and in several cases I insert the base of the term for the behavior that expresses a feeling. While these terms by no means exhaust the Utkus' emotional vocabulary, they are among those most commonly in use. The circumstances of their use are summarized in an appendix to the book.[4]

Secondly, in addition to describing what the Utku themselves say about feelings, I draw on more personal data. On the one hand I describe my observations of Utku behavior and the feelings that the behavior seemed to me to portray; and on the other hand I describe the feelings that I myself had in particular situations. My justification for this is that I was an intrinsic part of the research situation. The responses of my hosts to my actions and my feelings, and my own reactions to the situations in which I found myself—my empathy and my experience of contrasts between my feelings and those of my hosts—were all invaluable sources of data.

Conscious of the pitfalls of misperception to which such a personal approach is subject, I shall try throughout to distinguish explicitly among the various kinds of data on which my statements are based and not to extrapolate from my own feelings to those of Utku without cautioning the reader that I am doing so. I hope, moreover, to present the material vividly enough so that the reader, sharing to some extent my cultural background,[5] can also experience empathy and contrasts between his feelings and those of Utku, thereby enriching his understanding of the situation that is described and making his own interpretations.

It is important to emphasize that the picture of Utku life that is drawn here is very much a still life: a product of a particular

4. See also the glossary of emotional terms. Where terms are not given in the text, it is occasionally because they would be redundant: the term has been given once already on the same page and in the same context. But more often it is because they are not available; either the conversation quoted was in English or I do not know how the Eskimos labeled the situation.

5. In interpreting my statements, readers may find it useful to know that my background is that of a middle-class, urban, Protestant New Englander.

situation, a particular set of human relationships at a particular moment in time. I could never write the same book again, nor could any other observer have written exactly the same book. This point was brought home to me vividly on a return visit to Chantrey Inlet in 1968, when my relationships with the same people were quite different: more familiar and more peaceful. As a result, I saw, or attributed to the Utku, quite different behavior and motivations and hence observed somewhat different characters, in certain respects. They saw new qualities in me, as well, and attributed a somewhat different personality to me. This is not to say that our earlier views of each other were false, simply that they were a product of a different situation.

The book is a still life also in the sense that Utku life, like that of other Eskimo groups, is changing. Some of the practices and attitudes described here already at this writing belong to the past; and there is no telling how long the Utku will remain in Chantrey Inlet. But having made it clear that the book describes a particular moment in time, for simplicity's sake I shall avail myself of anthropological privilege and refer to that moment in the present tense.

The book focuses on a few individuals who, I think, illustrate exceptionally well in their relationships with other members of the camp the points to be made concerning the patterning of emotion. None of these central characters is an "ideal" Eskimo. On the contrary. I have chosen for two reasons to describe people whose behavior or character deviates markedly in one way or another from the ideal. My first reason for this choice is that it is often easier to learn what good behavior is when it is thrown into relief by misbehavior. Secondly, the description of individuals whose behavior is considered inappropriate gives me an opportunity to describe the way people try to control these undesirable tendencies, in themselves and in others.

The introductory sections of the book describe the geographical and historical setting of the group and the circumstances of my arrival at Back River. The seasonal nomadic cycle and Utku family organization are also briefly outlined. Following the introduction, chapters devoted to descriptions of individuals and their social relationships are interspersed with more general chapters intended to provide the ethnographic background necessary in order to understand the behavior of the individuals with whom the book is concerned.

The first person to be described is Inuttiaq, the religious leader of the Utku and my Eskimo father. He is considered by his fellows to be a "good person"; in important ways his self-expression remains within acceptable limits. But I think it probable that he maintains his reputation at some personal cost, as he seems to be a highly tempestuous person internally, and in this respect is far from the Eskimo ideal. People of Inuttiaq's type may recur fairly frequently in Utku society. I have the impression, both from Eskimo literature and from conversations with Eskimos about the personalities of shamans, that such people often became shamans in the old days. In any case, Inuttiaq, in his relationships with his family and with others, and in his role as religious leader illustrates most of the acceptable modes of personal expression, as well as a few that are subject to criticism.

Following a chapter on family life, Inuttiaq's children are described in an attempt to show how the proper patterns of expression are inculcated in children and how deviations from this proper behavior are handled. Utku, like many other peoples, expect children, at least small ones, to behave badly. Allowances are made for them because they do not yet "know better" or are not yet motivated to conform to adult standards. Nevertheless, attempts are made to train children in the way they should eventually go, and to observe this training is to observe what Utku believe the proper adult personality should be and what methods are appropriate in this culture to control and to educate children to grow in that direction.

The fourth chapter describes in general terms the ways in which members of different kin groups behave toward one another. This chapter is followed by one that centers on two specific kin groups: Inuttiaq's and Nilak's. Nilak's wife, Niqi, appears to be the least intelligent of the Utku; she is also the least able to control her emotions. Nilak, like his wife, is reputed to have a bad temper, as well as other unpleasant qualities such as stinginess. Between the two of them, therefore, Nilak and Niqi illustrate a good many of the unacceptable modes of personal expression and the ways in which these are dealt with by the community.

The last relationship to be described is my own with Inuttiaq's household. Like Niqi's and Nilak's, my behavior illustrates mainly the unacceptable. However, the origin of the difficulty is different. Whereas Niqi failed to conform because she lacked the mental ability, I failed because I had been educated to a different pattern. Some of the ways in which my offensive behavior was handled by the Eskimo community reflects this difference in cause: the fact that I was not, after all, an Eskimo. Nevertheless, the Utku measured my behavior by their own standards; they disliked and criticized it, as they did Niqi's.

The situations described in these chapters are obviously quite different from one another. The common denominator is the fact that all these forms of improper behavior attract critical notice and provoke attempts to control them. I am considering children, volatile Utku adults, and foreigners together in this way in order to point out similarities and differences in the ways in which Utku deal with the inappropriate behavior of these different categories of people. Let me stress that with regard to the particular forms of emotional behavior, the expressions of hostility and affection, with which this book is concerned, there is, as far as I could tell, only one ideal, which is applicable to all human beings, Utku or not, over the age of three or so. I judge this from the fact that the emotional behavior of all human beings is criticized in the same terms. This does not mean that in all respects a child is expected to behave like an adult, or a woman of twenty like a man of fifty, or a foreigner like an Utku, but the rule of even-tempered restraint does apply to all categories of people (except for the smallest children); and deviations from that rule are very likely to attract disapprobation, regardless of how common such deviations are.

An appendix to the book will summarize the kinds of behavior that are classified under each of the major emotion terms that occur in the text, and outline the situations in which the various kinds of behavior are or are not appropriate.

II. The Setting

Northwest of Hudson Bay, along the northern shore of the American continent and southward to the tree line hundreds of miles away, lies an immense open tundra. The feel of the tundra is that of a vast mountaintop—the same exhilarating, wind-clean space, low-scudding clouds, and the peculiar silence, almost audible in its intensity, that exists only where there is no tall growth for the breeze to ruffle. It is a severe country, but one of moorlike beauty and dramatic change.

In the Arctic each season sets its stamp sharply on the land, as well as on the lives of the people who inhabit it. In spring and summer, that is, from about the middle of June to the middle of August, the thin soil nourishes a luxuriant though tiny growth. The tallest plants, willow and birch, with twigs perhaps three feet long at most, lie spread-eagled along the ground in the marshy hollows or pressed flat against the ledges, where they seem much shorter than they are. The ground itself is covered with a hummocky mat of lichens and Alpine flowers, none more than a few inches high; and lichen-covered rocks are like elaborate Japanese fabrics in orange, green, and black.

In these months, the tundra harbors other life, as well. Insects swarm from the marshes, clogging eyes, ears, mouth, and nose, and pattering like rain on one's jacket. Ptarmigan whir up witlessly in front of one's feet, an easy target for the stones of children; and plovers run swiftly over the tundra on their long sandpiper legs, uttering the thin frightened cries that give them their Eskimo name: "Qulliq-quliik, qulliq-quliik."

In August when the berry leaves redden, the land glows rusty in the low sun till the first snow transforms it overnight into a charcoal drawing. Every day, flocks of birds pass across the gray sky, and once in a while, a loon, lost in the autumn land, cries a shivering complaint. "He is cold," the Eskimos say.

Winter comes rapidly. Snow falls thinly during the nights of September and October, driving in ribbons across the black ice surfaces of the lakes and rivers to freeze there, sculptured into graceful tongues by the wind. After the sea has frozen, the cloud blanket lifts, and the black-and-white landscape of autumn becomes suffused with the colors of the sinking sun. Then, too, the moon reappears. In the strong light of summer it had been a shadow, unnoticed, but now, radiant even at noonday, it seems the one living thing in a world whose silence is broken only by ⌐ie rustle of the ground-wind on the frozen snow and the thunder-crack of ice. Animal life has withdrawn into the whiteness; only the tracks of invisible ptarmigan, fox, and rabbit pattern the snow, and an occasional crow, startling in its blackness, flaps heavily above the ground in search of food.

Finally, with the returning warmth and the beginning of the long summer day in May and June, the year is complete. The long-forgotten gurgle and rush of water, cloud reflections, the plash of fish rising to insects, earth-fragrant wind, and endless sun bring liberation from an imprisonment felt only in the contrast.

This is the country through which Back River flows. Rising near Contwoyto Lake, on the edge of Indian country, it flows northeast to the Arctic coast, where, more than two miles wide, it empties into Chantrey Inlet.

From any hilltop near its mouth the river dominates the scene. No matter where one looks it is there, winding broad, peaceful arms around knolls of islands, or racing narrow and turbulent between confining granite bluffs. In the spring, torrential with melting snow and ice, the roar of Itimnaaqjuk, the Franklin Lake Rapids, can be heard at a distance of twelve miles or more, a bass murmur underlying the frenetic little freshets, and their surf shows as a white line of breakers on the horizon. In the summer the churning surf subsides, but the current never slackens. Even in winter no scab of ice forms over the rapids; and in autumn their breath hovers as a black vapor over the hole of open water.

The river derives its English name from that of the British explorer, George Back, who first traveled its length and mapped it. Back himself (1836) called it the Great Fish River, a translation of the name, Thleweechodezeth, used by the Indians who lived near its source at Contwoyto Lake. But the Eskimos call the river simply *Kuuk* (river).

The Utku are one of three Eskimo groups who have inhabited the lower reaches of the river. The territory of the Utkuhik-halingmiut (the people of the place where there is soapstone) lies between Chantrey Inlet and Franklin Lake. Beyond, where the river widens to form lakes Garry and Pelly, was the home until recently of the Ualiakliit (the westerners) and of the Hanningajuqmiut (the people of the place that lies across), that is, the river bend.[6] For generations these three groups hunted the great herds of caribou that migrated, spring and fall, through their territory, and fished for the trout, char, and whitefish for which the Indians named the river.

The early history of these three Eskimo groups is not clearly known. Current Utku traditions say that their own ancestors, and probably those of the other two groups also, came from the north, from the sea called Ukjulik, off the west coast of Adelaide Peninsula. The reasons given for the move are various. Knud Rasmussen, who visited the Utku briefly in 1923, was told (1931: 473–474) that following a famine in which many of their number had died, the remaining Utku families moved south into the uninhabited river country, seeking better game. Utkuhikhalik, the country of the river mouth, was rich at that time in caribou, musk oxen, and fish, and seal were plentiful where Chantrey Inlet widened beyond the river mouth. The Utku told Rasmussen that when they first moved into their new country, they used to go sealing every winter and spring in Chantrey Inlet; but that when they obtained guns, which they did in 1908 or thereabouts, they gave up sealing and turned to trapping fox, which at Baker Lake, two hundred miles to the south, they could trade for modern tools and white men's goods, including the valuable guns. For food, they fished and hunted caribou, ranging in search of the latter deep into the interior, as far as Garry and Pelly Lakes, the country of the Hanningajuqmiut and Ualiakliit.

An encounter of the explorers Gilder and Schwatka with Utku in 1879 supports the story of a move from Ukjulik, though the old man they spoke with said that he and others had moved from

6. Robert Williamson (1968) tells me that there are really only two groups: the Utkuhikhalingmiut and the Hanningajuqmiut. According to his sources (Eskimos from the interior who are now living at Baker Lake and on the west coast of Hudson Bay), the Ualiakliit are a subgroup of the Hanningajuqmiut, who live in the southwestern part of Hanningajuq. However, as my Utku informant explicitly and emphatically distinguishes the Ualiakliit from the Hanningajuqmiut, I shall continue to speak of three groups for the moment, as Rasmussen does.

Ukjulik not because of famine but because they were driven out by a neighboring band of warlike Netsilingmiut (Gilder 1881:77). Nowadays one sometimes hears Iluiliqmiut (whose traditional territory also bordered on Ukjulik) claim the credit for driving out the Utku. My elderly Utku informant, on the other hand, while telling me about the move from Ukjulik, mentioned neither famine nor warlike neighbors; he told me that the Utku came south in order to obtain guns, and when they had guns they gave up sealing and turned exclusively toward the interior, living on caribou and trapping fox to trade— a change in subsistence which agrees with what Rasmussen was told.

Accounts are least in agreement concerning the reasons for the move to Utkuhikhalik and the period when it occurred. My elderly informant thought that the Utku had moved at about the turn of the century; his older brother, he thought, had been among those who moved "to obtain guns." Rasmussen, too, says that the famine, which Utku told him had precipitated the move, was "not so very long ago" (1931:473). However, one gathers that he means it was several generations before 1923, which would place it well before the turn of the century. I think most other evidence also points to an earlier date, most probably a date prior to 1833. The old man, Ikinnelikpatolok, with whom Gilder and Schwatka spoke in 1879 (Gilder 1881: 77–78) said that "his family comprised nearly all that was left of the tribe which formerly occupied the west coast of Adelaide Peninsula and King William Land." It may be assumed that he himself had moved from Ukjulik, since he referred to himself as a person from there; but he must have been already living on Back River as a small boy, since he remembered having shaken hands with Back when the latter passed through Utkuhikhalik in 1833. Back, in his travels down the river in that year, met two camps of Eskimos and found traces of Eskimo habitation all along the river, from the inland lakes to the mouth, in the places we now know as Ualiakliit, Hanningajuqmiut, and Utkuhikha-lingmiut territories (1836:333–438). Back in 1833 (1836:378–386; 432–433), Anderson in 1855 (Rasmussen 1931:468), and Schwatka in 1879 (Gilder 1881:198) all found camps of Utku in the vicinity of the Franklin Lake Rapids, where Utku live today.

And these seem not to have been just transient families, moving through a foreign territory. The continuity of the Utkus' residence in Utkuhikhalik is shown by the fact that Ikinnelikpatolok's son-in-law, whom Schwatka met in 1879 (Gilder 1881:79) had been among those in the camp seen years earlier by Anderson. Another fact that supports a sizeable move prior at least to 1855 is that M'Clintock (1859:251) was told in 1859 that "formerly" many natives had lived at Ukjulik ("Oot-loo-lik," in M'Clintock's orthography), but "now very few remain."

All of these contacts with explorers seem to argue that the Utku moved into their present area early in the nineteenth century, in flight from famine or from enemies. But one report is difficult to reconcile with this view. Rasmussen's Utku informants told him of an "ancient tradition" which says the Utku were once a warlike and arrogant people, a "great nation, so numerous that all the hills looking over Lake Franklin were sometimes enveloped in smoke from the many camp fires round the lake" (1931:481). How is this possible if the Utku really moved into Chantrey Inlet just a few generations before Rasmussen was there and within the memory of the old man with whom Schwatka spoke in 1879?

Whatever their origins, within recent times these three inland groups have had a harsh history. In 1923 Rasmussen (1931:473) counted a total of 164 Utku and Ualiakliit combined, of whom 135 were Utku, or living with the latter in Chantrey Inlet.[7] But according to Utku with whom I spoke, at some time within

7. Rasmussen (1931:473–477) thought he had included the Hanningajuqmiut in his census, too, but according to contemporary Utku informants, he was mistaken. We therefore do not know how many Hanningajuqmiut there were in 1923.

In designating people as "Utku" I have followed the Utkus' own definition, as Rasmussen apparently did in the census referred to here. The term *Utkuhikhalingmiut* (people of the place where there is soapstone) seems to be essentially, but not wholly, a territorial concept. A person is Utku if he is born in Chantrey Inlet and lives there during his childhood, but he may lose his Utku affiliation by moving away and staying away for a number of years. Then he will be referred to as "formerly Utku." On the other hand, a person who was born and raised elsewhere, then moved to Chantrey Inlet as an adult, may or may not be referred to as an "Utkuhikhalingmiutaq," depending on the context of the conversation. Sometimes he will be referred to as "an Utkuhikhalingmiutaq—but not *really (-marik,* genuinely) an Utkuhikhalingmiutaq." I did not push the concept to its limits in discussing it with Utku.

their memory[8] famine and illness destroyed many of the Ualia-kliit and Hanningajuqmiut. Those who were left moved away to join other groups, such as the Utku at the river mouth and the Qaiqniqmiut at Baker Lake. Utku say that when the last remaining members of the "real" Hanningajuqmiut had left the area, then some of the Utku moved in, since Hanningajuq was usually very rich in caribou and fish. But between 1949 and 1958 there were again several famines in Hanningajuq, and in 1958 the government evacuated the survivors, taking them to Baker Lake, to Rankin Inlet, and to Whale Cove, communities on or near the Hudson Bay coast (McGill 1968; Williamson 1968). A few families have since moved in and out of the area, but no one, to my knowledge, has returned permanently to Hanningajuq (McGill 1968; Thompson 1967; Williamson 1968).

In the spring of 1958 there was a famine in Utkuhikhalik at the river mouth.[9] At that time, people did not depend on fish for food in all seasons as they do now. Instead of catching fish in the autumn for use in the spring when the river is empty, they used to go inland in search of caribou. But in 1958 the caribou failed to come. By the time this was apparent, the fish had gone. People tried to hunt seal, but owing to bad weather, hunting was poor. A few people died; others moved away: to Baker Lake, to Spence Bay, to Gjoa Haven. Before the 1958 famine, too, some Utku families had moved away: to Hanningajuq and to the kapluna communities. In 1956 there had been 100 Eskimos, mostly Utku, living in Chantrey Inlet, but during the winter of 1963–1964, when I lived there, there were eight households in the camp,[10] a total of thirty-five people at maximum count, excluding three adolescent children who were away at school. Of these eight households, two were only peripherally attached to the camp; they did not join the Utku every winter. They may possibly have come only to share the novelty and the resources of the anthropologist. The following year, 1964–1965, there were only twenty-one people, five households, in the winter camp; the two peripheral families were camping

8. Robert Williamson (1968) thinks it was around 1927.
9. The information in this paragraph was obtained from various sources in Gjoa Haven and Chantrey Inlet.
10. Household composition is shown on the charts in Appendix III.

elsewhere, and a third had disintegrated. Three of its six members had died of illness, and the survivors had moved away.

Once in a while Utku remark on their shrunken numbers as they walk among the old tent rings or along the top of the bluff where in former days long rows of fish were hung to dry in the sun; or as they sit drinking tea beside the tents in the summer nights, looking out over the blue river to the empty hills. Twenty-one people in an expanse of thirty-five thousand or more square miles, their nearest neighbors several days' travel distant.

To the foreigner who is accustomed to having all the space within his awareness filled with people, the Utku world can seem either lonely or refreshing, depending on his inclinations. I do not know whether the remaining Utku have either of these feelings. Of the land itself, with its plentiful fish and occasional caribou, they speak, so far, with contentment. They are grateful for the kapluna goods that make their life easier—and they have a surprising number of these, ranging from Coleman stoves to cameras—but they have not yet learned to value a kapluna way of life above their own. "Gjoa Haven," they say, "—dreadful (hujuujaq) place, there's nothing to eat there. But here we never lack for food; the fish never fail." They see beauty, excitement, and pleasure in their world, too. Their eyes shine as they describe the thunder of the rapids in the spring and the might of the river when it lifts huge ice blocks and topples them, crashing, into itself. When the first ice forms in September adults and children slide, laughing, on its black glass surface. "When winter comes you will learn to play," they told me—vigorous running games on the moonlit river. And the men, mending torn dog harnesses with long awkward stitches, sway heads and shoulders in imitation of a trotting dog, as they discuss a coming trip. Other men, whittling a winter fishing jig out of a bit of caribou antler, jerk it up and down tentatively in the hand, imitating the gesture of fishing, while humming a soft "ai ya ya," as they do while jigging, then laugh at themselves. "It's pleasant (quvia) to fish," they say. And in the spring, when the breeze loses its bite, there are endless hills of the sort "one wants to see the far side of."

III. Arrival

I was flown in to Back River at the end of August 1963 in the
single-engined plane that the government chartered in those
days to service the remote camps and villages of the Central
Arctic. In the ordinary course of a year the plane made just four
trips down to Back River. In late winter (weather permitting) it
brought the Utku population out to Gjoa Haven for chest X-rays
and medical examinations and took them back again. In the fall,
children who wished to go to boarding school were picked up
from all the villages and outlying camps in the Central Arctic
and flown to the government school in Inuvik, a thousand miles
away on the Alaskan border. In the spring they were brought
home again.

It was the school pick-up trip that took me in to Back River,
a fact that had uncomfortable implications for me. Though I had
spent the month of August in Gjoa Haven, trying to learn some
of the rudiments of the Eskimo language, my success had not
been so spectacular that I could regard with equanimity the
prospect of being abandoned in a completely non-English-
speaking community. The two or three school children who
would leave on the plane that brought me were, I knew, the
only Utku who had had any exposure at all to the English
language.

I had other cause for trepidation, too, as I watched Gjoa Haven's
warm wooden houses recede beneath me. Flurries of snow had
fallen for a week or more already, and the ground crunched
frozenly, though it was only August. Would I be able to survive
the Arctic winter without benefit of any of the accoutrements
of civilization? All too few of the kind and anxious people, both
white and Eskimo, who had given me advice had really thought
my project feasible. A blessed two or three did think it was;
a few others fervently hoped it was. (And I noted with relief
that optimism tended to be positively correlated with experience in the Arctic.) But, like "civilized" people everywhere,
the majority of my advisors cherished horrendous images of
the "primitive." One got the impression that the Chantrey Inlet
Eskimos were all morons and murderers. Some said there were
no Eskimos living there at all any more; they had all died of

starvation. And whatever their views on the local population (and their less directly expressed views on my motivations and sanity), my advisors were agreed on the impossibility of the climate. I was visited one day in Gjoa Haven by an Utku acquaintance who was living there. Uunai had heard that I planned to spend the winter at Back River. With vivid shivers dramatizing her words she told me: "It's very cold down there; *very cold*. If we were going to be down there I would be happy to adopt you and try to keep you alive." The expression she used, I later learned, was one that mothers use when exhorting their children to take good care of the baby birds they find and adopt as pets.

The image of myself as a perishable baby bird did not increase my peace of mind as I looked down from the plane at the empty expanse of broken ice, a gigantic green-edged jigsaw puzzle, that lay below us. It was expected that we would find the Eskimos settled in their traditional summer campsite just beyond the foot of Chantrey Inlet and beside the rapids at the mouth of Franklin Lake.

As we flew over the inlet, land reappeared, first on one side, then on the other: low sandy promontories, rocky islets jostled by the floating ice, and high capes, whose weather-ravaged faces dropped sharply into the water. The ice thinned and gave way to choppy water, dull under a gray sky. From the air the land seemed so barren, so devoid of life, that when we landed partway down the inlet to cache some of my supplies near the expected winter campsite, it was startling to find there two families of Eskimos from Gjoa Haven camping for the summer to net whitefish.

The country grew more rugged as we flew south, with small lakes sunk in hollows among granite knolls. The pilot and the interpreter in the cockpit began to scan the landscape, looking for signs of life. The interpreter pointed. Looking down at the camp that was my destination I was pierced by its fragility: racing water between two steep bluffs and two white toy tents side by side on a narrow gravel beach under one of the bluffs. Nothing else but tundra, rolling russet and gray to the horizon. A tiny knot of people, perhaps six or seven, stood clustered in front of the tents, watching the plane circle to land in a quiet backwater.

They were waiting by the plane in the same quiet knot when the door was opened, the men and boys slightly in the forefront. As the pilot, the interpreter, and I emerged, the Eskimos smiled and, smiling, came silently forward to shake hands, the "shake" no shake at all but a gentle squeeze almost entirely lacking in pressure. At the time I read it as the shy greeting of strangers, of Eskimos for kaplunas; but later I found husbands and wives, fathers and children greeting one another after an absence with the same restrained, tentative-seeming gestures. Even a newborn baby is welcomed into life in this way by its family and neighbors.

I was embarrassed when the plane began to disgorge my gear without so much as a by your leave or any sort of explanation offered to the Eskimos. But I was helpless, for the first of many times, in my ignorance of the language. The Eskimos obligingly, unquestioningly, caught the bundles as they emerged and laid them on the beach. I could only smile, as they did, hoping for acceptance, and trust to the later efforts of the interpreter.

I had with me letters of introduction from the Anglican missionary and his wife in Gjoa Haven. This missionary, an Eskimo deacon named Nakliguhuktuq, was overseer not only of the Gjoa Haven Anglicans but also of the Utku, and he and his wife, Ikayuqtuq, had very kindly taken upon themselves the responsibility of introducing me to the Utku. They had written to the latter in the syllabic script in which most Canadian Eskimos, including those at Back River, are literate. The letters said that I would like to live with the Utku for a year or so, learning the Eskimo language and skills: how to scrape skins and sew them, how to fish, and how to make birch mats to keep the caribou mattresses dry on the iglu sleeping platforms. They asked the Eskimos to help me with words and with fish and promised that in return I would help them with tea and kerosene. They told the people that I was kind, and that they should not be shy and afraid of me: "She is a little bit shy, herself"; and assured them that they need not feel, as they often do feel toward kaplunas, that they had to comply with my every wish.

They said, finally, that I wished to be adopted into an Eskimo family and to live with them in their iglus. And in order to forestall any errors, Nakliguhuktuq specified that I wished to be adopted as a daughter and not as a wife.

The idea of being "adopted" into an Eskimo family had been suggested to me in Ottawa by two Arctic scholars, both of whom had traveled as members of Eskimo families. In addition, I had read an account written by a man who had lived for a year as a "son" in an Eskimo family to learn what it felt like to be an Eskimo. There were logistic advantages to the idea: it would be warmer living with other people than living alone in an environment where body heat is a major source of warmth. And I thought vaguely it might be "safer" if one family had specific responsibility for me. The idea had a romantic appeal, also, as since early childhood I, too, had wanted to know what it felt like to be an Eskimo; and secretly I thought of this trip partly as a fulfillment of that dream. On my two previous field trips to Alaskan Eskimo villages I had identified strongly with the Eskimo villagers by contrast with such elements of the kapluna population as I had had occasion to meet. I had had no problems of rapport, and I expected the same to be true again. Indeed, never having felt very American in my outlook, I rather hoped I might discover myself essentially Eskimo at heart.

I voiced no such romanticism aloud, however. I was rather ashamed of my "unprofessional" attitude; and I had a number of qualms concerning the wisdom of being adopted, in terms of loss of "objective" position in the community; drains on my supplies which would result from contributing to the maintenance of a family household; and loss of privacy with resultant difficulties in working. Therefore I was not—so I thought—seriously considering the idea of adoption.

Nevertheless, when one day in Gjoa Haven Ikayuqtuq asked me why I wanted to live at Back River for a year, I spontaneously told her that I wanted to be adopted by an Eskimo family in order to learn to live like an Eskimo. I put it this way partly because I wanted—I think now, wrongly—to conceal from her that I would be "studying" the Eskimos. I was embarrassed by the scholarly analytical aspect of the enterprise, thinking she would consider it prying. Eskimos do not like to be asked questions;

they have an extremely strong sense of privacy with regard to their thoughts, their feelings, and motivations; and I feared to offend it.

I particularly wished to avoid telling Ikayuqtuq that the projected subject of my study was the traditional shamanistic practices of the Utku. My feeling that this was a delicate area of investigation was strengthened by tales I had heard about devoutly Anglican Eskimos in other areas who had committed suicide from guilt after being persuaded by an anthropologist to discuss the ancient practices and sing shamanistic songs. I did not intend to mention shamanism to anyone at Back River until people voluntarily mentioned it to me, which they presumably would after a certain amount of acquaintanceship and development of trust with regard to my intentions. Thus my naïve thought. As it turned out, ironically, the Utku never were willing to discuss shamanism with me; and Ikayuqtuq herself became my most interested and helpful informant on the subject. But at the time I could not foresee this; I saw her stereotypically as the wife of the Anglican missionary, the most unlikely of persons with whom to discuss pre-Christian traditions. So I withheld my professional purposes from her and told her only in the most general terms what I was doing in her country. I told myself, again with vast naïveté, that after I had "learned the language" and "developed rapport" I would be able to explain the other aspects of my work to the Utku.

Later, at Back River, I sometimes remembered that conversation with Ikayuqtuq and the resulting letters to my Eskimo hosts, and wondered in my frustration whether I would have been less rigidly defined as a learner-of-words-and-skills if I had been more open with Ikayuqtuq in the beginning. But perhaps not; perhaps in any case the Utku would have defined my role in some such narrow, relatively harmless way in order to keep me safely to one side of their lives, to keep their privacy inviolate. Or perhaps these tangible aspects of my role were simply the easiest for the Eskimos to see, as I never did discover how to tell them that I wanted to learn their "ways of life" until two years later when I was on my way home to my own way of life.

Ikayuqtuq had counseled me that on my arrival at the Utku camp I should tell the people through the government interpreter who would accompany the plane that I would like to live with them for a year; I should, however, withhold my letters of introduction until after the plane had left. "Tell them once," she had said, "then give them time to think about it."

Ikayuqtuq had written a letter to each adult woman; Nakliguhuktuq had written his letter to all of the men collectively, but had addressed the envelope to Nilak, who, he thought, would be the most appropriate father for me. There were only two suitable fathers in the group, since there were only two mature householders who had wives alive and at home. One of these was Nilak; the other, Inuttiaq. Nilak had a wife and an adolescent daughter. Ikayuqtuq and Nakliguhuktuq thought that I might be less of a burden on Nilak than on Inuttiaq, who had three daughters to support in addition to his wife. However, Nakliguhuktuq's letter told the men that they should talk about it among themselves and should decide among themselves who wanted to adopt me.

I was uneasy about this arrangement. While I agreed in not wanting to be a burden to anyone, I had discovered that Nilak occupied a much more peripheral position in the group than Inuttiaq did, in terms of his family ties and his camping habits. Nilak, it was said, sometimes camped alone in the summer when the Utku customarily scatter into small widely distant camps. Moreover, I had heard that Nilak's wife, Niqi, was "kind of different"—a characteristically Eskimo euphemism for negative traits. The condemnation was somewhat unspecific, but I had the impression that Niqi preferred sociability to hard work. In any case, all these factors combined to make me wish to postpone any decision until I had had an opportunity to look my prospective parents over *in situ*. It also made me anxious to reserve the decision to myself; but Ikayuqtuq assured me that I could veto the men's decision if I wanted to. I could even change my mind about being adopted if circumstances warranted it. I was much reassured.

On that first day, however, no adoption problem arose, as both Nilak and Inuttiaq, together with all the other able-bodied Utku, were somewhere out in the distant countryside, hunting caribou for winter clothing. The camp in which I was deposited, Itimnaaqjuk (the Rapids), had been the summer fishing site of four of the eight households that were living in Chantrey Inlet in 1963, and had I arrived a week or so earlier I would have found all four households there. As it was, only the two elderly brothers, Pala and Piuvkaq, remained, tending a small agglomeration of dogs, daughters, and granddaughters who would have been superfluous on the hunt.

My introduction to the community was quickly over. We sat hunched on stones under an uncomfortably slanting tent wall while the interpreter checked the registration numbers and parentage of the departing students, then proceeded to account for my presence. I told him to ask whether the Eskimos would mind if I stayed with them for a year to learn their language and ways; whether they would help me. The younger of the two old men smilingly assured me they would help me. The interpreter called to me: "Have a good winter," and the plane was gone.

It was only as the hum of the motor faded into the snow-heavy clouds that I fully realized where I was. Realization came in the form of a peculiar sense not of loneliness but of separateness, of having no context for my existence. With the plane had vanished the last possibility of access to my familiar world until the strait froze in November, and as yet no bond of language, of understanding, or of shared experience linked me with the silent Eskimos behind me.

The feeling remained with me that night as I lay in my sleeping bag and listened to the flapping of my tent, accented now and again by a staccato gust of sleet on the thin canvas barrier. But already a new context was beginning to form. I felt it in the warm welcoming courtesies of the Eskimos, their smiles, and their amused attempts to bridge the linguistic gulf between us. It was also in the physical warmth of the sleeping bag, the snug brightness of my tent—its kerosene storm lantern suspended from the ridgepole. Flaps tied against the windy darkness, boxes and duffels ranged along the walls to serve as seats for the ever-present visitors, primus, cooking pots, and cups set out tidily by the door, the tent seemed very much home, a molecule of the familiar and personal in the wilderness.

Later I often felt this fragile cosiness of Eskimo camps at night, seeing the glow of a tent illuminated by a fish-oil flame, the translucent dome of a traveler's iglu on the sea ice, or a covey of sparks darting up from a campfire—pockets of human warmth in the blackness.

Our camp of three tents lay at the edge of a quiet inlet, a backwater of the rapids whose roar was a pervasive undertone to the yippings and clatterings of camp life. The rapids were confined on either side by granite bluffs; on one side, crowned with rows of small stolid cairns, stood Itimnaaqjuk, the bluff that gave the area its name, on the other side Haqvaqtuuq, on whose shoulder my tent was placed.

The Eskimo tents stood below by the shore, at a little distance. Peeking out between the flaps of my doorway, fastened against the icy wind, I could look down to the tents with their flaps open on the inlet; the gulls dipping and soaring over the fishnets, whose rows of tin can floats patterned the water; the chains of ragged dogs curled in sleep; the frozen piles of tea leaves set to dry on boulders; the little cluster of women and children by the twig-banked outdoor fireplace, one crouching to blow at the reluctant blaze or to encourage it carefully with a twig while the others watched or chased each other, laughing, around the fire. Stones clattered underfoot as one of the women or children crossed the beach and bent from a boulder to fill the teakettle in the water; a paddle clunked against the side of a canoe as one of the men pulled wriggling whitefish out of the net with his teeth and dropped them into the boat; then as the boat approached the shore came the frantic yipping of the dogs, tugging at their chains in anticipation of a meal.

Life in the waiting camp moved with the same stillness as the waters of the inlet, rising and falling in their faint tides. Every morning shortly after dawn, Pala, the younger and more vigorous of the two brothers, made himself a kettle of tea, then, taking his kapluna fishing reel or a coiled throwline, he went to cast from the ledges where the surf foamed over the gray rocks. His catch, two or three or four salmon trout or char, each weighing between ten and twenty pounds, provided the camp's food for the day.

Meanwhile Piuvkaq and his widowed daughter, Maata, woke, and Maata brewed tea for her father, herself, and any of the children who might have wakened. Pala, bringing one of his fish to contribute to the meal, joined the others at their tea. Later in the morning, or perhaps in the afternoon, the men, each with a cargo of daughters and granddaughters in his canoe, paddled out to check the fishnets. Piuvkaq might take his line and go to fish in the rapids. And sometimes the two women, Maata and Pala's grown daughter Amaaqtuq, seeing that the high bank of twigs around the fireplace had dwindled, would take their *ulus*, the half-moon knives that all Eskimo women use, and a rope, and go off across the tundra in search of dwarf birch bushes, stopping in the lee of knolls to rest and eat the tiny seed-filled crowberries that grow there; then plod slowly home again bent beneath loads so big that the bearers were almost invisible beneath the burden. "Heeaavy!" they laughed. "Tiiiring!"—their vowels drawn out for emphasis. "But after one has felt tired for a little while one will stop feeling tired." At home they collapsed jokingly on top of the cast-off load, then refreshed themselves with tea and large slices of raw trout.

Late afternoon was the busiest time. Then, as the sun was sinking behind Haqvaqtuuq, the women took their ulus again and went down to the beach where the men had tossed the netted whitefish into a silver pile. Drawing into their parka hoods for protection against the icy breeze and sucking their wet scaly fingers to thaw them, the women gutted the fish, slicing out the oily belly flesh in two smooth cuts and tossing it into a bucket to be boiled for food and fuel. Now and then somebody would remark with a little laugh: "Uuuunai (it's coooold)!"

With fish gutted and dogs fed and watered, people gathered around the blaze of the twig fire while Maata or Amaaqtuq boiled the remains of the morning's catch for the evening meal. Only Piuvkaq, because he was old and tired, lay on his bed, smoking his pipe as the light faded or crooning "ai ya ya's"—brief songs in which people speak their thoughts and feelings. The songs had a poignancy out of all relation to their monotonous four-or-five-note structure.

The evening meal was eaten together, the steaming fish heads ladled with a caribou scapula into a single tray, around which people crowded sociably; only Piuvkaq, if he were in bed, was taken a separate bowl. The day ended as quietly as it had passed. The evening fire darted its arrows into the night and faded as a half-invisible figure carried a steaming teakettle into a tent;

shadows moved against the glowing tent wall as people drank their tea; and the camp faded into darkness.

My arrival in Itimnaaqjuk altered, if not the tenor, at least the pattern, of the day's activities. Visiting the kapluna woman became the major diversion. My tent was never empty, from the time I awoke in the morning (and sometimes before) until, frayed to exhaustion, I retreated into the warm protection of my sleeping bag, leaving my departing visitors to tie the tent flaps behind them. Life in those first days was a matched battle between anthropological conscience on the one hand and an overwhelming desire for recuperative solitude on the other, and every night I was as tired as if I had in fact waged battle all day. I felt wooden within and without: my face from smiling; my mind and tongue from hours of struggling with unaccustomed and meaningless sounds; and my body from endless sitting in a frigid tent, entertaining visitors. I was still burdened by the illusion that it was necessary to "entertain" visitors, in the kapluna tradition, and to stay with them as long as they chose to remain. It was some days before I made the happy discovery that the Eskimos themselves rarely adapted their activities to the presence of a visitor. They exchanged smiles with a visitor when he appeared, and talked a bit now and again if there was something to talk about. Eventually, if the visitor stayed long enough, as he usually did, the hostess would probably serve a kettle of tea. But for the most part the visitor either spontaneously joined the family's activities or sat quietly on the periphery, ignored, to my foreign eye. If the host had business elsewhere he simply announced the fact and went out, whereupon it was incumbent upon the guest to leave also.

My neighbors were the most benign and considerate of visitors. I knew it at the time, even as I wearied of their presence; and I realize it more vividly now, hearing my colleagues' accounts of the very different peoples they have lived with. The Eskimos, unlike these others, never begged, never demanded. They frequently offered to trade bone toys for tobacco or for bits of my carefully hoarded food supplies, but they rarely complained of the amounts I gave them. They were never noisy or obtrusive; they just sat, quiet and observant, around the edges of my tent. If, out of concern for my dwindling tea and kerosene supplies, I let them sit unfed for more than two or three hours, one of the adults might remark on the warming qualities of tea or, more indirectly still, ask if my water supply was low and offer to replenish it. They noticed when my fish was all eaten and brought me more. And if I was a bit slow in attacking the slimy raw body, they assumed I did not know how to cut it, so they filleted it for me. They laid a gravel floor in my tent to lessen the dampness. They lit my lamp when my fingers were too stiff with cold, they fixed the primus when it clogged, and sharpened my knife when they saw it was dull—all without my asking.

Their unfailing anticipation of my needs (even when my needs did not coincide with theirs) was immensely warming. I felt as cared-for as a three-year-old, and I am sure that is precisely one facet of the light in which the Eskimos regarded me. Their attentions also awakened in me guilt concerning the one need that would never occur to them: my desire for solitude. I knew I should regard their constant visits as a sign of friendly acceptance and curiosity, as well as hunger for the luxuries of tea and bannock, and so I did; but I could not help seeing them also as an invasion of privacy. I felt trapped by my visitors. I longed to see the view from the bluff-top, to explore the ledges by the rapids; I would even have welcomed an opportunity to pay a return visit to the Eskimo tents. Nothing depresses me more than inactivity, and when the site of the inactivity was a tent permeated with the dank chill of autumn the situation quickly became unbearable. I resented the fact that the Eskimos, when they felt cold, could go out and do some warming work or chase each other around the tents, whereas I had to sit and smile at the next relay of visitors.

Six days passed before I escaped. For once the relays of visitors had not quite overlapped. Piuvkaq with his five-year-old granddaughter had shared my breakfast and left; I was enjoying solitude when I heard a cough ominously close to my tent and the crunch of a foot on the frozen lichen. Clutching a berry can under my arm in the hope of obscuring my motives and feigning ignorance of my approaching visitor, I fled to the tundra and wandered there all day, memorizing Eskimo words and feeling homesick.

It was when I came back into camp late that afternoon that I first realized how important to me my Eskimo neighbors were and how dependent I was on the warmth of their acceptance. Coming over the ridge behind camp I looked down on the two women. Maata was airing quilts and mattress hides while Amaaqtuq boiled fish for the evening meal. They greeted me with smiles, and when the fish was cooked, Amaaqtuq brought me a large piece.

They did not invite me to eat with them, however, as they had the day before; and that evening for the first time I had no visitors. Wondering guiltily whether people had correctly read my disappearance, I decided to make amends. It was a gray windless evening, the temperature a balmy forty degrees. I found the women on the bluff-top, picking mountain cranberries. They smiled a welcome and began to drill me on the tongue-twisting names of the plants that grew on the bluff, convulsed with laughter at my pronunciation—laughter in which I joined with real relief. They were willing to overlook my hostile withdrawal, I thought, or—happy possibility—perhaps they had not even noticed it. I had been there a year or more before I realized the vanity of that hope. At the time, secure in my innocence, I felt the giddy joy of being, to all appearances, accepted. More, for the first time I really enjoyed the company of my new acquaintances. And it dawned on me how forlorn I would be in that wilderness if they forsook me. Far, far better to suffer loss of privacy.

An icy breeze rose and the women shivered on the hilltop. I invited them in for tea and bannock and was happy when they came.

IV. The Seasons

I had been at Back River for two months before I met all of the eight households that would constitute our winter camp. The Utku are nomadic, and their camps fluctuate in size and membership with the season as they move in pursuit of the fish and other game on which their life depends. Each family has a fairly predictable annual pattern of moving.[11] During the winter all the families who live in Chantrey Inlet camp together in an area

11. A table of seasonal activities will be found in Appendix II. Usual camp-sites are shown on Map II on p. 30.

known to them as Amujat, near the mouth of the Hayes River. Here, where the scanty snow has drifted and packed hard in the lee of the riverbank, they build an iglu village and set nets for whitefish under the ice. And from here the men go out every few days, each in a different direction, to check traplines for the fox whose skins buy tea, tobacco, and a variety of other goods in Gjoa Haven.

In March, when the sun returns, the whitefish disappear from the river mouth, and the surplus, frozen and stored in snow caves for the lean spring, is quickly depleted. Then people scatter, each family according to its custom. Some go to camp near the fish caches they made the previous autumn for use when the winter supplies should be exhausted. Others go to spots where they hope that by jigging with a hand-line through the ice they will be able to catch enough salmon trout to carry them from day to day. Later, in May or early June, when the seals come out to sun on the ice of Elliot Bay, a few families go north to hunt them. In spring people may be almost constantly on the move. Between the end of April and the middle of July the camp in which I lived moved thirteen times, distances ranging from four feet to forty miles. The long moves were determined by the need for fish. The short ones were dictated by the thaws, which first melted our iglus, then transformed the snow patches where our tents were pitched into waist-deep quagmires of slush and sent us down to exposed gravel strips along the river's edge, and finally flooded our gravel strips, forcing us uphill in retreat from the advancing water.

In July, drawn by thoughts of migrating salmon trout, the dispersed families walk and paddle back along the river to the fishing spots where they will pass the summer, singly or in groups of two or three, occasionally separated from one another by as much as a hundred miles or more. One or two families may travel north as far as the Adelaide Peninsula; one or two others habitually return to the mouth of the Hayes River, near the winter site. The majority, with whom I lived, move much farther south, to Itimnaaqjuk by the Franklin Lake Rapids.

People usually remain at the summer campsite until the frosts set in, in late August. This was the season in which I arrived, to find the able-bodied off in the interior hunting caribou for

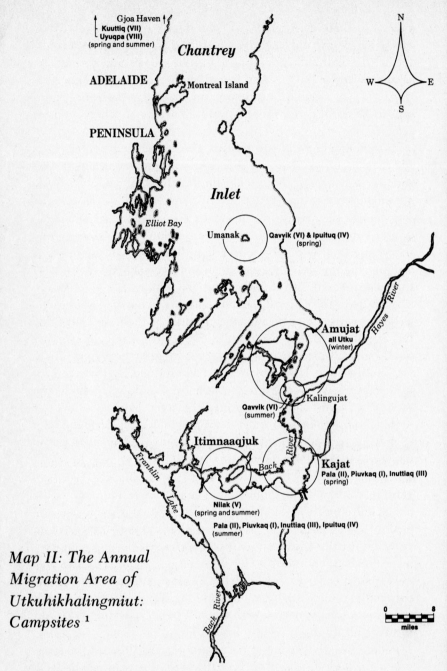

Gjoa Haven
Kuuttiq (VII)
Uyuqpa (VIII)
(spring and summer)

Chantrey

ADELAIDE

Montreal Island

PENINSULA

Inlet

Elliot Bay

Umanak   Qavvik (VI) & Ipuituq (IV)
(spring)

N
W — E
S

Heyes River

Amujat
all Utku
(winter)

Qavvik (VI)
(summer)   Kalingujat

Itimnaaqjuk

Back   River

Kajat
Pala (II), Piuvkaq (I), Inuttiaq (III)
(spring)

Franklin   Lake

Nilak (V)
(spring and summer)
Pala (II), Piuvkaq (I), Inuttiaq (III), Ipuituq (IV)
(summer)

*Map II: The Annual
Migration Area of
Utkuhikhalingmiut:
Campsites* [1]

Back   River

0   8
miles

1. Roman numerals correspond to the household
numerals on the charts in Appendix III.

winter clothing, while the old people and some of the unmarried women and children waited at the fishing place. The hunters are usually gone for one to three weeks. If they have been successful, they return with hides for the women to work into clothing, and a little marrow and tallow as a treat for those who stayed behind. Most of the meat is cached at the site of the kill, to be fetched by sled in late autumn or winter, when it makes a welcome change from a diet of frozen whitefish.

By the time the river begins to freeze, usually in early October, the canvas tents are crackling in the bitter wind, and the men think of building *qaqmaqs*. A qaqmaq, among the Utku, is a round, tent-roofed dwelling, walled with ice blocks cut from the river, or sometimes, if the snowfall has been sufficient, with a combination of snow blocks and ice blocks. A qaqmaq is much warmer than a tent, as the wind cannot penetrate the solid walls. However, one is at the mercy of the erratic autumn thaws, which cause the slush mortar between the ice blocks to melt, and sometimes even threaten to melt the walls themselves. Through the holes the wind drives fine snow (or sleet or rain) over the occupants and their bedding. "Snow" falls also from the canvas roof; the steam from boiling tea collects there and freezes into long frost-feathers which precipitate in fine cold prickles on one's face as the dwelling cools.

The Eskimos accept these minor annoyances with equanimity. They agree that it is unpleasant *(hujuujaq,* not *quvia)* to be cold and wet, but what can one do *(ayuqnaq)?* So when a sudden rain makes a sieve of the canvas roof they laugh: "We are wet like dogs."

And there are compensations. The river in Itimnaaqjuk teems with salmon trout in October. Often twenty and occasionally as many as forty trout, each weighing between ten and forty pounds, may be caught by one fisherman in a day's jigging through the ice. A few of these are eaten fresh, but most are cached in hollow cairns to freeze for use in winter and spring. Autumn is also the season when caches of whitefish are made for spring dogfeed. As in winter, nets are set under the ice near the camp, and sometimes as many as fifty whitefish are caught daily in each net.

There are still quantities of fish in Itimnaaqjuk at the end of October and early in November, but by this time the desire for the warmth of iglus begins to outweigh the pleasure of the daily meal of boiled trout. Salmon trout are much scarcer in Amujat; there the daily fare consists almost entirely of the inferior frozen whitefish. "On whitefish we grow thin," people joke. But iglus can be built much earlier in Amujat, where snow falls sooner and more heavily than in Itimnaaqjuk to the south. So one day the ice-walled shelters stand open to marauding foxes. The sleds are off for Amujat to join the other families gathering there for the winter.

V. Nomadism

Nomadic life holds much pleasure for the Utku. Arduous as moving sometimes is—when the sled runners bore into thawing drifts and stick fast; when the river snow becomes water-logged so that dogs and people slosh deep in slush and are soon drenched; when winds bite at noses and toes so that the children tied atop the load whimper with cold or shrink silently into the protective quilts that shroud them—nevertheless a move to a new campsite is a memorable punctuation in the ordinary flow of life. People look forward to the change of scene or of dwelling, just as they look forward to each turning season. In the autumn the talk is about how good *(quvia)* it will feel to move into an iglu. The night before we set off for Amujat, my first October at Back River, Inuttiaq, my father, lying in bed, pantomimed in the air the motions of cutting snow blocks and improvised a little "ai ya ya" song about tomorrow's iglu building. In the spring, when the iglus have been transformed by long occupancy into burrows of filthy gray ice, the talk turns to the pleasures of the spring moves: "Iglus are unpleasant *(hujuujaq,* not *quvia)* in the spring; the water of Amujat tastes unpleasantly of salt; it will be good to go to Itimnaaqjuk and fish." And people pantomime the motions of jigging for trout.

Even the process of moving holds excitement. A happy bustle pervades a camp that is preparing to move. Packing is done at double-quick tempo, orders given and obeyed with a vigor rarely seen in the quiet life of a settled camp. In the spring, when thawing weather and the search for fish required that we be constantly on the move, the spirit of impermanence seemed to infect people, so that, from my point of view, they seemed to make the maximum rather than the minimum necessary number of moves. At this season, unlike any other, tents were shifted for the slightest reason: because the gravel floor had become soiled with bits of paper and fishbones, or because a shift in the breeze was filling the tent with mosquitoes. Shifting was not done with quite such abandon in the more permanent summer camp; there, the unwanted foreign matter was picked out of the floor and the mosquitoes were simply endured. In spring, too, when the flooding river forced us uphill, the retreat was always made foot by foot as the river rose. For several days we moved camp at least once a day and sometimes oftener, and always when the water had arrived within inches of our doorsteps. Once as we were setting up the tents for the third or fourth time, I asked the friend who was helping me: "Does the water come up this high?" (I indicated the spot where we were placing the tents.) "Sometimes it does and sometimes it doesn't," was the reply.

I do not know what prompted people to move in this way. It may have been optimism; weakened by measles, as the Utku were that spring, they may have hoped that each minimal move would be the last. But then why shift the tent to escape the mosquitoes or improve the flooring? It sometimes seemed as though moving—rearranging the environment—were a form of play for the Eskimos, a pleasure in itself. Whatever the explanation, I never completely shared the Eskimo spirit. I found it a strenuous job to strike a tent, move all its contents uphill by armfuls, set up the tent again, and rearrange the interior. Once it was done, I enjoyed the freshness of a new home, a tent floor carpeted with reindeer moss and cranberry blossoms. Still, moves were a nuisance that disrupted my work and, worse, shifted my world as a kaleidoscope shifts its bits of glass, making me uncomfortably aware of the pattern's fragility. So, in retreating from the rising water, had I followed my own preference, I would have moved, once and for all, the few hundred feet to the top of the hill and sat there securely, looking down at the flood.

The fact that the moves were always made with no time to spare I sometimes found a little harrowing, too. I was never quite sure when I went to bed with the water two feet from my door whether I was going to wake up afloat. One such evening I observed to Inuttiaq that the dogs, who were chained to boulders at the water's edge, were going to get wet during the night. "Yes, they are," he said. And sure enough, in the morning several dogs were standing belly-deep in the flood, their noses pointing stiffly skyward.

In the course of many years of moving up and down the river, from campsite to campsite, from one fishing place to another, the countryside that seemed so limitless to me and at first sight so empty, had become to its inhabitants as grooved with associations as a familiar face. In the recognition of this familiarity, as well as in the excitement of change, may lie some of the pleasure the Utku find in their way of life. Like other wandering people, the Utku have a remarkable memory for the details of their territory, and the accuracy with which they observe and mentally record the contours of the terrain are proverbial; their map-making (and -reading) abilities are phenomenal. I showed several Utku men maps of the entire North American Arctic. They pointed out and named correctly all the major rivers, lakes, inlets, and islands from Baker Lake in the south to King William Island in the north, and from Perry River in the west to the west coast of Hudson Bay in the east, a territory approximately 135,000 miles square. One man even pointed out Bathurst Inlet and Southampton Island correctly, from hearsay. He had never been to either place, but he had heard them described by other Eskimos on his travels. Rasmussen's volume (1931) on the Netsilik contains maps of approximately the same area that were drawn by Netsilik Eskimos at his request. The Eskimos need these abilities, not only to find their way up and down the river in their sometimes lengthy travels, but also to relocate the caches of game and of belongings that they leave behind them as they move.

I was shown the country through Utku eyes the first time I traveled with Utku companions. While still camped at the summer site in Itimnaaqjuk, we had gone, two men and I, to replenish our supply of tea from the cache I had made in Amujat for winter use. This entailed a two-day round trip of sixty to eighty miles, on foot and by canoe. I was awed by the granite silence of the shores between which we paddled. The dip of the paddles and the quiet remarks of my companions were the only sounds. The stone fingers of cairns protruding into the gray sky to me accentuated the emptiness, the loneliness of the scene. But the Utku build cairns to *lessen* the loneliness, to create company for themselves. My companions knew the builders of many of the cairns; some had been built by people already familiar to me as well. The men pointed out to me on the hilltops and peninsulas we passed the many traces of their habitation: "That's Pala's cache, that oil drum"; "Piuvkaq built that cairn"; "people fish here in the autumn after the ice comes"; "Nilak has two caribou cached on the far side of those two steep knolls." Every point of land, every rise, every island and backwater was known and named, had its use and its associations.

Often a reminiscent mood was roused by a move to a new campsite, even when in my view people should have been exhausted and miserable after hours of shoving and tugging heavily loaded sleds through impossible country and worse weather. Once, I recall, it was five in the morning before we had our new camp made and tea drunk. It was June, just before break-up. We had traveled all night through wet snow, sleet, and slush, and had been without sleep for twenty-four hours. Even so, instead of going to bed people sat and shared memories of this campsite—some memories more than forty years old. They talked about places where they had fished and what they had caught. They showed me landmarks, including the place where Rasmussen had camped in 1923, though no visible trace remained of it, and taught me the names of all the points of land that now and then emerged as shadows behind the veil of sleet. It was rare, this eager talkativeness; it belonged to the peak moments. I heard it also when the men returned from a trading trip to Gjoa Haven in the winter, or when two households were reunited after a seasonal absence. Finally silence fell—but there was still no sleep. The men went fishing, picking their way out across the slushy river, while the women went for a slow ramble up over the hill among the oblongs and circles of stones that marked old tent sites, each in her own path, thinking her own thoughts. Only the children went to sleep, one still holding her half-drunk tea.

VI. The Society

Although the location of fish is the primary consideration in the Utkus' choice of campsites, nevertheless, within the limits set by their need for food, people still have considerable latitude to choose where and with whom they will live. There are many places where salmon trout and char are plentiful during the summer and where caribou can be hunted in autumn. Choice, within narrower limits, is even possible with regard to the winter campsite. Utku camping patterns, therefore, reveal not only the location of fish, seal, and caribou but also the shape of Utku social life; the preferences of the various families that compose the group and the quality of their relationships with each other.

It was in the pattern of the summer dispersal that I first, and most concretely, saw the lines along which Utku society is divided. The basic division is between "real family" (*ilammarigiit*) and "less real" or "not real family" (*ilammarilluangngittut* or *ilammaringngittut*). In the Utku view, everybody in the group is related to everybody else, and everybody addresses, or refers to, everybody else by terms of kinship. Kinship is the most important bond in Utku society. The dyadic contractual relationships—the hunting, meat-sharing, joking, and dancing partnerships—that are prominent in many other Eskimo groups play no role in contemporary Utku society, as far as I was able to determine. It is possible that there may have been hunting, joking, or dancing partners in the days when the group was larger, but I doubt that there were sharing partnerships even in the old days. The neighboring Netsilik did have such partnerships. In their winter camps, seals used to be distributed according to complex rules by which two men always gave each other a specified part of every seal caught. And throughout their lives the partners addressed each other by the name of the seal-cut which they shared: "My buttock," or "My head" (Van de Velde 1956). But Rasmussen (1931:482), writing of his visit to the Utku in 1923, describes them as lacking any such special sharing relationships at that time.

The Utku establish kinship bonds in four different ways: by birth, by betrothal or marriage, by adoption, and by naming. Formerly, bonds were created in a fifth way, as well: two friends would exchange wives for a period of time. Traces of previous wife-exchanges can be seen in the kinship terms used by certain people today. One woman, for example, calls two men "father," because they were joint husbands of her mother. Nowadays, however, since the practice of exchanging wives is in disrepute, it is difficult to obtain information either on the previous extent of the practice or on its present existence.

Wife-exchange aside, most Utku are related in two or more of the four other ways mentioned. Marriage relationships overlap with and complicate blood relationships, since Utku parents almost always, when possible, betroth their children to relatives, especially to cousins, that is, to the sons and daughters of the parents' brothers, sisters, and cousins.

Adoption is a complicating factor in kinship, too. As in other Eskimo groups, adoption is common, and the adopted child tends to retain certain kinship bonds, both terminological and behavioral, with his genealogical family in addition to acquiring membership in his adoptive family. For example, he continues to call his genealogical brothers and sisters by sibling terms and to treat them as informally as genealogical siblings treat one another. So complex do consanguineal and adoptive relationships become that there is even a kinship term (tamajrutik), which people resort to in certain cases when they do not know which of two equally applicable terms to choose for a given relative.

The fourth way in which Utku create kin relationships is by bestowing on a baby the name of some other person. A belief widespread among Eskimo groups is that a person acquires along with his name various characteristics of the previous owner or owners of the name: the latter's physical, mental, or moral traits, his skills and abilities. In a sense, he becomes the previous owner or owners of the name. The belief in name-souls and behavior related to the belief appear to vary in detail from group to group. Among the Utku, a baby may be named either for a living or for a dead person; in both cases the child is thought to acquire physical characteristics and mannerisms of previous owners of its name, including animals, if the name happens to be that of an animal. For example, a child who cocked her head to one side when listening was said to do so because her name was

Tulugaq (Raven). I do not know whether Utku believe, as some other Eskimos do, that the previous owners of a child's name protect their namesake (Gubser 1965:206; Stefansson 1951: 398–400), or transfer to the latter their skills and other characteristics (Guemple 1965:328–329). An Utku namesake does, however, acquire the network of kin relationships that belonged to his "name," that is, to the name's last owner, the person for whom he was named. He does not entirely substitute the terms appropriate to his "name" for those that would be genealogically appropriate for him to use; he may still use genealogical terms for many of his relatives; but for other relatives he uses the terms that his "name" would have used, and is in turn addressed by the terms that his relatives would have used in addressing his "name."

Among some Eskimos, name-sharing influences other behavior besides the use of kin terms. It may lead to an especially close friendship (Gubser 1965:162) or entail responsibilities for economic support (Guemple 1965:326–327). The extreme indulgence shown to Eskimo children is also sometimes explained in terms of the name-soul belief: punishing the child would be an affront to the deceased person for whom the child was named (Stefansson 1951:398–400; Thalbitzer 1941:600). The Utku, however, usually explain their indulgence of children in different terms; and though I did not inquire concerning ideal behavior associated with the Utku name-relationship, in practice I noticed no special behavior between name-sharers, other than the use of the name-sharing term in address and reference.

In any case, the complexities of name-relationships do not obscure the all-important bond among those who consider themselves *ilammarigiit* (real family). In one context—when talking about kinship terms—the expression *ilammarigiit* may be used synonymously with *ilagiit* (family in general) to refer to all relatives to whom one is linked, or assumes one is linked, genealogically. But in other contexts, when talking, for example, about sharing property, *ilammarigiit* is defined more narrowly, as an extended family consisting of genealogical or adoptive siblings *(nukariit)* and the children of those siblings. To be sure, the Utku are no less flexible in matters of kinship than in other matters. Residence and personal likes and dislikes are both important in determining whether a potential bond will be activated or ignored. When I inquired about relatives who had moved away, I was told, "We don't use kin terms for those people; they don't live here." One elderly man did not know by what term he would address his genealogical sister if she should return; he could not recall her name, either, because she had married and moved away before he was born. My data seem to indicate, too, that bonds between the children of siblings tend to weaken after the death of the connecting relative or relatives. But whatever the precise composition of the *ilammarigiit* in a particular case, it is in most contexts a subcategory of *ilagiit* (family in general). And it is in this sense that I shall use the term throughout the book. People outside the *ilammarigiit* are considered "less real" or "not real family" *(ilammarilluangngittut or ilammaringngittut),* even though, because of shared names or because of distant or putative consanguineal relationship, these outsiders are addressed by the same kin terms that are used for "real family." Whenever possible, it is with their "real family" that people live, work, travel, and share whatever they have. Moreover, it is only with their "real family" that they appear to feel completely comfortable and safe.[12]

When I lived with them, the Utku were divided into three kin groups, whose central figures were, respectively, Pala and Qavvik (both elderly widowers) and Nilak (a married man of about forty). Of these groups, Pala's was the largest. Whereas in 1963 Nilak's and Qavvik's families each had a core membership of three persons, Pala's kin numbered sixteen and comprised three households: Pala's own, and those of his older half-brother, Piuvkaq, and his nephew-cum-son-in-law, Inuttiaq. Piuvkaq and his wife were frail with age and illness ("tired," the Eskimos called it) and so were dependent on Pala's help, the more so, as they had no grown son or son-in-law to support them. Inuttiaq, like Nilak, was a vigorous man of about forty. He was related to Pala in two ways: as the son of one of Pala's brothers

12. Hereafter, I shall refer to members of an *ilammarigiit* or "real family" in various ways: as "kin" or "close relatives," as a "kin group" or as an "extended family." When I use the unqualified term "family," it may refer either to an *ilammarigiit* (an extended family) or to one of the nuclear families that comprise the latter. Which is meant should be clear from the context.

and as the husband of Pala's eldest daughter, Allaq. In addition, Pala's son Mannik was Inuttiaq's close friend; so Inuttiaq's household and Pala's were inseparable. Pala had a second son-in-law, too, a young man in his twenties named Ipuituq, whom he would have liked to count among his own. But Ipuituq, being a half-brother to Qavvik, had divided loyalties and was not always as obedient to Pala as the latter would have liked.

There were in addition two other households who, departing from their usual pattern, camped with the Utku during the first of the two winters I spent with them, but the Utku considered these families to be "not real Utku," in one case because the head of the household, Uyuqpa, though married to an Utku, was himself a Netsilingmiutaq; in the other because the head, Kuuttiq, though born an Utku, had become a Catholic and was now tied more closely to Catholic Netsilingmiut in Gjoa Haven than to Anglican Utku in Chantrey Inlet. These two peripheral households constituted a fourth kin group, because Uyuqpa's wife was the mother of Kuuttiq's wife; and there were also bonds of a complicated nature between them and Qavvik's family.

Though, as I have said, all three kin groups were interrelated in various ways, and clear lines were hard to draw, each nevertheless considered itself somewhat separate from the others, and frequently separated itself physically. When the Utku dispersed to their spring and summer camps, each of the three kin groups tended to go its own way, and when two or more shared the same campsite, as they did in the winter and occasionally at other seasons, one could usually see the lines between them in the spacing of the iglus or tents. Ipuituq's household, drawn both to Pala and to Qavvik, lived sometimes with one man, sometimes with the other, and occasionally by itself.

1

Inuttiaq

The autumn camp in which I was deposited on my arrival at
Back River consisted entirely of members of Pala's family group.
And it was with Pala's (more precisely with Inuttiaq's) family
that I was destined to remain during my year and a half at Back
River.

I had been camped at the Rapids for a week when the caribou
hunters returned—first Nilak's family, then, two days later, Inuttiaq's. And within another day or two Inuttiaq had adopted
me. Inuttiaq was to become the most significant figure, both
personally and anthropologically, in my life at Back River.
When I think of him now, my feelings are a complex blend of
admiration, affectionate gratitude, and a helpless desire to compensate him somehow for the difficulties that my un-Eskimo
behavior created for him and his family. At the time, however,
my predominant feeling toward him was, all too frequently,
irritation. Inuttiaq was not a typical Utku: he was more assertive
than most, and from the outset I came into conflict with this
quality in him. But it was from Inuttiaq that I learned most about

the ways in which the Utku express their feelings toward one another. It was partly his very atypicality that made it possible for me to learn from him what the proper patterns are. Most other Utku were so well controlled that my untutored eye could not detect their emotions. But Inuttiaq was, if I have read him correctly, an unusually intense person. He, too, kept strict control of his feelings, but in his case one was aware that something was being controlled. The effort of his control was caught in the flash of an eye, quickly subdued, in the careful length of a pause, or the painstaking neutrality of a reply. Occasionally, when he failed to stay within acceptable bounds of expression, I learned from the disapproval of others what behavior constitutes a lapse and how disapproval is expressed. Living in Inuttiaq's own dwellings, as I did for two winters, I watched him with others: as father and husband, as host to his neighbors, and as religious leader of the community. The turbulence of my own relationship with him also gave me many opportunities to observe his efforts at control. By seeing what annoyed him in my behavior, what pleased him and made him feel proud or protective, I learned how he showed these feelings and how he tried to influence *my* feelings or control their expression.

I. Dominance and Intensity

In a society in which people seem to blend harmoniously with the brown tundra, Inuttiaq stood out. In a different society he might have been a leader; but Utku society allows little scope for would-be leaders. The Utku, like other Eskimo bands, have no formal leaders whose authority transcends that of the separate householders. Moreover, cherishing independence of thought and action as a natural prerogative, people tend to look askance at anyone who seems to aspire to tell them what to do.

Neither was Inuttiaq a man of informal influence. Sometimes an Eskimo who has a reputation for wisdom, for skill in hunting or in other matters, may acquire influence within the band; he will be known as an *ihumataaq* (one who has wisdom) and his views may weigh more than other men's, when plans are being made. But Inuttiaq, although perfectly capable of keeping his family fed, was not remarkable for his hunting ability, nor were his opinions particularly prized. The one outlet he had for leadership was provided by the Anglican church. He acted as the band's lay leader, conducting the triweekly church services and the occasional funeral, and reading prayers over sick people if called to do so. For the rest, he stood out solely on account of his individual style.

There was nothing mild about him. Even in photographs his personality is so vividly communicated that people who have never seen Eskimos single him out of a group, asking who he is. I, too, noticed him before I knew who he was. I had been waiting with considerable suspense for his return to the Haqvaqtuuq camp, wondering whether I might find in him my Eskimo father. Nilak, my other potential father, had already returned to camp and, I am sure with an eye to my tea and tobacco, had been most hospitable in offering to adopt me. However, both because of his socially peripheral position in the group (he was even camped on the opposite side of the river from the other households) and because the doubts concerning his wife, Niqi, which I had acquired from Ikayuqtuq's criticisms now had derived substance and strength from my negative first impressions, I had postponed making a decision until Inuttiaq should return.

When I was called from my tent by the announcement that Inuttiaq had arrived, I found the camp in turmoil: dogs burdened with back packs, tent poles, and cooking pots milled around the tents and were discouraged from thieving entry by shouts and well-aimed rocks. The number of the newcomers was magnified in my view by their strangeness and by the uproar; but confused though I was, my eye was drawn to a man of about forty, who stood with straight barbaric arrogance (so my fieldnote described it), surveying the commotion. My instant premonition was chilling; I determined on the spot that under no circumstances did I want to live in that man's household. It was, of course, Inuttiaq.

I thought him haughty and hostile in appearance, very un-Eskimo in both feature and expression. He did not smile; he looked hard at me in the few moments before we were introduced, making no move. He did smile as we shook hands, but I could not read in the smile either the warm friendliness or the gentle shyness that I had come to expect from unknown Eskimos. Later I found that Inuttiaq did have great warmth; I had a glimpse of it that first day when I watched him greet his small daughter Raigili. They shook hands in silence, but there was affectionate softness in Inuttiaq's eye as he looked at her. Nevertheless, the predominant impression was of a harsh, vigorous, dominant man, highly self-dramatizing; a personality set off almost as sharply as that of a kapluna against the backdrop of his self-effacing fellows. Kaplunas, in general, with their aggressively loud voices, vigorous, jerky gestures, and noisy bravado create a highly discordant impression in an Eskimo group. To a lesser extent, so did Inuttiaq, even though, if one analyzed his voice and gestures they were Eskimo, not kapluna.

When kapluna sportsmen visited the Inlet during the summer, it was Inuttiaq who initiated most of the Eskimo visits to the kapluna camp and who took charge of distributing to the other households the boatload of food the kaplunas left for the Eskimos on their departure. Indeed, he was so much more self-assertive in his trading than either Nilak or Pala that some of the kaplunas felt quite chary of him and protective toward the other Eskimos.

I do not mean that he was aggressive in the way a kapluna would have been; he expressed dissatisfaction with a poor trade only when I encouraged him to do so, and then in the most tentative way. Once a kapluna offered Inuttiaq pink beads when he had asked for tea and tobacco, and I asked Inuttiaq: "Is it enough?" Inuttiaq looked uncomfortable and said, "Almost enough—just a *little* bit more, maybe." But instead of shyly retreating as others did when confronted by the language barrier, he played clown and communicated in pantomime. He was always in the forefront of the group of men who were displaying their articles for trade and he, unlike the others, was never loath to state what he wanted in exchange for his bone toys. And whereas other men presented an amiably acquiescent face to a drunken sportsman who patronized them, Inuttiaq quietly refused to shake hands. He stood with his hands at his sides, just smiling slightly.

Later, innumerable small incidents contributed to strengthen my initial impression of Inuttiaq's self-dramatization. There was the forceful way he drove his dogs, his voice rising and falling at top volume over several octaves as he told them picturesquely what he thought of their slowness, their contrariness, or the odor of their feces. "Smells like sugar!" he would roar, then turn to his passengers and laugh. I noted the commanding jerk of his chin as he whistled an inattentive congregation to its feet at the start of a church service, instead of quietly saying to its members, "May you stand up"; his habit of reserving his best laughter for his own jokes (which were exceptionally numerous and often exceptionally lewd); and his way of introducing himself at the beginning of a tape-recording session: "I, Inuttiaq, am going to speak," or (when I taped a church service) "Inuttiaq is leading." No one else ever gave his name when recording or volunteered to sing a song he did not know just for the sake of being heard. Inuttiaq was also one of the very few people who was positively eager (as distinct from merely willing) to have his picture taken; the other two who displayed similar eagerness were Inuttiaq's elderly father-in-law, Pala, and the former's three-year-old daughter, Saarak. Pala and Saarak would come to join any group at which I aimed my camera. Inuttiaq asked me to take a picture of him for him to keep, and he posed for it with care, planting himself, very erect, next to his lead dog and calling for his ice chisel and scoop to hold.

The theatrical quality of his manner is typified for me by his return one winter morning from a two-week trading trip to Gjoa Haven. He arrived while the camp was asleep and so was not greeted as usual by dark knots of people clustered outside the iglus to watch him anchor his sled with a flourish at the foot of the slope. I woke to hear a most tremendous pounding of fist and snow knife on the wooden inner door of the iglu, a banging much greater than necessary to unstick it from its icy frame; he might have been sounding brasses. Then, crawling through, he heaved himself up and stood very straight and solid in his snow-encrusted furs, staring at us from under icicled lashes, as if announcing by his bearing: *"HERE AM I!!!"*

I quickly came to share the Utku view of Inuttiaq's pretentiousness and his antics. People considered him a show-off. No derogatory reaction was ever visible when he was present, and one sometimes heard people commend him for being a great joker and very funny *(tiphi)*. His reputation as a joker had even reached Gjoa Haven; it was the first thing I heard about Inuttiaq on my way to Back River. People laughed with merriment when he played his favorite comedian role—making faces, grabbing playfully for adolescent penises, or graphically describing the size and shape of his feces or the life history of his urine—but behind his back they also gossiped about his fondness for being at the center of the stage. "He is not very shy *(kanngu),*" they would remark.

Nevertheless, Inuttiaq was considered a fine person. It seemed to me curious that it should be so in a society that places a high value on mildness and gentleness. Perhaps it was partly that people enjoyed watching Inuttiaq play a role that they themselves would have liked to play. Very important, too, I think, was the fact that control of temper is a cardinal virtue among Eskimos, and Inuttiaq never lost his temper.

This was a remarkable feat if my impression is correct that internally Inuttiaq was a highly tempestuous man. Perhaps it was partly his self-dramatizing behavior that gave that impression when contrasted with the much milder, retiring manner of the others. Partly, too, it was the unusual ferocity of his dog-beating. All the Utku beat their dogs; they saw it as a necessary disciplinary measure: "We all do it; we know it makes the dogs behave; everybody knows it," they emphasized in justification. They beat them with boots, rocks, frozen fish, hammers, tentpoles, or anything else that came to hand, and as the dog was usually chained or harnessed, escape was impossible. They got a good deal more than pedagogical satisfaction out of the process, too; I saw gleaming eyes and smiles of delight as dogs cowered and whined with bruises and bloody heads. I also saw a woman's face absolutely set and expressionless as she pounded and pounded a thieving dog from a distance of two or three feet with a boulder, which she picked up and threw again every time it bounced off the animal's ribs. But Inuttiaq sometimes beat his team mercilessly for no offense whatever. One day he broke a tentpole over the back of one dog because the team, having had, as usual at that season, nothing to eat for two or three days, was howling in anticipation of an approaching armload of ptarmigan. No power on earth could have stopped the team from howling at that moment, but Inuttiaq beat them, anyway.

Inuttiaq also had extremely violent fantasies, full of stabbings, whippings, and murders. He usually voiced them on occasions when he felt helpless to cope with kaplunas. I do not know that these fantasies were peculiar to him. Others may have shared his views; but Inuttiaq was the only one who expressed them to me.

Moreover Inuttiaq, far more frequently than other adults, had audible nightmares. Young children often had them: dreadful nightmares from which there was no waking them. Inuttiaq's six-year-old daughter, Raigili, often screamed and sobbed in her sleep, raising her head from the pillow and writhing in a most agonized way, while her parents pummeled her and shouted at her to go to sleep, usually to no avail. She never woke; her sobs gradually subsided as she slept. It is Utku belief that only children have nightmares, and indeed all of the adults I knew except Inuttiaq slept extremely quietly. I asked an old lady one day if adults ever had nightmares; she laughed heartily and joked: "That would be frightening (kappia)! Are you going to have nightmares here?" But Inuttiaq slept restlessly and often talked in his sleep in an anxious, defensive tone; I could not understand the words.

Other people seemed to have a sense, similar to mine, of Inuttiaq's inner intensity. They feared him for the very reason they admired him: because he never lost his temper. They said that a man who *never* lost his temper could kill if he ever did become angry; so, I was told, people took care not to cross him, and I had the impression that Allaq, his wife, ran more quickly than other wives to do her husband's bidding.

Looking back, I wonder if Inuttiaq might have been partially aware of people's fear of him. It occurs to me that a desire to reassure people, in addition to the obvious desire to attract attention, might have been one of the motives behind his joking. One day when he was teasing a fourteen-year-old by grabbing for his penis—a favorite game of his, and his alone—he said to me: "I'm joking; people joke a great deal. People who joke are not frightening (kappia, iqhi)."

The feeling Inuttiaq was expressing is one that is very characteristic of Eskimos: a fear of people who do not openly demonstrate their good-will by happy (quvia) behavior, by smiling, laughing, and joking. Unhappiness is often equated with hostility *(ningaq,*[1] *urulu)* in the Eskimo view. A moody person may be planning to knife you in the back when you are out fishing with him, claiming on return that you drowned. In the old days he might have been plotting to abscond with your wife—a common occurrence prior to the introduction of Christ and the Royal Canadian Mounted Police. Even without harboring specific evil designs an unhappy person may harm one, merely by the power of his moody thoughts. It is believed that strong thoughts *(ihumaquqtuuq)* can kill or cause illness; and people take great pains to satisfy others' wishes so that resentment will not accumulate in the mind. A happy person, on the other hand, is a safe person. I wondered whether Inuttiaq felt an exceptionally strong need to show himself a happy person because he was not.

II. Religious Leader: Assertiveness

The quality of Inuttiaq's assertiveness, and the community's reaction to it, appeared clearly in the manner in which he exercised his religious leadership. The Utku have been exposed to a minimum of missionary influence, so little that in Ottawa, in Cambridge Bay, and even in Gjoa Haven I had been told by knowledgeable kaplunas that the people were pagan. My first hint that this was not the case came from Ikayuqtuq in Gjoa Haven, who told me that the Utku, far from being pagan, were "too religious." They are devout, if not exactly orthodox, Anglicans, and their religion is one of the two or three central interests in their life (others being hunting-and-fishing, and eating). They were converted to Christianity some twenty-five or thirty years ago, largely through contact with Christian

1. At the time this fieldwork was done (1963–1965) I was under the impression that there was just one word, *ningaq(tuq),* which meant both "he is angry" and "he fights." On my return visit to the Utku in 1968 I discovered that I was mistaken. These two ideas are conveyed by two different words: *ningaqtuq,* which can be glossed as "he fights," and *ningngaktuq,* "he is angry." In spite of this error, I have decided to leave the base *ningaq* in the text, considering that this is preferable to giving no indication at all of the Utku concept to which the text refers. The reader should bear in mind, however, that wherever the base *ningaq* occurs in the text it may represent either the word *ningaqtuq* or the word *ningngaktuq,* and in no case do I know which of these words was actually used by the Utku speaker.

Eskimos whom they met on trading trips to Repulse Bay and Baker Lake. Occasional white missionaries, Catholic and Anglican, had passed through Chantrey Inlet on proselytizing trips, but none had ever stayed with the Utku. The nearest resident missionaries were in Gjoa Haven: a European Catholic priest and the Eskimo deacon, Nakliguhuktuq. Nakliguhuktuq was responsible in turn to a kapluna missionary in Spence Bay, a community somewhat under a hundred miles northeast of Gjoa Haven. One or the other of these men made the long trip down by dogsled to visit the Utku once every year if possible (it often was not possible), and it was Inuttiaq's job to conduct the every-day religious observances of the band under Nakliguhuktuq's tutelage.

I never found out how Inuttiaq had been chosen lay leader. Nakliguhuktuq did not know, either. I gathered that Inuttiaq had been leader for two years or less at the time I came there. Two, and possibly all three, of Nilak's brothers had preceded him, but when two of these men died and the third was hospitalized for treatment of tuberculosis, Inuttiaq became the leader.

Inuttiaq's duties were to conduct two services on Sunday, at 11 A.M. and at 7 P.M., and a prayer meeting on Wednesday evening at seven. Deviations from this ideal pattern were frequent, however. Inuttiaq canceled or rearranged services not only when practical exigencies required but also when it suited his personal inclination. If it got dark at five o'clock and fuel was scarce, or merely if Inuttiaq were impatient, we would pray at four instead of at seven; and if someone happened to be busy building an iglu on Wednesday we could pray just as well on Thursday. Inuttiaq sometimes decided not to hold services, saying that he was tired or had a bad cough. Occasionally, when he was planning to leave for Gjoa Haven on Monday, he would even cancel a Sunday service in order to prepare the dog food for the trip, in spite of the fact that work of any sort was forbidden on Sunday. At other times he gave no explanation at all for omitting a service. No one ever inquired or commented.

Such irregularity was perfectly in line with the pragmatic adaptability that characterizes much of Eskimo behavior. If circumstances make it difficult to realize a plan, well, it can't be helped (*ayuqnaq*). But I read more than pragmatism into Inuttiaq's behavior. I was annoyed by an intuition that when he exercised his prerogative in ordering religious observances he *enjoyed* the power inherent in his right to direct community behavior. He held the community in his hand, and it seemed to me that he savored the fact in a way that was quite improper in Eskimo eyes. It is difficult in retrospect to say exactly what gave me that impression. I question whether perhaps I saw Inuttiaq's motives through the blur of my own dislike of arbitrary orders. There was little to criticize in the manner in which he made and communicated his decisions. When he dismissed the congregation, saying, "We aren't going to pray today; I have a cough," his quiet matter-of-factness was exemplary. Yet others besides myself had the impression that Inuttiaq enjoyed telling them what to do; they complained to Nakliguhuktuq that Inuttiaq was overzealous in his attempts to regulate their behavior.

Sunday was Inuttiaq's day of leadership. I felt the weight of his presence more on that day than on others, possibly because work was forbidden on Sunday, so he was more at home. Possibly, too, the fact that Anglicanism is uncongenial to me increased the oppressiveness of the atmosphere. I object more powerfully to being told to say "amen" than I do to being told to make tea.

The day used to begin pleasantly enough. We slept later than usual, as there was no need to harvest the daylight hours. Similarly, because there was no rush, the usual three or four mugs of morning tea might be followed by a kettle of coffee, if we had any. Coffee in turn was followed by the element of Anglican ritual that held strongest appeal for me: a wash and hair-combing. The iglu smelled delightfully of soap on Sunday mornings. The only drawback to the procedure was that all the dormant itch in my scalp was roused by the combing. There was nothing to prevent one from washing one's hands and face or combing one's hair in midweek, too, but usually people did not—except for the young girls who, perhaps for the friendliness of it, liked to comb each other's hair out and rebraid it.

Inuttiaq's daughter Saarak almost always objected violently to having her hair braided. Allaq, her mother, lulled her by talking to her throughout the process in a low, saccharine voice whose flow never stopped, telling her how pretty she was going to be and how lovable (*niviuq*) and cute, and how her father and her mother's brother and her mother's sister were going to see her and tell her how pretty and lovable and cute she was— and so on and on till the braiding was accomplished. Then Allaq would tell Saarak to show Inuttiaq the stiff new braids and Inuttiaq would obligingly admire with a warm "vaaaaaa!"

By this time people were usually beginning to gather for church, which was held in our home unless one of the other dwellings happened to be larger or better lit. Church was held promptly at eleven by whichever of the three watches in camp, Nilak's, Inuttiaq's, or mine, happened to suit Inuttiaq best. If he was still washing or felt like having another cup of tea when his watch said eleven, he went by mine, which was an hour slower. It must be admitted, though, that he rarely kept people waiting very long. He would order us, his wife and daughters, to hurry up, and we would hastily straighten the bedding and push the duffel bags to the wall to make room for the women and children to climb onto the sleeping platform with us. The men and boys stood jammed together on the floor, seats of oil drums and boxes being brought only for a few of the older men. Everybody in camp, except for the few Catholics, came to church on Sunday mornings, so there were twenty-nine people at church in our ten-foot iglu during my first winter there.

In the main, Inuttiaq imitated Nakliguhuktuq's ritual and manner in conducting a service. The various parts followed one another in orthodox Anglican fashion; Inuttiaq read from more or less the same passages as Nakliguhuktuq in the prayer-book, used the same formulae in his extemporaneous prayers, and painstakingly followed the weekly schedule of Bible readings that was circulated to all outstations by the mission in Spence Bay. Both Nakliguhuktuq and Inuttiaq created a tone that was much less dramatic, more muted, and a tempo that was slower than that of a kapluna service. I was reminded of Eskimo services I had witnessed in Alaska. The leader's presence never dominated the congregation, as a kapluna clergyman's does. Hymns were announced and the sermons or textual explanations delivered in a voice as quiet as inward musing.

Inuttiaq preached very seldom, except when he had just come back from visiting Nakliguhuktuq in Gjoa Haven, and his sermons were necessarily less sophisticated than Nakliguhuktuq's. Nakliguhuktuq was well versed in Anglican doctrine; Inuttiaq, like the other Utku, was relatively untutored. He almost always covered the same basic points in his sermons, without elaboration. Satan wants us *(piyuma)*, he used to say, but God, who loves *(naklik)* us as a father, will protect us as long as we pray regularly and don't get angry *(ningaq, urulu)*, steal, or lie. We should try to learn more and more of God's words—you should and I should, too. Otherwise we will burn forever and it will hurt very much. We all know that; you know it, and I, too.

It was some time before I realized that Inuttiaq did occasionally preach, since he always did it after announcing the closing hymn and without raising his eyes from the page. As the sermons were always very short, I thought he was reading the words of the hymn before starting to sing. Nakliguhuktuq's manner of preaching was equally quiet, but there was a difference; he, unlike Inuttiaq, looked at his audience as he talked. At the time I thought nothing of this difference; but now, fitting together the bits and pieces of Inuttiaq's behavior, I wonder whether it might have been an unconscious suppression of a wish to impose himself, to dictate, that kept Inuttiaq's eyes lowered.

In one other significant respect Inuttiaq's manner of conducting the services differed from Nakliguhuktuq's: Nakliguhuktuq allowed the congregation to choose almost all of the hymns in the two evening services; Inuttiaq almost always chose them himself.

But it was not only the differences between Inuttiaq's services and Nakliguhuktuq's that imbued the former with Inuttiaq's assertive spirit. The ritual elements that he chose to imitate and his manner of teaching them to the other Utku were also significant. I particularly remember two innovations in ritual: one in Inuttiaq's own behavior, and a second that affected the whole congregation. Though I am unsure of Inuttiaq's reasons for making these changes, it seemed to me in both cases that the effect of his act was to enhance his visibility.

The change in Inuttiaq's personal ritual occurred during my first winter in Chantrey Inlet. We had moved church from our iglu to Pala's because the latter was brightly lit by a gasoline pressure lamp. Inuttiaq had recently returned from a trip to Gjoa Haven where he had attended a service at Nakliguhuktuq's. Nakliguhuktuq held services in the large main room of his house, which ordinarily served as living room, kitchen, and chil dren's bedroom. Within the limits imposed by these quarters, he adhered as closely as he could to orthodox Anglican practice. While the congregation gathered, Nakliguhuktuq used to sit sociably at the kitchen table, which doubled as altar and prie-dieu, but shortly before the service was to begin, he would disappear into the little back bedroom. When he reappeared in his white deacon's robe, clasping his prayerbook formally in both hands, the congregation rose and he announced the first hymn. Inuttiaq, like Nakliguhuktuq, had used to sit chatting with the congregation while they assembled; but after he came home from his midwinter trip to Gjoa Haven, I noticed that he no longer did so; though he had no robe to don, he now sat silently at home, reading his Bible, ritually washing his hands or merely idling, until the rest of us had had time to gather—and usually to wait a little. Then he appeared and took his seat on the oil drum reserved for him in the center of the floor, and the service began.

I will never know what was in Inuttiaq's mind when he made this change, since, so far as I was aware, he himself never remarked on his innovation, nor did the others give any sign that they had noticed it. To be sure, it must have seemed to Inuttiaq only right and proper that the ritual behavior of Nakliguhuktuq, the religious teacher, should be imitated. The Utku do have a conception of propriety in religious behavior; in certain respects they follow quite closely the proper Anglican procedures, removing their caps or hoods in church, and praying with folded hands and lowered head. Inuttiaq in a communicative moment once showed me the way the Utku used to sing hymns in the early days of their Christianity, jogging rhythmically from foot to foot: "We thought we should do it that way; we were very confused," he laughed, with some embarrassment, I thought.

But it seems to me that mere conscientiousness concerning ritual detail is not enough to explain Inuttiaq's innovation. As I have said, Inuttiaq was often irregular in his adherence to ritual.

I think, therefore, that his adoption of Nakliguhuktuq's manner of entry into church must have had a more personal meaning for him, and three thoughts concerning this have occurred to me. I wonder whether perhaps he sensed in the act and found appealing its ritual meaning: the formalization of the religious role of the lay leader and the separation of this role from his everyday secular life as husband, father, and neighbor. A second possibility is that he wished, unconsciously, to be more like the powerful leader he imagined Nakliguhuktuq to be. Inuttiaq, like other Utku, appealed to Nakliguhuktuq for support when neighbors (and kaplunas) became too difficult to cope with; he believed that Nakliguhuktuq wielded a bigger whip and had the ear of more powerful "kings" than he himself did. Might he not, then, have wished to adopt Nakliguhuktuq's behavior as his own? This second speculation, of course, would apply as well to any behavior of Nakliguhuktuq's that Inuttiaq adopted. My third thought has reference specifically to Inuttiaq's new manner of entry and was inspired by the effect that the innovation had on me when I first saw it. I sat among the women on Pala's sleeping platform, waiting for the service to begin. Inuttiaq was late. The other women read their Bibles silently on either side of me or exchanged quiet remarks with the men standing close and patient in the tiny floor space. The gasoline lantern tacked to the snow wall glared and hissed aggressively, melting the dome so that it dripped coldly down our necks and messily onto our prayerbooks, and soaked our parkas so that later they would freeze. "Iq (ugh)," someone said in a neutral voice, and from the block in readiness by the door cut a square of frozen snow to attach as a blotter to the offending drip. The wooden door of Inuttiaq's iglu across the way slapped against its frame and footsteps creaked vigorously across the snow while the men squeezed closer together on either side of the door to make room for Inuttiaq's entrance. Conversation stopped and eyes lifted from Bibles as Inuttiaq dove with a flourish through the knee-high entrance, stood for a moment to let the young men dust the snow off his back, then took his seat with a smile and a joke on the central oil drum. There was no doubt that Inuttiaq had arrived.

The effect of the other innovation I recall was equally assertive to my eye. I am no more certain than in the other instance that

Inuttiaq was motivated by a conscious desire to dominate, but in this case the reaction of the congregation seemed to show that the innovation offended their dignity as it did mine. Whereas people took no overt notice of Inuttiaq's new manner of arriving in church, seeming to define it as Inuttiaq's own business, it was another matter when he tried to alter *their* behavior.

It happened in early November, after I had been at Back River two months. The Utku had just assembled at the winter campsite and we were holding our first service of the winter season, all twenty-nine of us crushed into Inuttiaq's ten-foot iglu, contorted by the curving walls, by the uncomfortable proximity of foreign elbows and feet, and by the attempt to avoid the most relentless drips from the dome. It was under these awkward conditions that Inuttiaq suddenly decided to bring our ritual more into line with what he had observed in Gjoa Haven. Whereas previously the whole service had been conducted without change of posture, the women sitting and the men standing or sitting as room allowed, now we were to conform to more orthodox practice, standing, sitting, or squatting (in lieu of kneeling on the snow floor) during appropriate parts of the service.

I am not sure what triggered Inuttiaq's decision; though he had had many opportunities to observe the Anglican ritual in Gjoa Haven, he had not been there since the previous spring. The innovation seemed to be a spontaneous thought, as it occurred not at the beginning of the service but toward its close. Inuttiaq had conducted almost the entire service as usual: the opening hymns, the responses, prayers, and Bible reading. Then, as he opened the hymnbook for the closing hymns, he instructed the congregation to stand. Everybody except Piuvkaq's wife and I obeyed. Huluraq was sitting on the edge of the sleeping platform and could have stood up on the floor; but she was elderly and frail. I was jammed against the sloping rear wall of the iglu and could not have stood except curved double against the wall. But my situation was different only in degree from that of the other women who did stand on the sleeping platform; they too had to stand with bent heads in what looked like a most uncomfortable position. Inwardly, I seethed at the "inconsiderateness" of Inuttiaq's order, but nobody protested.

Later, however, a reaction that looked to my foreigner's eye like passive resistance gradually developed. What happened during the first month following the innovation I do not know, as I was away in Gjoa Haven. When I came back in mid-December I had the impression that standing for hymns, responses, and the creed had become standard behavior. People stood, on the whole, without being told to. But within a week of my return the rebellion (if that is what it was) had set in. I do not know whether I was the cause of the resistance; certainly I may have strengthened it by concurring in it. In any case, at each service now about a third of the women in the congregation remained seated, and by mid-January, services in which nobody at all stood alternated with ones in which four women rose: three pious adolescent girls and Nilak's always unpredictable wife, Niqi. The end came in February. For several services Inuttiaq seemed to ignore the fact that the congregation remained seated; he made no sign that they should rise. The following Sunday he *whistled* the congregation up with an imperative jerk of his chin; but only the three faithful young women, Inuttiaq's young brother-in-law, Ipuituq, and Niqi, obeyed. He never ordered them up again; the status quo ante prevailed. And all without one word, to my knowledge, being spoken.

This was not an isolated case; Inuttiaq's other attempts to influence Utku behavior and belief tended to meet equally sad fates, except when he could credibly cite the higher authority of Nakliguhuktuq and, through him, the authority of Goti (God). The emphasis is on "credibly." Though most of the Utku are enthusiastic students of Anglicanism, they are not easily convinced of the validity of new doctrines. The basic doctrines they understand very well: that the many people who get angry, lie, or steal are used by Satan as firewood and that the happy few who refrain from such evil activities will be taken up to heaven by Jesus when He returns. They know that shamans are to be feared *(kappia, iqhi)* because their power is from Satan, but that they need not fear as much as they used to because Jesus has more power than any shaman and he, like a good elder brother, "will love *(naklik)* and protect us if we pray." I found that people freely admitted that their knowledge of the Bible and of the proper Anglican behavior prescribed by the Bible was still limited, and they were eager to learn. They liked to be certain, however, that the doctrines they were taught really originated with the Lord and not with some overbearing minion with an urge to tell other people what to do. Local voices were suspect. Nakliguhuktuq, on the other hand, was trusted to speak for God and not to lie for the purpose of self-aggrandizement. But so great was the reluctance to be led by mortal man that people were careful to make certain I knew it was not Nakliguhuktuq himself they were attending to; Nakliguhuktuq was only expounding the Lord's words as written down in the religious texts by God's people in heaven "because they love and care for *(naklik)* us." All words found in the Bible, prayerbook, and hymnal were to be faithfully believed, whereas those in my Eskimo-English dictionary which, they knew, had been published by the Oblate Fathers, were in mortal error.

Inuttiaq was the first to insist that he learned his doctrines from Nakliguhuktuq and through Nakliguhuktuq from God, but sometimes the community seemed unwilling to accept his statement. "Have you heard?" he said once on his return from a trading trip to Gjoa Haven, "Jesus says we should knock on iglu doors before entering when we go visiting." (Most iglus nowadays do have waist-high wooden doors if wood is available and, as a result, are much warmer than in the past, when the entrance was left open all day.) I asked Inuttiaq if Nakliguhuktuq had said this. "I heard it from Nakliguhuktuq," he replied, "but it's Jesus who says we should do it." For the next few days, whenever anyone came in to visit, he reported the news to the visitor, very matter-of-factly, as though he were reporting the day's fish catch. "Have you heard? When we visit we should knock; I heard it." And he added with a laugh, "Uyuqpa too." Uyuqpa was one of the less convinced Anglicans in the community; he vacillated between Anglicanism and Catholicism, a fact that may have exacerbated the dislike in which he was held because of his bad temper.

But somehow the doctrine never gained a foothold in the community. Uyuqpa was not the only one who ignored Inuttiaq's pronouncement. Nilak and Qavvik, leaders of the two other family factions in the community, questioned it, but unfortunately I did not know enough Eskimo at the time to understand either the questions or Inuttiaq's answers. Other people, when instructed, merely murmured "eeeee (yes)," indicating with the customary bland impassive smile that they heard. Inuttiaq's wife, Allaq, alone of the people I observed, received the doctrine with apparent enthusiasm, helping Inuttiaq to instruct her younger sisters and me. But as she rarely went visiting except to Pala's household, which had no door that winter, she had no occasion to put the doctrine into practice. Once in a while during the next few weeks, Inuttiaq's good friend Mannik, and once Mannik's brother Putuguk, both humorous young men, did knock when they came to visit us, then entered, laughing. Whether they were obliging Inuttiaq or teasing him, I do not know. But within six weeks the only sound that announced a visitor was the approaching creak of his feet on the hard-frozen snow.

A year later, when I went back to Gjoa Haven, I inquired into the origin of the doctrine that Inuttiaq had tried unsuccessfully to introduce at Back River. I found that Ikayuqtuq and Nakliguhuktuq had decided it would be a good idea to teach the Gjoa Haven Eskimos something of kapluna manners so they would not annoy kaplunas, like the priest and the teacher, by walking unannounced into their houses. Moreover, said Ikayuqtuq, "people are beginning to be shy about having others see them when they're sitting on the urine pot; and if people knock before they come in, one can get ready." The suspicions of the Utku were well-founded; Jesus had nothing to do with the doctrine in its original form. And Inuttiaq had not heard the teaching from Nakliguhuktuq at all, but from Nilak's brother, who was living in Gjoa Haven.

The question is, how did Jesus come to be associated with the teaching in Inuttiaq's mind? Did Inuttiaq—or Nilak's brother— misunderstand the informal nature of Nakliguhuktuq's suggestion to the Gjoa Haven Anglicans, confusing his secular with his religious teachings or assuming that because it was Nakliguhuktuq, the missionary, who spoke, the words were therefore from God? Or do all rules, of whatever source, ultimately have a religious sanction? Perhaps the Utku do not make the distinction we do between religious and secular rules. This possibility occurred to me on another occasion when Inuttiaq told me that the police and God forbid the shooting of musk oxen except in case of starvation.

A fourth possibility is that Inuttiaq consciously or unconsciously embroidered Nakliguhuktuq's dictum in order to present it with greater forcefulness to the community. There were a number of occasions on which Inuttiaq appealed to an imaginary superior power to support him; and I think that this behavior may have been characteristic not of Inuttiaq alone but of people in his position of religious leadership. In the old days it was not unusual for a shaman to elaborate on the formal fundamentals of belief to enhance his own power or prestige, or to strengthen the force of his words; and in more recent times, Anglican lay leaders have done the same thing. It was said that one of Inuttiaq's predecessors used to make journeys into the sky to talk to God, and he once preached to the Utku that if they persisted in pagan ways a very black man would come and eat them. In this case, too, people were skeptical; they searched their Bibles to see if it were true, and when they found nothing they wrote for confirmation to the kapluna missionary in Spence Bay.

The most dramatic instance of Inuttiaq's appeal to superior force was the time he was lecturing me on his role as religious leader. Nakliguhuktuq had appointed him king over the Utku, he told me; the deacon had told him that if people resisted his, Inuttiaq's, religious teachings, then Inuttiaq should write to him and he would come quickly and scold (*huaq*) the disbelievers. Moreover, Inuttiaq added, "If people don't want to believe Nakliguhuktuq either, then Nakliguhuktuq will write to Cambridge Bay, and a bigger leader, the kapluna king in Cambridge Bay, will come in an airplane with a big and well-made whip and will whip people. It will hurt a great deal."

III. Father to Kapluna: Protective Dominance

Self-assertiveness was not Inuttiaq's only salient trait. As husband and father he showed a much gentler face than he did as religious leader; even his authority when expressed toward his wife and children was molded into a strong protectiveness. In adopting me, he extended his fatherliness toward me, as well. The manner in which the adoption was carried out—indeed, his treatment of me from the very first—exemplifies the interplay of warm concern and dominance that characterized his relationships with his own family.

It was with characteristically Eskimo indirection that Inuttiaq accomplished my adoption, but with the highhanded twist that I later found to be his trademark. He and his family came to visit me for the first time almost immediately on their return to the Rapids following the autumn caribou hunt. As soon as their tents had been set up, the dogs chained, and the welcoming tea drunk in Pala's tent, Inuttiaq's sun-browned face appeared in the crack of my tent flap. Behind him appeared all the rest of his newly arrived family, accompanied by the already familiar households of the two patriarchs, Pala and Piuvkaq. The fourteen people silently filled my eight-by-ten tent to the point of explosion; the canvas bulged, and I trembled for the primus and cups balanced on a none-too-flat rock perilously close to the shifting feet. But Inuttiaq very shortly had people sorted out onto duffel bags and boxes, and I breathed safely again. In addition to Inuttiaq there were five strangers: Inuttiaq's gentle-smiling wife, Allaq, who, they said, was Pala's eldest daughter; Inuttiaq's youngest daughter, Saarak, carried as always on her mother's back, inside her parka; Pala's two adult sons, Mannik and Putuguk, who had accompanied Inuttiaq on the hunt; and Putuguk's wife, Kanayuq, a girl remarkable for her cascading giggle . . . usually directed at me. Saarak, gazing over her mother's shoulder, screamed with terror *(kappia, iqhi)* at the strange kapluna and was put to nurse in the comfortable darkness of her mother's parka. Inuttiaq's six-year-old daughter, Raigili, who, rather against her will, had been left during the hunt in the care of her grandfather, Pala, and her young aunts, had now deserted Pala's company for her father's and was leaning against his knee. I noted with surprise and a slight feeling of offense that Inuttiaq seemed oblivious of her presence; but he allowed her to lean.

I offered tea and bannock, a fried bread that is an arctic delicacy not often enjoyed by the Utku during the long season of open water when they are cut off from Gjoa Haven. Inuttiaq and

Pala took care of the distribution, each man seeing first to the wants of his small children and liberally covering their bannocks with jam. Inuttiaq saw to it that I got a proper owner's share (an embarrassingly large one) of the feast, telling me to pour my tea before my guests' and not to distribute the last bannock but to keep it for my breakfast. He was in general very much in charge, then as on later occasions: suggesting that as my teakettle was very small we would do well to make another kettleful; sending one of the young men to fetch water for it from the river; offering to light the primus stove, which I was quite capable of doing myself; making sure I had a fresh fish for my breakfast and filleting it for me, which I was not quite so capable of doing myself. He also constituted himself my language teacher, with laughing assistance from the two young men, Mannik and Putuguk, who served as his stooges. Together they acted out words while Inuttiaq asked me, "What are we doing?" When I confessed ignorance he would tell me the answer, speaking slowly and clearly, paring all superfluous elements from the word, and repeating with infinite patience until I had written down some semi-intelligible variant of what he had told me: "He is jumping/spitting/burping/lying-with-his-feet-toward-the-door/wrinkling-his-nose," and so on. He was a jolly and ingenious teacher, but he endeared himself to me even more by his imaginative capacity for understanding my efforts to communicate. Indeed, all the adults of the Piuvkaq-Pala-Inuttiaq contingent had an astonishing ability to communicate with me, though at the time I knew at most twenty words of Eskimo. Their perceptiveness was set off the more vividly by the absolute lack of any such quality on the part of Nilak's household. Nilak, the other man who had been suggested as a possible father for me, had returned from caribou hunting two days before Inuttiaq and, like Inuttiaq, was eager to adopt me for the winter. The lengthy visits of Nilak and his wife to my tent were always a misery to me. Not yet aware of the friendliness of silence, I could only sit woodenly smiling, with chilblained fingers tucked into my sleeves, alternately shivering and brewing the kettles of tea that Nilak, it seemed to me endlessly, hinted at, while I brooded on the alarming depletion of my fuel supply.

Inuttiaq and his family came to visit me at great length several times a day—oftener than Nilak, who lived on the far side of the river; and with far more imagination than Nilak, Inuttiaq courted me as a daughter, by waiting on me, anticipating my every wish and some that I did not have at all, by teaching, and by understanding me. Several times during this first day or two Inuttiaq asked me whether I wanted to be his daughter; but still unsure of the wisdom of being adopted by any family, I put him off, telling him as well as I could that I would decide after a while.

Two or three days after Inuttiaq's return to the Rapids, while the decision was still unmade, I went to pay Inuttiaq's family a return visit. I had not been to his tent before, and my view of it and its occupants was still that of a foreigner. It was a tiny ragged tent, stained with turf and caribou blood. The worst rips had been pulled roughly together with sinew, but drafts jabbed at the dim flame in the lamp, intensifying the murkiness of the place. I had a sinking impression of damp, sticky, animal filth: greasy quilts, caribou bones, and remains of fish strewn on the gravel floor. Involuntarily, my thought flew thankfully to my own bright tidy new tent up on the bluff. The whole family was at home, waiting for Allaq's sister Amaaqtuq to brew the evening tea. Allaq was skinning fish bellies to cook for oil and food; holding one end of the oval belly skin between her teeth, she pulled it down to the ventral fins, bit each fin neatly through, and ripped the skin the rest of the way off the flesh with four quick movements; then she tossed the flesh into a fire-blackened oil-drum pot. Her chin was shining with oil to which milky scales had stuck. Inuttiaq was writing with a scrap of pencil on the salvaged inner lining of a tea package, the paper carefully spread out on the cover of his Bible. The children played around their parents, and Pala sat on a rock by the entrance, visiting. Saarak, seeing my strange face, screamed and ran to thrust her head, ostrich-like, inside her mother's parka; but Inuttiaq and Allaq welcomed me with warm smiles, and Inuttiaq indicated a seat on a soft duffel bag, handing me his folded parka to make the seat even softer. He told me that since Putuguk and his wife were leaving the next morning for Kalingujat at the mouth of the river, he was writing a letter to Nakliguhuktuq to send with them. Perhaps one of the Gjoa Haven Eskimos fishing near Kalingujat would take the letter along when he went home later in the autumn. "I am telling Nakliguhuktuq that you are going to live in my household; he wants to know." I docilely agreed, and so the decision was made.

My sense of relief told me then that for reasons both personal and anthropological I had been leaning toward adoption by Inuttiaq's household ever since they had arrived, in spite of Saarak's screams, my initial impression of Inuttiaq's "arrogance," and my general qualms about the wisdom of being adopted at all. Inuttiaq's genial and patient helpfulness to me and Allaq's gentle warmth, appealing to a shame-faced wish to be taken care of in that wild land, overruled my doubts—the more so when contrasted with my growing feelings about Nilak and his wife, Niqi. Not only was communication hopeless in their case; I was also very much put off, I was ashamed to realize, by the way Niqi giggled at me. Everybody laughed at me; she was not unique in that; Putuguk's young wife, Kanayuq, laughed with her whole body. But whereas all the others laughed openly and, I felt, warmly, Niqi tittered behind her hand and whispered to the others. Fortunately for my prejudices, the suspicion that I had earlier acquired in Gjoa Haven, to the effect that Nilak was a relatively isolated member of the Utku band, had proved correct; his household was camped across the rapids, a quarter of a mile or more from all the other households, which belonged to Pala's group. There was no question in my mind that both anthropology and I would benefit more if I lived with Inuttiaq. Still, it was clear that it was Inuttiaq who had chosen me, rather than vice versa.

When I accepted Inuttiaq's pronouncement, he gave a quick nod which I read as satisfaction and said with disarming warmth: "Our daughter, have some tea." In that moment the physical surroundings that I had just been loathing faded in importance, suddenly and permanently.

From that time on, I was "Inuttiaq's daughter" in the community, insofar as I would permit myself to be so defined. With much laughter I was taught the kinship terms by which it was proper for me to address people: grandfather, mother's brother, little sister, and so on; it became a game, as it was with the tiniest children, to see whether I would recognize the terms— though I noted that it was only my parents and sisters who used such terms with any consistency when addressing *me*. Mostly the others addressed me by my own first name, "Yiini" in their speech, and when they referred to me they called me "kapluna." Inuttiaq saw that I did not lack for fish, and Allaq sent me large family-member-size hunks of caribou tallow, which was eaten like candy, and which I, too, much later came to savor. Allaq also became my "leader," as a mother should; she decided the extent to which I should be permitted to join the daily activities, an extent determined by my limited abilities and stamina. She took charge of my education, teaching me how to cut out fish bellies (I never learned to skin them), how to scrape the caribou hides that I would use as winter sleeping skins, and how to recognize the difference between brittle birch twigs good only for firewood and new growth suitable for use as under-mats on the sleeping platforms of the winter iglus. If I wandered away from the others when we were out twig-gathering among distant knolls, Allaq sent her sister Amaaqtuq after me to make sure I did not lose my way; but she never told me she had done so; it was Amaaqtuq who, a year later, told me about it.

Inuttiaq watched my progress as a daughter, sometimes approvingly, sometimes not so approvingly, and I learned much about equanimity from his reactions to my struggles. I found skin-scraping more difficult to learn than some of the other skills, as unaccustomed muscles were used; and my slowness was aggravated by the frequent interruptions I made to record vocabulary. Inuttiaq, coming in from a day's fishing, would look at the small square of skin I had scraped in his absence and say in a neutral tone: "You have written more than you have scraped today." And he would sharpen the blade of my scraper encouragingly. Occasionally, though skin-scraping is largely woman's work, Inuttiaq would even take the hide and work on it briefly himself, showing me how to hold it and demonstrating how much force I should exert. Once in a while, exerting a little too much energy, he would push the blade through the hide by mistake instead of along its membranous surface. "Eehee! I am a bad person!" he would exclaim cheerfully, and laugh. When I made the same mistake, as I often did in my clumsiness, my exclamations reflected none of Inuttiaq's equanimity—rather, intense frustration, alarm, and sometimes poorly suppressed rage, born of the ridiculous conviction that my sleeping skin was all that stood between me and death from exposure. Once I remarked that it was frightening to ruin one's winter sleeping skin by poking it full of holes, and Inuttiaq comforted me by saying matter-of-factly, "It's not frightening *(kappia)*; the holes can be sewn up."

But my successes were also noted. When, forcing myself to disregard my chilblained fingers, I joined the fish-gutting circle on the icy beach, or when I carried home a heavy load of birch twigs from a distant hill. Inuttiaq looked on and a woman said to me: "He is watching his daughter." Once in a while on such occasions he would look at me with warmth in his eyes and make an approving remark of which I understood only the tone and the word "daughter." And when in October I caught my first fish, jigging as he had taught me through the ice, the pleasure in his eyes and in his voice made me glow, though all he said was: "You caught a fish."

During the two years that I was Inuttiaq's daughter, I felt this warmth gratefully many times: when my nose turned dangerously white with frost, Inuttiaq noticed and thawed it in his hand, always warmer than my own; if I innocently walked too close to thin black ice, Inuttiaq warned me; if, when we moved camp, no one offered to help me carry my heavy boxes to the sled or canoe in which they would be transported, Inuttiaq saw and directed one of the younger men or some of the older children to help me. Looking back, I now realize with intense respect and gratitude how very willing Inuttiaq was to adopt me as a daughter, not merely as a superficial gesture—for the novelty of being father to a kapluna or to enjoy the rewards of my tea, tobacco, and kerosene—but in a profoundly genuine sense, with responsibility and warmth. I realize this with dismay, too, because I was so much less able than he to fulfill the obligations of the relationship. To be sure, unlike Inuttiaq, I had to learn my role: he already knew how to be an Eskimo father; I did not know how to be an Eskimo daughter, and the proper docility was hard to learn.

My feelings toward Inuttiaq's fatherliness were complex. I was grateful for his many small solicitous acts: when he had filleted my hard-frozen fish as he would have done for Saarak,

I was only too happy to respond when he later asked for a handful of raisins "for Saarak" or told me to make bannock. But my gratitude was sometimes soured by a suspicion that the responsive warmth engendered in me by Inuttiaq's concern had been in a sense engineered by him. I felt his solicitude was prompted partly by a wish, conscious or unconscious, to foster in me feelings of obligation. When he was so fatherly he left me no alternative but to *want* to be daughterly—or to be needled by guilt when I could not be. And I was irritated both by what I felt to be a "crass" expectation of reciprocity and by the indirection with which he phrased his wishes, so much more devious even than the manipulative tact that annoys me in my own culture. It rankled that he took for himself a small share of the raisins he had asked "for Saarak"; I asked myself why, if he was hungry for raisins, he didn't say so directly. And when he told me I was not to go fishing with him because my feet would freeze or because I would hurt myself when the sled bumped over rocks, I mentally accused him of using concern for me as an excuse for relieving himself of unwanted company.

The situation became particularly tense when daughterliness required that I submit *unquestioningly* to his decisions concerning me. When, without explanation of any sort, he told me to leave my precious fieldnotes in their heavy metal case and my equally precious and unwieldy tape recorder on the top of a knoll during flood season while we moved downriver for an unstated length of time, I felt not daughterly trust but frightened fury at the expectation that I should relinquish control to anyone—least of all to one who, I could be sure, did not share my view of the value either of material possessions in general or of fieldnotes and tape recorders in particular. After I had learned something of the language, I was sometimes so rude as to question: how long would we be gone? and would the water reach the knoll top when the river flooded? But I thought I read in the terseness of Inuttiaq's polite answer a controlled resentment at my presuming to question his judgment.

I puzzled over how to interpret Inuttiaq's treatment of me. It occurred to me that my anxiety concerning dependence and my dislike of deviousness were leading me to read more manipulativeness and autocracy into Inuttiaq's behavior than were there.

Did I only imagine that expectations of reciprocity underlay his solicitude and that he used the latter as a cloak for the expression of his own wishes? Did I imagine that Inuttiaq wanted unquestioning obedience from me? I think not. My intuitions were quite consistent with others' descriptions of Eskimos; the elements of the situation: the strong value that Eskimos place on responsiveness to others' needs and on reciprocity, the indirect manner in which they habitually express their wishes, and the public subordination of women to men, have been remarked many times by other observers (Freuchen 1961; Gubser 1965; Jenness 1922; and Vallee 1962, among others). Though I have not seen described the particular concatenations represented in Inuttiaq's behavior, I noted them many times among Utku other than Inuttiaq, in situations in which I was not personally involved: kind, obliging behavior toward others *was* expected to generate similar behavior toward oneself; concern for others *was* used as an excuse to obtain something for oneself; daughters *did* obey their fathers without question.

But though I was ultimately convinced that the behavior that, in Inuttiaq, I defined as "manipulative" and "autocratic" was both real and Eskimo in its general shape, I am still unsure whether in some elusive manner Inuttiaq infused the Eskimo patterns with his own assertive spirit, whether in some subtle ways he went too far in his dominance or exerted on me more pressure than others did to be submissive.

It was an Eskimo friend in Gjoa Haven who initially led me to suspect that this might be so. I had spent the month of November 1963 on holiday in Gjoa Haven, and now Inuttiaq had come to fetch me, as he had reassured me he would "when we run out of tea and tobacco." My friend heard him tell me to get up at six the next morning so we could make an early start on our long sled trip to Back River. Waiting until he had left to go to bed, she asked me: "Does he always order you around like that?" I hesitated, thinking of all his warm, helpful acts. "Sometimes," I said, "but he's very good to me; he takes very good care of me." We continued to chew on the lining of my fur parka, which had become rigid as wood because I had ignorantly kept it in a hot dry house for three weeks. After a few minutes she said: "Do you mind if I tell you something? Inuttiaq is a show-off. Maybe he likes to tell other people what to do." I agreed inwardly that that might be so, and from that time on for many months I always felt a cautious hesitation when he told me to do something: was the order appropriate—legitimized by cultural expectations —or was it an "Inuttiaq-order"? Was he taking advantage of my ignorance of proper fatherly behavior? Did he enjoy, perhaps a bit too much, exerting power over a kapluna—a situation in which the usual Eskimo-white relationship was reversed? I wanted to be a good daughter, but I did not want to be used by Inuttiaq for his own ends, however kind he was to me. I noted, perhaps with exaggerated sensitivity, the tiniest differences between Inuttiaq's behavior to me and that of other fathers to their daughters. Other fathers issued orders with quiet confidence. Inuttiaq's orders were also quiet, but to my suspicious ear had an added fillip of assurance. And whereas other fathers might express concern with a question: "Are you tired? Shall I carry your load?" Inuttiaq tended to do it with a command: "You are tired; Mannik will carry that for you." (It was characteristic of Inuttiaq, too, that it was his cousin Mannik, about fifteen years younger than himself, who was his best friend. Inuttiaq fed him, joked with him, traveled with him as friends do—and ordered him around as was his right as an older man.)

I could never be sure that the difference I sensed between Inuttiaq's fatherliness and that of other men was real, partly because of my personal involvement in Inuttiaq's behavior with all the attendant feelings I have described, and partly just because I had much greater opportunity to observe Inuttiaq than I had to observe other men. The hint given me in that conversation in Gjoa Haven was the only one I ever had from another person; never once did I see a telltale flicker in an Utku eye when Inuttiaq gave me an order. It was not proper to react openly to interactions in which one was not directly involved. But I did learn that Inuttiaq was not singling out his kapluna daughter for special domination. When fourteen-year-old Kamik, one of his favorite daughters, came home from boarding school in May, I found that Inuttiaq was even more peremptory toward her than he was toward me. He had been expecting the obedience of an adult daughter from me, but his directiveness had been tempered by quick concern for my kapluna weaknesses—

a concern that, of course, he did not need to show on Kamik's behalf. In this open solicitude he was treating me, I saw, much as he treated his three- and six-year-old daughters—not as an adult. I learned, too, in the last months of my stay, that by no means all of Inuttiaq's concern for me was dominating or manipulative. In those months, when I had nothing to offer him materially and when, because of a misunderstanding, my company was anathema to him as it was to the rest of the community, he nevertheless consistently warned me away from thin ice and made sure that I had enough to eat and a warm place to sleep.

IV. Father to His Own Children: Affection

Inuttiaq's warmth was most evident when he was with his own children. Eskimos are reputed to be devoted to their children and very indulgent of them, and the Utku are no exception. But Inuttiaq had an unusual reputation for even-tempered affection. Both his wife and his father-in-law told me several times what a good father Inuttiaq was: "He loves *(naklik)* his children deeply; he is never angry *(ningaq, urulu)* with them." "Inuttiaq is the only parent who is never angry with his children," Allaq said. And Pala said that because Inuttiaq was never angry with them, his children loved *(unga) him* very much. It was highest praise.

Inuttiaq and Allaq had had seven daughters, the last born while I was with them, but three of these had died in infancy or early childhood. I wondered sometimes how Inuttiaq felt about the fact that he had no son. Utku, like many Eskimos, tend to want sons perhaps more than daughters. Inuttiaq, as he himself occasionally observed, had no one to help him in his work except his young friend Mannik. Mannik's primary obligation was to his own father, Pala, and it was for Pala that Mannik traveled, fished, and hunted; nevertheless it is possible that Inuttiaq's lack of a son intensified his fondness for Mannik; perhaps in some small measure Mannik's company was a compensation to Inuttiaq.

But if Inuttiaq inwardly wished for a son it did not seem to detract from his affection for his four daughters. The warmth Inuttiaq felt for these children charmed me totally, especially as it was expressed toward the two youngest: Saarak and the newborn, Qayaq. At first it was sometimes more difficult for me, as a foreigner, to perceive his affection for Raigili and for Kamik, when she came home from school for the summer. It is toward small children that Utku express affection (*naklik, niviuq*) most openly, most completely. They are snuffed, cuddled, cooed at, talked to, and played with endlessly, the men as demonstrative as the women. In part, the tenderness felt for small children is a protectiveness born of their smallness and helplessness. In households where there are no small children, young puppies sometimes receive the overflow of this desire to protect and nurture; instead of being kicked and cuffed in the usual fashion and turned out to fend for itself, a pup in such a household may be as lovingly treated as a baby. The Utku have a word for objects that rouse their protective feelings: *naklingnaqtuq (naklik)*, "it is lovable or pitiable [the word has both connotations] and to be taken care of." This word is not restricted to small children and pups, but is used for anything that one feels a desire to protect: a frost-bitten ear, a lone kapluna woman in the wilderness, a person who is very sick. At least, sick Eskimos are *naklingnaqtuq;* Inuttiaq told me that sick dogs are not, and he was not sure whether sick kaplunas are: "Because I've never seen any sick kaplunas," he said.

There is also another word for objects that rouse affectionate feelings, and this second word *is* largely restricted to small children: *niviuqnaqtuq (niviuq)*, "charming." Allaq once defined the difference between the two words in this way: "When somebody is *naklingnaqtuq* one wants to feed him, keep him warm, keep him safe; when somebody is *niviuqnaqtuq* one wants to kiss him." When children first begin to respond to others—when they smile or gurgle, when they begin to try to talk or walk—they are said to be *niviuqnaqtuq*, kissable. As they grow older they stop being so charming, and gradually, in theory, they become a little less *naklingnaqtuq*, too.

Theory does not prevent affections among the adults of a family from being very strong; when Utku talk about their relationships with husbands or wives, parents and children, brothers and sisters, it is clear that they often love (*naklik*) each other deeply. But Utku do not feel altogether at ease with affectionate feelings, other than those that are directed toward young children. Though, ideally, concern *(naklik)* for others is good and commendable, nevertheless, among adults other values and feelings conflict with affection, inhibiting both the feeling and the expression of tenderness. One such conflicting value is that placed on reason *(ihuma).* Adults are expected to keep their feelings under the control of reason. The physical display of affection among adults is considered unpleasant *(hujuujaq)* to see, and the very feeling of affection *(naklik, unga),* when too strong, is derogated because it is painful for the person who loves. The person for whom concern is felt may also be of two minds about it, because of the value placed on independence. An Utku adult wants to be self-sufficient, and not a cause of concern or an object of pity to others.

My first hint of these complicated attitudes about affection *(naklik)* lay in a puzzling remark that my friends often made to me. "We'll miss *(hujuujaq)* you when you first leave," they used to say warmly, and then they always added matter-of-factly: "But it will be all right *(naamak);* only Saarak will be unhappy *(naamangngit),* poor dear *(naklik)."* I never failed to be startled when I heard this, and a little wounded. But I think really people were reassuring me that I need not worry about causing them pain when I left, because all of them who were old enough to reason would understand and accept my departure. They were expressing the facts as they saw them: emptiness does heal, and it is good that it should be so.

The same attitudes are even more clearly expressed in the idea of loving *(naklik)* someone "too much *(-pallaaq-)."* It was Allaq and Inuttiaq who described this to me. They were explaining the feelings that parents have for their children, telling me that the strong affection *(naklik)* one has toward a small child gradually lessens as the child grows up. "But sometimes people love *(naklik)* their grown-up children very much too," said Allaq, blushing. "My father, Pala, was like that; he used to love me too much. But it's all right now; he has stopped loving me so much."

Because the idea of loving a child *too* much struck me as strange, I asked Inuttiaq and Allaq about it. Inuttiaq said, indicating his daughters: "I love *(naklik)* Saarak and Kamik a little bit more than I love Raigili and Qayaq. I love them too much.

When I am away on trips, hunting or trading, I want to see them. I sleep badly. When Kamik is away at school I miss her; it makes me feel uncomfortable (*ihluit, naamangngit*). If I love a child too much I am concerned (*naklik*) if she cries a lot; otherwise I don't mind (*huqu*). People don't like to feel uncomfortable. If one doesn't love too much it is good."

Inuttiaq may have regretted loving Saarak "too much," but I found his tenderness when he was with her very endearing. His presence was important to her too. Though Saarak was considered too young to feel mature, protective affection (*naklik*), people said of her love for Inuttiaq: "She wants to be with him (*unga*)." She was always cranky when he was away on trips, crying over "who knows what," as they said. Allaq explained then that Saarak was lonely for her father. When he came home she was transformed, bouncing with excitement and making sweetly coy faces till he shook her hand and took her on his lap to kiss her. He sometimes played with her and always at night he cuddled her beside him in bed, cooing at her tenderly as she slept. One of the techniques for persuading Saarak to go to bed at night was to tell her Inuttiaq wanted to nurse at her breast, which he would jokingly pretend to do. For a while after her baby sister was born Saarak would not go to bed at all unless Inuttiaq were in bed to cuddle her.

Raigili was past the age of being kissed or held, but her life also revolved around Inuttiaq. In January she drew me a picture of the August afternoon when Inuttiaq had taken her fishing—just the two of them in his canoe. One night she dreamt that he had scolded (*huaq*) her; we found out about it the following afternoon when, remembering the dream, she burst into tears. At first, the seeming indifference of Inuttiaq's treatment of Raigili froze me. When she leaned against him or stroked his hand, as she often did, he seemed not to notice her touch. When, in bed beside him, she stroked his naked back softly, he would occasionally tell her to scratch an inaccessible louse bite; but I detected no tenderness in this command. As my eye grew accustomed, however, I saw affection in other acts: in the mountains of jam he put on her bread and the two heaping spoonfuls of sugar he put in her tea, in his making her a little sled and straightening out the string figures in which her fingers were hopelessly tangled. Once in the spring when traveling was easy he took her with him and Mannik on the long trip to Gjoa Haven. I can imagine them crossing the empty white sea, Raigili a tiny silent glowing-eyed bundle in a cocoon-quilt tied onto the top of the sled load. She was only about five at the time.

Inuttiaq's eldest daughter, Kamik, was, like Saarak, loved (naklik) "too much." Eldest children are often loved "too much" among the Utku; they say it is because they look forward so much to having children that when one finally comes it makes them very happy (quvia). Kamik, at her own request and for the first time, had gone away to school on the plane that took me in to Back River in August 1963. One day in December, traveling between Gjoa Haven and Chantrey Inlet, I happened to ask Inuttiaq and his friend Mannik what they were talking about over the evening meal. "About my affection (naklik) for Kamik," Inuttiaq said. In April they began to talk about her return for the summer. Inuttiaq bought a sleeping bag for her and flannel for a new parka cover. And for her arrival he saved one of the eight caribou he had killed the previous August. All through May we waited for the government plane, but it did not come. We did not know that it was marooned for much of the month by bad weather in Spence Bay. Inuttiaq thought that the plane might have left Kamik by mistake with Qavvik, who was sealing at an island called Umanak about halfway down Chantrey Inlet, instead of bringing her all the way south to the Rapids where we were; and he went to look for her, traveling three days through soggy spring snow. He found neither Kamik nor Qavvik. He was very silent on his return. He lay in his place in the tent, smoking, drinking tea, and seemingly oblivious of the family around him. But when that afternoon the hum of a motor was at last heard in the distance and Allaq and I from the top of the hill shouted out the camp below: "Plane! Plane!" Inuttiaq was the first to appear in his tent entrance and was in the forefront as we floundered down through the soggy, knee-deep snow to meet the plane, which was bouncing to a stop on the river ice. The greeting between parents and daughter was as shy, as restrained as Utku greetings always are; I am not sure they even shook hands, and nothing was said. But Inuttiaq showed his pleasure by taking Kamik's light duffel bag from her to carry it up to the tent; and only on the second day after her arrival did he, brusque in his ebullience, order her for the first time to make tea and to perform other daughterly duties. On that first afternoon he stayed at home, participating in the welcoming feast of tea and bannock and silently listening to his daughter's tales of the strange kapluna world where people are always loud and angry *(ningaq)*, where they hit their children, let babies cry, kiss grown-ups, and make pets of dogs and cats. And that night I heard the figures in Inuttiaq's restless dreams shout the English phrases with which Kamik, to impress her uncomprehending relatives, had punctuated her speech.

2

Family Life: Expressions of Closeness

It was October when I moved in with Inuttiaq's family. As long as the camp was housed in tents, I had lived alone in my own; but as soon as the river froze and the round, ice-walled qaqmaqs were built, Inuttiaq and Allaq invited me to join them. Allaq pointed out as mine the wall-edge opposite hers in the sleeping area and helped me lay my twig mats on the gravel floor. I spread out my bedding on the twigs and settled down as the eldest daughter of the household.

An Eskimo dwelling, whether tent, qaqmaq, or iglu, is divided into two parts by drawing a line parallel to the entrance. The *ikliq*, the family's sleeping and living area, occupies the rear half or two-thirds of the dwelling; the front part of the dwelling, just inside the door, is the *natiq* or floor. The latter is a general utility area: larder, kitchen, and storage space; it is also the area where visitors stand—or sit on bags of clothing or piles of defrosting fish, the latter hospitably covered by the host with a burlap bag or scrap of hide to protect the guest from chill and damp. In a snow iglu the ikliq is a platform built up often two

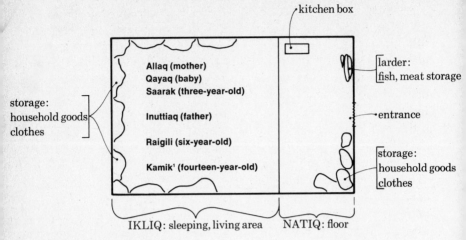

Plan of Inuttiaq's Tent

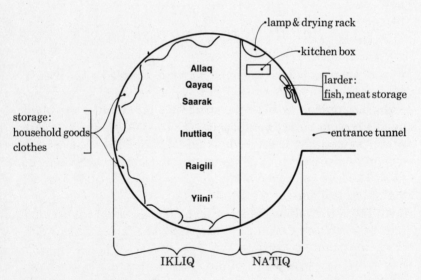

Plan of Inuttiaq's Iglu

1. This is the place of the eldest child or of a guest. Kamik occupied it when she was at home. I occupied it in her absence.

or three feet above the floor, but in tents and qaqmaqs it is at floor level, separated from the latter only by a row of stones or a tentpole laid down to serve as edging. Only specially privileged guests such as old people, close friends, or kaplunas are invited to sit on the ikliq with the family, unless one of the family members is absent, in which case his place may be temporarily occupied by a visitor. Each member of the family has his own place on the ikliq, by day and night, and the ordering of these places is standard in all Utku families, as it is, with occasional variations, in other Eskimo groups, as well.

The arrangement of our qaqmaq was typical. On one side, next to the wall, was the place of my mother, Allaq, and beside her that of the youngest child, Saarak. Saarak's place was not quite as established as other people's; she tended to roam a bit: to seek a kiss from her father, to snatch a toy from her sister or, after she grew accustomed to me, to beg raisins from me. But at night she slept on one side or the other of her mother, and often she played beside her mother during the day, when she was not actually inside Allaq's parka. Next to Saarak was Inuttiaq's place, more or less in the middle of the ikliq, and on his other side was Raigili. Finally, between Raigili and the wall, opposite Allaq, was my place, the place appropriate both for an oldest child and for a house guest.

That spot, just the length and breadth of my sleeping bag, very quickly became my home, in a real sense. I possessed my spot, and from it I always looked out on the same view. The sameness of it gave me a sense of stability in a world of shifting dwellings, a feeling of belonging in a family; it even gave me a sense of privacy, since no one ever encroached on my space without permission, and sitting there I could withdraw quietly from conversation into an inner world, reading or writing, or observing the doings of the rest of the family and their friends without disturbance.

Sitting in my corner of the ikliq, I watched each member of the family in his accustomed orbit. Inuttiaq, ensconced in the center of the ikliq, held court with the visitors ranged along the edges of the floor, enjoying his jokes at least as much as they did. Home from a cold morning of fishing or net-checking, he cradled his enamel mug gratefully in both hands as he drank his strong sugarless tea before taking out the afternoon's craftwork. I never tired of watching him work—though when he was in an uncommunicative mood he occasionally irritated me by nose-wrinkling refusals to answer my rude questions about what he was doing. If I had been polite I would have waited to see for myself when he had finished: a new pipestem or a handle for an ice-fishing line whittled out of a bit of caribou antler, the key of a powdered milk can transformed into a needle, a nail into an elegantly barbed fishhook, or half of a primus valve into a new gunsight. His tools were a penknife and a file, his workbench a flat rock laid across his thighs. I could never accustom myself to the Utku right-angled sitting position: legs stiffly outstretched, back straight—no bending at the knee and no back rest—but Utku seemed to find it perfectly restful.

Allaq, too, spent much of the day in her corner of the ikliq, her hands deftly busy while she listened, silent but attentive, to the men's conversation, gossiped with her visiting brothers and sisters, and kept a sixth sense tuned to Saarak's mood. Her work varied with the season, but there was always something: worn boots and mittens to be mended or new ones to be made, caribou hides to be scraped and softened for winter parkas and trousers, or yards of dried sinew to be braided into fishline. If Inuttiaq were home there was tea to brew and, with luck, bannock to fry or fish to boil; Inuttiaq rarely let more than two hours go by without suggesting something to eat, and the frequent visitors had to be offered tea, too.

Saarak, a little rabbit in her fur suit, revolved around her mother or was wooed by an aunt with a morsel of caribou tallow. More often she stood securely resting inside Allaq's parka against her back, the naked flesh of each warming the other while Allaq sewed or smoked, rhythmically rocking her body back and forth and humming to quiet Saarak's restlessness. It was some time before I had a closer view than this of Saarak, because although she soon stopped shrieking with terror at the sight of me, as she had in my first days in camp, it was a month before she dared to approach my side of the ikliq or ceased to shrink away, whimpering, if I approached hers, and it was midwinter before she came to sit on my lap.

Raigili was the least visible member of the family in those

October days; often I was hardly aware of her existence. For large parts of the day she was out playing or "visiting" in other homes with her slightly younger cousin Qijuk and her ten-year-old aunt, Akla. Children do not really visit, Utku say; they never stay; they duck in through the low doorway and stand shyly smiling, looking to see who is there and what they are doing, and perhaps stopping to accept a cup of tea or a bite of fish before darting on to the next home. They are like waterbugs, skimming erratically over the surface of camp life. Even when Raigili was home, her presence was rarely distracting. Gentle and unobtrusive, she sat beside me on the ikliq, arms drawn in out of the threadbare sleeves of her parka for warmth, and quietly watched the gathering, humming hymn tunes or talking to herself, as she waited for the tea to brew.

I. The Inner Circle: Intimacy and Informality

The atmosphere of Inuttiaq's household was entirely different from the way I had imagined it in the days when I ventured out from my tent on the bluff to visit in the camp below and then returned safely to my isolation. Savoring solitude during those evenings in my tent, after the camp was asleep and I lay warmly reading in my sleeping bag, I had dreaded the lack of privacy that I thought would be my lot in Inuttiaq's household. Life in a ten-foot room with two children under the age of seven! And it was not only noisy children that I imagined would irritate me —just the mere presence of people from waking to sleeping, the lack of respite from low-voiced, giggling, constantly cheerful conversation, the absence of a place or a time in which to be unmannered. My fears were groundless. To be sure, there were moments, even days, of depression which only a long walk in the empty windiness of the tundra could assuage. But on the whole, to my surprise, the human warmth and peacefulness of the household, and the uncanny sensitivity of its members to unspoken wishes, created an atmosphere in which the privacy of my tent came to seem in memory a barren thing.

In my first days in the qaqmaq it was during the evening, when our visitors had gone home and we were preparing for bed that I felt most strongly the special warmth of the family, its closeness as a unit. During the day, when the houses were full of visitors, I had the impression that Eskimo men and women largely ignored each other, except when a man gave instructions to his wife (or daughter or sister) to perform some service for him: make tea or boil fish, pick lice out of his undershirt, or fetch him a little tobacco from next door. Women did not participate in men's conversations; they sat at the periphery and listened. Or else while the men were gathered in one circle, playing cards, joking, reminiscing, and planning hunting and trading trips, the women brought their sewing to another spot, where they gossiped together, reminisced, and played with their babies. But at bedtime, or at other times when close relatives were alone together: early in the morning; on stormy days when our iglu entrance was buried in drifting snow; or in leisurely weeks in remote spring camps which we shared only with Pala's family, the separate circles meshed. The division then was not between Men and Women but between Family and Outsiders.

When our visitors had one by one excused themselves with yawns and with references to pressures on the bladder, Inuttiaq, too, would decide it was bedtime. "One is so sleepy!" he would remark, yawning dramatically and straining at his boots, which had molded themselves like living skin to his feet. It was a struggle to get them off at night, even when exercising the proper technique: one foot crossed over the other so that the ankle of the upper foot can be pulled against the lower while pushing on the instep with the hands. I found this impossible to do when my boots were wet; so did Inuttiaq when he was lazy with fatigue. "Pull my boots off," he directed Allaq, and she did, losing her balance when the boot slipped off and toppling backward with a startled giggle into the pile of fish by the door. "Weak!" Inuttiaq teased. "Here, wrestle with me!" and he held out a crooked wrist. Allaq, embarrassed, demurred, wrinkling her nose, laughing. "Wrestle with me!" Inuttiaq was insistent. Allaq crooked her wrist with his, and they tugged apart, laughing, till Allaq, quickly vanquished, fell toward Inuttiaq and broke away, giggling.

Inuttiaq, too, laughed quietly and resumed preparations for bed. Swiftly standing up on the ikliq, he bent over so that his parka, falling forward, would shield his genitals, pulled off his two or three pairs of trousers as one, knelt under the quilt, pulled his parka and shirts over his head, rolled his clothes into a pillow, and tucked them under the caribou mattress. The whole process was accomplished in a few seconds, as one smooth efficient gesture. "Cover me up, child," he directed Raigili and, glowing with pleasure at the request, she tucked the quilt carefully around his naked back. Inuttiaq's next order was to Allaq: "Move the tea things over here before you take your boots off so I can make tea in the morning when I wake up, while you lazybones [jokingly] are all still asleep." Allaq, too, complied, then undressed the waiting Raigili, who hunched sleepily on the edge of the ikliq. She made the child's pillow and tucked her in between Inuttiaq and me, pushing the quilt-edge firmly under the mattress hide so that Raigili would not roll into me in her sleep. Last to undress was Allaq herself, Saarak having been tucked in on the other side of Inuttiaq as soon as he lay down. Allaq had to wait until we had drunk our bedtime tea so that she could refill the kettle with fresh water for the morning. Had I been a proper daughter I should probably have fetched the water myself, but I did not know that. I often sought the warmth of my sleeping bag even before Inuttiaq gave the signal for bed.

While Allaq went about her end-of-evening tasks, Inuttiaq lay with his head on the pillow beside Saarak, making tender overtures to the daughter he loved (*naklik*) "too much (*-pallaaq-*)." Saarak was just learning to repeat, recognizably, the sounds of Eskimo speech, and Inuttiaq, in these bedtime moments, enjoyed coaching her in the sounds of the syllabary: the system of symbols in which Canadian Eskimo speech is written. Adults recite the syllabary in a patterned, slightly nasal, singsong, always in the same quadruple form: "Ai-ee-u-ah, pai-pee-pu-pa, tai-tee-tu-ta, mai-mee-mu-ma," and so on through all the consonants of the language, the voice rising as if inquiringly after each quadruplet. Inuttiaq, teaching Saarak, repeated the syllables one after the other, waiting for her to mimic him in her docile chirp before continuing with the next: "Ai." "Ai." "Ee." "Ee." "U." "U." And so on. Allaq, Raigili, and I always listened with soundless absorption to these exchanges, and when occasionally Saarak took a step ahead of Inuttiaq or stumbled on the step behind, saying "pu" when she should have said "pee," or "tai"

when she should have said "tee," a murmur of affectionate giggles arose. After the syllabary the lesson would continue with
names: family names and those of the family's dogs—mostly far
too complicated for Saarak's tongue: Allaq, Raigili, Piuvkaq
(that was one of Raigili's names), Amaaqtuq (her aunt), Inuttiaq,
Pala (her grandfather), Yiini (my own name). She pronounced
these last three very well, and her success drew warm "vaaa"s
from her parents. But Inuttiaq seemed to take a mischievous
pleasure in inserting now and again an absolutely impossible
name or term of kinship: Qijuaaqjuk (one of Saarak's own names),
Qiqnariq (a dog), aqnaqvinnuara (a kin term meaning "my
mother's sister"). "Avavi?"—Saarak's inquiring little echo.
"Aq-naq-vi-nnua-ra"—Inuttiaq patiently laying each syllable
before her again. And so on and on, until Inuttiaq tired of the
game or, as often happened, the pupil fell asleep. Inuttiaq's
voice stroked her endearingly as she slept. The words I never
understood; it was baby talk he cooed (aqaq) at her so gently;
but the tone diffused a tenderness over all of us.

Evenings were a time for story-telling, too, especially in the
iglu months of winter, and in spring, when families were lonely
in their dispersed camps. Only once did I hear Inuttiaq tell one
of the traditional stories that other people told, the histories of
ancient days when there was little difference between animals
and people. Allaq said he never had told those tales. He claimed
not to know them and always responded to my inquiries with a
curtness that I read as embarrassment. But I never understood
his feeling. That he really knew as little as he claimed seems
highly unlikely, as everyone else in camp over the age of fifteen
or so knew many stories. Perhaps he had learned some hesi-
tance about repeating "pagan" beliefs from his brief contacts
with missionaries or had heard that kaplunas laughed at such
notions. Pala, too, was reticent in my presence; I never heard
him tell ancient stories, though he did know them, and people
said he told them in other winters. Once, in a more than usually
open moment, Inuttiaq asked me whether it were true that there
are two kinds of Indian: the human-looking sort that people
meet when they are taken to the hospital and an animal-like
variety that lives in the tundra, where kaplunas hunt them like
wolves, from airplanes. He must have seen the quick surprise

in my face, though I merely said that I had not heard about the second variety and asked him to tell me what people said about them. He replied that he had not heard the stories very well. And he never again shared any cosmological ideas with me, other than Christian ones; he merely said he did not know.

But in other respects Inuttiaq was most communicative with his womenfolk in the evenings, and much of my best understanding of Utku life comes from these family hours when Inuttiaq, who often largely ignored me during the day, questioned me about life in my country, recalled past events in his own family's life, and explained Utku ideas and words. Sometimes small Raigili, in her quaintly prim little voice, described her sojourn in the kapluna communities of Baker Lake and Chesterfield Inlet when she was taken out to the hospital. (Could she possibly have remembered? She was only two or three at the time.) And when Inuttiaq's adolescent daughter, Kamik, came home for the summer—frenetic, sulky, pretending deafness—these private evening hours were almost the only time of day in which she permitted herself to speak to her parents at all; then, while they lay in bed, she told them long tales about Inuvik, the big government school near the Alaskan border where she had spent the winter. I had moved into a separate tent for the summer, but I heard the sound of her voice next door. Her parents said she even spoke English to them then, something she could never be persuaded to do in public.

Allaq, unusually self-effacing wife that she was, rarely initiated conversations in these hours, except when Inuttiaq was away on trips. But she added threads to her husband's stories, correcting him when he made mistakes, answering his queries when he could not remember, and inserting additional facts. In the easy companionship between the two of them at these times I felt something of the bond that common experience can create between a husband and wife. It is occasionally said that the major ties that exist between Eskimo spouses are those of sex and economic cooperation.[1] Of the marriage I knew best I had a quite

1. E.g., Spencer (1959:249). A number of authors, however, present a fuller picture of the relations between Eskimo spouses, one that is more in accord with my own observations. These include Gubser (1965), Jenness (1922;1928), Lantis (1946), and Washburne (1940). This is not to gainsay the probable importance of

different impression, one compounded of a hundred small incidents: a note that Inuttiaq, stormbound one day on the sea ice halfway to Gjoa Haven, wrote to Allaq and sent back with a returning dog team: "You [he meant his wife and daughters] who remain behind are people to be cared for (naklik)"; the quiet pleasure that I felt in Allaq's smile when she repeated to me: "He says we're to be cared for"; and the prayers she offered on evenings when Inuttiaq was away: "God, be with the travelers, hold their hands, and let them come home"; the question Inuttiaq asked me one day when I was inspecting the dainty, precise sinew stitches in the pair of caribou boots Allaq was making for me: "Do you think you'll be able to sew like that when you leave here?" I felt closeness in the shared eagerness with which Inuttiaq and Allaq pored over my maps together, pointing out distant lakes and rivers in whose vicinity they had hunted autumn caribou "before we had children," and in their mutual amusement at the memory, years old, of the stone-walled qaqmaq that one night shed its stones onto their sleeping heads. And I felt it in the suddenness with which Inuttiaq one evening said to me, breaking a long silence with a brusque nod in Allaq's direction: "I saw her being born."

Hardship was a thread in the memories, too. One story was particularly vivid. It was about the famine of 1958, "when Raigili was a baby on Allaq's back." Inuttiaq and Allaq together told me about it. It happened when the days were getting longer, and the Utku had dispersed to their spring camps. In those days they depended on the migrating caribou to provide them with food during the fish-scarce weeks of spring. But the caribou did not take their usual route that year. When the food was gone, Piuvkaq, the old man, was left alone in a tent in Amujat because he was too weak to walk. He had one cartridge with which, from his bed, he managed to shoot one ptarmigan. With that he survived till help came. The rest of his household: his more vigor-

---

economic cooperation and sex as binding forces in Utku marriages. Of the former there is certainly a great deal. Of the latter I cannot speak, since as a woman I was not in a good position to be told about it. Sexual attitudes and behavior are not subjects of conversation among Utku women, and the inquiries I tried to make of Allaq, concerning the spacing of children, for example, drew only blushes. Moreover, whatever sexual activity there was was completely inaudible.

ous wife, his daughter, and small grandson, went off on foot up the Hayes River to look for caribou. Inuttiaq had six .22 cartridges and that was all. He set up a tent on the ice over a hole that somebody else had cut, as he himself had no ice chisel; there he fished all night from his bed while the rest of his family slept. He caught five fish: "It made one very grateful *(hatuq).*" He also saw caribou but was unable to shoot them. "It made one feel like crying," Inuttiaq said in a voice without apparent emotion. After a while the government learned of the famine and sent a plane to drop supplies to the stranded people: food and caribou hides and ammunition. Piuvkaq's life was saved by the drop; and Inuttiaq, with a fresh supply of ammunition, set off up the Hayes River to hunt, with Allaq, Kamik, then about nine years old, and Raigili. All but one of their dogs had died, so they had to carry their goods on their backs. Eventually, far up the river, they shot fifteen caribou. Inuttiaq carried the skins, most of the meat and tallow, and the raw fat. Allaq carried Raigili, the tent, the sleeping skins, and a little meat. Kamik carried one hide and some of the tallow. "She was lovable *(naklik),*" said Inuttiaq. "Starving is not pleasant *(quvia).*"

Such memories of dependence, of sacrifice, of happiness, private jokes, too, were threads in the intimacy that I felt binding and giving security to the members of Inuttiaq's family in these private hours. Another important strand was religious. I felt the family's closeness not only in the prayers that Allaq, sometimes haltingly assisted by Raigili, said for Inuttiaq's safety when he was out in the night, but also in the prayers that Inuttiaq led when he was at home. Households varied in their private religious exercises; not all held evening or morning prayers. During the summer, when sound traveled from tent to tent, Nilak's heavy voice, counterpointed by his adolescent daughter's softer one, was heard regularly every evening at bedtime: "Ataatavut qilangmiitutit . . . (Our Father, Who art in Heaven . . .)." Pala, on the other hand, though he and his children seemed among the most devout of the Utku, never to my knowledge led prayers in his household. Instead, the members of his family read their Bibles or their prayerbooks silently to themselves in peaceful moments during the day, and often they sang together hymns from the book. Inuttiaq's household quite often prayed aloud together, to ask protection or to give thanks, not regularly every evening like Nilak's but as the spirit moved Inuttiaq. Occasionally his prayers were so informal, his voice so ordinary, so conversational, that in the early days, when I understood few words, I did not realize he was praying till Allaq stopped buttering the bannock for which Saarak was whimpering, clasped her hands in her lap, and bent her head. Once I lacked even that clue, because Allaq for some reason did not join in as usual. Inuttiaq had made a remark—talking to himself, I thought, or perhaps to Allaq—in which I heard all our names listed: "Piuvkaq [that is, Raigili], and Yiini, and Allaq, and Saarak . . ." When I asked what it was he had said, he replied, "I'm praying."

But usually Inuttiaq's devotions were not so completely casual as this. And usually Allaq and Kamik, if she were at home, each in turn added a prayer of her own to Inuttiaq's. Small Raigili rarely contributed a prayer, but always, faithfully and to the best of her ability, she joined in the chorused formulae that framed the extemporaneous prayers: the Lord's Prayer, and a benediction from the prayerbook: "The grace of our Lord Jesus Christ be with us all evermore, amen." Saarak, too, if she were awake, would add a birdlike "amen." If she did not, Inuttiaq might prompt her: "Amen, Saarak."

The sense of family intimacy that I had at these times derived partly from the fact that the prayers were shared—that Allaq bowed her head and hushed Saarak with a persuasive murmur: "Look, we're going to pray." I felt closeness also in the very spontaneity with which religious feelings were expressed within the family circle; I never heard Utku spontaneously pray aloud in the presence of strangers or aliens. And there was solicitude in the prayers themselves: for Piuvkaq, that she should grow and learn; for Saarak, that she should learn not to cry; for Allaq, that she should be safe while Inuttiaq was away; for me, that I should not forget the Eskimo words I learned; for all of us, that we be protected while we sleep.

Pala's family, alone among the other Utku households, shared in the family intimacy of Inuttiaq's household. The other families had their own circles. Pala's family belonged to us, because Pala was Allaq's father and Inuttiaq's uncle. The two families were very close. Allaq's grown sisters, who lived much of the time with Pala, were her confidantes; one of them, her still-unmarried sister Amaaqtuq, about eighteen years old, had slept in Inuttiaq's household instead of in her father's until I took her place; and her brother Mannik was Inuttiaq's constant companion. Inuttiaq and Pala almost always camped together, even during the spring and summer dispersal, often setting their tents or building their iglus so that they opened into each other, forming a two-roomed dwelling: one room for Inuttiaq's family, the other for Pala's. One of the times when this was done was during my second winter at Back River.

On the whole, during the year and a half of my stay, the two families lived side by side but their dwellings were not contiguous. It was the younger members of Pala's household: his youngest child, Akla, a girl of about ten; his son Ukpik, about fourteen; and his granddaughter Mitqut, somewhere between her young aunt and uncle in age, who, to my annoyance, woke us in the morning, letting the wooden door slam against its frame as they entered. They stood silently by the entrance, shifting from foot to foot till Inuttiaq, roused by the door's thump, raised a groggy head and ordered them to make tea. It was Pala's sons and daughters who stayed latest in the evening or who ran in at bedtime to fill their father's pipe from our tobacco can, to borrow our frying pan in which to make bannock, or to fetch Saarak for a visit. But though we saw a great deal of Pala's family, there were still moments or hours of separation, when the members of each household sewed, skinned fish bellies, and drank tea alone, joking and gossiping in privacy.

There was no separation during the second winter. In October of that year, Pala and Inuttiaq decided that when they moved to the winter campsite at Amujat they would build a double iglu. It was then that I saw most vividly that the two families were halves of one whole. The creation of our joint household was an expression of the affection that bound them; only the closest of friends ever built together like this. But there were practical as well as emotional reasons for the move. The explanation I was given was that it would save Inuttiaq the trouble of shoveling out the entrance when the snow drifted into it, as all too often happens in winter winds. A joint iglu such as Inuttiaq and Pala proposed to build has only one entrance tunnel, which leads from outdoors into the first-built iglu of the pair. The second iglu has one wall contiguous with the first and opens, like an inner room, into the latter. In our case, Pala's was the outer iglu, Inuttiaq's the inner one. Perhaps for this reason, and certainly also because Inuttiaq was older than the two young men of Pala's household (Pala's son Mannik and son-in-law Ipuituq), he was less directly in line for the unpleasantly heavy task of shoveling.

And this was not the only practical consideration, I think. The extent to which both goods and activities are shared among the Utku varies considerably under different living conditions and in different seasons. During the spring and summer weeks of the year I am describing, the members of the small tent camps sat or worked together most of the time outdoors. They also cooked and ate together: in the spring in order to make sure that all had a share of the fish, which are often scarce at that season, and in the summer I think partly in order to make efficient use of the limited supplies of birch twigs and lichen that the women collected for fuel after the winter's purchases of kerosene had been exhausted.[2] Some of the lines between households and between families were blurred then; on the surface the camp seemed almost a communal unit, whether or not the families that comprised it were closely related. In winter, on the other hand, when the scattered families of the band drew together on a common hillside, the camp lost its semblance of communality. Paradoxically, when the families joined one another, each iglu-household to some extent withdrew, economically and socially, from the others. Even close kin withdrew from one another in this way, so that relatives who shared their work and their meals during the summer now worked and ate separately—unless they had a joint iglu.[3]

2. During the summer of 1968 both plants and kerosene were used for fuel. When plants were used, we cooked and ate our main meal of the day communally, as described here; when kerosene was used, we did not.
3. The Utku pattern of seasonal variation that is described here contrasts with that of certain other Eskimo groups, in which winter camps are said to be more communal in one way or another than summer ones. In some cases it is the housing that is described as more communal in winter (e.g., Boas 1888; Jenness 1922; Freuchen 1961:61). In these groups, joint iglus, or even communal iglus, in which each family has its own sleeping niche around a central floor space,

During the first winter, when Inuttiaq and Pala lived separately, their two households were economically distinct entities. Mannik and Ipuituq served Pala's household, checking their fishnets together; and together the women of the household, Amaaqtuq and Ipuituq's wife, Amaruq, cut out the fat fish bellies and boiled them up for oil. Inuttiaq, lacking male assistance, checked *his* nets with the help of Allaq and myself; and when oil was needed, Allaq, with clumsy help from me, prepared the fish bellies. Mannik and Ipuituq stored their fish together in a hole cut into the entrance tunnel of Pala's iglu; Inuttiaq stored his fish in his own vestibule. Pala's iglu was cold that first winter, while Inuttiaq's was usually warm with the heat generated by the frequent brewings of tea made possible by my kerosene supplies. Pala's children came often to ask for cardboard or paper scraps so that they could make a tea-fire in their stove, a sawed-off oil drum; but they rarely asked for kerosene, and they never had enough fuel so that they could brew tea on a whim, as we could. Neither did Pala's household share equally with Inuttiaq's in my kapluna food and tobacco supplies, in spite of their frequent visits and more frequent small requests; they received little more than the other chance visitors, who shared nibbles, but certainly not equal portions, of whatever meal they happened in on.

are usual. In other cases communal hunting is described, or rules for the distribution of meat in winter camps, such that each household in the camp has the right to claim a share of any animal caught (e.g., Balikci 1964; Rasmussen 1931; Van de Velde 1956). In still other cases, communality of both housing and food distribution are described (e.g., Holm 1914). Mauss (1904–05) bases his ingenious argument concerning seasonal variations in Eskimo social structure on data such as these. Among the Utku, however, joint iglus are rare; I saw only three in two winters. And there is only one sense in which food is more communally shared in an Utku winter camp: there are more people to solicit from. Summer and winter, the rule holds that anyone who feels a desire for a certain food that he does not have, or who lacks tobacco or fuel, may occasionally request "a little bit" from one who does have some. In the summer there are few people around to ask from; in the winter one may ask from anyone in the band. But requests are always modest in the extreme, and never come close to equalizing the food supply. Rasmussen (1931:482) did describe the Utku as living (in 1924) in a "state of pronounced communism" both summer and winter, all meals being eaten in company by all the members of a village. If this was true in Rasmussen's day, the situation has now changed. I think it is possible, however, that Rasmussen was extrapolating from the "communism" he observed in the late spring camp he visited.

In our joint iglu, the situation was strikingly different. We lived almost as communally within our snow wall as we had lived in our summer tent camp. Not only did Mannik and Ipuituq take it upon themselves to shovel out the entrance, they also helped Inuttiaq (and he, them) with the daily net-checking chore; and Inuttiaq's fish were stored with the others'. Allaq and I no longer helped with the outdoor work at the net, but when the fish were brought in we worked with Amaruq and Amaaqtuq at the oil-making. Most significant of all the changes, from the point of view of the kapluna provider, was the fact that in our joint household, all cooked meals were eaten in common. Whereas in Inuttiaq's household of three adults and two small children a twenty-five pound bag of flour had lasted two weeks, our joint household of twelve (not counting Inuttiaq's new infant) used sixty pounds of flour for bannock during the one week in which that amount was available.

The two months during which I lived in this common household were the last two of my stay at Back River, and perhaps it was partly the imminence of my departure—the loosening of my involvement and, simultaneously, my desire to hold every moment permanently—that caused the ordinary domestic scenes of those days to take on something of the quality of a stage set. Every detail was sharp with the clarity of distance, but by the same distance it was made unreal. As always, I watched the comings and goings from my corner of Inuttiaq's ikliq. From that position the round, waist-high hole through which one stooped into Pala's iglu gave me a truncated view of his early morning visitors, all of whom I learned to recognize by their boots as they stood in front of the hole, drinking their mugs of tea before setting out to check their nets or their fox traps. When the men left, Pala's daughters—Allaq, too—began their morning housekeeping activities: chipping away the filthy gray layer of frozen mucus, fishbones, and other remains that had accumulated underfoot and resurfacing the floors with fresh white snow, or stripping the bedding off the ikliqs to spread snow or gravel in the uncomfortable hollows melted by warm buttocks. The return of the men from the nets was announced by the thud of frozen fish—several hundred of them—tossed down the entrance tunnel into a smoking pile on Pala's iglu floor, the men in frost-crusted furs following after to warm themselves with tea before going out again to feed the dogs or repair a sled. As our ikliq was at right angles with Pala's, all I saw of the men as they ate and drank was a row of caribou boots protruding stiffly along the edge of Pala's ikliq. (Only visitors sit tentatively on the edge of an ikliq with their feet on the floor; contact with the snow floor is too cold. The family sits well back with legs outstretched, a warm height above the floor.) The women, bent in a circle around the huge pile of fish on the floor, gutted each one with two smooth strokes of an ulu and tossed it toward the storage hole in Pala's iglu wall, handing up choice fatty morsels to the men on request.

In the afternoon, when outdoor work was finished and darkness falling, family and visitors gathered to talk and eat, or just to sit together in sociable silence. Then the unreal quality of the view from our iglu into Pala's was intensified. People and fish were almost invisible in the gray dusk that weighted the ice-block window, a gloom made deeper by the mingled steams of breath and tea and boiling fish, and by the smoke from numerous cigarettes. The fish-oil lamp, a thin line of yellow light, only deepened the murkiness of the scene. But my view was a foreign and a personal one. Cheerful reality lay in the quiet flow of guttural conversation and in the sounds of a card game: the playfully aggressive slap of cards on a board, a mock-annoyed exclamation: "E he!"—followed by runs of giggles.

I had feared that the presence of Pala's family in our second winter home would destroy the relaxed evening hours, which in the first winter I had valued both as expressions of family camaraderie and affection and as sources of data. I had thought that perhaps with seven additional people in the iglu the daytime barriers between men and women would be maintained even after visitors had left, which would prevent Inuttiaq from engaging in the long informative conversations we had formerly had. I had once asked Inuttiaq and another, younger, man about the reasons for this social separation between the sexes. They had been telling me about the feasts that the Utku used to have when the group was large, and how the men and women ate separately "because there were so many people." Rasmussen (1931:66) says that in the old days, among the Netsilik neighbors of the Utku, men and women used to eat separately, because they believed that unclean women could endanger the hunting if they ate with men. He says (1931:482) that Utku men and women also always used to eat separately. Though at present there appear to be no menstrual restrictions among them, I had assumed that formerly there had been, and that, as in the case of the Netsilik, these had influenced the eating patterns. Inuttiaq and Putuguk, however, said that Utku men and women had eaten separately (as they still do when both sexes are present in numbers) because each sex feels freer to talk and laugh when it is by itself—not because they are shy *(kanngu)*, or unwilling to have their words heard by the other sex, but merely because that's the way it is: "It's pleasanter; together we are unhappy *(hujuujaq)*." But the feelings that urged separation did not seem to apply to the extended family any more than they did to the smaller household of parents and children. The presence of Pala's family did not detract, as the presence of outsiders did, from the intimacy of private hours. For reasons not clear to me there were no longer any family prayers, but in other respects, closeness seemed enhanced and extended: there was a great deal more joking than when we lived alone; there were delightfully exclusive midnight feasts of scarce and hoarded commodities like rice and bannock; and in other respects, too, some of the more formal aspects of the relations between men and women seemed in abeyance.

I often wakened in the cold pre-dawn gloom to hear Pala quietly making the rounds of the household cups, pouring out the morning tea while Inuttiaq, still sleep-fogged, fumbled for his pipe under the pillow. Others, Allaq especially, seemed to sleep more soundly than the two senior men, but if the clink of the mugs as Pala placed them in position near their owners and the metallic splash of the tea failed to rouse his wife, Inuttiaq might prompt her: "Allaaq! Tea!"—nudging her verbally until she groggily raised her head from the pillow to grasp the mug Inuttiaq handed her. I sometimes needed prompting, too. Though always awake by this time, I never found it easy in the early morning chill of the iglu to disturb the cocoon of warmth in which I lay. "Yiini! Are you asleep? Have some tea!" I used to resent this arousal, on Allaq's behalf as well as my own, but perhaps there was more kindness in Inuttiaq's act than I felt: concern lest we forfeit our share of the precious, heat-producing tea. Or perhaps it was simply proper that when the head of the household got up, the other members should also rouse themselves.

The first cup was drunk in sleep-heavy silence; but by the time Allaq, or more often Ipuituq's wife, Amaruq, bestirred herself to make the second kettle of tea, the two iglus were coming gradually to life. One person, then another, pulled himself up out of the quilts, slipped his parka on over his head, and sat with sleeves dangling empty while his arms sought the warmth of his bare belly. I was never among the first to dress, and once, in the guise of teaching me a new word, Inuttiaq chided me jokingly for my laziness: "You are still-in-bed-in-the-morning-when-the-first-visitors-come," he said.

Banter flew between the iglus while we waited for the tea to brew. "Yiini was very funny *(tiphi)* last night," Amaaqtuq reminisced, "when she said *putuqariik* instead of *putuqliriik*—very funny." And she dissolved into giggles, followed by everybody except Inuttiaq, who scorned to join in the laughter of women, unless he had initiated the joke. Mannik, Ipuituq, and Pala had no such inhibitions; they laughed gaily. "Saarak!" Allaq coaxed. "How did your elder sister [she meant me] fart last night? Imitate it again, you're going to be very cute *(niviuq)* and have a piece of bannock and jam." Saarak obliged with a loud bronx cheer, which was greeted with more gales of laughter, from everybody but Inuttiaq. But attention returned to Inuttiaq when he said, "Listen!" and proceeded to break wind himself with elaborate vigor. "It stinks in here," he said, turning to me. "Did you cause it?" Then he was the first to laugh. And pulling himself up to dress, he shielded his genitals carefully from women's view with an edge of quilt, whistled to draw the attention of the men in Pala's iglu, displayed himself briefly, and laughed again with his audience.

Rather to my surprise, Inuttiaq tended to play as dominant a role in our large, joint-iglu household as he had in his own smaller one. Though Pala directed activities only in his own room of the iglu, while Inuttiaq remained master in *his* room, I had imagined that the immediate presence of the older man, who was at once his father-in-law and his uncle, might inhibit him somewhat. I was wrong, with the possible exception of the family prayer sessions that were no longer held. Pala, a quiet and rather inert man who, when among other men tended to follow rather than to initiate activities and who often preferred to sit at home, smoking his impressively large and curving kapluna pipe rather than engage in active pursuits at all, was very much in the background. It was Inuttiaq who, on a day of few visitors or in the evening, after the visitors had gone home to bed, would suggest: "Let's make bannock, yes?" or, "One feels like rice," whereupon one of the women with a delighted smile would hasten to comply, and we would have a delectably selfish feast.

Family conviviality was even greater at such times than in the cold and busy mornings. In the morning, as soon as tea had been drunk, the household scattered to the work that had to be done while the short daylight lasted. In the evening there were no such pressures. There were many ways of whiling away the time until the food was cooked, although the Utku, not as restless as kaplunas, do not feel the need to fill *every* moment with an activity. One day Allaq, her brother Putuguk, and Pala spent a giddy hour shooting a paper plane at the ventilator hole in the iglu dome. Often the card games were renewed, and at these times only Pala was a bystander, watching, pipe in hand, over a player's shoulder. In sharp contrast to the exclusively masculine games of the visitor-filled afternoons, all the younger members of the household: brothers and sisters, brothers-in-law, parents and children, played together with much hilarity. Sometimes even Saarak screamed to play and was permitted to disrupt the game, though Inuttiaq would tell her, teasingly, "You don't play well."

One card game was especially hilarious, though not very frequently played. It was not exclusively a family game, but the one time I saw it played there was only one outside visitor present, an adolescent girl friend of Amaaqtuq's, who played with the rest. The humorous object of the game, quite obviously, was to insult. One player suggested in advance an offensive label with which the loser was to be tagged: "The one who loses is too lazy to make morning tea"; "cries easily"; "wets his pants"; and so on. Then they drew cards, compared them according to a principle I never fathomed, and laughed at the loser, who laughed as heartily as any.

Once in a while, when there were no visitors in the house, the women would laughingly try an acrobatic stunt that was usually for men only. It was during the Christmas season, when the men had set up an *uyautaut* in Pala's high-domed iglu. An uyautaut is a rope stretched taut between two points, above the head of a man. In this case it was passed through the walls of the iglu and fastened outside. A man grasps this rope with both hands and pulls himself up and over the rope in a somersault or series of somersaults. Most of the young men could complete three or four revolutions without touching the ground, and even Pala and Qavvik turned an occasional stiff somersault to the accompaniment of huffs and laughing groans. The adolescent boys, urged on by their elders, wrinkled their noses in shy *(kanngu)* refusal, or else rushed at the rope, clowning in parody of a successful predecessor, dangled briefly with wildly thrashing legs, and dropped off into the laughing audience. Women never tried the stunt on these public occasions; they performed only privately, spurred on by their husbands and brothers with much amusement. They always failed—as I'm sure the men were aware they would. Inuttiaq urged even his self-effacing wife to try it, but when she reluctantly did make a comical half-hearted attempt, he watched the female nonsense with characteristically expressionless face, not joining in the general laughter.

It was when we were all in bed at night, drinking our final mugs of tea and searching our underwear for lice, that the joking reached its climax. It was Inuttiaq's game, with Saarak his willing stooge. "Saarak," he whispered, "say 'Pala'!" "Pala!" The old man's name had an oddly impertinent sound in Saarak's tiny voice. I was never sure whether this impression derived from my own world, where the children I know do not call older relatives familiarly by their first names. But in Utku society almost everyone uses terms of kinship more frequently than names, and ordinarily Saarak called Pala "Grandfather."

"Louder—much louder," Inuttiaq urged her.

"PALA!"

"WHAT, Saarak?" Pala's scratchy old voice called back.

"How many lice do you have?"

"*I* haven't got any lice; how many do *you* have?"

Again, Inuttiaq whispered: "Call your mother's brother." (That was Mannik, Saarak's favorite uncle and Inuttiaq's friend.)

"Mother's brother!"

"What, Saarak?"

"You have no testicles."

"You're mistaken. It's you who have no testicles."

And so on, until Saarak's tongue tangled with sleepiness. Pala and his married daughter Amaruq, who occupied opposite wall-edges of their iglu, had already blown out the lamps beside them; the voices came out of the darkness weighted with sleep, and one by one were silent. Allaq, bent over the one remaining lamp, pored inch by inch over the gray-brown surface of Inuttiaq's erstwhile white longjohns, cracking all visible intruders between her teeth. Finished, she laid the garment aside, undressed with the same smooth quick movements as her husband, pulled the quilts over her and, raising herself on her elbow in a final gesture, blew out her lamp.

I liked being the last to sleep at night. I savored the darkness that swallowed the daytime jumble of boxes, cups, clothing, and oil cans, the soot-grayed, icicled walls, corroded into burrow-like ugliness by the ordinary processes of life. Gradually, as my eyes adjusted, the empty blackness was replaced by a suffusion of moonlight which glowed through the ice window at my head so faintly that its blue glimmer served mainly to heighten the sense of darkness. In those few moments before sleep the iglu, filled with visible night and quiet breathing, was filled also with peace.

II. Men and Women: The Warmth and Luxury of Male Dominance

The easy conviviality that I saw among the members of the family in their private hours revealed an important aspect of the warmth that underlay the formal, somewhat distant, public relationships between the sexes. In a more literal sense, too, warmth was enhanced when the men and women of a family were together. "Iglus are cold when the men are away," people told me, but the words meant little to me until in January of my first winter Inuttiaq went to Gjoa Haven to trade.

The Utku looked forward to trading season. In late August the breeze began to bite and the ground to crunch underfoot; the drums of boiled fish bellies stored in the tent entries became granulated with ice, and the used tea leaves froze to the flat rock on which they had been piled to dry for re-use. Then the men, sitting flat-legged around their card games, and the women, rocking their babies on their backs and tucking stiff fingers into the hollows of their necks to limber them for sewing, began to talk about Gjoa Haven and what they would buy there when the strait froze in November and the men made the long sled trip in to trade. The lists were always the same: fresh tea to replace the jaded old leaves (and the weed-stalks that we brewed up as tea-substitutes when there was no life at all left in the old tea leaves); flour for bannock to supplement the staple fish; real tobacco and cigarettes to replace the bits of twig and trouser pocket that the people were smoking in thimble pipes; duffel for a new parka; cartridges . . . These trading trips were the events of the winter, the peaks of an otherwise even-flowing life. As Amaaqtuq, her eyes shining, told me once during my first autumn: "You will see: when the men come back from Gjoa Haven we stay up all night. It's *tiring!*" Feasting on bannock and more bannock, she meant; drinking tea, coffee, cocoa, one after the other, while listening to news of the world across the strait, a world accessible only during the winter. Any one Utku man would make the trip only once or twice in a winter, but somebody was always coming or going, and usually two or three traveled together, as without companions the journey of a week or two across jagged, empty sea ice would have been arduous and lonely.

The women appeared to look forward to the trips as eagerly as their men. They reported to each other again and again what their brothers and husbands had been overheard to tell the other men about their plans: how many sleeps they calculated the trip would take, and what they planned to trade their foxes for. If a woman was fortunate enough to have caught a fox or two on her own trapline—always shorter and laid closer to camp than a man's line—she, too, would outline her projected purchases, her pauses seeming to give weight to her choices as she listed each item thoughtfully against a finger: powdered milk for the children; jam; butter; embroidery thread for decorating cloth boots . . . On the eve of a trip, women sat late at night over their lamps, scraping and cleaning the foxskins, while the travelers prepared dogfeed for the trip, stuffing burlap sacks and ragged old caribou hides full of the woodenly frozen whitefish without which a trip was an impossibility.

Gear for the trip had to be settled too. "I'll take one of Yiini's primus stoves because mine is cached in my trapping shelter," Inuttiaq would decide. (He referred to the tiny iglu at the far end of his trapline, a day's journey from home, where he was accustomed to spend the night when he went to check his line.) "I'll take the frying pan so I can make bannock on the way home, and the big teakettle for the trip home, too, because I'm going to buy tea. The little kettle will be all right for you while I'm gone because you won't be in a hurry; when you want tea you can heat water several times in that little pot and it will be enough." Allaq never demurred at these decisions which always, I am sure unjustly, seemed to me so highhanded. Without comment she packed everything Inuttiaq designated in the wooden box that ordinarily served us as kitchen table. She seemed completely involved in the bustle and excitement.

Sleep was short on the night preceding a trip. On the morning of his departure, Inuttiaq always roused Allaq long before dawn had grayed the ice window. The sequence of events was almost always the same. "Allaaq! Make tea." Allaq, clumsy and speechless with sleep, dressed—parka and trousers—then pulled the primus toward her and filled its tray with alcohol. While the blue flame burned she pulled on her boots; and when the primus was roaring steadily under the kettle, Inuttiaq, still comfortably in bed with his pipe, spoke again: "Go out and look." Allaq, as on every other winter morning, obediently went to test the weather, of which neither sight nor sound penetrated our snow walls. "It's still completely dark," she reported, ducking in again; "magnificent weather; no wind; no ground drift." "It makes one grateful (hatuq)!" Inuttiaq, suddenly electrically awake, threw off the quilts and pulled his parka on over his head. On the morning of a trip Inuttiaq never waited quietly in bed, as he usually did, to sip his first cup of tea in lazy relaxation. Fully dressed and booted, he gulped the tea as fast as its temperature allowed, then, catching his snow knife out of the wall by the door as he passed, he ducked out to see to the sled. Allaq, abandoning her tea, hurried to collect her husband's gear. Sometimes—I regret to say, not always—I, too, shamed into activity by the general bustle, dressed and helped Allaq. Together we pulled one of the two mattress hides out from under the sleeping children. Saarak stirred. "Kahla!" her mother whispered. "Careful! She's waking up." She laid a hand on Saarak's head, transferring quiet through her touch till the child once more slept securely. One mattress; one quilt pulled off the children and stuffed into a bag with Inuttiaq's Bible and prayerbook; the wooden kitchen box, which had to be hammered and wrenched free of the floor to which it was frozen—one by one I passed the things to Allaq, who shoved, tugged, and carried them along the passage to the slope outside where Inuttiaq waited to arrange them on the sled. Packing the sled itself was the driver's work. Allaq hurried, so as to be in time to lay out the harness in a neat pattern on the ground in front of the sled, before Inuttiaq should be ready for her to help him with the final tying-on of the load— tossing the rope back and forth to each other across the sled and hooking it firmly under the crossbars. The final job was harnessing, and this Inuttiaq and Allaq also did together, dragging and kicking the reluctant dogs one by one down the slope to the harness, while those still chained above clamored and leapt at their chains, their enthusiasm completely out of keeping with the resistance they would show when their turn came to be harnessed. Most of the dogs had settled positions in the tandem harnesses, but Inuttiaq occasionally shifted two or three of the animals around. "Where to?" Allaq would ask, with difficulty collaring a wildly cavorting pup, and Inuttiaq would tell her.

I stood helpless and embarrassed during the hitching-up. In the beginning I had tried to learn, but, though unharnessing was easy, the reverse process I found impossible. Simple as the harness seemed when I helped to lay it out on the snow, as soon as I straddled a prancing dog the bands lost any semblance of pattern; the head went through the tail hole, the leg through the head hole; the poor dog yelped and struggled to escape. If I took off my mittens the better to unravel the puzzle my fingers started to freeze, and finally in the fury of frustration I roared, "Stand still!" and kicked the dog as brutally as my soft boots would allow, in emulation of Inuttiaq and Allaq. Several times Allaq had tried to demonstrate the proper technique, stretching the harness between her hands so that I could observe its pattern, moving her arm through it as if inserting the head of a dog so that my slow eye might follow, then with painstaking deliberation placing the dog in the harness. Emphasizing each move— "like this, like this"—she slipped one loop over the animal's head, raised the right leg and inserted it in the second loop, raised the left leg and inserted it in the third loop, and pulled the whole contraption straight over the tail. It was no use; I was all blind thumbs, my natural clumsiness with ropes aggravated by the atmosphere of haste. Then the others left me alone to struggle with my one dog while they dealt with the rest of the team, until finally, ready to start, Inuttiaq came, took the harness out of my hands, and expertly slipped it over the dog. He never commented on my ineptitude, but his silence humiliated me more than any joke or criticism could have done. I was grateful when he assigned to me the far less taxing job of standing on the clawed anchor, which dug into the snow beside the sled, adding my weight so that the dogs in their early morning enthusiasm could not run away with the sled before Inuttiaq was ready.

Meanwhile other iglu doors slammed, other teams yowled and leapt on their chains, and the frozen snow creaked underfoot as Inuttiaq's traveling companions—almost always Mannik, sometimes Putuguk or Ipuituq, more rarely Nilak—assisted by their households, made similar preparations for departure. There was never any farewell and rarely a backward glance; neither did any man wait for any other, but as soon as his last dog was in harness the driver leapt for the anchor, yanked it up out of the snow, shoved at the side of the sled to dislodge it, and breathing a hardly audible command to his team—"ai (be off)!"—flung himself sideways onto the sled and was off, careening at a gallop down the slope and out onto the flat river ice. Wives, sisters, and fathers, who had helped to harness, stood singly in front of their own iglus or moved to join one another, women to women and men to men. Full light was just growing on the southern horizon, infusing sky and snow alike with the soft winter brilliance of blue and rose. Arms withdrawn from their sleeves for warmth, women watched the sleds dwindle and be absorbed into the distant landscape. The old man Qavvik was a still silhouette alone on the hilltop by the farthest iglu, watching his adopted son, Putuguk, disappear. "Inuttiaq has climbed up," Allaq observed, her eyes intent on a moving speck that, veering to the west, had ascended the river bank and disappeared across a neck of land on the horizon. She stood silently for another moment. "On the far side of Sunday," she said, "we will see him coming again." She waved in imaginary greeting at the empty river and smiled at me. "Uunai!" she said. "It's cold. One feels like drinking tea." And she followed her sisters indoors.

From the beginning I shared in the excitement of these trips to Gjoa Haven, but I did not at first appreciate what life was like for those who stayed at home while the men were away. The events that should have given me my first insights into the chill discomfort of these occasions I misinterpreted. Two such misunderstandings occurred, the first at the very beginning of the autumn traveling season, about two months after my arrival at Back River. In need of a holiday and unaware that, except in the spring, the Utku ordinarily considered the trip to Gjoa Haven and back too arduous for women, I had asked and received from Inuttiaq permission to go along on the first trading trip that was planned in November. He was not going himself at that time, but he arranged for me to go with three other, younger, men. He said that when he went to trade in December, he would bring me back. Inuttiaq and Allaq supervised my preparations regarding equipment and provision: a sleeping bag, a mattress hide, sugar to drink in our tea—"for warmth," said Allaq. But when I mentioned that I planned to take my kerosene storm lantern and primus stove I thought I sensed a flicker of disconcertion pass between my parents. Perhaps I imagined the fleeting expression, it was almost nothing, but it moved me to explain that I would need these things in Gjoa Haven because I would probably be living by myself in an iglu there. I imagined simply that they did not like relinquishing the kapluna luxuries to which they had become accustomed since I had moved in with them. It did not occur to me that my independence in taking my own stove and lamp instead of using those carried by the men I was to travel with might be unusual behavior for a woman. Neither did it occur to me, since Inuttiaq and Allaq themselves owned both a primus stove and a fish-oil lamp, that I might be working hardship on them. Because the Utku, when they felt cold, generally chose to stoke their own bodies rather than to heat the air around them, and stoves were therefore almost never run steadily throughout the day but were used only periodically for brewing tea, I was unaware how great a difference my equipment could make in the temperature of the iglu.

The second incident that I misinterpreted happened as I was returning to Back River with Inuttiaq and Mannik after my holiday in Gjoa Haven. It was early in December; the dark and cold were bitterer than when I had traveled north three weeks earlier, and, after an interlude in overheated houses and warm beds, I was feeling somewhat less hardy than usual. Inuttiaq, having predicted that the trip would take three sleeps, was now pushing to cut it down to two, driving Mannik and me vigorously from dawn till long after dark each day. "Raigili and Saarak are cold," he explained. Resentful of being urged out into the black midwinter morning after only four hours' sleep, I privately accused him of using that unselfish pretext to cover his desire to rush home and display his new acquisitions. The meticulous honesty of Eskimos does not extend to public expression of one's motivations, and it is common practice to phrase one's own wishes in terms of concern for others.

Only when I was left for the first time with Allaq and the children in the iglu during Inuttiaq's absence in Gjoa Haven did I realize how genuine was the concern with warmth that I had crudely interpreted as an excuse for self-display. And then I realized, too, how complex were the causes of the chill that prevailed when the men were away.

My first experience of this chill was unusually impressive. It was, as I have said, in January of the first winter, when Inuttiaq, Allaq, the children, and I were living by ourselves. Though I enjoyed the cosiness of our life, the private family hours, and the conversations with Inuttiaq and Allaq, nevertheless I had looked forward to the trip Inuttiaq proposed making to Gjoa Haven in January as a much-needed opportunity to bring the typing of my fieldnotes up to date, unplagued by the changes in iglu temperature that Inuttiaq's presence caused. When he was there, it was impossible to maintain the iglu within the temperature range of twenty-seven to thirty-one degrees at which typing was feasible; either the iglu steamed and dripped so that my work was lost in a wet fog as a result of his demands for tea, boiled fox, bannock, and soup in rapid succession, or my fingers and carbon paper froze as a result of his drafty comings and goings at jobs that seemed to necessitate propping the door open. Allaq never initiated eating orgies, never suggested that I interrupt my typing to cook just when the temperature had arrived at twenty-eight, rarely hinted that a contribution from my kapluna family's latest gift of soup might be welcome. She never came and went through the door with such abandon as Inuttiaq, nor sat in the open door to drink her tea. Many were the frustrated moments when I heartily wished him gone. But only when he was gone did I learn how essential his presence was to us, how dependent we were for warmth on the very demands I so resented.

In his absence that January, life seemed almost to be in abeyance. Perhaps it was partly the weather, of a solid, tangible cold that seized face and feet and hands in a burning, dry-ice grip. Indoors the cold, though much less intense than outdoors, had an aching, relentless quality that, in my first experience of it, I felt as a physical weight—the weight of the snow dome drawing down over me and numbing my energy. One of our two primus stoves had gone with Inuttiaq and one of our two kerosene storm lanterns; but it was not just the cold weather and the absence of some of our accustomed heating equipment that lowered the iglu temperature so spectacularly. It was Allaq's behavior, too. She became a different person; her passivity was beyond belief. She never boiled fish, rarely brewed tea, and never lit the lamp to dry clothes—any of which activities would have heated the iglu. Neither did she go out to warmer iglus to visit. She just sat in her corner of the ikliq, waved her feet, blew on her hands, and endlessly observed that the iglu was cold. She decided that one reason for its temperature was that she had not banked it thoroughly enough with loose snow when it was built; but she did nothing about it beyond pointing out to me the thin spots. She merely blew on her hands and remarked that they were too cold to sew, as she would like to do. One day when the temperature was eight degrees indoors (a full twenty degrees lower than when Inuttiaq was home) Allaq spent the entire day searching for lice in Saarak's sweaters and her own and remarking that her knees were cold. We did not eat, because the fish on the floor were frozen too solidly to cut and Allaq did not light the lamp, which would have thawed them. I retreated to my sleeping bag during this period, and even so I froze the gloved fingers which, in order to hold my book, protruded from the sleeping bag. The children also stayed in bed most of the time, playing quietly and apparently happily under the quilts. Allaq never stayed in bed, even when there was no practical need for her to get up, a fact curiously out of keeping with her other behavior, I thought. She slept late—we all slept about sixteen hours as compared with the usual nine or ten—but then, having drunk her morning tea, she would say reluctantly but with a smile: "I ought to get dressed. The cold makes one lazy but one ought to get dressed." And she would pull on her parka and her thin boots and sit blowing on her hands and searching for lice.

But when the dogs' howling signaled Inuttiaq's return, bleak passivity vanished in a flash; the iglu filled with visitors come to share the feast and hear the news. Allaq made tea, coffee, bannock, tea and more tea, till the thawing dome dripped again, while Inuttiaq, enthroned on the ikliq with Saarak on his lap, recounted the Gjoa Haven news and the comic vicissitudes of the trip, and listed his purchases in detail to all comers.

Looking back on this incident, I find it even more puzzling than I did at the time, so contrary was Allaq's behavior to her usual quiet industry. Perhaps her pregnancy, then unknown to me, ate at her energy, intensifying the numbing effect of the cold and making it seem too effortful even to go next door for a visit and a cup of tea in Pala's iglu. She did visit, I thought, far less often than usual that winter, whether or not Inuttiaq was at home, and once she explained to me that she did not feel like visiting, because standing, as visitors do, was tiring and made her feet cold. But this does not explain why she rarely visited in her father's iglu, where she was privileged to sit down familiarly on the ikliq. Allaq's failure to make more than the minimal morning and evening tea while Inuttiaq was gone was also puzzling. Perhaps it was because both the primus and the tea belonged to me; perhaps in the absence of her usual leader,

Inuttiaq, Allaq, still a little shy of me, was waiting for *me* to give directions, as Inuttiaq usually did, concerning the use of my belongings. I, on the other hand, curious to find out to what extremes her passivity would go, had refrained from interfering or from taking the initiative myself.

In other camps and at other seasons the effect of Inuttiaq's absence was less dramatic. Whether that was because the weather was warmer on other occasions; or because Allaq had had her baby; or because in most other camps we lived in closer association with Pala's household, and Pala's requests for tea and food substituted for the absent Inuttiaq's, I do not know; in any event, I experienced then some of the pleasure I had anticipated in vain on the occasion of Inuttiaq's January trading trip. True, it was chilly because the primus or the Coleman had gone with the travelers; but life proceeded at a more relaxed and leisurely pace than normally. "We will sleep late when Inuttiaq is gone," Allaq said, smiling; and so we did, every day, undisturbed by Inuttiaq's early morning monologues and tea-brewing clatter. Inuttiaq never liked to be behindhand when the men went out to their morning tasks. When the men were gone, only a minimum of fishing and net-checking had to be done, because there were fewer mouths, human and canine, to feed.

Allaq, except on that first occasion, seemed closer to her own family during Inuttiaq's absences. Her sisters Amaruq and Amaaqtuq, always freely in and out of our iglu in any case, seemed at these times to visit longer and more talkatively, occupying Inuttiaq's place on the ikliq with comfortable familiarity. Once, during the winter when we lived in a joint iglu with Pala, Amaaqtuq announced that she would spend the night on our side of the wall for the pleasure of it, and she did. She lay awake for a long time after we were in bed, gazing up at the dome and dreamily telling Allaq, as she had countless times before, the story of her household's recent trip from autumn camp to winter camp: ". . . It was very cold . . . the wind was blowing the snow along the ground, and then it began to storm . . . and one of the puppies climbed out of the box where we were carrying them and fell off the sled and we had to go back for him . . . it was funny *(tiphi)* . . ."

I enjoyed the enhanced conviviality of Allaq's family at these times: the family presided over by Pala, a benign patriarch, placidly puffing at his enormous curved pipe while he watched the activities of his children and grandchildren, laughed with them at their amusements, and periodically reminded Saarak of his love for her. "Ee ee! Did you mistakenly think you weren't lovable *(niviuq, naklik)*? Ee ee!" I enjoyed also the respite that Inuttiaq's trips gave me from what I perceived as his "domineering self-centeredness." I have mentioned already the difficulties I personally encountered when my interests clashed with his: when, for example, he destroyed the painfully achieved typing temperature of the iglu. In addition, I was irritated by his peremptory manner toward Allaq and the children and by the lack of consideration I felt he showed them. He seemed to have no compunctions about interrupting their activities, and occasionally even Allaq's sleep, to order them to do things for him: make tea, make bannock, fetch his pipe, help feed the dogs, chip the stalactites off the walls. If the wall developed a hole and snow began to accumulate on the bedding, or if a dog broke loose from its chain during the night, it would always be the soundly sleeping Allaq, not her wakeful husband, who had to go out and repair the damage.

Once I myself was unwittingly the occasion for Inuttiaq's disturbing Allaq's sleep. It was toward the end of my first winter when, frustrated to the point of desperation by the typing situation in the iglu, I had set up a double-walled tent behind the camp, a delightfully cosy cranny just large enough to hold the three boxes that served as desk, stool, and lampstand, and the primus with which I heated the tent. I often spent seven or eight hours a day there in January and February, trying to complete the notes that I had not been able to bring up to date, as I had hoped, while Inuttiaq was in Gjoa Haven. Coming home then late at night when the rest of the family was already asleep, I occasionally indulged in the luxury of frying my supper fish. Somehow, it was harder to eat it raw when I was alone than when I was surrounded by other raw-fish-eaters. Moreover, fried (as opposed to boiled) fish was a treat impossible to have during the day, both because the frying pan did not hold enough so that everybody could have a share and because the smoke from the frying smothered the other occupants of the iglu. In order not to disturb the sleepers on these midnight occasions, I used to carry the primus out into the unheated storeroom and cook there, jogging from foot to foot as I had been taught, to keep my feet from freezing while the fish fried. One such night when I came into the iglu bearing my smoking fish, I found Allaq sitting up in bed, eyes bleared with sleep, mixing bannock. Inuttiaq lay beside her, smoking a cigarette. He explained, "I told her to because I'm famished."

If Inuttiaq's intention was to make me feel the pinch of guilt for my private feast, he was successful; but I never found out whether his midnight demand for bannock was indeed a reproach to me or whether he was merely awakened by the smell of frying fish (very like that of frying bannock) and was, as he said, famished.

Inuttiaq rarely went so far as to make Allaq cook for him in the middle of the night; and most, if not all, of the demands he made were quite within the rights of a man in his position as independent head of a household. On one occasion I nonplussed Allaq by asking why it was that men "bossed" women and made all the daily decisions. Allaq, very resourceful when confronted with idiotic kapluna questions, was silent for only a minute, then said: "Because the Bible says that's the way it should be." Wanting to know whether the situation was rationalized in terms of women's inferiority, I prodded her, telling her that some kapluna men also boss their women because they believe that women have less *ihuma* (judgment or mind) than men. She assured me that this was not the case among Eskimos: "It's just because the Bible says women should obey men; that's the only reason." She did not, of course, mean that in pre-Christian days women obeyed men less. She meant that it is in the natural ordained order of things for men to boss women, and always has been.

Utku women, as far as I could tell, did not feel beleaguered by the demands of their men. A woman did not resent it when her husband took the best of the lighting and cooking equipment with him on his trips to Gjoa Haven, leaving her to suffer from the cold. She did not feel unjustly put upon when her husband waked her in bitter darkness to chase a loose dog, usually in vain, through the camp. She rationalized these vicissitudes in terms of the feeling that it is the men who have the hardest work to do, going out in the coldest weather to fish or hunt and making long difficult sled trips under the most adverse conditions. "We want to do what we can to help them because they take care of us," was the way Ikayuqtuq put it to me. She was not an Utku, but the latter also phrased their performance of everyday duties in terms of "wanting to help." Whenever Amaaqtuq abandoned a half-sewn seam or a half-written letter and rushed out at the sound of her brother's approaching team, it was because "I want to help Mannik unharness." And when Allaq, once achingly, wheezingly ill with a grippy infection, refused to take off her boots and lie down, it was "because I want to help Inuttiaq unload," when he returned from a trapping trip.

Moreover, I had the impression that many of the demands men made were welcome for their own sake. A woman who would not have presumed to cook a rare delicacy like rice on her own initiative was delighted when her husband or brother told her to do so. Even tea was drunk in greater quantity when the men were around to order it. A woman herself would modestly claim to be satisfied with one cup; but if her husband were thirsty for a second kettleful, she would be more than happy to have a second cup.

Playing the recorder in imitation of Yiini

Returning from the autumn caribou hunt: unloading the dogs

Late summer at the Rapids

Setting off on the autumn caribou hunt

Making tea: younger sister imitating elder

3

Inuttiaq's Children

I. Saarak: Temper and Reason in Child Nature

Next to Inuttiaq himself, the most important person in Inuttiaq's household during my first winter at Back River was Saarak, the three-year-old baby of the family.[1] Indeed, in some respects

1. During my 1963–1965 field trip, I had occasion at one time or another to observe seventeen Utku children, six boys and eleven girls, who were divided by age as follows:

Age	Boys	Girls
Under 2 years	2	2
3–4 years	0	3
5–6 years	0	2
10–15 years	4	4

There were also two boys and two girls who were considered almost adult (sixteen to nineteen years old) and whom I therefore do not list as children. Unfortunately, of these seventeen children, only six lived for more than a few months in the camps in which I lived, and these were all small girls. Many of my impressions of child life were thus based on the behavior of these six little girls, although, as far as possible, I checked my intensive observations of them against my more irregular observations of the others.

Saarak was more important than her father. She was the lodestone not only of her household but also of her whole kin group. Members of Pala's family: Saarak's grandfather, aunts, and uncles, often excused themselves after a visit to my tent that first autumn by explaining: "I want to see Saarak." Similarly, coming in to visit in Inuttiaq's iglu, they would announce: "I wanted to see Saarak." Saarak, small, pretty, eagerly responsive, was greeted with snuffs and endearments and courted with specially hoarded delicacies: fish eyes and skin, bannock, jam, and spoonfuls of dry milk. Every wish was catered to if at all possible or soothed away tenderly if not. And when the source of her trouble could not be determined or when she refused to be assuaged, people, hearing her rending wails, murmured sympathetically, "Naaaaklingnaqtuq (poor dear)." Small wonder that in Saarak's view her family existed to serve her. Small wonder, too, that, being a child of vivid moods, she expressed her feelings both frequently and strenuously.

Long before it was time for me to leave, Saarak had bewitched me as completely as she had bewitched the rest of her family. People had taken for granted that this would be so: "You'll remember Saarak after you leave," they predicted, "and will want to see her." And so I did, intensely. But at first I found her far from enchanting. When others were a little slow in bending to her will, she screamed in anger and frustration, and when confronted with the unfamiliar, she screamed in fear. The pity of it all and the effort not to show my feelings left me breathless.

During my return visit in 1968 I saw again eleven of the same children. In addition, six children had been born, two boys and two girls under the age of two, and two girls between two and three years old. On this second trip I saw more variation in child-rearing practices than I had observed before, variations both among families and within one family in the treatment of different children. However, these were all variations on the theme described here, and consisted mainly in the timing and severity of the training in emotional control. Tears and demands on the part of favorite children tend to be tolerated considerably longer than the same behavior on the part of less favored children. Saarak's public behavior is now very much like the behavior of Raigili that I describe here, but in the privacy of her family she is far less controlled than her sister was at the same age, and her lack of control is indulged to a far greater degree, even though she now has two younger sisters.

Ages given in the text are approximate, as has been mentioned earlier, as Utku do not keep track of birthdays.

Worst of all was the fact that in the early days the screams were very often directed at me. Saarak was terrified of me, as she was of all strangers—perhaps doubly afraid in my case, since every detail of my appearance and manner was so foreign to her. If her mother, Allaq, brought her to visit in my tent, she whimpered, a tiny, tentative sound, mounting shortly to an insistent wail. Allaq would try in vain to soothe the child at her breast, and I, knowing the lure of kapluna delicacies, would contribute raisins or a bit of bannock, to no avail. In a few minutes Allaq would give in. "Saarak wants to go home," she would say, smiling an apology, and home she would obediently go. If I tried to visit in Inuttiaq's tent the situation was similar. Usually my head had hardly appeared in the entrance before a screech of anguish shattered the peace, and I hurriedly withdrew to the neutral company of my books and papers.

Saarak's Eskimo family and neighbors took a more objective and tolerant view of her temper than I did. The Utku expect little children to be easily angered (urulu, qiquq, ningaq) and frightened (iqhi, kappia) and to cry easily when disturbed (huqu), because they have no ihuma: no mind, thought, reason, or understanding. Adults say they are not concerned (huqu, naklik) by a child's irrational fears and rages, because they know there is nothing really wrong; they are concerned only when a child is hungry, cold, ill, or in real danger. They may laugh at a child's fear or anger; nevertheless, at least while the child is small, there is affection in the amusement, an affection expressed in caressing words and tones: "Naaaaklingnaqtuq!" Because children are unreasoning beings, unable to understand that their distresses are illusory, people are at pains to reassure them. And similarly, because children cannot understand the exigencies of the real world: shortages of food and needs of other people, people feel it is hard (ayuqnaq) for them to be deprived of anything they may want.

In the Utku view, growing up is very largely a process of acquiring ihuma, since it is primarily the use of ihuma that distinguishes mature, adult behavior from that of a child, an idiot, a very sick or an insane person. Ihuma has many manifestations. When a child begins to respond to the social world around him: when he begins to recognize people and to remember, to understand words and to talk, when he begins to be shy and self-conscious *(kanngu)*, to learn restraint in self-expression, and to want to participate in socially useful activities, people remark affectionately that the child is acquiring *ihuma.*

Utku consider, I think, that the growth of *ihuma* is internal and autonomous to a degree. They believe that *ihuma* needs to be informed, instructed, in order to develop along proper lines, but that there is no point in trying to teach a child before he shows signs of possessing it. So in many respects the child is permitted to time his own social growth. The belief is that the more *ihuma* the child acquires, the more he will want to use it. Adults just wait for him to conform, or say "I told you so" when he burns himself or is bitten as a result of ignoring warnings. By the age of five or six the child has usually given evidence of possessing considerable *ihuma.* Then if he misbehaves in some egregious way—if he loses his temper, for instance—one of his elders may inquire with scathing quietness: "Does one think, mistakenly, that he is using his ihuma?"

Saarak, during that first winter at Back River, was beginning in small ways to acquire *ihuma,* but she had not yet become subject to criticism. Soothed and indulged, her tempers and fears still reigned in their full vividness. However, Allaq was pregnant that winter, and the birth of a baby sister in April was to mark the fading of Saarak's innocence. Watching Saarak, the outspoken princess, with her successor, and contrasting Saarak's life with that of her predecessor, her quiet, shyly sweet sister, Raigili, taught me much about the growth of adult restraint and about proprieties of self-expression.

II. Saarak's Charm: Spontaneity; The Expression of Affection toward Small Children

I became aware of Saarak's charm only gradually. That first autumn my journal curtly noted that Saarak was one of the two least lovable children I had ever met, the other being Saarak's small cousin Rosi, whose moods were even more violent and who enjoyed similar freedom of expression. It was, not surprisingly, when Saarak began to court me that I discovered how very delightful she could be.

Saarak's affection for me was initially purchased with raisins and chocolate; her love for these delicacies preceded by weeks her affection for me. It was immoral to deprive a child of Saarak's age of anything she set her heart on. Saarak exploited that situation to the full, and I resented it, since Saarak's appetite was insatiable and my supplies finite. In my early days with Inuttiaq's family I was unaware of Saarak's growing passion for kapluna sweets. She was much too afraid of me then to make her wishes known directly to me as she later did, holding out her hand and chirping like a petulant sparrow: "Mmm? mmm?" Instead, she demanded the goody from her mother, who was herself so shy (*ilira*) of me at first that she tried, usually in vain, to substitute a fish eye or a bite of caribou tallow for the coveted raisins, without calling my attention to the situation. Only when importunate wails arose and I looked up from my writing to find out what was the matter, would Allaq apologetically explain: "Saarak wants raisins; she hasn't enough sense (*ihuma*) not to ask for things she wants; she's funny (*tiphi*)." I always produced the raisins then from their hiding place in my knapsack and doled out a half-frozen handful to Saarak and another to Raigili. Raigili had already learned not to make demands of people other than her mother; she never gave a sign of wishing to share in the bounty, even when the box was brought out, but when I handed her her share the silent shine in her eyes was expressive enough. Her less restrained sister bounced and coquettishly pursed her lips with pleasure, while Allaq murmured to her a warm "vaaaa," a long release of breath like a sigh of fulfillment. It was Allaq's idea that the raisins be kept hidden in my belongings; she hoped, on the whole vainly, that Saarak would think of them less frequently this way. And whenever the box was emptied, which happened quite often, she showed it dramatically to Saarak, murmuring with a sympathy that was partly guile: "Look, they're all gone, no more raisins, all gone." The maneuver rarely worked for long; Saarak was convinced that if she screamed importunately enough, another box would materialize from some mysterious corner. She continued to be convinced of this long after my supply was really gone.

It was on an afternoon about a month after I had moved into Inuttiaq's qaqmaq that another dimension first appeared in my relationship with Saarak. I was sitting, as usual, in my place on the ikliq, my chilblained hands thankfully tucked into the shelter of my wide duffel sleeves. Tea was brewing on the primus. The thread of steam from the kettle's spout mingled with the breath of the visitors, and the warming hum of the stove underlay the murmured talk of the day's catch, the impending move to the winter campsite, and the trading trip to Gjoa Haven which would follow the move. Saarak was, as usual, entertaining with tricks that her aunts and uncles had taught her. Children of her age were the adults' playthings. People amused themselves by teaching the children to sing fragments of hymns and to repeat with perfect adult inflection phrases whose syllables their unaccustomed tongues hopelessly stumbled over. Saarak's stock phrase for almost the entire winter of 1963 was an imitation of my own most joyful phrase. "Oh oh!" Saarak would say with a kapluna lilt in her voice, "Tukihivu-u-unga (I understand)!" That phrase she had picked up by herself, to the amusement of the adults: "What? What did you say, Saarak? 'Oh-oh-tukihi-vungaa'? Say it again, Saarak, you're going to be so cute and lovable (niviuq) and have a piece of bannock to eat. Do tell us again what it is your elder sister is always saying: 'Oh-oh . . .'" And Saarak would obligingly repeat, rewarded by laughing snuffs and perhaps by the promised bit of bannock.

Saarak and Rosi were also taught to make comical faces on request (one, with down-drawn mouth and raised eyebrows, reminded me of an arrogant English butler) and to imitate a variety of gestures, some invented for the occasion, others characteristic of all Utku. Thus, as a game, Saarak was taught how to say "yes" as Utku do by raising their eyebrows and how to say "no" by wrinkling the nose. She was taught to groove her tongue in the manner of an adult tending a campfire or blowing out the lamp at night, a gesture vastly more effective than my flat-tongued blow, which the Eskimos found entertainingly inept. Saarak was also taught how to rock back and forth from one foot to the other, bouncing a bundle of rags or a limbless and headless rubber doll pressed into the back of her fur suit, like a mother bouncing her baby to sleep. Occasionally Saarak's mother or one of her aunts tried to tuck a live puppy into the back of Saarak's suit, but this Saarak resisted with screams, to the amusement of the adults.

The children were taught these gestures by example. "Do it like this," the adult would say, rocking back and forth, or grooving her tongue so that the child could see. Saarak and Rosi were extraordinarily observant; after a few tries both children usually produced comically accurate facsimiles of the adult's gesture. I noted the same keenness of observation in older children and adults, all of whom were much more skilled in imitation than I, accustomed as I am to verbal instruction. The imitative attempts of the small children, both the successes and the failures, were greeted with warm laughter and affectionately drawn-out murmurs: "Eeeeeee eeee!"; "vaaaa!"

On this particular afternoon, instead of responding to adult directions to do this or that, Saarak had reversed the procedure and was directing her family and visitors to do as *she* did. She pattered from person to person in the qaqmaq, stopping in front of each, folding her hands into her neck as adults do to warm them, and instructing each person as she herself was wont to be instructed: "Do this! like this!" Each person obediently tucked his hands into his neck in imitation of Saarak and laughed with her. Usually when Saarak ran around the qaqmaq, summoned to sit on an uncle's lap or to be kissed by an aunt, she made a wide detour around me, but on this day, to my delighted astonishment, she included me in her circuit. "Do this!" she instructed me, and when I, like her other admirers, docilely tucked my hands into my neck, she beamed and chirped at me as happily as if I were really a member of her family. She had never smiled at me before; I was elated, suffused by a warmth I had not previously felt for her.

After that, there were many incidents that drew me to Saarak. There was the night in midwinter when I came home after one of the first days that I had spent working in my writing tent, pitched on the slope behind our iglu. The tent was a blessing, but it meant that I was at home much less often than formerly, and Saarak noticed the change. She met me, on this particular night, when I crawled through the low iglu doorway, shoving ahead of me all the unwieldy paraphernalia that anthropologists need to keep them happy: primus stove, lantern, tin box of field-notes, typewriter, teapot, cup, ulu for scraping the previous night's accumulation of frost off the tent walls. Saarak bounced, pursing her lips in the self-conscious gesture that her parents interpreted as "being a child: wanting to be loved *(niviuq)*." She ran to take each object as it appeared in the doorway and with amusing but precarious dispatch carried it over to my side of the iglu, where it belonged. The primus landed wrong-side-up, the storm lantern clattered on its side, while Allaq, laughing, instructed Raigili to repair the situation. Then Saarak ran for the snowbeater, the wooden stick used to knock the dry snow out of clothes before it has time to thaw and soak the clothing. She laid about my legs with such enthusiastic warmth that I feared for my shins and toes. "Do this," she ordered me, squatting down. Allaq, anticipating Saarak's next move, hastily substituted a large fur mitten for the wooden stick, and when I obediently squatted on the floor, Saarak beset my shoulders and back with the mitten like a determined little whirlwind.

"That's enough, Saarak," Allaq laughed. "Enough! Enough!" I echoed, laughing. But Saarak chirped, "Just a minute!" and continued to beat me, thoroughly enjoying the performance. Saarak (and her elders) used "just a minute!" the way American children use "no!"—but she always said it in the most enchanting, birdlike voice; one could not help laughing. And nobody tried not to laugh.

I was profoundly refreshed by the fact that people did *not* try to suppress their amusement at the antics of small children like Saarak and by the fact that the children were permitted to enjoy the entertainment together with their audience without fear that they would become "self-conscious" or "spoiled." When Saarak bounced for attention like a quaint rabbit, nobody seemed to worry that she was learning the bad habit of showing off; she was merely expressing a childlike wish for affection *(niviuq)*, a wish in which her family happily acquiesced, nodding their heads at her lovingly and murmuring, "Eeeeee eeeee," in the soft cadence of affection. Later, when she developed reason *(ihuma)*, restraint and shyness *(kanngu)*, a wish to be properly inconspicuous, would, in their view, grow naturally. The adults' freedom to express enjoyment and admiration, and Saarak's freedom from soul-shriveling disapproval, were, I am sure, important elements in my enjoyment of Saarak. I was simultaneously Saarak and parent, in both roles reveling in a spontaneity unfamiliar to me.

In another way, too, the relaxed warmth between Saarak and her elders was delightful to me. Utku husbands and their wives, children older than five or six and their parents, never embrace or kiss, never sit with arms entwined, do not hold hands or lean against one another, and rarely touch one another in any way, except insofar as they lie under the same quilts at night. I missed the clasped hands, the comfortably leaning shoulders that in my own society I was accustomed to in these relationships. I felt frozen, isolated, by restraint, and so the love so tangibly bestowed on Saarak was a balm. It was a joy to watch her with her family, and I, like her family, delighted in luring her onto my lap, in feeling her warm, wriggly little body in my arms, and in snuffing her small dark head. I delighted in society's permission, more accurately, in its injunction, to respond to all Saarak's commands—except, now and then, to her commands for raisins.

I do not know whether the relief that was a part of my love for Saarak was shared by her Utku family. Perhaps not, since I, unlike the Utku, suffered from the contrast between the restrained Utku ways of expressing affection: the glance or the smile, the matter-of-fact offer of a cup of tea, or the unasked attention to a ripped mitten, and the ways that were a part of my own nature. Moreover, for the Utku, not *all* physical warmth was channeled into these relationships with small children. Though it was lacking in the relationship between husband and wife and between parent and older child, where I missed it, there was some in relationships among brothers and sisters, who sometimes rough-housed gaily with each other, leaned close together to look at a picture, or deloused each other's shirts, pulling the garment up, section by section, to inspect it under the lamp while the wearer bent patiently into the light. I saw it among little girls, who walked hand in hand or leaned against older people, who never appeared to notice; among older girls who, as a friendly gesture, combed each other's hair out and carefully braided it again; and among young men who, idling away the evening in a tiny travel-iglu out on the sea, lay with their arms around one another or sprawled across one another as they laughed over word-guessing games or told each other again and again what they would buy with the foxes they were taking to Gjoa Haven. Still, all of these demonstrations had a much more casual tone than the affection shown to Saarak, and to Rosi by *her* family, and I think it is possible that the intensity of these relationships with small children may be in part a reaction to the restraint so prevalent in other relationships.

III. Raigili's Charm: Mildness

Raigili, on first acquaintance, was as mild in manner as her sister Saarak was forceful, as docile as Saarak was unruly. Paradoxically, it was her very invisibility that made me notice her and that in the first months drew me to her more than to the vividly assertive Saarak. In the first weeks Raigili's normal quietness was intensified by fear of me; she never spoke to me unless I spoke to her, and then her answers came in the tiniest of whispers. Often she did not even manage a whisper but replied to my questions only with an affirmative lift of her eyebrows or a negative wrinkle of her nose. Strangely, though I remarked the intensity of her shyness, I was not clearly aware that I was its cause until weeks later, when the fear had lessened. I must have sensed something of her uneasiness, so strong was the protective warmth that I felt for her; but consciously I thought her soft unobtrusiveness a natural gentleness with which all Utku children seemed, however incredibly, to be favored after the age of five or so. The other children of Raigili's age and older seemed equally retiring; even their play, from the distance at which I first observed it, seemed noiseless, the laughter and the cries of excitement absorbed by the huge tundra spaces.

In part, my impression was right: the older Utku children *were* usually gentle-mannered, even when they did not feel shy (*ilira*) and afraid (*iqhi*). They were never chittery in the noisy manner of children in my own world, never buzzed inside the tents and iglus with the young restlessness that would have been so distracting in those close confines; but normally there was a gaiety, a spontaneity—a childlike aliveness—in their quietness, which was obscured at first by their fear of me. And perhaps not only by fear. In retrospect, it seems to me that even after the fear was allayed, I was blind for some time to these other qualities in the children. I think the vividness of the contrast between the children's quietness and the clamor that I had hitherto, with a mixture of irritation and resignation, expected of children may have exaggerated my perception of the silence. It was peaceful; I accepted it gratefully and unanalytically, inwardly blessing and ignoring my small benefactors.

But if I was slow to discover Raigili's aliveness, I was more than ever charmed by her when I did so. The bubbling giggle that convulsed her when I attempted bumblingly to talk to her was very endearing, and so was the funny little air of maturity with which she told stories of her life in the hospital or made solemn pronouncements: "The weather doesn't feel cold to *me* because *I* am a child." It was delightful to hear her beside me on the ikliq, humming and talking, often to herself, as she rocked idly back and forth or amused herself in small ways. I never ceased to be amazed at her capacity for absorbing herself in scarcely perceptible pursuits for hours on end, sitting or lying quietly on the ikliq and demanding no attention from anyone. She might scrape a discarded bit of hide with her mother's scraping tool, wave a sock vaguely in the air, twist and untwist an empty plastic bag, or run cardboard dogs, which her mother had made for her, up and down the tent pole that edged the ikliq. One of her favorite activities was drawing. Sometimes, early in the morning, when I opened my eyes and rolled over in my sleeping bag to face the rest of the family, I would find myself looking into Raigili's wide dark eyes. Lying silently beside me, she was waiting for me to wake. "Titiraut . . ." With a hardly audible whisper that trailed off into silence before the word was finished, she would beg a pencil from me, and, pulling out from under her parka-pillow the discarded cover of a lard package or a grimy scrap of cardboard the size of a pocket mirror, she would draw—mostly figures of parents and children—or painstakingly attempt to write her names and those of her relatives in the syllabic characters that her parents and aunts were teaching her. I found her shy glow completely captivating when, after she was finished, she explained to me in her trailing whisper what it was she had written or drawn.

Raigili responded to the warmth I felt for her—as well as to my frequent small gifts of raisins and chocolate. She showed her liking first with characteristic quietness. One night at bedtime, about a month after I had moved in with Inuttiaq's family, she appeared in front of me as I was writing in my place on the ikliq. Clutched to her chest she held my urine pot, a tin can almost half as big as she herself was, and over the frosted top of the can her wide eyes, very like Inuttiaq's in their contour, smiled at me with melting warmth. During the day it was customary for all except the very young and very old to go outdoors to urinate, but at night large cans: a gasoline drum for Inuttiaq's family and a smaller powdered milk can for me, stood in front of the ikliq. In the evening, after the family went to bed, a smaller can was passed around, and each member of the family filled it in the privacy of his sleeping bag or quilt and emptied it into the communal can. It was an efficient and inoffensive system, since the indoor chill quickly canceled any odor. Raigili was often sent at bedtime to bring in her family's can from outdoors, where it lay during the day, but she had never brought in mine, nor had anyone asked her to on this occasion. Raigili said nothing, but the beaming smile that appeared over the rim of the can made her mother's explanation superfluous. "She likes you *(pittiaq),*" Allaq said. "The children like you because you give them kapluna food to eat."

IV. Raigili and Her Family: The Expression of Affection toward Older Children

I was slow in sensing the quality of Raigili's relationship with her own family. She was past the age when affection for her could be exuberantly expressed, as it was toward Saarak, and many of its manifestations were too subtle for my unpracticed eye and ear to catch. My initial impression was that, except for attending to her physical needs, the members of her family were as unaware as I was of her gentle presence on the periphery of their activities. During that first winter, Allaq still boned Raigili's fish for her and cut it into bite-sized pieces, as she did for Saarak (and occasionally for Inuttiaq when he remarked that he was feeling lazy). Daily she dried, stretched, and mended Raigili's clothes, and when Raigili had lost her fur mittens or worn holes in her boots, as frequently happened, Allaq made her new ones out of whatever scraps of hide were available. At night the sleepy Raigili would sit hunched on the edge of the ikliq or stand immobile in the middle of the floor, her parka sleeves dangling limp and armless, while she waited for her mother to undress her. Allaq, usually without a word, would come and lift the inert child into bed, folding her parka and trousers under her head for a pillow, and pulling the quilt over her shoulders. "Have you peed, child?" Inuttiaq would ask her, and when she murmured that she had not, he would pass her the can: "Pee, so you won't wet the mattress."

It seemed to me in my first weeks that most of Raigili's exchanges with her parents were of this matter-of-fact, overtly unemotional sort. It was not that I thought her unhappy or rejected; she never gave that impression. She was simply there—pleasantly, comfortably, taken for granted, to be responded to or overlooked as convenient, never intrusive or obstreperous. Unlike Saarak, Raigili seldom, if ever, insisted that her parents respond to her remarks or play with her; she rarely pressed *directly* for any sort of notice, except when she was hungry, and even then her apparent patience amazed me. If Allaq were sewing busily or scraping the floor, she might simply ignore her daughter's soft-voiced request for tea or fish. Raigili would repeat her request at intervals: "Uuumak! [her word for "mother"; literally, "Hey you!"] one feels like tea," but she seldom grew insistent and even less often petulant. If she did, her mother might respond with a sound of disapproval in her voice like the mooing of a cow: "Mmmmmmm, Raigili! Always hungry!"

But Raigili was by no means unloved, and her parents were explicitly concerned that she should feel their affection. Inuttiaq, voicing this concern one autumn day, taught me how wrong I had been in thinking that Raigili was ignored. He was standing with some of the members of Pala's household on the bluff above the camp, keeping Allaq company while she boiled fish for the camp's supper on a wind-sheltered fireplace built into the cliffside. Raigili, who had been playing down by the shore, started to come up to join the group on the bluff, but Inuttiaq, seeing her coming, called to her to fetch his parka from the beach and take it home. Not hearing Inuttiaq's shout clearly, Raigili started to bring the parka to him on the cliff instead, and he redirected her to the tent. Obediently she carried the heavy parka to the tent, from our height a tiny figure waddling almost invisibly behind the bulk of duffel. Again she started up toward the cliff, and again Inuttiaq sent her back, this time to fetch his pipe from the tent; but at the same time, watching her retreating back, he remarked to his wife in a low voice: "We'd better not send her on any more errands. If we send her away every time she gets close she'll think we don't like to have her near us *(niviuq)*."

As I learned more of the language, I became increasingly aware of the affection that was expressed for Raigili. Often it was the little signs of her growing up that elicited the affection. When she offered for the first time to fill the big teakettle with water from the river, her mother watched from a distance. Seeing Raigili, small and inept, slip on the stones at the river edge and spill the water half out again, Allaq called to her: "Rai! That's enough!" And watching the child approach across the gravel, tilted heavily to one side under the weight of the half-empty kettle, she murmured, while the child was still too far off to hear, a warmly amused "vaaaa!" When Raigili went fishing in three feet of water with a hookless string for a line and a stone that refused to stay in place for a sinker; when she wandered off to hunt ptarmigan, as small groups of children often did, but this time going by herself much farther than children of her age usually cared to go; when, staggering and falling, she carried a nearly adult-sized load of plants for fuel up to the fireplace on the bluff; when she heated water for tea on the lichen-fed fireplace—her parents, her uncles and aunts, her grandfather, noted her behavior from a distance with affectionate murmurs: "Vaa-aaa!" "Eeee eeeeee!" "Naaaaaklingnaqtuq (she is lovable)!"

A good deal of the solicitude that people felt for Raigili seemed to be expressed at a distance in this way—so much so that I did not always see how Raigili could be aware of the affection that her parents wished her to feel. There were isolated occasions on which, I am reasonably sure, she was *not* aware of being affectionately observed. When one day Allaq noticed her daughter vomiting behind the qaqmaq, she only said to me: "Naaaak-lingnaqtuq (poor dear), she's vomiting"; she did not approach the child. And when, another time, Inuttiaq noticed Raigili outdoors by herself, without playmates, he too said only, "Naaaaklingnaqtuq! She's all alone"; he did not inquire into the situation or take steps to alter it.

But in general I think she could not fail to feel the love that surrounded her. Hearing other children privately remarked on by their families, she may have guessed that she was, too, even when no direct sign was given; and on many occasions when she was observed, echoes did reach her. People would ask her later with a smile: "Raigili made tea today?" or: "How many ptarmigan did you get?" She would beam, and the adult would smile: "Vaaa!" Once in a while I was refreshed by a communication of more than usual directness: the pleasure Allaq several times expressed as she listened to Raigili singing and talking beside her on the ikliq; the note Inuttiaq sent once when he was away on a trip to Gjoa Haven: "Kiss Saarak for me and speak lovingly (aqaq) to Raigili."

One incident is especially memorable. It occurred one winter day when, going outdoors on an errand, I noticed Raigili in the distance, helping her mother to carry big chips of ice for drinking-water up to the iglu from the river, several hundred yards away. It was not an easy task; the ice, as I knew well, had an unpleasant propensity for freezing one's fingers, even through fur mittens. Admiringly (and a little guiltily, because I was not myself helping with the job that day), I mentioned Raigili's helpfulness to Inuttiaq. "Eeeee," he said, in the flat monotone characteristic of Utku. It always baffled my untrained ear, that tone; remarks were engulfed by it and vanished without a ripple of response. But when an ice block dropped with a thud in the storeroom outside and Raigili's small, red-clad form appeared in the door, Inuttiaq looked up from his filing: "Were you fetching ice?" And when she raised her eyebrows: "Yes," he took her hands out of their mittens—"vaaaa!"—and held them against his naked belly to warm them.

To be sure, under ordinary circumstances, Raigili had outgrown this physical form of tenderness as she had outgrown being kissed, and explicitly affectionate words, too, would become increasingly rare as she grew older. Most expressions were already very discreet—chillingly so to me, by contrast with the lavish cuddling and cooing that Saarak reveled in. Conscious that Raigili's feelings for her sister were not always of the friendliest, and hungry for affection myself in my isolation, I wondered whether Raigili felt her diet as thin as I would have in her place. I think, on the whole, she did not. Discretion was inherent in the adult way of expressing feeling to which Raigili was being assimilated and, as a child of her people, she must have been attuned to it as I could never be. Even to me, the matter-of-fact questions and comments, the smiles, the silently considerate acts, spoke clearly enough when I was the recipient. And the glow that I felt at such times I thought I sensed also in Raigili's smile when she reported how many ptarmigan she had stoned or when she responded to Allaq's pleasure at hearing her chatter.

Moreover, not only did Raigili understand adult ways, she also wanted, like other children, to be part of them. She must have felt some pang at the passing of childish privilege, but perhaps for that very reason her tolerance for those more extravagant forms of affection was nil. Nilak, a frequent visitor of Inuttiaq, took advantage of her reticence for his amusement. The ritual was always the same. Lowering his handsome face toward Raigili, he would tease: "Want a kiss?" At this Raigili would always draw away in silence, wrinkling her nose, while her tormentor laughed. I noted Raigili's behavior, thinking it an expression of the shyness characteristic of her age. Raigili's small cousin Qijuk was subjected to the same joke and responded similarly. But I had no suspicion of how deeply Raigili felt about being kissed until one day when her own mother teased her. Allaq's baby, Qayaq, was several months old at the time and, enthroned on her mother's back, she already received a good deal of affectionate homage. On this occasion Raigili had lifted her face toward the baby, who stood looking down at her, over Allaq's shoulder. "Kunik (kiss)?" asked Raigili, tenderly. But Allaq joked, "Raigili wants to be kissed," and she raised her face in imitation of her daughter: "Kunik . . ." Raigili's face contorted in furious shock. With a loss of control startling in her, she shrieked, "My little SISTER!" (not you!) and, crushing her eyes shut, stuck out her tongue at her mother, who giggled.

Raigili's parents showed their affection for her in one fundamental and consistent way that would probably not be outgrown: in responsiveness to their daughter's own feelings of affection (*unga*) for them, her wish not be separated from them. The sensitivity that Inuttiaq showed on the day when Raigili tried to join the sociable group on the bluff was not unusual in his relationship with her. One of the other occasions on which I observed it occurred shortly after Qayaq was born. A night or two after the event, Inuttiaq remarked that the family quilt under which he, Allaq, Raigili, Saarak, and now Qayaq all lay, had become a bit small. The usual solution in such cases is to suggest to the oldest child that he or she might use a separate quilt. Inuttiaq said nothing specifically to Raigili that night, but next morning, lying in my sleeping bag beside Raigili, I heard her father murmur a question to her. The words were unfamiliar to me, and her reply, a wrinkle of the nose: "No," gave me no clue to what he had asked. Later, when Inuttiaq and Raigili had gone out, I asked Allaq for an explanation. She said, "Raigili should sleep separately, but she wants to be with us (*unga*). When Kamik comes back from school next month, they two will sleep together." In fact, Raigili was still sleeping under the same quilt with her parents nine months later when I left Back River.

Raigili's wish to be with her parents was heeded also at the time of the autumn caribou hunt. Every August, when the able-bodied members of the camp went off into the tundra for a week or two to hunt caribou for their winter clothing, most of the children and old people were left behind. In the first autumn of my stay Raigili had been left behind at the Rapids with her grandfather, Pala, and her aunts Amaaqtuq and Akla, but in the second autumn, little as she was, she went along. She was a valiant little figure in her red parka as she plodded off over the hummocky tundra, already far behind the others before they were out of sight of the camp. I wondered why she had gone, instead of remaining behind again with Pala and the other children. Pala told me: it was because she had been so sad (*hujuujaq*) last year when she was left behind.

V. The Lives of Children: Sibling Relationships

In the weeks before I saw Raigili very clearly, I thought her life idyllic. There seemed to be no pressure on her to be anything other than what she was: a charming little girl with shyly glowing eyes and a cascading giggle that erupted at the slightest amusement. Casually, in the interstices of my day, I watched her with her two friends Qijuk and Akla; I was aware of the trio in the background of my other concerns—giggling together, darting through the camp on unknown chases, or bending together over various absorbing occupations. They seemed never to lack for amusement. Sometimes they accompanied the adults on their fuel-gathering, net-checking, or fishing expeditions. If the spirit moved them, they might gather a few handfuls of lichen or heather, pull a fish or two from the net, or take a turn at jigging; if it did not, they would occupy themselves with their own pursuits at the edge of the adult group or wander off by themselves. In the autumn they slid on the smooth fresh ice of the inlet or harnessed themselves to a toy sled, taking turns in pulling one another over the river, urged on by the shouts of the "driver": "Ui! ui! ai!" Sometimes the three little girls harnessed themselves together to the sled while a young uncle, or perhaps Saarak, rode in style; and sometimes an older uncle harnessed himself and gave them all a ride. Crouching in imitation of the adult hunting posture, they would stalk the clucking ptarmigan that ran ahead of them over the uneven ground and that finally stood stupidly waiting to be stoned. They chased lemming and ermine with wild torrents of giggles in and out and around their stony burrows, prodding the animals out with sticks whenever the cowering little things thought themselves safe under a rock; or else they took turns at being caribou, stalking, "shooting," and "butchering" each other in the field behind camp. They played at being dogs, allowing themselves to be chained to a rock as the real dogs were, watered, and fed with fish, which they ate in canine fashion, holding the fish on the ground with both "paws" and tearing at it fiercely with their teeth. Sometimes they walked on all fours with the aid of bird legs or caribou rib-bones for front paws and pretended, never very ferociously, to snarl and snap at each other.

Often, too, their games were domestic. The adolescent girls made stuffed dolls out of scraps of cloth and hide, sewing tiny skin boots and fur-ruffed parkas for them with minuscule stitches that spoke well for their future prowess as seamstresses, and sometimes the younger girls would clumsily imitate them, to the silent amusement of their elders. At other times the little girls fried bannock for themselves and for the children who were still too young to play, miniature bannock cooked on a tin plate precariously balanced on three pebbles that served as a fireplace. And in the long spring and summer nights when the sun never set and the air was heady with light, the children wandered on the tundra or along the water's edge, occasionally until nearly morning, before they retired to the rickety play tent they had built out of canvas and quilts behind the camp. In the tent, which they filled to bursting, they lay close together under their quilt, giggling or telling each other stories, and the adults, hearing a child's soft voice in the background, would smile as they sat together in front of the tents, drinking tea and chatting: "Raigili. She's telling a story."

Accustomed as I was to the ordinary frictions of American child-life, I was refreshed in those early weeks by the apparent peacefulness of Raigili's life. Though some of the children's entertainments were, literally or figuratively, murderous, there seemed remarkably little strife among the children themselves: little competition and less quarreling. I was refreshed also by Raigili's apparent freedom of action. I heard none of the adult directives, the "do"s and "don't"s, that constantly prick at children in my world. Raigili was asked to run errands occasionally, but beyond that she was not called on to take a consistently useful part in social life. There seemed remarkably few things that she was not permitted to do, and if she did rummage in the household storage box, eat the lump of tallow that had been saved for Saarak, or fail to run an errand, her small misdemeanor never earned her more than a passing titter or a moo of disapproval, and often it seemed to be ignored altogether.

Raigili's peace and freedom were not as pervasive as I had at first thought. It became clear later that what seemed to me a "mild" note of censure or of amusement was not necessarily so to Raigili. But at first, as unattuned to the highly modulated expression of friction as I was to the discreet expression of affection, I failed to note either the signs of tension or the context in which they most often occurred: Raigili's relationship with her sister Saarak.

During much of the time when I knew Inuttiaq's family, the relationship between the two sisters was highly turbulent. Raigili did not welcome intrusions on her activities, and most often it was Saarak who, so far innocent of restraint, was the intruder. Moreover, Raigili, being older, was always required to submit to her tyrant-sister. In later years, when Saarak acquired more reason (*ihuma*), Raigili, as the elder, would be rewarded by having Saarak at her beck and call; but for the moment her satisfaction must lie in her own knowledge of having used her reason maturely and in the approval of her relatives.

Raigili's behavior was, of course, not always guided by reason. She was only six or seven; her unhappiness and displeasure could not always be concealed. But so angelically demure was she on first acquaintance that it was some time before I realized that the lesson of control was still imperfectly learned.

During my first weeks with Inuttiaq's family, Raigili and Saarak seemed to me to have little importance for each other. Even when Raigili was at home, which she often was not, Saarak's activities rarely seemed to interest her; and Saarak was still far too attached, physically and emotionally, to her mother to pay attention to Raigili except when Raigili had something that Saarak wanted. She seldom turned to Raigili when she wished something to eat or needed to be placed on the urine pot. As I recall, she did not always include Raigili in her attention-seeking games either, and Raigili for her part rarely admired or laughed or cooed at Saarak, nor did she usually help, as other children did, to offer distraction when Saarak was in a temper. Much of the time I had the impression that the two sisters lived in separate worlds. Increasingly, however, as winter limited Raigili's roamings—or perhaps it was partly that my senses became more keenly attuned—there were moments when the two orbits impinged on one another. The collision was sometimes resounding, but not always. Sometimes, snug under the quilts on a cold morning, or on a day when Raigili was awaiting the repair of her boots, the two children played together quite happily, singing snatches of hymns, poking each other teasingly in the navel, playing "cards" with little squares of cardboard, in imitation of their elders—throwing the cards down one after the other, picking them up and repeating the process—or running the cardboard dogs that Allaq cut out for them along the edge of the ikliq. Sometimes, pulling the quilts up over their heads, they just lay and giggled together.

The peacefulness of the children, lying together in bed, and their ingenuity in entertaining themselves on such occasions was as amazing to me as Raigili's own capacity for solitary absorption. Their elders were amused by the games. One of the words for play, *pinnguujaqtuq*, means to "pretend to do," that is, to imitate; and the children were marvelous mimics. I was one of their favorite models; all aspects of my behavior were copied and, as far as possible, my speech as well. One morning, a few weeks before I left Back River, I was working to fill in a few of the most flagrant gaps in my data, when Allaq, with a low-voiced "Yiini" and a surreptitious nod toward the children, pulled my attention from my notebook. Raigili was lying in bed on the ikliq and Saarak was sitting astride her sister's stomach, tapping absorbedly with all her fingers on Raigili's chest. Raigili's folded arms moved slowly across her chest as Saarak tapped, until they extended far to one side, at which point Saarak abruptly shoved them back again so that they protruded on the other side. Then the process was repeated. Intermittently, Saarak interrupted her tapping to tug the neck of Raigili's undershirt a little higher up on her sister's chin. She was typing, with Raigili a most efficient instrument!

There were other games, too, that mirrored my behavior in illuminating ways. There was the asking-for-raisins game, for example, in which one of the children, Saarak, or Raigili, or perhaps their ten-year-old aunt, Akla, sat "typing" on an imaginary machine at an invisible box-table while the other player came and stood beseechingly beside her. "Kaglali (berries)!" the petitioner pleaded in a thin baby voice that stumbled over consonants; but the typist blandly continued to type, ignoring the increasingly importunate voice at her elbow. Finally, she leaned down, rough with impatience, pulled an imaginary box of raisins from inside the "box" on which she was "typing" and brusquely thrust it at the importuner: "Uvva (here)!" Over this game, too, Allaq and I exchanged secret smiles, but I felt more than a twinge of guilt, witnessing the all-too-accurate portrayal of my kapluna selfishness.

Of all the roles the two sisters played, perhaps the commonest were those of mother and child. The game took various forms. Often in the mornings, when the two were playing together in bed, Raigili would suggest to Saarak that she "carry" her (using the word that refers to the act of a mother carrying her child on her back). Saarak would climb onto the back of her crouching sister, and Raigili would attempt to cover them both with the quilt. And when Saarak fell off, as she always did, the game would begin over again with happy giggles. Or if one of the family's bitches had recently whelped, the children would plead to have a puppy or two brought to them in bed, and they would play with the tiny, half-blind things as if with babies: snuffing their noses lovingly, feeding them bits of cut-up fish, holding them in their laps and tapping their penes to make them urinate, as mothers do with their infants.

Occasionally, Raigili and Saarak played together in these ways for an hour or more at a time, but oftener the games ended abruptly in mutual outrage. The events precipitating the clash were rarely visible to my eye; Saarak in some imperceptible way would annoy (urulu) Raigili, who would retaliate by surreptitiously shoving Saarak, or merely by ignoring some demand Saarak made of her, and Saarak's shriek would effectively summon the adult world to her aid. It was, of course, always Saarak's aid and not Raigili's to which people came, since Raigili, as the elder, should have known better than to annoy (urulu) her still irrational (lacking in ihuma) little sister.

VI. Raigili and Saarak: Sibling Friction

According to Allaq, Raigili's clashes with Saarak occurred excessively often. Though jealousy between sisters seemed an ordinary enough feeling to me, Allaq denied that it was usual for Utku children to feel consistently hostile toward their brothers and sisters. The word tuhuujuq (tuhuu), which denotes adult "jealousy" and "envy," is not used to describe children's feelings about their siblings. People are aware that a child who is displaced from its mother's breast and back by the birth of a younger sibling may feel distressed (ujjiq), and reassurances of food and attention are offered to assuage its suffering; it is recognized that children get annoyed (urulu) with one another at times, and also that children may love *(naklik, niviuq)* some of their siblings more than others, just as parents love *(naklik, niviuq)* some of their children more than others; but these phenomena are seen as quite different from the consistent antagonism that Raigili showed toward Saarak. Raigili, rightly or wrongly, was said to be an unusual case. As Allaq put it, when Saarak was born Raigili "didn't acknowledge her as a younger sister," and often she did not "feel like an older sister," affectionately protective *(naklik)* and amused *(tiphi)*, toward Saarak.[2]

I was not convinced that Raigili's feelings for Saarak were as unusual as her mother claimed. Allaq's statement may have been an expression of the Utkus' embarrassment in the face of hostility, their inclination to minimize it or to deny it altogether (like the English-speaking informant who, when I asked him to translate the word "hate," flushed and denied that there was such a word in Eskimo). Though Allaq could not conceal Raigili's antagonism to Saarak while I lived with the family, she may nevertheless have wished me to believe that in general the Utku did achieve their ideal of amity. Or possibly, prompted by a mother's irritation at her daughter's slowness in learning to control her feelings, she really did believe Raigili unusually difficult. Allaq's mild smile gave me no clue to her thought.

My doubts concerning the idiosyncratic nature of Raigili's feelings stemmed in part from the remarks people made about their "less loved *(naklik, niviuq)*" siblings. Though variations in the quality of affection *(naklik, niviuq)* felt for one's siblings was taken for granted, and though remarks made about the less loved brothers and sisters were always temperately phrased, there was occasionally something in their quality, or in their context, that made me wonder how much more was felt than said. Allaq's remarks about her own siblings are illustrative. Pala had had twelve children, of whom Allaq was the eldest and a favorite

2. Inuttiaq's daughter Kamik, who was as dear to him as Saarak, also behaved most of the time in a very "unsisterly" manner toward Saarak: stepping on her foot, snatching her toys, deliberately tormenting her to the screaming point, which, in Saarak's case, was always quickly reached. But because Allaq averred that Kamik's teasing of Saarak had been much worse since her return from boarding school, and because the school experience had made her behavior aberrant in other ways, I have not considered Kamik illustrative of ordinary Utku child behavior.

with her father. Five of her brothers and sisters were dead and a sixth brother, Putuguk, had been adopted as a small child by Qavvik and his wife, who had no children of their own. Once, watching the two men, Putuguk and Qavvik, steer their loaded sled down the river on their way to a new camp, Allaq remarked that Putuguk had been a very sweet *(niviuq)* little boy. And she named her baby, Qayaq, for another brother who had drowned a few years earlier: "Because I loved *(naklik)* him very much." But she remembered less affectionately *(niviuq)* the babyhoods of her three youngest siblings, two sisters and a brother, who were still living with Pala. The youngest of all, Raigili's playmate Akla seems to have been the least favored *(niviuq)*, both by Allaq and by her brother Mannik, who was a few years younger than herself. She was recalling one day the endearing *(aqaq)* phrases that Mannik had used for his various small nieces and for his younger sisters, years ago, when they were of an age to be caressed. These forms of endearment are highly individual refrains, affectionate links between two people, one older, one younger. Occasionally, they may even replace a kinship term as a way of addressing or referring to a person. Once, on an earlier day, Allaq had amused herself by prompting Saarak to recite in their characteristic, tender tones the affectionate phrases by which she, Saarak, was addressed.

"What does Qavvik say to you?" Allaq had asked Saarak.

"Dub-dub; dub-dub." (These were tender but meaningless syllables.)

"What does your father say to you?"

"Taipkuat, taipkuat (those, those)."

"What about your grandfather?"

"Niviuqnaittuhugilutiit (did you mistakenly think you weren't lovable [*niviuq*])?"

"How does your mother's sister [Amaruq] speak to you?"

"Nu. Nivi." (These were the first syllables of "sister's daughter, sweetheart [*niviuq*].")

I was startled to hear my own name in the recital, as I had been unaware of the affectionate refrains in my speech. "What does your eldest sister say to you?"

"Saaaaarak qaplunaatut uqaluttiaqtuq (Saarak speaks English beautifully)."

Allaq remembered the phrases that Mannik had used for all of his younger sisters and sisters' daughters, except Akla. "He didn't speak lovingly *(aqaq)* to her much," said Allaq. "She wasn't very charming *(niviuq)*."

Another time, when Allaq was discussing the comparative prettiness of various infants, she mentioned her other younger sister and brother disparagingly: "I didn't care much for *(niviuq)* them as children; they weren't very pretty; Ukpik had a big nose." I asked whether she had loved *(niviuq)* all of her other brothers and sisters. "Yes," she said, "all of them." I reminded her of her earlier remark about Akla: "You said she wasn't lovable *(niviuq)*; Mannik didn't find her charming *(niviuq)*." Allaq corrected me, as she occasionally did when I neglected to modulate my expression: "I said he didn't find her *very* charming." But she added, "I didn't find her very charming either."

There were, to be sure, experiences in Raigili's life that might conceivably have caused her to find Saarak even less charming than Allaq found *her* siblings: Amaaqtuq, Akla, and Ukpik. In the first place, while Raigili was still very small, she had a severe illness and was flown out to the hospital in Chesterfield Inlet, three hundred miles to the south. She was gone for about a year, not in the hospital all the time, but staying with her future mother-in-law, Ukalik, in Baker Lake, near Chesterfield Inlet, while she awaited transportation home. Ukalik's own children were fairly well grown; in her household Raigili had probably been the baby, treated with all the tenderness usually lavished on children of her age. When she finally came home, Allaq said, she was severely distressed. Her parents seemed unfamiliar to her at first, and she cried to go back to Ukalik; she cried for milk and candy and gum—all the delicacies to which she had become accustomed in the kapluna settlements in the south; she suffered from nightmares and from unusually intense fears *(kappia)*. "It's all right now," Allaq told me; but Raigili had not forgotten her experience away from home. In the evenings, when the family lay in bed comfortably talking, Raigili sometimes told us fragmentary stories about the hospital and about her future mother-in-law's family at Baker Lake.

It was while Raigili was away that Saarak was born. Small wonder, I thought, that she should resent her; not only had she been violently torn away, she had been supplanted in her absence. She had gone away a pampered baby, had probably been adored and pampered as a baby in Ukalik's household, and then had been transplanted suddenly into a family in which she was not princess, a family not even clearly hers, in her childish mind. But Allaq never phrased it this way, and it is impossible for me to know what Raigili really felt when she returned to find a newborn sister.

A second reason why Raigili may have felt unusually antagonistic toward Saarak is that her parents loved *(naklik)* Saarak, as Inuttiaq put it, "a little bit" more than they did her. This may also be another reason for Allaq's sensitivity to Raigili's hostility. Though the preferences parents felt for some of their children over others were, in general, accepted as straightforwardly, spoken of as matter-of-factly, as were the preferences that siblings felt for one another, nevertheless, for some reason, Inuttiaq and Allaq did not at first tell me of their preference for Saarak (and for their eldest, Kamik). Allaq did one day ask me which child I preferred *(pittiaq)*, Raigili or Saarak. It was only about three weeks after I had moved in with Inuttiaq's family. I was still at that time far more charmed by Raigili than by the whiny, demanding Saarak, but, inhibited by the kapluna sense of indiscriminate "equality" that seeks to deny differences, I was embarrassed to admit the truth. Even though Raigili was not at home and Saarak was too young to understand, I said I liked *(pittiaq)* them both. Allaq then candidly remarked: "My younger sister Amaruq likes *(pittiaq)* Raigili best." I was surprised to hear of Amaruq's preference, because my impression had been the reverse: she, like everyone else who came to visit, always made much of Saarak, cooing *(aqaq)* at her, holding her, teaching her cute tricks with which to entertain the adults; and almost every morning she came to carry Saarak to her grandfather's qaqmaq for a visit, tucking the child under her parka for warmth and crawling out through the low doorway with Saarak clinging like a huge protuberance to her belly. To Raigili she seemed to pay no attention at all beyond addressing her with an occasional teasing remark to which Raigili responded with a self-conscious grin. But Allaq said no, Amaruq liked Raigili more; she knew because when Raigili was younger and kissable, "at the darling *(niviuq)* age," Amaruq had snuffed her with deep, long, vigorous intake of breath—Allaq demonstrated by snuffing Saarak—whereas when Amaruq snuffed Saarak (which she frequently did) she did it, said Allaq, with less ardor. Moreover, as Allaq demonstrated, there was less intense affection in Amaruq's tone when she cooed *(aqaq)* at Saarak than there had been in the days when she cooed at Raigili.

Why Allaq was reluctant that day to disclose her own preferences, I do not know. Possibly such favoritism, though more easily accepted than it is with us, is nevertheless not quite ideal. Or perhaps she was embarrassed by my own reluctance to name Raigili. Though I flattered myself that my hesitation had been invisible, I did not allow for the extraordinarily sensitive antennae that Utku have for others' expressions of feeling. In any case, when in turn I asked Allaq about her affectionate feelings for the children, she told me that she loved *(naklik)* both children sometimes and was annoyed *(urulu)* with both sometimes. "Everybody is like that," she said, slightly embarrassed, I thought, at admitting annoyance; *"everybody* gets annoyed *(urulu)* at children sometimes—except Inuttiaq; he loves *(naklik)* his children, so he is never annoyed *(urulu)* with them and never scolds *(huaq)* them."

It was a year later that Inuttiaq and Allaq, discussing with me the feelings parents have for their children, agreed—in Raigili's presence—that they loved *(naklik)* Saarak "a little bit more" than Raigili. Raigili, quietly occupied as always, showed no sign of distress. Knowing of her "unsisterly" feelings for Saarak, I felt a tug of sympathy for her. But again I have no idea what passed in her small dark head just then, whether resentment was a strand in her feeling as she sat beside her father, listening to our conversation. Perhaps her parents' preference for Saarak was unrelated to her own feelings about her sister. Perhaps Raigili, like her parents, accepted individual differences in the quality of affection as part of the natural order, an acceptance warmed by Inuttiaq's further explanation: that he loved *(naklik)* Saarak and Kamik "too much," so much that it was uncomfortable, whereas his love for Raigili, and for the baby, Qayaq, was comfortable and good *(naamak)*.

But even if her parents' preference for Saarak, or her own

difficult hospitalization, did not give Raigili unusual cause to dislike Saarak, it seemed to me there was ground enough for antagonism just in the ordinary nature of the relationship between Utku siblings. Sibling relationships are extremely important in the life of an Utku child. Though in adulthood, and in the later years of childhood, too, these relationships may be very close—the bond between siblings is said to be one of the strongest in Utku society—nevertheless, when a child is small, his brothers and sisters are responsible for many of his growing pains, a fact that makes even more interesting the Utku view that hostility between siblings is unusual.

Three important lessons in particular are related to the birth of a younger sibling: [3] learning consistently to walk instead of being carried, to eat adult food instead of being nursed, and to control feelings.

Utku children are usually born about three years apart. How this spacing is managed I do not know; I found no evidence either for abstinence or for infanticide, and direct inquiries about birth control elicited only embarrassed smiles. Utku are aware that kaplunas and the Netsilik Eskimos who live in Gjoa Haven sometimes have babies more frequently, "even before the elder one can walk!" Allaq once disapprovingly remarked; and they feel strongly that this must be difficult *(ihluit)* not only for the child who is still unable to walk easily but also for the mother. "Too much crying, I should think," Allaq observed. In the Utkus' own practice, on the other hand, since a child is ordinarily both nursed and carried by its mother whenever he wants to be until the next baby is born, the latter's birth represents to the older child a double crisis; he is simultaneously weaned and set on his own feet.

Control, the third and perhaps most difficult lesson the small

3. The toilet training that is considered such a critical experience in the life of a kapluna child does not appear to be a crisis for the Utku child, who from the time he is born is held over a can at appropriate moments: when he wakes, after (and sometimes while) he eats, before he goes to sleep, and in general whenever he shows signs of discharging. I did not observe the transition from this stage to the next, in which the child learns to call attention to his need for the can. Allaq told me that children learn a verbal signal by themselves, by imitating slightly older children, and this seems quite in line with the autonomy that children are granted in other areas of their development.

child learns, is not physically connected with a sibling's birth, but it is related in other critical ways. It often happens that by the time the baby is born the elder has acquired enough *ihuma* to warrant pressure, just a little, at first, being placed on him to begin to moderate his demands and control their expression a bit. The baby's birth may well provide an incentive to begin this training, not only because the crying of two children is hard to bear, as Allaq observed, but because the mother has the needs of a younger, more helpless being to attend to now. Furthermore, and herein lies the most direct cause of friction, it is toward this younger sister or brother himself that the elder child is first taught to exercise control, to practice the Utku virtues of generous self-subordination, patience, and helpfulness. More and more, as the younger child's demands increase, he unwittingly provides the elder with opportunities for improving the control of his temper. It is not easy to learn to relinquish one's toys or one's chewing gum to an insistent little hand, or laughingly to permit the baby to destroy one's proud handiwork.

VII. Raigili's Troubles: Hostility in Older Children

Control did not come easily to Raigili, but so strongly was antagonism disapproved that she took care to express it with utmost surreptitiousness: a pinch under the quilt, a snatched toy when the adults' backs were turned. More often her hostility took the form not of attack but of sullenness: a passive, but total, resistance to social overtures. Her feelings were never considered justified; all of the adults and older, more socialized children agreed that when Saarak ordered Raigili to give or to take, to do or not to do, Raigili should obey.

Although Raigili very rarely resisted these pressures actively, some incident or other almost every day attested to her displeasure. One of the few instances of open conflict that I noted concerned a plastic bag that Raigili was playing with as she lay in bed, absorbedly turning it inside out and back again, blowing it up and pressing the air out again, laughing at its squeaking reluctance to be forced. Saarak, lying beside her sister, was fascinated; but when she tried to appropriate the marvelous bag Raigili, amazingly, held fast. Saarak characteristically tried to enforce her will by battering at Raigili, who, uncharacteristically but exasperated this time beyond endurance, hit her back. Allaq quietly instructed Raigili to give her sister the coveted bag, but the instruction was lost in the commotion. Allaq, giggling, remarked on the humor of the situation, and for a while she waited for the problem to dissipate itself, or for Raigili to use her reason; but when neither child showed any sign of weakening determination, Allaq mildly cautioned Raigili against hurting Saarak and tried to distract her attention from the battle. Raigili, enraged, broke into loud wails, most unusual for her, which were promptly echoed by her sister. Allaq with soothing murmurs took the weeping Saarak onto her lap and offered her breast in consolation, while Raigili, her tears ignored, lay reproved.

The same plastic bag featured in a second incident as well. As before, Raigili had it and Saarak wanted it. This time Inuttiaq intervened. "Give it to Saarak," he said quietly. Raigili sat immobile with lowered head, while Inuttiaq waited. "Give it to Saarak," Inuttiaq repeated in the same still voice. Raigili sat, frozen. Saarak danced shrieking on the ikliq, flailing her arms in the direction of her sister. Inuttiaq took hold of the end of the bag that Raigili held unyielding in her hands and gradually, but equally unyieldingly, tugged, fixing his recalcitrant daughter with a steady stare but saying nothing. Raigili held tightly and silently to her possession, but Inuttiaq was stronger; the plastic bag changed hands. But then, perhaps moved by a twist of sympathy for Raigili, he divided the bag in half and gave one half to each child—a rare gesture, which Raigili accepted, still in silence.

Silent sulkiness was Raigili's characteristic response not only to problems caused by Saarak but to all the distresses to which she was subject, and a dramatic response it was. I had never imagined that sulking could be such an aggressive act, that one could feel so directly attacked by inertness. In such moods Raigili might stand for an hour or more facing the wall, her arms withdrawn from her sleeves—the latter pose a characteristic Utku expression of hunger, cold, fatigue, and grief. If her mother tried to tempt her with a piece of jammy bannock she dropped it or ignored it. If her father tried to move her she was limp in his hands. Only gradually, very gradually, would the mood lift, and when she finally turned around in acceptance of a cup of tea her wet face would betray her silent tears. And Raigili was not the only child who behaved in this way; I was struck by how little overt hostility was expressed by Utku children of Raigili's age and older, as compared with our own children. To be sure, of the seventeen children who lived in our camp at one time or another there was only one other of Raigili's own age, her cousin Qijuk, with whom to compare her; but the behavior of Qijuk, who was a few months younger than Raigili, was comparable to the latter's in every way; when she was happy, her gentle spontaneity was charming; when she was unhappy, her silent tears were as devastating as her cousin's. In the older children: in Akla and in her fourteen-year-old brother, Ukpik, I saw traces of sulkiness in the impassivity with which they sometimes countered requests that they fetch a kettle of water from the river or help to harness the dogs. Looking straight ahead with blank eyes and chewing vigorously on the gum that circulated eternally from mouth to mouth, pulling it in long pink strands from between their teeth, wrapping the strands around grimy fingers and thrusting them back between their teeth, they would appear totally engrossed in their private activity and unaware of their elder's request. Kamik carried withdrawal to an extreme on her return from school. Apparently intensely unhappy at home after her winter in a kapluna settlement, she pretended for most of the summer that she was deaf. The noise in the school diningroom (which *was* certainly louder than any she had previously heard) had deafened her, she claimed. And toward the end of my stay I could see the same pattern developing even in Saarak when, suffering from a fall, a slight, or a frustration, she would sit motionless on the ikliq with her arms withdrawn from her sleeves, unresponsive to affectionate inquiry.

To be sure, the silence of childish rebellion was not absolute; there were outbursts. But even the occasional shriek that tore the silence was wordless. Only once during the time I lived with the Utku did I hear a child shout reproaches at anyone (and that child was Kamik, during the difficult summer after her return from school). I never heard a child say "I won't!"; though when accused of a misdemeanor, they frequently did moo a denial: "I'm not!" or "I didn't!" And the hostile flailings with which

Raigili and Qijuk occasionally emphasized their resistance were never more than the most ineffectual of symbols: a swat with a wool sock or a slash of the arm, which carefully fell several feet short of the offending elder.

The responses of the more socialized children and of the adults to these displays of hostility seemed on the whole as mild as the displays themselves. Often, childish misbehavior was met by silence, not the heavy silence of gathering tension but an apparently relaxed and rational one that seemed to recognize that the child was not being reasonable but that sooner or later he would come to his senses and behave more maturely again. Compliance with adult demands in any specific instance was generally not enforced; though obedience was valued, parents rarely made issues out of incidents by *insisting* on obedience. Inuttiaq's duel with Raigili over the plastic bag was an exceptional case.

It was with some sense of shock that I contrasted this relaxed attitude toward discipline (which most kaplunas visiting in Eskimo communities distortedly view as "spoiling" the children) with our own insistence on parental consistency, our feeling that parental demands ought to be "followed through" on pain of punishment. If an Utku child played with fire or wandered too close to a dog, an adult might reinforce the painful consequences by unsympathetically reminding the child that he had only his own folly to blame; but the child was not punished in our sense of the word. Adult disapproval of children's actions was often clear to see, and sometimes, especially if a child were persistently obstreperous and tended not to heed ordinary instruction, strong pressure to conform might be exerted in the form of false threats, repeated often, even when the child was not being unruly at the moment: "The kapluna will adopt you, he likes disobedient children." "Do you know why it's gotten dark? It's because you're disobedient." "Watch out! Yiini has adopted a pet marmot and she keeps it under her sleeping bag." And very rarely: "We'll tie you to the dog chain." But often adults seemed to make a sort of game out of the threatening situation, smiling secretly at each other over the head of the wide-eyed solemn child, and finally letting the child into the secret: permitting him to look under the sleeping bag or reassuring him that they had been lying to him. And if the child chose to pay no attention, the subject was dropped; penalties were not inflicted on him, either in retribution for his wrong-doing or to "teach him a lesson."

Nevertheless the Utku methods of bringing up their children were, in their own way, highly consistent. Their consistency lay in the nature of the demands themselves, the requirements for maturity. They were always the same: control of emotion-ality, generosity, helpfulness, honesty, independence. There was never any doubt which aspects of the child's behavior were reprehensible; and sooner or later the child, with the help of his reason *(ihuma)*, would take the initiative in bringing himself to conform. There was consistency also in the calmly rational quality of the adults' responses to childish misbehavior. To me, the adults seemed refreshingly relaxed, though my for-eign eye may have misled me. Was it amusement born of tension that was responsible for the secretive smiles exchanged by Raigili's family behind her sulking back? Allaq, passively per-mitting Saarak in her lap to assault her in a tornado of fury be-cause the chewing gum was all gone, laughed, as did the visitors, at the buffets, screams, and bites while she offered her the breast. When Saarak hit at her face with a spoon, she turned her head away, saying calmly, "She has no reason *(ihuma).*" And when Saarak was finally nursing peacefully, laughter released the audience.

Laughter, like silence, was a common response to childish misbehavior, not only as a reaction to the ruffling of the smooth social surface, but also sometimes as a device for encouraging more mature behavior in the child. After once or twice witness-ing the merciless teasing to which Raigili was subjected when, overcome by some unspoken woe, she stood staring into the lamp, almost inaudibly sobbing behind the wall of her misery, I no longer envied the lot of Utku children or thought them blessedly untormented by adult pressures. At first her elders would ignore her, smiling behind her back, but if the mood did not quickly dissipate itself, and usually it did not, her parents would intervene. The sobs were often so silent that I, on the far side of the ikliq, was not aware she was crying until Allaq or Inuttiaq, in a voice as neutral as if they were asking Raigili to hand them a fish, said, "Stop crying. You are loved *(naklik).* Drink some tea. Stop crying." If these efforts to thaw Raigili's barricade were unsuccessful, then they would say, "Listen! There's a dog howling—Maktak, I think"—to which Raigili would respond with redoubled sobs, vehement and angry now, and Inuttiaq, laughing slightly, would imitate each inflection of her tone, every catch in her voice, until the poor child was shrieking wordless fury at the wall. Inuttiaq would reply to each shriek with an amused "thank you; thank you" and then quietly start to sing hymns to himself, while Raigili relapsed into muffled sobs and finally silence.

Inuttiaq's hymn-singing seemed primarily a way of demonstrating to Raigili that she was being ignored, and perhaps also a way of soothing his nerves. Occasionally, religion was invoked more directly as a sanction against Raigili's outbursts. One incident in particular stands out. It was a chilly November afternoon, shortly after we had moved into our new winter iglu. Raigili and I were alone at home while the others were out, visiting neighbors. Raigili, feeling the pressure of several cups of afternoon tea (and perhaps imitating the lazy and not altogether approved habits of her kapluna sister) had urinated into the indoor pot, volunteering the excuse that it was too dark to go outdoors into the snow as she should have. Unfortunately, when Raigili rose, the hem of her parka snagged on the edge of the pot, overturning it and spilling warm urine all over the snow floor. Raigili surveyed the pocked yellow floor, and with truly adult calm observed: "How annoying," or "Too bad"— the word *(urulu)* has both meanings; and with equally adult matter-of-factness she proceeded to repair the damage. Pulling the snow knife—nearly half as big as she was—from the wall where Inuttiaq had stuck it, she went out, cut a block of hard snow—also half as large as she was—struggled in with it, hacked it into pieces with the knife, just as her mother did when she repaired the floor, and spread it evenly over the concavities. She surveyed the floor critically: as good as new. Beaming at me, she ran out to play. When Allaq came home and noticed the fresh floor I explained what had happened. "Eeeee," said Allaq, smiling in amusement. And when after a while Raigili reappeared, her mother looked up from her sewing and said to her with a trace of smile: "I dreamt last night that Raigili urinated in the pot, saying it was too dark to go outdoors, then spilled the pot on the floor, brought in snow, and fixed the floor." Raigili looked blank; then a sheepish grin grew over her face as her mother and I broke into laughter at her puzzlement.

But alas for Raigili's pride in her housekeeping prowess. At that season it was Saarak's custom every evening for an hour or two to run wild over the iglu, round and round the floor, burrowing in the larder, poking at the fish, piling up the cups, trying to light the primus, hacking with her mother's ulu at the box that constituted our kitchen; she was into everything, to the helpless amusement of the adults. "She buzzes," they observed, using the word that is used for the circlings and divings of mosquitoes. "Saarak!" her mother and aunts would protest, laughingly trying to distract her from her most destructive goals. On this particular evening, her goal was Raigili's proud new floor, and she attacked it with absorbed persistence, wielding Allaq's ulu. Unfortunately, while she was so engaged, Raigili came in from one of her many visits. She said nothing but kicked once ineffectually at the ulu in Saarak's hand and stood sulking. When Saarak paid no attention, Raigili tried, at considerable peril, to interpose her foot in her sister's hacking. Saarak shrieked in wordless fury, and Allaq, as usual, quietly instructed Raigili not to interfere. Raigili's sulks ended of their own accord, and later that evening when, cheerful again, Raigili was sitting in her place on the ikliq, turning the pages of the religious comic book that her uncle had brought back from boarding school, Allaq took the opportunity to teach her daughter a lesson. "Look," she said in a soft, pious voice, pointing out a lurid picture of Jesus on the cross, "Yisusi was crucified because he loved *(naklik)* people. It hurt very much. His head hurt and they made holes in his hands and put nails in. It hurt very much. If he hadn't loved us he wouldn't have been killed. He says to love *(naklik)* one's little sister." Raigili questioned her mother with interest on the details of the crucifixion but gave no sign of having heard the admonition.

It was difficult to tell how Raigili responded to this training in the use of reason. I often had to stifle pity as I watched her small figure standing in motionless distress on her mother's side of the iglu or noted the dampness of her lowered face beside me on the ikliq. The demand for control, though clothed in the mildest voice, was so relentless, and Raigili was still so little. The lesson takes a remarkably short time to learn, judging from the almost infallible control of the children I knew who were ten years old or more. But the learning must entail suffering.

One hint that this was so lay in Raigili's nightmares. Adults, as I have mentioned, are said not to have nightmares, and the suggestion that they *might* have them was met with a laughing shudder: "O-h-h-h! how frightening *(kappia)!*" Though some people do have dreams that they characterize as "unpleasant *(hujuujaq)*" or "startling *(tupak)*," I rarely heard any adult except Inuttiaq actually cry out or talk in his sleep. But children— "some" children, they told me with characteristically Eskimo concern for accuracy—do have nightmares. Inuttiaq did when he was a child, and Raigili often did. Toward the end of my stay, the dreams seemed to plague her more rarely but Saarak was beginning to be afflicted. The Utku seem to believe that nightmares are caused by too intense emotion (or perhaps it is by too intense emotional expression), whether the emotion concerned is giddy lightheartedness or anger. Often when Raigili and her playmates were convulsed in giggles over their games, an adult or an older child would caution them: "Careful, you're going to have nightmares!" Once I even heard Raigili cautioned at a time when she was *not* excited. "Don't have nightmares," Allaq said to her in the saccharine, persuasive voice in which she more often spoke to her other daughter, Saarak, "it's so noisy." It was as though *ihuma*, reason, the governing principle of behavior by day, could also be invoked to control nightmares.

I never heard Raigili warned that her hostility would cause her to have nightmares, but Saarak, shrieking with rage, was once so cautioned, in the time when her baby days were beginning to come to an end. Perhaps in the Utku view Raigili's outbursts of distress were already mild enough so that she need not fear nightmares on their account. But I did associate her frightening dreams with her hostility: with those very struggles to contain the anger that had almost no legitimate outlet.

Though often it was impossible to guess what visions caused Raigili to shriek out in her sleep, there was one night when her woe was quite explicitly expressed. Bedtime had not been peaceful that night. Allaq had, as usual, undressed Saarak with coaxing endearments *(aqaq)*, whereas Raigili, her arms withdrawn in fatigue, had sat silent, motionless and ignored, in her place on the ikliq. This was the first winter in which Raigili had been expected to undress herself, and the expectation was too much for her when she was tired. For a while her unvoiced request for help received no response; but eventually, with protest in the brusqueness of her touch and in her characteristic mooing murmur of disapproval, Allaq did pull off Raigili's tight boots and fur trousers, fold her clothes into a pillow, and settle her under the quilts beside Saarak. "Your little sister can take off her boots better than you can," Allaq mooed at Raigili. Almost immediately Saarak broke into a wail, and Allaq chided Raigili: "Raigili annoys *(urulu)* her little sister." Raigili, her cheeks wet with silent tears, fell asleep. Suddenly she reared up, as she always did in her nightmares, her body tensed into an arc and her head weaving, emptily searching from side to side as she wailed over and over: "Mother, mother! Bad bad Saarak! I'm bad, bad! Saarak is bad! I'm bad!" She was, as always, frozen in her vision; it was impossible to wake her. It always seemed to me incongruous, and not a little cruel, that her parents habitually responded to her misery by shouting at her to go to sleep—a command that Inuttiaq reinforced, especially if Raigili's cries had waked him, by pounding her on the back with his fist or roughly shoving her, not in anger, perhaps, but with force. The treatment never waked her. Allaq and other observers rarely struck the unconscious child as Inuttiaq did, but laughed as they urged her to "lie down and go to sleep!" Eventually, without waking, Raigili, her cries fading into whimpers, subsided onto her pillow and slept quietly.

Sometimes traces of these dreams remained to mar the day. One afternoon, Raigili, at home in the iglu, was overcome with silent tears. Her tears were ignored, as they often were; but that evening, when Raigili was again playing happily, Allaq asked her: "Why was Raigili crying this afternoon?" The shy smile that I found so bewitching came into Raigili's face as she looked up at her mother and in her soft voice explained: "I dreamt last night that my father scolded me, saying, 'Stop wanting to eat!' and when I remembered it I cried." It was a cruel dream, as eating is one of the greatest delights of Utku life. Moreover, the dream father may have been understood to tell his daughter to restrain her demand not only for food but also for affection, since affection often takes the tangible form of food. The dream accorded well with the realities of Raigili's world. Though I never saw Raigili or any other child threatened with loss of food as a punishment, it was true that since Raigili had out-grown the "darling (niviuq)" age, she *was* learning restraint with regard to affection and patience with regard to food.

VIII: Saarak's Changing World: Recalcitrance in Small Children

During the time I was at Back River, Saarak was largely immune to the griefs that her older sister suffered, but toward the end of my stay her world was beginning to change. It was possibly Allaq's pregnancy as much as the coincident growth of *ihuma* in Saarak that brought about the change.

For a long time I did not suspect that Allaq was pregnant. Her voluminous parka camouflaged her condition the more effec-tively because Saarak was so often sheltered inside the garment with her mother, playing on Allaq's warm dark lap or watching the world from Allaq's back, cheek to cheek with her mother. Allaq was not the only woman to conceal her pregnancy. Her sister Amaruq, who lived next door to us and visited us daily, had given birth to her child before the neighbors, including Allaq, knew she was pregnant. But Amaruq's behavior was ex-treme. And in any case Saarak must have sensed, though ob-tuser adults did not, that her mother had changed. Youngest children cry a lot and eat a lot when their mothers are pregnant, Allaq told me. She guessed that one reason for the child's hunger might be the loss of its mother's milk as it dries up during the course of pregnancy. By the time Allaq was four months preg-nant I noted (though I did not know the reason at the time) that Saarak was being nursed much less frequently than her cousin Rosi, who was Saarak's own age, but whose mother was a widow. More and more frequently, when Saarak sobbed in rage or misery, Allaq soothingly offered not her breast but substitute delicacies: a spoonful of jam or dried milk, a fish eye, or a bit of bannock hidden away especially for such emergencies.

In another way, too, Saarak's growing up was proceeding faster than Rosi's. Both Saarak and Rosi had had winter suits of fawnskin made for them in the autumn of their third year, charming one-piece garments so constructed that the fawn's head formed the hood of the suit. The fawn's ears tucked into the hood and the perky triangular tail of the suit, left open for practical purposes, gave the children the air of small brown rabbits as they bounced about the ikliq. But Rosi did not often wear her suit that first winter; she preferred the familiar warmth and closeness of her mother's back. Saarak liked to be carried too; but whether because she was uncomfortably heavy for Allaq to carry, weighed down also by the baby in her womb, or because Allaq wanted gradually to accustom Saarak to her approaching displacement, more and more frequently during the winter, she encouraged Saarak to dress. Often now in the morning, Allaq, her voice saccharine with blandishment, would try to induce Saarak to put on her fawnskin suit and "run-run" around the iglu or go visit her relatives.

Saarak did not always take kindly to this innovation. There were days on which she demanded to be dressed in her suit, but there were other days on which she protested vehemently when the suit was brought out. "It feels cold!" she would screech, "it feels cold!" and with reason, since, in the midwinter chill of the iglu, donning one's frosted clothes gave one the gasping, cringing sensation of an icy plunge; it required an effort of will. So I always silently felt Saarak's protests as my own. On only two or three occasions did I ever see Allaq try to impose her will physically on Saarak, and in each of these instances Saarak ultimately won; her mother laughed, snuffed her, and said tenderly, "How lovable (naklik) she is." Nevertheless, Allaq did employ all sorts of techniques short of physical coercion to manipulate Saarak's will. Inducements of all sorts, false and true, were urged in that honeyed tone, which was characteristic not only of Allaq but also of all adults and older children when addressing Saarak and her peers: "You'll be so sweet and lovable and cute (niviuq); you'll go to visit your uncle; you'll run and play; you'll have bannock to eat . . ." Mother and aunts coaxed together. Sometimes Allaq would instruct one of her sisters to carry Saarak and her clothing off to her grandfather's iglu in the hope that getting dressed might prove a more attractive prospect over there. One day Allaq, her sister Amaruq, and a neighbor woman spent the better part of the short morning trying to persuade Saarak to dress, so that she could be left in her aunt's care while her mother attended to the daily chore of removing the fish from the nets. The two women drained their repertoire of inducements: a bottle of deodorant Saarak could play with when she was dressed; another toy; a playmate, a little girl that Amaruq was also tending, to "run-run" with in the iglu; goodies to eat; but the only sign of impatience Allaq vouchsafed was a meditative remark addressed to the teakettle: "Bad Saarak —sometimes a sweetheart (niviuq), sometimes a nuisance (hujuujaq)."

On other occasions threats, all false, were used to bring Saarak's will into line with her mother's, and then Allaq invariably played the role of protector. Sometimes she invented animal bogies: wolverines, mad dogs, or lemmings, from whom to "protect" Saarak. More often she invoked Saarak's fear of strangers. One little drama in particular was often enacted. "Listen!" Allaq would murmur in a conspiratorial tone, buzzing in imitation of an airplane motor: "Wissy-wissy-wi [that was what Saarak called kapluna fishermen] are coming. 'Hello, hello,' they're going to say [demonstrating the way they would shake hands]. 'Is that Saarak crying?' they're going to ask. 'Give her to us, we want to adopt her,' they'll say. So, hush, then they won't hear you; come, put on your suit, then they won't see you." This often had an effect. Saarak would murmur a questioning "hmmm?" in her baby voice and stand listening for approaching sounds, then docilely, though without sign of anxiety, permit Allaq to pull the cold suit over her naked body.

The kapluna fishermen who visited the Inlet during the summer were not the only bogy foster parents. Until Saarak stopped being afraid of me, I was a convenient scapegoat. "Shhh," Allaq would whisper protectively, "your elder sister over there will hear you and adopt you." Or perhaps one of the other women might hold out her hands in mock enticement to the recalcitrant child, or raise the edge of her parka as if to take Saarak inside, fully aware that the gesture would frighten her: "Come, let me carry you!" she would say, coaxingly; "do you want to come home with me? Come, climb into my parka." Saarak would shrink, whimpering, against her mother while the adults laughed, mildly. The effects of this "joke" seem to persist for years in the fear of being adopted by someone outside the family. I saw it in both of Saarak's older sisters: in the stricken look in Raigili's face when a visiting police officer swung her in a friendly way in his arms; and in Kamik, when Nakliguhuktuq and Ikayuqtuq, with whom she was temporarily staying on her way home from school, teased her by offering to adopt her permanently. But the adults had little sympathy with the social fears they inculcated or fostered in the children; they laughed, both at the fear and at its expression: "She really believed she would be adopted," they would tease; "she almost cried."

Fears of adoption were invoked in a variety of situations in which Saarak was of contrary mind and not only when Allaq wanted to get her dressed. But there was one other social fear that was exploited, indeed, in Saarak's case, learned, primarily in the dressing situation. That was physical modesty. Though adults were extraordinarily modest, even when dressing and undressing in the close confines of the iglu, small children, carried naked on their mothers' backs, were exempt from these prescriptions. Saarak, when I first knew her, and later her tiny sister, Qayaq, were encouraged to display themselves; and a great deal of affectionate admiration was focused on their bodies. When Qayaq was only a few months old her mother, playing with her, pulled her upright in her lap and held her there, facing outward, each tiny fist clinging tightly to one of her mother's fingers; and as the baby's wobbly body arched out toward the audience they greeted her movement with admiring "vaaa!"s. "She is increasingly female," they explained to me, and when a baby boy makes the same gesture they say, "He is increasingly male."[4] The baby smiled with responsive delight. Saarak had outgrown this baby gesture, but she was still urged

4. I am uncertain whether to translate the words, *aqnaq* and *angut*, as "female" and "male," respectively, or as "woman" and "man." The words have both meanings.

by her affectionate relatives to offer her navel or her breast, her armpit, nose, or cheek for a kiss. "Let me kiss you, let me kiss you, here, here," they would coo, and she would smilingly comply, rewarded by warm laughter. Her cheeks and her nose were all jokingly "named" with her several names, and when someone inquired of her, "Where's Qijuaaqjuk?" "Where's Aqnariaq?" "Where's Saarak?" she would present the appropriate segment of her face to be kissed, amid general applause at the accuracy of her response. One of her favorite games consisted of poking and being poked in various delicate and always naked regions, especially in the navel, on which a good deal of Eskimo sexual interest focuses.[5] "Laah! Laah!" somebody would tease, advancing on the happily frightened child with outstretched finger, while she danced on the ikliq, screaming with laughter, uncertain whether to expose her belly or to hide from the searching finger. Sometimes she descended on her tormentor in turn, seeking a spot to "laah," while her victim pretended to squirm away, laughing.

But the day came when these games were turned against Saarak and became, indirectly, a means not of gaining attention and love but of learning modesty. The issue was never phrased as one of decency. Training in modesty seemed largely a byproduct of attempts to secure obedience, for family convenience, in dressing and undressing. But the fear of being seen, exposed, was nonetheless successfully inculcated. Previously, Allaq had laughed encouragingly when Saarak's aunts and uncles, sisters and cousins had coaxed the child for kisses and for pokes; now, when the iglu was cold and she wanted Saarak to dress, Allaq began to warn her in the familiar protective whisper: "Watch out, your uncle's going to poke you if you don't cover up and get dressed! He's going to poke you here and here and here." Whereupon her uncle obligingly appeared with outstretched finger to support Allaq's tale, and Saarak shrieked at him in fear and rage, hastening to dress. Similarly, if the rest of the family were ready to go to sleep and Saarak resisted being undressed, Allaq or Inuttiaq would whisper: "Your uncle's going to kiss you!" Or if there were a visitor in camp, they might capitalize

5. Personal communication from David Damas. He was speaking of the Perry River and Bathurst Inlet areas to the west of Chantrey Inlet.

on Saarak's fear of strangers, warning: "Nimiqtaqtuq is going to see you!" And Saarak would hurry to undress and cover herself with the bedclothes.

There was nothing sudden or drastic about the changes in Saarak's life before her sister's birth; the quality of her life seemed much the same as it had always been. She still lived in a private world insulated from annoyance: soothed and gratified more often than not; cuddled and cooed at (aqaq) by all her relatives; bounced to sleep on her mother's back when restless and tired; nursed often when she asked and always when she insisted. In January, four months before Qayaq was born, Saarak caught a feverish cold that was going the rounds of the camp, and it was then, when I saw her ill, that I realized how far she had grown during the time I had known her. While she was sick, and even for a time after she was better, she was again in every respect the infant she had been when I came. For three weeks Allaq never left her sick daughter. The fawnskin suit lay untouched in the pile of household goods that lined Allaq's edge of the iglu. Saarak, by turns passively content and crankily demanding, lay under the quilts beside her mother's seat, leaned against her mother's naked back, or sat cradled on her lap in the shelter of the voluminous parka while Allaq talked to her tenderly (aqaq), made sure that she was warm, made her bannock whenever she cried for it, and carried her to her grandfather's iglu when she cried to visit there.

At the time, I was impressed by Allaq's solicitude and by her willingness to let Saarak return to babyhood at will, but it did not occur to me to question her reasons. Only now in retrospect I wonder whether perhaps she was afraid that Saarak would die. Though, on the whole, Saarak did not seem very ill to me, she was nevertheless not very hungry and often refused the diced bits of fish that Allaq offered her. "Eat some fish? Don't you want to eat? Mmm?" Later I learned that loss of appetite is considered an ominous sign; when a sick person is no longer interested in eating, he is close to death.

I do not know whether Allaq was in fact so concerned about Saarak; she may simply have felt sympathetic with her daughter's discomfort. Inuttiaq's absence on a trading trip—the January trip described earlier—and Allaq's resulting lethargy may also have played a part in prolonging the period of Saarak's babyish behavior beyond the week or two when she was really sick. Inuttiaq left while Saarak was still convalescing, and Allaq, in her chill, may have felt no desire to do other than sit and hold Saarak warmly against her. In any case, Saarak eventually recovered and Inuttiaq returned; and the evening that he returned, when Saarak was ebullient with the joy of seeing him, she was coaxed into putting on the fawnskin suit once more.

IX. Saarak's Crisis: Loss of Mother's Closeness

Qayaq was born on the night of April 28. Looking back afterwards, I was amazed that she had not been born a week earlier. We had moved on April 21 from the winter camp at Amujat to our spring camp with Pala and Nilak at Itimnaaqjuk, near the rapids. It was about a six-hour sled trip, and the going was arduous. The outsize load created by the addition of my goods to Inuttiaq's was always difficult, but this time the spring weather made the situation worse than usual. The sun, already above the horizon for much of the night, had a balmy feel, and the breeze, too, was exhilaratingly gentle after the constricting chill of the winter wind. Unfortunately, the sled runners also felt the effects of the new warmth. The thin layer of ice that glazed their turfing quickly melted, so that instead of slipping smoothly over the surface we ground resistingly forward, sullying the snow with a trail of two parallel brown lines. Moreover, the snow itself was no longer frozen solidly through, as it was in winter, when its surface was as trustworthy as that of the earth itself. On the contrary. Every time the sled encountered a rise, a dip, a bump, a drift, the runner tips bored deep into the snow and had to be hacked and heaved and tugged out again to the accompaniment of bellows and blows aimed at the struggling team.

I was, to my shame, no help on these occasions. In fact, I was a decided hindrance because, owing to the ignorant instructions I had given Allaq when she sewed my caribou traveling clothes, the fur socks were so bulky around the knee that I was unable to move freely. As a result, if I jumped off with the other adults to help strain and push at the sled, I was unable to scramble up again when the sled started up with a lurch and careened away at six or seven miles an hour. There was nothing for it but to stay perched ignominiously in my place atop the high load, ineffectually trying to alleviate the feeling that I was a burden by taking charge of one of the squirming puppies that almost always shared our trips, a job usually bestowed on children of Raigili's age, who were too young to walk. Given my propensity for sliding off in my slippery caribou trousers when the sled leaned too far to one side, it was a wonder that I avoided the ultimate disgrace of being tied onto the load as Raigili and Saarak were, wrapped snugly in quilts.

In any case Allaq, advanced in pregnancy as she was, took a full share of the rigors of the trip. For a good part of the way she jogged beside the sled, as adults do to lighten the load, and whenever the sled stuck fast in the snow she jumped down with Inuttiaq and exerted all her force to get it moving again. And when suddenly the efforts took effect and the sled lurched into motion again, she would run beside it for a moment or two while it gained momentum, then throw herself belly first onto the load, pulling herself up, bit by bit, with the help of the lashings, as the sled bumped forward.

The exertions of the move did not end with the sled trip, either. There was still an iglu to be built and moved into, and Allaq's task, after we had drunk a welcoming cup of tea in Pala's iglu, was to bank the walls with loose snow as Inuttiaq and Mannik cut the blocks and raised them. To be sure, she was helped by her younger sister Amaaqtuq, by Nilak's wife, Niqi, and by me. But Amaaqtuq, who was still a girl, and Niqi, who was childish, rarely concentrated long on any piece of work; and I, though eager to atone for having sat like a clod on the load most of the way from Amujat, was nevertheless not very adept at tossing the heavy shovelfuls of snow up over the highest parts of the iglu in such a way that they stayed where they were thrown instead of cascading down again to the ground. So, as before, the heaviest work fell to Allaq. And on her devolved, as always, the responsibility for building the sleeping platform, once the iglu was finished: she arranged the snow blocks that Mannik cut for edging and shoved in to her through the entrance hole; she filled in the inner area of the platform with loose snow obtained from other blocks, which she heaved into the area and hacked into powder with the two-foot snow knife; and when the platform was filled to a depth of about two feet, level with the top of the edging blocks, she climbed up onto it and trampled it down hard and even with her feet before arranging on it the twig matting, the caribou mattresses, and the various boxes and bags of household goods that unseen hands, Inuttiaq's and others', thrust through the entrance hole into a helter-skelter heap on the floor.

None of this work was out of the ordinary for Allaq, and she had not behaved as if it cost her undue effort. Nevertheless, the activity was so foreign to my middle-class American prejudices concerning the way a pregnant woman should behave that, looking back on it all later, I was, as I have said, surprised that Qayaq had not made her appearance that very night.

The baby was born in the middle of the night, and Inuttiaq was the only person who shared the experience with Allaq. None of the other women in camp: the adolescent Amaaqtuq, the childish Niqi, and the inept kapluna, was roused. It had been an exceptionally pleasant evening. The festive mood that we had brought with us when we moved from the deserted camp at Amujat, the elation of unaccustomed company, was still with us. Allaq had spent the evening frying bannock for our household and Pala's while the tape recorder blared Inuttiaq's favorite music: "Il Trovatore." "The music that makes one want to cry," he called it, and he always wanted it played at a volume that jarred my eardrums and severely taxed the capacities of the tape recorder. Allaq had been fully one of the company; she had shared in the feast, had joked with her sisters as usual when they came in to share the bannock, had nursed Saarak tenderly to sleep at her breast as always, blown out the lamp, and apparently settled down to sleep. That was at 11:30. At 1:30 I woke to hear the wavering cry of a newborn baby. A short length of wick had been relit; the fresh snow wall glimmered in the light. Allaq, dressed in her parka, knelt in her place on the ikliq, bending forward with her elbows resting heavily on a pillow built of a rolled-up sleeping bag with Inuttiaq's parka folded on top of it. Inuttiaq, dressed except for his boots, was standing barefoot on the ikliq, near Allaq. He was leaning forward with one hand on Allaq's pillow, saying something in an unusually rapid, vigorous voice. "It doesn't come out," he explained, seeing me watching him; "the bad placenta doesn't come out." And he continued rapidly and emphatically to "call it out": "Hurry up! Bad placenta! Hurry up!" There was more to the exhortation, which I did not understand. Allaq knelt against her pillow with an air of fatigue and silent concentration. After a while Inuttiaq stopped talking, sat down beside Allaq and lit his pipe; but now and again he interrupted his puffing to ask Allaq in a low voice a question to which she murmured a response. In a little while he pulled on his boots, stood up on the snow floor by his wife's head, and prayed to God: ". . . because you are God . . . because you are able to do all things . . ."; I understood only this much of the brief prayer. Very shortly after that the placenta came. Inuttiaq sharpened Allaq's ulu, the same knife with which she performed all household chores, and she cut the cord, tying the end with a bit of sinew.

The baby all this time had been lying on the caribou mattress hide between Allaq's knees, under the dark warmth of her parka. Waiting for the placenta, Inuttiaq had once lifted the edge of the parka and peered in at his baby daughter. "Naaaaklingnaqtuq (lovable)," he had murmured, drawing out the vowel tenderly. Now Allaq took the baby up, wiped her fragile body softly with a bit of caribou fur, and handed her to Inuttiaq, who drew his arms in out of the sleeves of his parka to hold the baby, with a gentleness extraordinary in so vigorous a man, against his warm, naked belly. Allaq slowly, moving with effort, cut out the square of mattress hide on which the placenta lay, folded it over the placenta without touching the bloody mass, and tied it up with string. Then Inuttiaq, with another murmur of affection, gave the baby back to the warmth of Allaq's belly, took up the bundle of hide and his snow knife, and went out.

This was not the first daughter Inuttiaq had helped to deliver. Though often older or experienced women are called upon to assist, sometimes there are none in the vicinity. Saarak, like Qayaq, had been born in the spring, the season at which people are most dispersed. That spring Inuttiaq's family had been camped completely alone, so Inuttiaq and Kamik, who must have been about ten at the time, had helped with her delivery, Inuttiaq warming Saarak against his belly, as he now had

Qayaq, while the cord was cut. Perhaps he had delivered other daughters, too; certainly he was practiced and efficient and seemed not at all ill at ease in the situation. And his absorption—the intensity of the support he gave Allaq when the placenta was delayed, the tenderness in his voice when he lifted the edge of the parka to look at his child and in his arms when he held her—was wholly touching. I watched him as he worked, wondering what his reaction was to the appearance of a seventh daughter in place of the son I knew he would have valued. The one remark he made, next day, concerning the baby's sex was impossible to read, said, as it was, in his ordinary, matter-of-fact voice: "Lots of daughters." But there was no doubt of his feeling at the moment of her birth; there was no hint of indifference or dismay, nothing but protective tenderness. And when he returned from burying the placenta, his mood was one of festivity.

It was three o'clock by then. Allaq rested, sagging, against her high pillow, the baby still held in her arms against her body. I lay in my sleeping bag, suppressing yawns. I was chagrined that I had slept through the actual birth; doubly so because it was the third and last that could possibly occur among the Utku while I was there, and I had missed the others, also: the one through ignorance that Amaruq was pregnant (so voluminous was her parka), the other through a probably unnecessary reluctance to intrude. So this time, sleepy though I was, I was determined to miss nothing else that might occur. There was no question of sleep. Inuttiaq was ebullient: unusually energetic, talkative, busy. He heated water to wash his hands and face, and with what remained of the water, he made tea for the three of us, then bannock. We feasted there for nearly three hours in the middle of the night. Allaq, too, ate with appetite. And while we ate, the baby, in a manner as informal as that of her birth, received her first name: "Qayaq," in memory of Allaq's loved *(naklik)* brother, who had drowned a few years earlier.

The children were introduced to their baby sister also in the course of our festive meal, the one exuberantly, the other reluctantly. Raigili was wakened while our tea was brewing. Shaken into semiconsciousness by Inuttiaq in the efflorescence of his excitement, she raised a groggy head from her pillow. "Child! Look at your baby sister!" She gazed unseeingly for a moment in the direction her father indicated and grunted something unintelligible. "Do you love *(naklik)* her?" her father persisted. "Yes." Inuttiaq tried to teach her the kinship term by which she should address the baby, but her head had already sunk back to the pillow, and she was fast asleep again.

Saarak was another matter. She was allowed to sleep soundly, and when she did stir after a while, Inuttiaq rhythmically rubbed her back in an attempt to lull her back to sleep. His efforts were futile, and when he saw that she was really awake, he pointed out the baby to her. I held my breath. But there was no outburst, not for the first minute. Saarak chirped and cooed and poked at the baby with friendly interest. It was only when she saw her mother put the baby to her breast that the storm broke: a storm of wails and slaps. Allaq, holding the baby protectively, said in a tender voice, "Don't hurt her." Whereupon Saarak demanded her endangered right: to be nursed.

Tactful as I knew Utku to be, I had never imagined that the crisis, when it came, could be handled as gently as it was. Allaq assumed a tone that I was to hear often in the next few days, a false but sympathetic tone of disgust. "It tastes terrible," she said. And the tone surrounded the words with affectionate protectiveness. But when Saarak continued to scream and slap at her mother and the baby, Allaq gave in, took her distressed daughter into the accustomed shelter of her parka, and nursed her, albeit briefly, at one breast while she nursed the baby at the other. I neglected to notice whether Saarak came away from the breast voluntarily or by persuasion; in any case, a little later she began to wail again. This time Inuttiaq took a hand. "You're very much loved *(naklik),*" he assured his daughter, soothingly; but Saarak was too distressed to heed him. "Go to sleep!" Inuttiaq then said, loudly and more gruffly. "You're very sleepy!" And eventually she did cry herself to sleep. Inuttiaq looked at the little face on the pillow beside him, the cheeks still damply streaked and the small dark braids awry. "Poor little thing *(naklik),*" he said, "she realizes and she is troubled *(ujjiq).*"

When we finished our midnight feast, a little after 5:30, Inuttiaq went to visit (and doubtless to wake) Pala's iglu, presumably to announce the baby's birth, while Allaq and I, like Saarak, went back to sleep. But when Inuttiaq returned, three hours later, Allaq roused herself again, put on her parka, and sat for the rest of the day, dozing once or twice, but mostly supervising with her usual interest the activities of the household. Her sister Amaaqtuq came early in the morning with the rest of her family to see the baby and stayed most of the day to help, making tea and bannock again, fetching water, and attending to Saarak's and Raigili's needs, all under her elder sister's direction. Allaq, as usual, chatted with Raigili and played with Saarak, speaking to the latter always in her most tender *(aqaq)* voice.

Saarak cried four times to be nursed that day, and each time, when bannock and other distractions were rejected (once Allaq even fed Saarak water, mouth-to-mouth, as she fed the baby), Allaq complied with her wish, pulling her breast out of the neck of her parka for Saarak to reach. But each time, after Saarak had sucked briefly, her mother or aunt would try again to distract her attention, and after Saarak had had her way for a minute, it was not hard to do.

That evening, while Saarak was playing happily, her parents expounded the new doctrine to her. In the same false but sympathetic tone of disgust that Allaq had earlier used, Inuttiaq said, "Your little sister has nursed and gotten the breast and the inside of the parka all shitty and stinky; it smells [or tastes, the word has both meanings] horrible." Allaq murmured sympathetic agreement.

Saarak had no visible reaction at the time, but it was not more than four days after the baby's birth that she stopped asking to be nursed. Or so her mother said. It was true that during the day the pathetic wail "apopo-o-o-o" was no longer heard; but at night sometimes Saarak did wake and cry, restlessly, as if expecting to be offered a suck, as formerly she had been. The suck was no longer forthcoming; Allaq simply waited for her to go back to sleep, and once in a while Inuttiaq would add a sleepily gruff injunction to go to sleep. After the first of these incidents Allaq, to my surprise, observed: "Saarak didn't really want to nurse last night; she didn't cry much at all." And three weeks later, after a particularly prolonged bout of midnight tears, when I asked Allaq why Saarak had cried, she said: "No reason; she just cried spontaneously." I wondered. Could pity, or perhaps a characteristically Utku tendency to minimize crises, have urged Allaq not to notice Saarak's wish?

It was true, however, that Saarak did seem less intent on obtaining nourishment than on maintaining her closeness with her mother. It was not as difficult to divert her from the breast as it was to convince her that the dark sanctuary of her mother's parka was no longer desirable. The wish to be taken inside was expressed dramatically enough to leave no doubt of its presence fully a month after the baby's birth. In the first days, the storms, like those of weaning, had been daily affairs, and some had been violent—one especially when Saarak, weeping, had tried her utmost to invade the parka, tugging at the hem in an effort to raise it and lifting her leg up in an attempt to insert it in the neck of the garment. In the past she had entered both ways, from the top and from the bottom. This time, Allaq simply sat still, resisting her daughter's assaults with imperturbable immobility and silence, seeming neither to feel nor to hear her. After a bit, however, she softened and, speaking gently to the weeping child, she invited her to come and sit in her lap outside the parka, circled by her arms, a blanket, and a quilt—a position as closely as possible approximating the one Saarak had lost. But Saarak would accept no compromise, and eventually her mother gave in and took her in where the baby also lay. Immediately, Saarak was transformed; happiness itself, she cooed and chirped at the baby who shared the space with her. In a few minutes, Allaq suggested to Raigili, who was lying in bed, that she invite Saarak to join her under the quilt. Raigili did, and Saarak, to all appearance still perfectly happy, came to play with her.

Allaq dealt with all these early storms as she dealt with Saarak's desire to nurse, by turns resisting and soothing, sometimes laughing at the buffets, and briefly giving in before finding some way of distracting Saarak's attention. And as in the case of the weaning crisis, the daily upheavals had come to an end before the week was out. But the most difficult time was yet to come.

Toward the end of May, just a month after Qayaq's birth, Saarak came down with a bad cold. The men had made one last trip to Gjoa Haven before the summer thaws should cut us off; and always when they returned from Gjoa Haven they brought respiratory infections. "The disease travels on the sleds," people said. We were in tents by this time; we had moved on May 1 when our iglu melted away in a warm rain. I was in my own tent, set beside Inuttiaq's, since Inuttiaq's was too small for all of us, and I spent my newly solitary days mostly at home, surrounded by inch-long slips of vocabulary, which paraded precariously over the hummocks of my sleeping bag. I was trying to work more systematically than I had been able to before on the language; but on this particular day I found it exceptionally hard to concentrate, because from next door, off and on all day, came the sound of Saarak, sobbing. She cried steadily for at least an hour in the morning, and if Allaq offered consolation or distraction it was inaudible; I heard no sound but Saarak in the other tent, except that once in a while Allaq commented with an annoyed moo on the persistence of the tears. Once Inuttiaq, listening too, remarked affectionately, "She's lovable (*naklik*)"; but he was not at home to help; he was visiting me in my tent. And at length Allaq restored peace by taking the child to visit at her grandfather's.

In the afternoon, when I heard her sobbing again, I went to investigate. She was crying insistently and seemed to have some object in mind, which Allaq was doing her patient but frustrated best to determine and gratify. She offered her chewing gum, ordinarily Saarak's favorite sweet; Saarak so delighted in chewing the sugar off the outside of a stick, then discarding it in favor of a fresh one that Allaq used to keep the true amount of the supply a secret from her, so that it would not all disappear in one day. But this time gum availed nothing. Allaq asked if she wanted her clothes put on. No. She screeched. Inuttiaq offered to let her smoke the pipe he had just finished making for Raigili, and he filled and lit it for her. She hit it away. Inuttiaq went to Pala's to visit, and Saarak screamed at Allaq to stand up. She did. Then Saarak screamed at her to take her boots off. She sat down again and obeyed. *Then* it appeared that what she really wanted was to get inside Allaq's parka with the baby. As before, she tried forcibly to lift up the edge and crawl in; and as before, Allaq sat silently, impassively, preventing her entry simply by holding her parka down with her arm. Though she offered to call Amaaqtuq to come and carry Saarak inside her parka, Saarak would have none of it. Finally, Allaq did take her inside on her lap where the baby also was, and immediately peace descended. The happiest of voices could be heard from under the parka, chirping at the baby. But when, after a minute or two, Allaq in a tender voice persuaded Saarak to crawl under the quilts again, serenity was lost at once. Out and in and out again—the drama was re-enacted, but the second time Allaq admitted Saarak to the sanctum there was more annoyance than tenderness in her voice when she said "all right!" and the brusque gesture with which she lifted the edge of her parka was eloquent.

The ordeal continued for the rest of that day and the next. When Saarak was urged for the second time to lie under the quilts instead of under the parka, she seemed in a way to accept her eviction but not yet the loss of physical closeness with her mother. Her demand changed. "Get into bed!" she screamed at Allaq, over and over again, her words lost in the frenzy of sobbing: "Get into bed!" Allaq, as always, did her best to soothe, to offer other solace or diversion, to compromise. This time she did send for Amaaqtuq to come and carry Saarak on her back; but Amaaqtuq, too, had a cold and refused, saying that she was tired and Saarak was heavy. Allaq warned Saarak tenderly that she would injure herself by crying so hard. She sang hymns with determination—to drown the wails, I thought, as Raigili's much less violent sobs were sometimes drowned. And once, just once, on the second day she startled me by saying pleasantly but definitely: "I'm not going to lie down." The rarity of the direct refusal, mild though it sounded, gave it for me the impact of much harsher words. Allaq must have despaired of peace, I thought. I offered a precious square of chocolate, which would ordinarily have had a magical effect, but the distracted child hurled it away. I made her a paper bird with wings that flapped, and Allaq sailed it in front of Saarak, crying, "Kuttiiq, kuttiiiq," as the gulls did when they stole from our fishnets in the summer. Saarak shrieked louder. Allaq tried lying down beside Saarak with her clothes on, but Saarak shrieked louder still. Once Allaq actually undressed and lay down beside Saarak as she demanded, and there was peace for a moment. But shortly she had to get up again in order to bounce the baby to sleep in the back of her parka, and the sobs broke out anew. Once or twice in the course of the two days, Saarak cried herself to sleep and later woke, crying. Once, toward the end of the first day, she seemed to cry herself completely dry. She lay in bed under the quilts, perfectly quiet and passive.

In Pala's tent, and in Nilak's, they heard Saarak's distress. Amaaqtuq remarked on it the second day with the discretion characteristic of Utku: "She wants her mother to get into bed." That was all. The previous day, though she had been too tired to carry Saarak, she had gone in, briefly, to invite the child to come and visit in her grandfather's tent; but when Saarak rejected the offer she had gone home again. This second day neither she nor anyone else went to proffer assistance, whether from a fear of intruding, or from a feeling that the situation was beyond help, or from some other motive that I, with my outsider's understanding, could not guess, I do not know. Surely it was not indifference in the case of Pala's household; they were ordinarily so solicitous.

I found my own inability to help painfully frustrating; and painful also was my sympathy with Saarak as an older child and my knowledge of her loss. I contrasted her situation during this present illness with that which had obtained during her last illness, in January, when Allaq had cuddled her for hours on end at the slightest whimper. But inevitably the tears stopped; and when they did, the crisis was permanently over. A month later when Amaaqtuq, delighting, I think, in hearing her niece's newly learned word of protest, turned Saarak toward her mother and teased: "Have a suck," Saarak rejected the suggestion with shrill vehemence: "Nooo!" And when three months after that Allaq herself one day teased her: "Come, let me hold you on my lap inside my parka. Have a suck," Saarak paid no attention.

X. No Longer a Baby: Transition to Older Childhood

Saarak's desire for affection expressed in physical closeness did not simply vanish, however, and her family knew that it would not. The Utku have a custom that helps to ease the loss of the mother's lap. On the birth of the next child a member of the household other than the mother "adopts" the elder child, which means primarily that he or she sleeps in warm contact with the child, in the same way that the child has been used to sleeping with its mother. Sometimes such adoption can create a special bond that lasts into adulthood, and sometimes the cuddling itself lasts well into childhood. In the case of one of Allaq's sisters, who was adopted in this way by a blind uncle who lived with her family, it lasted until the girl was married. And Allaq's youngest sister, Akla, who was about ten, still slept under her father's quilts and was so closely bound to him (as possibly he was to her, as well) that she never slept with the other children in the play tents that they set up. Pala, looking at his sleeping child, once remarked in a tender voice: "Poor dear (naklik); she's very attached (unga) to me." On another occasion he told me that the affection of all of his children for him had intensified since his wife died, and it is possible that Akla's love was especially strong, since she was only a baby at the time of her mother's death.

It was Inuttiaq who took the place of Allaq for Saarak, and for a period her dependence on him was very strong. The night after the baby's birth, when we were all in bed and Saarak, lying, as always, between her parents, was absorbed in her mother and the baby, Inuttiaq spoke to her affectionately: "Turn over toward me." And a night or two later, when Saarak woke in the morning, she found herself lying on the far side of her father, between him and Raigili, instead of between him and Allaq. She resisted the change at first, scrambling over her father, back to her usual place as soon as she woke. Her parents did not insist; for as long as I was with them, Saarak more often slept between her parents than between her father and sister. But by the sixth or seventh week after Qayaq's birth, Saarak's attachment to Inuttiaq had become so strong that she refused to go to bed unless he also was in bed. And for three or four months she maintained her stand. Sitting there on the ikliq, fully clad, her eyes glazed and apparently unseeing, she clung to the remnants of consciousness with a touching stubbornness. Allaq would inquire in her tenderest, most persuasive tone: "Want to go to bed? Shall I put you to bed? Mmm?" No. The sagging little figure would not be seduced; she resisted until she toppled into her mother's arms, sound asleep. And even then, if she woke while Allaq was, as gently as possible, removing her clothes, she screamed to be dressed again and would listen to no contrary arguments. Once when Inuttiaq was at Pala's, Allaq, hearing Amaaqtuq come in to visit, tried to pretend that it was Inuttiaq coming home, but Saarak, her eyes only half open, was firm: "He's not here." Whether Inuttiaq was at home or out visiting, however, it was all the same to Saarak; she would not lie down until he did.

Saarak's attempted regulation of his bedtime was, I think, a little too much for Inuttiaq. When Allaq went, as she several times did, to tell him as he sat playing cards with Mannik: "Saarak won't go to bed' until you do," he did not always heed the summons. Even when he was at home, lying idly on the ikliq and obviously about to fall asleep himself, he more than once ignored his daughter's tears and the hints of his wife. But once he was in bed, no child could have had a more tender father.

Inuttiaq was by no means the whole of Saarak's world at this time, however. The horizon of her life was expanding rapidly beyond the confines of her own dwelling. It was spring when Qayaq was born, and for Utku children, spring and summer are seasons of growth.

The Utku world expands and contracts with the seasons, though not in the same way for everybody. Autumn is the most constricted and unpleasant season for everyone: windy, wet, gray, increasingly dark. The temperature hovers around the freezing point, never holding clearly enough to one side or the other to permit people to adjust their clothing, their housing, or their activities to the situation. But the wind is the worst. It ruffles the water so that the fish do not bite, and on some days there is nothing to eat except rotting whitefish from the dog-food caches—not bad for a change but still a less desirable food than the boiled heads of salmon trout and char that usually provide the evening meal in summer and early winter. Even when there *is* cooking to be done, the wind does its best to hinder, blowing the smoke from the twig fires in every direction so that the women, coughing and twisting to shield their watering eyes from its onslaughts, are hard put to keep the flame burning. The bite of winter in the wind feels doubly cold by contrast with summer warmth; people who have sat outdoors all summer in sociable clusters on the gravel beach now withdraw into their separate tents and barricade the entrances with windbreaks of quilts or last year's ragged tent. There is little activity outside of the tents at this season, except for the warming game of ball that is played by everybody nearly every afternoon on a nearby level space.

Conversation turns then to the comforts and pleasures of winter. When the frosts set in, the primus stoves and lamps that were left in the spring on convenient hilltops up and down the river can be fetched again to light and heat the qaqmaqs, and later the iglus, that will be built. Then, too, some of the caribou that were shot and cached far from camp at the time of the August hunting trips can be fetched for eating. Shortly, the season for trapping foxes will begin, and then will come the trading trips to Gjoa Haven, which mean tea and tobacco and flour for bannock: all commodities that people have been hungering for. For men, winter is in one sense the most expansive season; it is the season of mobility. When wind-packed snow and ice have converted tundra and water alike into a highway for their sleds, they will travel hundreds of miles up and down the river: fetching and carrying, visiting, fishing, hunting, trapping, and trading.

For the women and children, who share few of these sled trips, winter, however pleasant, is very largely an indoor season.[6] And even when they go out, they tend to stay considerably closer to home than in spring and summer. The children play on the slope of the camp among the iglus, or out on the flat expanse of the river, and only the older ones go over the hill, out of sight of home, to check an occasional trap or to follow the prints of a fox. The smallest children are indoors most of the time, and when they do view the white world outside it is almost always from the snug vantage of their mother's back. Women visit from iglu to iglu, or venture out to fetch water or to help in checking the

6. The difference between summer and winter may be more striking nowadays. Formerly, when caribou were plentiful, everyone had winter clothing of fur. Now the women and older children usually wear duffel clothing in winter, which, though warm, does not compare with caribou as a protection against wind and therefore does not encourage prolonged outdoor activity. Formerly, too, it was necessary for women to make lengthy excursions to find birch for fuel, even in midwinter. Nowadays, kerosene is available in winter, brought by the men from Gjoa Haven; unless kerosene is in very short supply, women gather plants for fuel only during the summer.

fishnets or in harnessing the dogs; like the older children, they may have a fox-trap or two within a short walk of the camp, but rarely are they beyond the shelter of an iglu for more than an hour or two at a time during the height of the winter.

It is in the spring and summer that the world of the women and children is widest. When the tents are set up again on emerging gravel patches, it is sheer delight to sit outdoors in the blinding spring sun, absorbing all the myriad life of the vast tundra; to search the wet-black hills for motion that might be caribou; to watch the men stalk the migrating waterfowl that land in the thawing ponds and on the swampy tundra; to stone ptarmigan on the knolls; even to gather plants again to feed the outdoor fires. The children's caribou suits are stuffed into sacks to be put away until next winter; now they wear cloth trousers and rubber boots under their duffel parkas. Secure in their boots, they go for long walks across the uncertainly thawing river snow to explore for ptarmigan or to gather rabbit dung to smoke in their pipes. And as the season progresses and the days become longer and warmer, their freedom is limited only by their fatigue.

It is at this season that babies learn to walk, that children of Saarak's age begin to roam, and that their older brothers and sisters increase their knowledge of adult skills. So many things are easier in the summer. Cloth clothes and rubber boots pull on and off without a struggle; fish, no longer frozen, can be filleted without the help of a stronger arm; lichen or heather can be gathered and tea brewed, if the weather is calm, on makeshift fireplaces of three stones; and if the children wander far away there is no danger of their freezing or getting lost in blowing snow and darkness. But when winter comes, some of this new independence will be lost again, since the frozen fish will still be too hard to cut, the wet hide boots will still be too sticky to pull off, and the dark and cold will still be dangerous.

About the time that we moved into tents, Saarak began to follow Raigili and Akla around the camp instead of staying at home with Allaq and the baby. Now and then Allaq would suggest to her: "Why don't you go visit your grandfather," or "Go tell your mother's brother to give me a cigarette." But often it was on Saarak's own initiative that she went trotting off after the others.

Her life was not made easier by this development. Allaq spent many hours sitting on the sun-warmed gravel by the tent, with Qayaq in her lap, a tiny bulge under the parka. From there she quietly watched the doings of the camp, or now and again, lowering her face into the wide neck of her parka, communed privately with her baby. Protective as always, she kept an eye or an ear attuned to Saarak, and often she would tell Raigili and Akla to watch the child: not to let her climb the boulders at the top of the hill, not to let her walk too close to the dog chain when she was carrying food in her hand, and not to leave her behind when she was trying to follow them. But the older children did not always take kindly to these instructions. Though at times Saarak could be an amusing playmate, often she was a burden. Unable to keep up with the others and used to having her own way, her cries reverberated from one end of the camp to the other whenever she was abandoned. Akla would say to Raigili, "Go get Saarak"; Raigili would reply, "You get her"; and neither would do it. A favorite trick of both was to lure Saarak into a tent, then run away and leave her—a trick that was sometimes ignored by their elders but that on occasion, when Saarak's screams were particularly rending, earned the girls a disapproving moo.

The changes in Saarak's life were watched by her family, a little proudly, a little regretfully. One evening when I went into Inuttiaq's tent, Allaq greeted me: "Tonight Saarak got undressed all by herself and made her own pillow." Her tone was warm, and she nodded (aqaq) at the sleeping child in the character-istic gesture of tenderness. She watched, pretending not to notice, these first efforts of Saarak's to manage her clothes by herself and "vaa"d her successes warmly, but she never inter-fered or proffered help unless frustration reduced her daughter to screeches. When once she saw Saarak, some distance off on the beach, whimpering with the effort of replacing a duffel sock and pulling up her fallen trousers, Allaq said, not loud enough for Saarak to hear: "Poor little thing (naklik)"—and permitted her to struggle until she succeeded.

One day Saarak decided to make tea on the outdoor fireplace.

It was her own idea, and she executed it almost entirely by herself, placing the very empty kettle (it had only about two cups of water in it) over the smouldering fire, feeding it with lichen, and prodding it awkwardly into a blaze with the metal-tipped stick used for that purpose. She was charming in her absorption, squatting on the gravel beach in her new white duffel parka, poking at the fire with her stick, and now and then, with a smile of delight, seeking recognition from the watching adults and older children, who responded with the most affectionate "vaaa"s. Once when she was a little too enthusiastic with her stick, the kettle tipped off the stones on which it was balanced, and Amaaqtuq came and replaced it; but otherwise no one moved. When the tea was hot, Saarak herself labored with the sooty kettle—huge it seemed beside her minute figure—up the incline to the tea-board, which was laid in front of the tents. People hurried to fetch cups, and Saarak, her motions cocky with pleasure, poured the tea as Allaq instructed, so that everybody had a tiny sip. "Go take tea to your grandfather," Allaq told her then, and the kettle bumped over the gravel as Saarak hurried off to the tent where Pala lay. Allaq, watching her retreating figure, which seemed so full of the happiness of accomplishment, remembered another small figure: "Raigili made a *full* kettle of tea year before last," she said. And from Pala's tent came the laughing echo of our own appreciation: "Eee eeeee! Did you make tea?! Eee eeeee!"

But Inuttiaq and Mannik one day took Saarak with the other children on a sled trip four miles downriver to visit a neighbor. Allaq, Pala, and I, the only three left in camp except for the baby, stood on the gravel spit and watched Saarak dwindle in the distance, only the peak of her white hood protruding from the wooden box in which Inuttiaq had placed her to protect her from the flying slush of the river surface. Then amused affection at her new venture was tempered by the tug of separation. We sat together in the sun. The camp was very quiet; the stuttering cries of an invisible loon only enhanced the stillness. Every now and then Pala's deep old voice sighed: "Eee eeee!" And once Allaq, sitting, as always, with the baby in her lap, remarked with a little laugh: "I feel left behind; I'm lonesome (*pai*) for Saarak."

Bit by bit, Saarak's babyhood was passing in another, most important, way: she was losing to her infant sister some of the attention, the open demonstrativeness, that she herself had formerly enjoyed. It happened so gradually that I was not aware of it until I heard Allaq one day coo at *(aqaq)* the uncomprehending Saarak: "My little Saa, your mother's brother no longer coos at *(aqaq)* you very much." Saarak made no response.

There were two games that Saarak's family played with her that seemed to me to dramatize this transition. It was in the autumn, when Qayaq was about five months old. Saarak at this time had begun to enjoy games in which she and her fellow-players took turns in assuming false identities, then pretended to discover their error. Thus, when Saarak entered her grandfather's tent for a visit, her aunt Amaaqtuq would greet her with mock ferocity: "Bad Kanunga! Bad dog! Get out of the tent!" Saarak, disconcerted not at all, would stand there, beaming, till Amaaqtuq, with equally mock surprise, suddenly said, "Why, it's Saarak!" Saarak would repeat her entry several times, each time telling Amaaqtuq to say "bad Kanunga!" Then she would take *her* turn at telling Amaaqtuq, at the top of her lungs, that *she* was a bad dog.

The two games that involved Qayaq were also identity games. In one, Inuttiaq and other relatives pretended to mistake Qayaq for Saarak. Bending over the baby as she lay in her mother's lap, Inuttiaq would coo *(aqaq)*: "Saaaraaaak . . ." I held my breath each time, but although this game never seemed to amuse Saarak as did the "bad dog" game she played with her aunt, her reply was rarely ruffled, only firm. "Here she is," she would announce, pointing a grubby finger at her own chest. And then her teasing relative would pretend to see her: "Why, *there's* Saarak!"

The second game involving Qayaq I considered even more perilous than the first, but Saarak did not seem especially threatened by this one, either. "Where's the charming *(niviuq)* little one?" one of her relatives would ask. "Here." Saarak would point to herself. "No," the other person would say gently, "*here*," pointing to Qayaq. "Here?" Saarak would chirp, pointing at the baby. "Eeee (yes)." But when, after a few repetitions, Saarak had learned to point to Qayaq, then her interlocutors asked her: "And where's the *other* charming *(niviuq)* little one?" Then when Saarak docilely pointed to Qayaq, they would correct her: "No, *here*," pointing to Saarak herself.

Saarak may not have been quite old enough to be alarmed by the implications of this game; she participated in it with exactly the same eager interest with which she participated in the kinship guessing game that it resembled, even when her relatives teased her by asking instead: "Where's the annoying *(urulu)* little one?" and laughing at her when she innocently pointed to herself. A month later when Amaaqtuq, whose Christian name was also Saarak, pointed out to her small namesake the similarity in their names, Saarak, to Amaaqtuq's immense amusement, shrieked in furious self-affirmation: "NO! *HERE* is SAARAK!!!" She would have nothing to do with any imposter. And when Allaq once at *that* time teased her daughter: "You're not charming *(niviuq)*; you're an old lady," Saarak cried, and was snuffed and comforted by her laughing mother.

In any case, once the initial crises had passed, Qayaq did not seem to be a major menace to Saarak. Saarak was never overtly hostile to the baby. When Qayaq was asleep, Saarak ignored the little bulge on her mother's back; when the baby woke and was shifted around to the front of the parka to be nursed, Saarak chirped and cooed, asked to see the baby, to kiss her, and sometimes to hold her (a gesture that Allaq always prevented for fear of the baby's safety) or to cuddle *(iva)* her in bed, as she herself was cuddled. Allaq said all small children, except Raigili, treated their younger brothers and sisters as Saarak treated Qayaq: "They feel protectively affectionate *(naklik)*."

There were only two signs that there was another side to Saarak's feelings about the baby. One I noticed only when Allaq pointed it out to me. When Qayaq was about six months old, I happened one day to ask whether children ever refused to eat. Allaq said, "Yes, when a child first has a younger brother or sister, that is, when the younger child is about Qayaq's age. Then the older child's stomach becomes small; if it is summer he will eat only the marrow and the tongue of the caribou [which are delicacies], and if it is winter he will eat only kapluna food, when the men come back from Gjoa Haven—as Saarak does."

The other clue lay in the nature of Saarak's favorite game, a game in which she impersonated, now a mother, now a baby. She had played this game before the baby was born; all children do, packing on their backs limbless fragments of dolls, or bottles, or puppies (Saarak one day twisted her own arm into the back of her parka, bounced it to sleep, then brought it around to her breast and nursed it); anything that will create the familiar bulge in the back of the parka will do. But now, since Qayaq's birth, whenever Saarak played this game, whether she was bouncing her legless rubber doll to sleep with realistically vigorous fist-pats on its buttocks, or was herself being bounced on the back of her young aunt Akla, invariably, her eyes and voice alight with pleasure, she called her mother's attention to the "baby": "Look, it's little sister!" And her mother would smile and nod *(aqaq)* with affection.

When I saw Saarak again, three years later, she and Qayaq were inseparable, and Allaq, watching the two playing together by the shore one day, remarked: "They are friends. That's the way it often is between brothers and sisters who are close in age." But what happened to the peace between Saarak and her little sister during the time when Saarak was learning the hardest lessons, I do not know. At the time I have described here, Qayaq was still so small, her wants so few, that Saarak was not yet called upon to give to her sister what she herself wanted. Neither was she called upon to control her temper with any consistency while I was there; the two lessons would go hand in hand; the one in restraint, the other in generosity. But harbingers of the change were visible. In the month before Qayaq was born, patience with Saarak's screams was already beginning to lessen. Though most of the time she was soothed as she had always been, she occasionally had to wait a bit before Allaq took notice of her howls; and if the first attempts to soothe did not prevail against the screams they were once in a while followed by an annoyed "ssssk," the noise that is made to discourage puppies from prowling around the entrances of tents, or by the order so often given older children: "Stop crying!" And already once or twice the path that Saarak was to follow had been pointed out to her.

Often it was done not when Saarak was in a blind rage but

when she was playing happily, oblivious of crisis. The day before we moved to join Pala's household in the spring camp in which Qayaq was born, when the household was electric with the happy bustle of packing, Allaq, in the sweet tone of persuasion, told Saarak: "You're not going to cry tomorrow; you're going to see your mother's sister." And another time, when the wet spring snow had soaked Saarak's caribou trousers along the tops of her boots, Allaq pointed out the dampness to her and said in the same tone: "Look, your pants are all wet with your tears. You mustn't cry; you'll make your pants wet and then you'll freeze." Occasionally, too, warnings were issued when Saarak was actually crying: "Don't cry; you'll hurt yourself; look, your eyes are bleeding." The warnings were almost always of the gentlest, but after the baby's birth the admonitions increased in frequency; and just once, with a startled, pitying twinge, I heard Allaq briefly imitate Saarak's wails, as Inuttiaq did Raigili's. The sound struck sharply through Saarak's immunity.

There was another sign, too, that Saarak's feelings were no longer considered quite as babylike as they had been. Although in Utku society, children are rarely the victims of genuine physical aggression, it does happen occasionally that adults play at physical attack with a small child, as they do with each other. The poking game (laah!) described earlier in this chapter is such an aggression game, but that game is enjoyed by the child "attacked" as well as by the attacker—until, eventually, adults teach the child to flee in earnest. There are other games, much more rarely played, which the child clearly does not enjoy. These games are always kept within the most careful bounds, yet they are nonetheless striking in contrast with the usual pervasive gentleness. Indeed, the aggressive nature of the games is enhanced by the fact that the players never exert any force; the caution seems to cry danger. One old grandmother was particularly given to these games. "Hit me," she would urge, holding out her face toward her granddaughter; "hit me." The child, Rosi, who was Saarak's age, would hesitatingly stretch out her tiny fist and lightly touch her grandmother's cheek. Immediately, the old lady would tap Rosi's face with her own fist, then again hold out her cheek: "Hit me again." Another of her favorite pranks was to tap her granddaughter lightly on her back or leg when she was not looking, then to pretend unawareness when the child turned to investigate. She would repeat the game until Rosi screamed in anger, whereupon her expressionless old face would wrinkle with laughter.

Saarak's family, too, had occasionally teased her in similar ways. They had offered her objects or activities she was sure to reject, for the amusement of hearing her shattering screech: "NOOOOO," as when Amaaqtuq had offered her Allaq's breast. Occasionally, they had pretended to do battle over her, Amaaqtuq "hitting" her while Inuttiaq or Allaq "protected" her by "attacking" Amaaqtuq in turn, batting their fists at the empty air. Sometimes Amaaqtuq would hit in Raigili's direction instead, while Saarak, apparently in great distress, waved her arms ineffectually at her aunt and shrieked until Amaaqtuq, whimpering as if in injury, retreated to the door. Allaq explained Saarak's actions to me with an amused smile: "She feels protective (naklik) toward her sister."

Inuttiaq once in a while teased Saarak by holding out his hand for a piece of food that she was about to put in her mouth, laughing when she whimpered in fear and gave the food to her mother to hold in safety. On one never repeated occasion he did something that I thought really cruel: he pretended to eat Saarak herself, snuffling with open mouth at her naked neck and breast like a hungry dog. The stricken child sat limp in his arms, while quiet sobs shook her body. Her father, to my horror, laughed gently and continued his sport for a while, but finally, still with quiet laughter, he took his daughter's hands and held them against his belly in a warming gesture of affection, and shortly Saarak, too, laughed.

These physically teasing games that are not enjoyed by the children are abandoned as children grow older. When older children are teased, as they often are, it is most often by subtler taunts, with rarely a physical overtone. The only physical attack game inflicted on Raigili was Nilak's: "Want a kiss?" and in the last months I knew her, Saarak, too, seemed largely to have outgrown these forms of joking.

To what extent Saarak felt the changes in the atmosphere I cannot say, but every now and then I began to see emergent in her behavior the outlines of a personality like her older sister's.

Raigili one day squeezed a longspur until its heart burst through its skin and, like the other children, she enjoyed killing the unwanted newborn puppies, dashing them with squeals of excited laughter against boulders or throwing them off the high knoll edge into the rapids below. Killing puppies was a child's job; adults said they found it too revolting to do themselves. Saarak one day, her eyes gleaming with pleasure, beat two small puppies with a stick until they cried piteously. Allaq paid no attention. Raigili had nightmares; Saarak now sometimes wept in her sleep, and one day she half roused from a nap, crying, "Uuuumak! uuuuumak!" (her word for "mother"). Allaq said tenderly, "Are you starting to have nightmares? I'm here," and Saarak went back to sleep. Like Raigili, too, Saarak one day in November spent the entire day in bed, by choice. She seemed perfectly happy, and though she was never actually alone in the iglu during the day, for long periods of time she asked no attention at all. Indeed, she resisted it. She buried herself, head and all, under the blanket, holding the edge down firmly and repelling with shrieks her aunt's sociable taps and laughing attempts to penetrate the barricade. A comical little bump on the ikliq, she sang and talked to herself, while Allaq now and then bent her head surreptitiously to listen, smiling, to the monologue.

Most of all like Raigili, Saarak was beginning to mope. The first time I noticed it was three weeks before Qayaq's birth. Raigili was lying in bed playing with an undershirt, drawing it over her head as a hood. Saarak watched her sister. "Laalaa too!" she demanded, her still babyish tongue stumbling over the consonants. "Laalaa too! Laalaa TOOOOO!" Her voice was shrill, but Raigili ignored her, and after a bit, Saarak lapsed into sulks, putting her finger in her mouth and pouting. The pathetic transformation of Saarak's expression, the sunless gloom that I had never seen darken her face before, struck me suddenly as funny, and I laughed. Inuttiaq, reached by the laugh as he had not been by Saarak's insistent voice, looked up from his work. "Vaaa, vaaa," he said, noting his daughter's expression, and immediately, warmed by her father's affection and my laugh, Saarak's face cleared. She bounced and pursed her lips, soliciting further attention, and the shirt was forgotten.

On the next occasion, six months later, the cause of Saarak's distress was different, and she was not so easily revived. She had fallen and hit her chin on the gravel floor of her grandfather's qaqmaq, and there I found her, in the company of Amaaqtuq, sitting motionless on the edge of the ikliq. Her legs in their caribou trousers stretched stiffly out before her, her sleeves dangled limp while her arms were wrapped around her body, her dark eyes stared at nothing, and her face was still streaked with tears. Amaaqtuq was sewing silently beside her. I was not amused this time; Saarak's expressionless face was desolate. "Saaraaaak," I said, offering the only solace I knew, "come sit on my lap." Saarak signified by the faintest wriggle that she had heard and accepted, and when Amaaqtuq helped her off the ikliq, she trotted, as if propelled without will, her empty sleeves flapping, across the qaqmaq to the oil drum where I sat; but in my arms she lapsed again into inertia; only the warmth of her little body and the rise and fall of her breath were alive.

There were other occasions, too. When Allaq went fuel-gathering and left Saarak behind in her aunt's care, Saarak knelt, ostrichlike, on the ikliq with her head buried in the bedding: "Because 'she's' not here." And when she was told not to fold the photographs she was looking at, pictures of herself that I had taken and given to her family, she sat with hanging head, batting at her mother and at me when we tried to touch her.

But for Saarak it was the exception still, and not the rule, this silent withdrawal in the face of adversity. Her parents had not yet begun to criticize her as they did Raigili in mooing tones when she sulked: "Always annoyed (urulu), always angry (qiquq)." Allaq, observing Saarak's hanging head, laughed at the nascent sulk, murmured, "Ee eeee," and snuffed her warmly. Perhaps her parents never became as severe with her as they were with Raigili. Amaaqtuq's letters for two years regularly reported: "Saarak still cries, poor little dear (naklik)."

4

Two Kin Groups: Expressions
of Separateness and Hostility

The closeness that marks relationships between households belonging to the same kin group contrasts with the social distance between households that belong to different kin groups.[1] As Inuttiaq's daughter I saw the contrast most clearly in the way my household related to Pala's on the one hand and to Nilak's and Qavvik's on the other. Pala's household was, of course, part of our own family circle; Nilak's and Qavvik's were not. The separateness of these three kin groups, Pala's, Nilak's, and Qavvik's, the feeling of "we" versus "they," that had first been expressed for me in the distance between camps and in the spacing of tents and iglus took many other forms, as well. Once, during the first August days at the Rapids before the caribou hunters had returned, I asked Amaaqtuq and her cousin, Maata, where the absent people were. They gestured in a northwesterly direction: "Over there." But when I asked whether Nilak had

1. A kin group, it will be remembered, consists of genealogical or adoptive siblings and the children of those siblings. See also section VI of the Introduction and Appendix III.

gone in that direction, they pointed to the opposite direction. It was their own kinsmen Inuttiaq and Mannik who had gone northwest. And during the spring, when Allaq looked forward to the return of the schoolchildren, it was not Nilak's nephew she spoke of; it was her daughter and her brother: "Soon, I think, Kamik and Ukpik will be coming." It was only when small Raigili asked: "And Tiriaq too?" that Allaq added the outsider to the list: "And Tiriaq." One's own family was always present in one's thoughts, as others were not. Even the dreams that were shared over breakfast tea were peopled with kinsmen, not with others.

Distance was expressed more tangibly, too. When Saarak began to venture out alone into the camp, Allaq would say to her: "Go visit your mother's brother," or "mother's sister," or "grandfather." She never said: "Go visit Nilak" or "Qavvik." Adults visited kinsmen more often than they visited others; they sat down comfortably on the ikliq with the family, helped themselves to the pile of fish in the corner if they were hungry, perhaps lent a hand with a fishnet that was under construction or with a pile of fish bellies that was being skinned, or brought their own sewing, plaiting, or toolmaking to work on while they visited. Outsiders, more formal in their behavior, usually stood just inside the door, unless invited to sit down; they ate when invited to do so (though they were not always averse to making their hunger known); and they watched but did not help spontaneously with the household work. If a mother wished to be relieved of her baby for a bit, while she went to check a fishnet or bring in a load of twigs, it was her sister, her mother, or her brother's wife she asked, not an outsider. If a man wanted a companion for a fishing or trapping trip he usually invited a close relative. If he needed to use a bit and brace or a saw, if his wife needed a frying pan or a cupful of fish-oil for the lamp, they would send to their parents or to their brothers and sisters before they approached others.

In certain respects, expressions of closeness and of separateness among households and kin groups varied with the season and with the size and membership of the camp. I have mentioned that during the time I lived with the Utku, summer camps were more communally organized than winter camps. Almost every activity was performed by a larger group in summer than in winter. In winter, the members of each iglu household checked their fishnets by themselves, cached their fish separately, and cooked and ate their own food in their own iglu, independently of close relatives who might live in nearby iglus. When visitors were present during a meal, they, too, were served, but their portions tended to be smaller than those of their hosts, even if the visitors were the host's own kinsmen. Only in the rare case when more than one nuclear family belonging to the same kin group shared a joint iglu did they collect and cache their fish together, or cook and eat as a single unit.

But when the same households joined one another in summer tent camps they ceased to be so independent. Then all the households belonging to one kin group checked their nets and cached their fish together; and all the women in the camp, whether or not they were kin, shared in gathering fuel and in preparing meals, which the whole camp ate together.

In another respect, too, summer camps were more communal than winter camps: there was less privacy. In winter, though the hillside under its snow covering swarmed with people as it never did in the summer, each iglu constituted a snow monad. Some clues to the activities of the neighbors came from the squeaking footsteps that passed nearby or overhead (depending on how deeply buried one's iglu happened to be); all footsteps were recognized. But the creak of snow underfoot and the faint howl of dogs heralding an approaching sled or meal were the only sounds that penetrated the muffling snow walls. Most news was brought by the children, who acted as messenger-scouts. All day, swallowlike, they darted in and out. When they came into an iglu they were always thoroughly interrogated. Inuttiaq used to do an exceptionally detailed job: "Where have you been? What were they doing? Do they have visitors? Who? Did you eat? What are they cooking? Boiled wolverine? Vaaaaa! Is there any left? I want to eat boiled wolverine!" and hastily pulling up his hood, out he would go to visit.

In summer there was no need for interrogation; the tent camps were porous. Much of life was lived outdoors. Even when one was indoors there was little private family life. Nilak saying evening prayers, Amaaqtuq chanting Responses from the prayerbook, Inuttiaq's nightmare and Saarak's temper tantrum, the anthropologist's tape recorder, and someone starting the primus for tea—all were audible.

Paradoxically, while the porousness of a tent camp erased some of the divisions between families, it accentuated others. In such a camp, the intimacy of communication among members of a kin group was publicly apparent as it never was in the winter. It was at night after people had retired to their tents that I noticed it. Then the silence that separated some households was eloquent in contrast with the spoken warmth that bound others. This was never more vivid than in the spring camp that Inuttiaq's household shared with Pala's and Nilak's after Qayaq's birth. If Allaq failed to wake when the baby cried, Pala next door would hear and shout: "Little daughter, wake up! One is crying and crying." Nilak's family never gave a sign of having heard the baby. Inuttiaq, feasting on bannock and jam, would call to his cousin Mannik: "Don't you want some?" and in a moment Mannik's smiling face would appear in the doorway. Usually one of his sisters would come, too, to fetch a piece for Pala. But Nilak's family was never summoned. Sometimes, lying lazily in bed, Inuttiaq would institute a question-and-answer game between Saarak and her relatives in the other tents, like that which they played during the winter in our double iglu. "Mannik!" she would call to her favorite uncle at Inuttiaq's dictation. "Are you asleep?"

"Yes," he would joke.

"Why?"

Was the rude question "why?" that Inuttiaq dictated to Saarak, a parody of my own persistent, impertinent questioning, intended for me to hear in my tent next door? I wondered. Laughter followed the nonsensical exchange, but Nilak's family never shared in it.

Again, Inuttiaq told Saarak to call to her grandfather: "Pala! Do you love me?"

"No," came the answer, with mock harshness.

"That makes one feel like crying."

More laughter followed, as Pala, in a voice of amused tenderness, called: "I was joking; I love *(naklik)* you very much, you're very sweet *(niviuq)*; did you think you weren't lovable *(niviuq)*?"

Or Saarak might call to me: "Elder sister! What are you doing?"

"Writing."

"Go to sleep!" and again laughter from all tents except Nilak's would follow the rudely imperious order.

Such closeness among kin was the embodiment of an Utku ideal. This was the way people should feel and act toward their kinsmen: with kindness and concern, helping them, sharing with them, and enjoying their company. A similar ideal of harmony, forbearance, and charity applied to relationships with all people. One should help anyone who required it—at least a little. One should be mild, sociable, and, of course, never under any circumstances angry or resentful. But the ideal did not prevent the separateness between kin groups, in itself acceptable and expectable, from being tainted, more often than not, by hostility. The hostility was subtly expressed and often strongly denied, but it was there.

Occasionally there were tensions among close kinsmen as well, but these, when they existed, were even more strenuously denied and rigorously controlled. To the superficial eye, harmony reigned within Pala's family circle. No discord was ever communicated directly or indirectly to the anthropologist in the house. I learned of the undercurrent of fear engendered by Inuttiaq's impeccable control of his temper not from the members of his family but from people in Gjoa Haven; and it was only after they had enlightened me that I read any deeper meaning into Allaq's docile behavior. When Pala's other son-in-law, Ipuituq, joined the household, the harmony seemed on the whole extended to him, although he belonged to the family only by marriage. Again it was in Gjoa Haven that I learned of the tensions existing between Ipuituq and Pala, with regard to Ipuituq's excessively independent tastes in residence. The story was that at one point Ipuituq's reluctance to live in Pala's household had nearly broken his marriage with Pala's daughter Amaruq. He left her; she followed him to Gjoa Haven; and there the marriage was formally cemented by the Anglican bishop on his annual visit. But Ipuituq and Amaruq seemed a most affectionate couple at the time I knew them, and no member of their family revealed their history to me. Once attuned, to be sure, one did hear occasional critical comments, very matter-of-fact in tone, to the effect that Ipuituq was unpredictable, lazy, or inclined to untruthfulness. But so subtly was the disapproval expressed that a foreign observer would have noticed nothing. No one ever shouted, or even sulked visibly, at anyone else. And if occasionally someone felt "too lazy" to do a job requested of him, no one seemed to take it seriously. It did not happen often—except in the case of the children, who, after all, could not be expected to obey consistently, since "their minds *(ihuma)* were not yet fully developed."

I did sense strain between the household of the old man Piuvkaq and the others of Pala's circle, but I never learned whether my feeling was correct. Though Pala and Piuvkaq were half-brothers and each considered the other a member of his kin group, Piuvkaq seemed somehow only formally accepted by Inuttiaq and Pala. I thought this might have been because Piuvkaq, through the frailty of age and the lack of an adult son, was to some extent dependent on the others. The two younger men, Pala and Inuttiaq, recognized their family obligations to share food with Piuvkaq and to help him move when they migrated, but the assistance rendered seemed more dutiful than joyful. Piuvkaq's tent, or his iglu, stood next to his brother's, but when Pala and Inuttiaq joined their dwellings together to form an intimate whole, Piuvkaq's small home seemed rather lonely.

Piuvkaq's household consisted of himself, his elderly wife, Huluraq, their daughter, Maata, who was about twenty-five and had already been twice widowed, and Maata's two small daughters, one from each marriage. There was also an adopted son, Pamiuq, about fourteen years old, the only cheerful, bouncy member of the household. He was actually Piuvkaq's grandson but had been adopted as a son when his own parents died.

Piuvkaq and Huluraq were sweet old people, but one did not see much of them because they were both "tired," as the Utku put it, that is, elderly and unwell; they spent most of their time at home. Their daughter, Maata, was often silent and aloof. The smiles with which she responded to the smiles of others were seldom reflected in her eyes. I had the impression that she was not well liked, or that she herself disliked people. She came occasionally to visit in Inuttiaq's household or in Pala's, but usually stood quietly by the door for a little while, without speaking or being spoken to, and then left. More often she came to beg a bit of tobacco for her mother or a little oil for the lamp, as her own household was always short of everything. Maata and Pamiuq between them did the best they could to help Piuvkaq provide for the household. They fished, they set a net, they ran a short trapline, but the three of them could not equal the work that would have been done by a young and vigorous man. The small requests they made of Pala and Inuttiaq were never refused, but on the other hand very little was spontaneously offered to Piuvkaq's household. The spirit of the relationship between Piuvkaq's household and these others was symbolized for me by an incident that occurred one day in the winter camp. Hearing Piuvkaq's approaching footsteps on the snow outside, Inuttiaq quickly cut off a small piece of an especially fat and desirable fish he had just caught and, laughing, hid the rest under a hide. The small piece he generously urged on Piuvkaq when he entered.

Piuvkaq and his wife both died of respiratory infections while I was at Back River, within a few days of each other. Maata and the children moved in with Pala for a little while, but then Nakliguhuktuq arranged for Maata to marry a man from another community, and she moved there, taking her daughters and Pamiuq with her.

The tensions that existed between one kin group and another were more visible than those that existed between the households of a single group. The loyalties that sealed the tongues of close kinsmen were less binding on remote relatives, so between extended families hostility found expression in gossip and slander, as it never did within the family itself. It was always the Others who were accused of untruthfulness, theft, laziness, stinginess, unhelpfulness, jealousy, greed, lechery, and bad temper. Qavvik stole, the other families said; he gossiped evilly; he talked a great deal about his plans but rarely carried any of them out. The picture was not wholly black. He was an excellent hunter and trapper, they said; he was industrious and kind. But on the other hand, he was not very religious and he had too great a fondness for women. "Those people are always wanting a woman," Nilak would tell me, jerking his head toward the other iglus: Qavvik's, Inuttiaq's, and Pala's. *"We* don't do that; we're all right *(naamak)."* And Allaq would tell me, "The men don't like to travel to Gjoa Haven with Nilak, because he never shares his tea and tobacco with the others on the way home. Inuttiaq and Mannik always say that. He is stingy and jealous *(tuhuu).* We are not like that; we are all right *(naamak)."*

Of course, there was sometimes a factual basis for these remarks. But often it seemed to me that the Outsiders were merely scapegoats for the release of hostility that had built up in the course of day-to-day living, regardless of the original cause of the anger. If Nilak stayed at home one day instead of going off trapping he was "lazy," said Allaq. If Inuttiaq stayed at home he was "tired."

Similarly, appropriation of other people's property was differently defined depending on who did it. The Utku have very clear concepts of personal property. However, in theory it is quite all right for someone who lacks a particular item, say, tea or flour, to take a little from the cache of someone who has a great deal of that item. Such behavior is defined as "stealing" only if the taker fails to report to the owner of the cache, or if he uses the cache all up. If Inuttiaq and Mannik, members of my family, helped themselves from my supply cache, my family viewed that as legitimate sharing, as long as the takers reported the act to me, the owner. But if Outsiders took something, my family invariably told me of the "theft," even though the takers had themselves announced their deed to me.

In actual fact, all of the Eskimos I encountered were punctiliously honest. Every accidentally spilled drop of kerosene and every teaspoonful of tea taken was reported. But when a tangible act like stealing was not involved, it was sometimes difficult to know whether an aspersion was true or not. I was never sure whether the Utku themselves believed their slanderous remarks; people occasionally seemed embarrassed by my tendency to take them literally. My family often told me that Nilak commented behind my back about how heavy the letters I wrote were and how reluctant he was to carry them to Gjoa Haven for me: "It is only Nilak who thinks they are heavy and who doesn't want to take them. Inuttiaq and Mannik and Ipuituq would agree to carry them." If I happened to be feeling beleaguered that day, I would believe them, and would meet their gossip with silently burning resentment: how could anyone consider five or six half-ounce letters heavy! But if I then agreed that perhaps I had better not ask Nilak to carry them, Inuttiaq or Allaq would say anticlimactically, "I think he will carry them if you ask him."

Similarly, members of my household would report to me that Qavvik did not want his adopted son, Putuguk, to carry on his sled the heavy load of flour I wanted to order from Gjoa Haven. But if these reports deterred me from making the request, somebody was sure to reassure me: "I think he will do it if you ask him." And indeed he did. When I went once, apprehensively, to ask Qavvik's permission for Putuguk to carry the flour for me, he said with utmost warmth: "You mustn't be afraid *(ilira)* to ask us to carry things for you; we are not frightening *(ilira)*. You are a kapluna, a woman, and alone here among people; you are someone to be taken care of *(naklik)*." I thanked him and went home to meditate on the meaning of Utku slander. Were Qavvik and Nilak really as reluctant to carry my letters and supplies as they were said to be? Were their warm reassurances to me merely a polite veneer overlying the reluctance that they expressed behind my back? If so, were the ungracious remarks that were reported to me to be taken literally? Did Nilak really think my letters were heavy, or was he, perhaps, expressing in figurative terms resentment against me because his household tended to receive less than Inuttiaq's of my kapluna benefits? Or, on the other hand, did Inuttiaq and Allaq simply invent Qavvik's and Nilak's ungracious words, perhaps attributing to their neighbors resentment that they themselves felt concerning my inconvenient requests?

5

Nilak's Family

During the months in which I lived as Inuttiaq's daughter, the
social world of my family was to a large extent my own world.
Though for the sake of my work I made some effort to visit in
other households more widely than my family did, the pattern
of their associations could not help but influence mine: my visits
were limited to the households that shared our camp, and I saw
more of the people who visited frequently in our home than I did
of others. Pala, with or without Ipuituq, was almost always with
us, as was Piuvkaq until his death. Qavvik, on the other hand, almost never shared our spring, summer, or autumn camps; we
saw him only in the winter, when all the households gathered
in Amujat. Of the families who were not closely related to us, we
were most in contact with Nilak's.

It was a small family, Nilak's, the smallest in the band. It consisted only of Nilak, his wife, Niqi, and their adopted daughter,
Tiguaq, a girl of about seventeen; they had no children of their
own. Nilak was the last remaining one of a group of brothers
who used to camp together in Chantrey Inlet. Two of the

brothers had died, and the third, crippled by tuberculosis, lived in Gjoa Haven, where life was not so rugged as it was in Chantrey Inlet. Niqi's parents and siblings, too, had all either died or moved south to Baker Lake, so Nilak's household was left without any close relatives at Back River. It was a lonely situation, and the loneliness was exacerbated by the personal peculiarities of Nilak and his wife. It was not that they camped far from other families, as I had been led to expect; they did not. Nilak was one of the "Itimnaaqjuk-people," those who habitually camped at Itimnaaqjuk, the Rapids, during the summer, as did Pala and the two associated households of Inuttiaq and Piuvkaq; but his isolation was all the more visible for that very reason. It was especially visible to me the autumn I first arrived in Chantrey Inlet, when his tent stood alone on the far shore of the river, facing, across the rapids, the clustered tents of the other families a quarter of a mile away. The howling of his dogs came to us on the breeze, and we watched the household like puppets coming and going about their toy tent, gathering their fuel, fishing, and setting their nets on their own side of the river. Within sight, as they were, and yet out of the range of immediate neighborly contact with the other tents, they seemed more distant than if they had been miles away.

My first meeting with Nilak's family occurred just a week after I joined the two elderly brothers, Pala and Piuvkaq, at the Rapids. Nilak, like Inuttiaq, was away inland, hunting caribou when I arrived, but snow flurries already whitened the ground at night, and the occupants of the camp at the Rapids daily scanned the empty tundra expectantly for signs of their missing kinsmen and neighbors. I, too, was expectant, but my anticipation was colored by anxiety. I wondered what my prospective fathers, the absent hunters, Inuttiaq and Nilak, would be like, and how they would react to the discovery that a strange kapluna woman had materialized in their midst during their absence. I felt, guiltily, a little resistant to the prospect of increased demands on my work-time and privacy, on my good humor, and especially on my limited food supplies, which the presence of newcomers would entail, so soon after I had become reconciled to the incursions of Pala's kinfolk.

About noon one day, Piuvkaq's daughter, Maata, and I were sitting together in my tent. I was trying with cold-stiff fingers to record vocabulary while Maata sewed me a pair of duffel socks as protection against the frostbite that I feared was imminent. Pala's daughter Amaaqtuq parted my tent flaps and gestured in the direction of the distant hills across the river: "Nilak." Pencil and sock in hand we ran to look. "Where?" My eyes are good, but they could not match the Eskimos' sensitivity to moving objects in the landscape. For some time my neighbors tried vainly to point the travelers out to me, but it was some minutes before I saw a white team of dogs running down toward the opposite shore. Watching them come, Maata and Amaaqtuq instructed me. "Nilak and his wife, Niqi, are called *nuliaqtaariik,* 'the married couple.' Niqi is little and her adopted daughter, Tiguaq, is biiig." They laughed.

Pala and Piuvkaq watched Nilak's approach with as much interest as their daughters, and as soon as the figures were seen to have reached the opposite shore, the old men, probably spurred by the startling news they had to impart, paddled over to greet them and to escort them across the river to drink tea with us.

The details of that first meeting are still vivid in my mind, partly because the warmth of the greeting the family received was so strikingly out of keeping, both with the expectations that had been engendered in me regarding Nilak's isolation and with the confirmation that these expectations received later that evening when I stood with Pala's and Piuvkaq's daughters on the beach and watched Nilak and his womenfolk organizing their camp again in the remote spot across the river where it had stood all summer. Later I found that an appearance of warmth characterized most Utku reunions, regardless of the tensions that would emerge when the euphoria of meeting had dissipated; and, as I look back now on that day, I see other tokens of Nilak's isolation in the welcoming atmosphere. At the time, however, I was blinded by preoccupation with my own feelings: strangeness and self-consciousness in the Eskimo world and anxiety regarding what my own future relationship with this newly arrived man and his family might be. Curiously, I recognize now that it was precisely to these personal concerns that I owed my first experience of the relationship between Nilak's family and the others, had I only been sensitive to it.

The newcomers were met on the same strip of shore where a week earlier I had been met. The same silent, smiling knot of Eskimos stood waiting for the canoes to be beached, then went forward to shake hands with the three who stood, also silently smiling, at the edge of the shore. The resemblance of the scene to the earlier one of which I had been the focus struck me, perhaps because as yet there were so few acts that were familiar to me in this new life. I felt, moreover, though it may have been a trick of my self-consciousness, that I was almost as focal an actor in this second scene as in the first. I had followed the two women of the camp when they beckoned me to go with them to the shore and had stood a little apart and behind them while the hunters shook hands with their welcomers and distributed presents of caribou tallow to the children. Then Pala summoned me from my shy retreat: "Shake hands." I obeyed, and Nilak, with a beautiful smile, handed me, too, a generous piece of tallow. Afterwards I had occasion to think longingly of that tallow, but at the time I had not the least idea what the grubby suet-like lump was; I feared only that I would be expected to eat it, as indeed I was. I felt that at that moment the reunion of Nilak's household with Pala's and Piuvkaq's was of less interest to the Eskimos than my own introduction and display. To Nilak I was a stranger, a person to be courted. At the same time, to Pala's family I was a curious acquisition to be shown off. I felt a protectiveness, perhaps a little possessiveness, toward me in the manner of my recent friends, which contrasted with the timid stares and smiles of the newcomers, and it is my memory now of that possessiveness, the feeling I had that suddenly I "belonged" to some people as distinct from others, that makes me realize that, unaware as I was of its real meaning, I experienced then the fact that the Utku are not a cohesive, unitary group.

The feeling that I belonged with or, better, *to* Pala's kin, a little in the manner of a pet, continued when the women beckoned me to the tents to share in the welcoming meal of tea and bannock, which Maata with hospitable haste ran to cook, and I felt only the exhilaration of gratitude even when, on the way,

Maata and Amaaqtuq, amused as always, put me through my linguistic paces, encouraging me to perform publicly all the words they had taught me in the past week—especially the plant names, which they knew I found impossible to pronounce. I had the impression that my friends also dictated silly or comic phrases for me to repeat, playing with me the way they sometimes did with small children whose tongues tripped amusingly over complicated words; but the laughter—I felt it excessive—that followed my obedient repetitions of their phrases may have been due simply to my execrable pronunciation, not to the verbal content per se.

Nilak and his family did not participate in these games. They seemed amused but were too shy, or perhaps too polite, to laugh at me loudly as the others did. Overtly, they paid no attention to me at all. The men swapped news, with occasional interpolations from the women: Nilak had shot twelve caribou; the gulls were eating the fish out of our nets; some kaplunas had come in a plane; I myself had come to live with them for a year. I understood little else and soon gave up straining to mold the stream of sound into words. The quietness of the talk, its slow tempo, and the running laughter on which the words were threaded lulled me. Silences were long, as is usual in Eskimo conversation, and few questions were asked. People waited for news to be offered.

Sitting as an honored guest on Piuvkaq's ikliq, I sipped the bitter tea and ate bannock that tasted overwhelmingly of the fish oil in which it had been fried. Surreptitiously, I observed Nilak, his wife, and adopted daughter, seeing them through very kapluna eyes. They eyed me in turn, equally surreptitiously with the exception of Niqi, who stared when she thought I was not looking. I was pleasantly impressed with Nilak, a handsome man of about forty (I thought him somewhat younger). He had a warm smile and a bowl haircut and was well dressed in a worn duffel parka and fairly new store clothes: jacket, shirt, chinos, and rubber shoe-pacs, all of which I later discovered had been presents from kapluna sportsmen who had fished in Chantrey Inlet earlier in the summer. Nilak's adopted daughter, Tiguaq, seemed charming, too. She was really his niece, Nilak told me, the child of one of his brothers. Eskimos who have no children of their own or whose children are grown often adopt children, partly just because they enjoy having children around and partly for the help that the child can render its adopted parents as it grows up. Nilak and Niqi, being childless, had adopted Tiguaq when she was still so little that she had to be carried next door to be nursed by her real mother. She was now a pretty adolescent with heavy, neatly braided hair and knee-length hide waterboots like a man's, which drew my eyes because of the thrifty way they were constructed. Sealskin, very scarce at Back River, had been used only for the soles, while the uppers were made of the less waterproof but more readily available caribou hide.

It was on Niqi, however, that my attention centered. My foreigner's eye was much less kind to her than to her husband and daughter, partly because of her unkempt appearance and partly because her uneasiness concerning me manifested itself in ways that irritated my kapluna sensibilities. She unwittingly deepened the gratitude I felt for the proprietary attitude toward me of Pala's and Piuvkaq's households. Her appearance was ludicrous and repellent. She was a funny little creature, with sparrowlike gestures, quick and jerky. Her age could not be determined from her appearance, but I calculated that she must be about forty, like her husband. She was unusually short, even for an Eskimo, and I think this may have contributed to the childish impression she created; as Maata and Amaaqtuq had told me, Nilak and Tiguaq both towered over Niqi by a foot or more. She was wearing an indescribably grimy, ragged cotton parka cover (filthier by contrast with the fairly clean clothes of her husband and daughter) and a dime store necklace of huge luminous beads which, like Nilak's clothes, was a present from the summer sportsmen. She was one of the very few Utku women who *preferred* pipe to cigarette smoking, and the first such woman I had met. She alternately smoked and spat incessantly, as did everyone else, but when Niqi spat she let the saliva roll out of her mouth onto the gravel floor at her feet instead of shooting it vigorously out the door like other people. To be sure, I later found that other people, on occasion, also spat on the floor, but it was Niqi in whom I first noticed this behavior. Perhaps others were more discreet at first, out of regard for my "civilized" weaknesses, or perhaps I was merely more aware of Niqi's spitting because I disliked her.

Niqi hid her shyness of me and her curiosity about me much less successfully than did the other Eskimos. Instead of laughing warmly and openly like the others at my execrable speech, Niqi snickered behind her hand and whispered to her neighbors. She also covered her mouth in an outburst of giggles and looked away when I smiled at her or when somebody pointed her out to me in conversation. I discovered soon enough that the manner that annoyed me so was in reality an expression of excessive, uncontrollable shyness *(ilira)*. When the shyness lessened in a day or two, she made efforts to teach me words, which, though unsuccessful, made me aware that her intent was friendly, however ineptly it was translated into action. In later months, warmer feelings for Niqi came to be mingled with my antagonistic ones, but at first, even when she was friendly, I could not like her. In spite of myself, I defensively felt her manner hostile. I missed the warm smile, however superficial it might be, that others, including Nilak and Tiguaq, controlled to perfection.

As I sat in the tent that first day, listening dimly to the quiet, humorous exchange of news, I felt alone in my hostility toward Niqi. To my ear no antagonism marred the friendly cheer the others seemed to share. But before many days had passed I found that Pala's kin shared my aversion. They disliked Nilak as well, and when I came to see the darker feelings that underlay the superficially gracious relationship between Nilak's family and the others, I appreciated more fully the quality of the isolation that was symbolized by Nilak's distant tent site.

It was possible, to be sure, that the situation of Nilak's tent that summer had a purely practical explanation. In other seasons and other years the division between Nilak's family and the others was less dramatic. We often shared the same campsite; but even when we did so, Nilak's tent or iglu was usually set at a relatively great distance from those of Pala's family. Pala's daughter Amaaqtuq, a year later, when we were all camped on the same side of the river, did give me a practical reason for Nilak's unusually isolated camp that first summer. In the spring of that year, members of Pala's, Piuvkaq's, and Inuttiaq's households had gone out to the coast to hunt seal. Walking back down the west side of the river after the ice had gone out, they had arrived at Haqvaqtuuq on the northern side of the rapids and had decided it was too much trouble to ferry the dogs across by canoe to Nilak's campsite on the other side. So they had stayed at Haqvaqtuuq while Nilak, who had not gone sealing, stayed at the more usual site on the southern side of the rapids.

Perhaps that was all there was to it. But I noted that although Nilak's family almost every afternoon paddled over to visit Pala's camp until nightfall or canine pandemonium sent them home again, return visits from the larger group were rare, and I suspected that Amaaqtuq's family had considered Nilak's company not worth the effort of ferrying the dogs across.

I. Unpleasant People: Utku Dislike of Volatility

I was never sure exactly in what manner the absence of close kin ties between Nilak and other Utku combined with his own and his wife Niqi's unpleasant personalities to make the other families dislike them. Nilak and Pala were cousins, Pala's mother and Nilak's father having been brother and sister; but this was not considered a very close relationship, and so it is possible that some of the gossip directed against "the married couple" was merely scapegoating, gossip of the sort to which people outside the protective pale of family loyalties were often subject. But my own observations of Nilak and his wife indicated that much of the gossip was based on fact. And the personal quality of the hostility was also attested by the fact that Nilak's adopted daughter, Tiguaq, a pleasant girl who gave no cause for offense, was exempt from the malicious gossip, even though her kinship connections with Pala's group were one degree more remote than Nilak's own. Both of these facts seem to indicate that personality rather than lack of kinship was the determining factor in the dislike. Pala's kin certainly perceived it so. On the other hand, I sometimes wondered whether some of the testiness for which Nilak was disliked might itself stem from his insecure kinship position in the larger group, though my friends in Pala's group assured me that he had been just as nasty in the days when his brothers were around: nasty to his brothers as well as to members of Pala's family.

In any case, the unpleasant characteristics of Nilak, and especially of Niqi, provided endless conversation in other households. Nilak's warm smile, I was told, concealed bad temper *(huaq, urulu, ningaq)*, stinginess, and unhelpfulness, three of the most damning traits that one Eskimo can ascribe to another. But it was his wife, Niqi, who bore the brunt of the attack. It is possible that even Nilak himself resented her and that her defects contributed to his own irritability. In my presence he was the most considerate of husbands. In the early days, the pair always came visiting together to my tent, paddling over from their camp across the river, and I was impressed by the solicitude with which Nilak sugared Niqi's tea and kept her supplied with bannock and jam as I cooked it. But people said: "Nilak doesn't love *(naklik)* his wife; he just wants kaplunas to think he does."

The neighbors' view of Niqi was summed up in two critical judgments: "She seems a child *(nutaraqpaluktuq)*" and "She hasn't much sense *(ihumakittuq)*." There was a real basis for these judgments in that Niqi seemed unable to behave in a properly adult manner. I think it probable that she was mentally deficient. She was the only adult under the age of fifty who was illiterate in syllabics; and I was told that she spoke incorrectly sometimes. She had had a brother who was clearly defective; people said he hardly spoke intelligibly.

Dislike of Niqi, like that of her husband, centered on her bad temper; she had a reputation for being easily provoked to angry tears or sulks *(qiquq)*. Once when I returned from a trip to Gjoa Haven, Allaq informed me that while I was away Niqi had assaulted Tiguaq, shaking her in anger *(ningaq)*. "Even though Tiguaq is a big girl," said Allaq disapprovingly. What truth there was in the story I do not know, but it indicates the low esteem in which Niqi was held.

I once asked Allaq whether other people "of little sense *(ihuma)*" were disliked, as Niqi was. I named two other Utku of recent memory who had been even more incapable than Niqi. No, Allaq said; they were liked as long as they were pleasant people and did not lose their tempers *(urulu);* it was only Niqi who was disliked, because she had no control of her temper.

Interestingly, though Niqi's bad temper was as much disliked as anyone else's, in one respect the reaction to hers was unusual: she was the only person whose anger did not alarm people. They just shrugged it off as they would the passing ill humor of a half-grown child, only perhaps a bit more scornfully: "Niqi is annoyed *(qiquq, urulu)* again; just like a child, she has no sense *(ihuma);* she's not frightening *(iqhi)."*

I knew one other notoriously bad-tempered person at Back River, a Netsilik man named Uyuqpa who, by marriage, had become a peripheral member of the Utku band. Uyuqpa's temper was also called "childish *(nutaraqpaluktuq)"* and "lacking in sense *(ihuma),"* but nobody ever said *it* was not frightening. Quite the contrary.[1] I wondered what made the difference. Perhaps people recognized that Niqi really was more like a child in many respects and that her behavior was as inconsequential as the latter's. Her irritations, like those of a child, tended to come and go in a flash.

An Eskimo friend of mine, a Netsilingmiutaq who had had considerable acquaintance with kaplunas, once characterized

1. The Utkus' attitude toward ordinary ill temper seemed different from their attitude toward the violence of insanity. Ukalik, the widow of one of Nilak's brothers (Tiguaq's real mother), was insane and, on occasion, murderous. She was in a mental hospital in Winnipeg during the time I was at Back River, so that it is difficult accurately to compare reactions to her rages with reactions to common anger, but the tenor of remarks about Ukalik was quite different from the criticisms directed toward Niqi and Uyuqpa. Though Ukalik was very much feared during her psychotic periods, she did not seem to be disapproved of in the same way as the others. She was not said to be a person of "little sense *(ihumakittuq),"* but when she was psychotic her reason was said to disappear altogether *(ihumaqaruiqtuq).* These episodes were thought to be caused by intrusion of evil spirits, and the fear in which she was held at these times did not seem to affect the regard in which she was held during her sane periods; both Pala and Qavvik were eager to marry her, should she return to Back River.

In one point, however, attitudes toward Ukalik and toward Uyuqpa (though not toward Niqi) seemed to coincide: Ukalik and Uyuqpa were both considered to have power to kill, whether with the help of evil spirits or merely by the force of their own angry thoughts (see below in this section), I am not sure, but I believe that both of these people owed their reputations for evil power to their evil tempers.

More detailed comparative data on attitudes toward varieties of rage remain to be gathered.

the difference between Eskimo and kapluna anger. "If a kapluna is angry with you," he said, "he can be angry with you in the morning and forget all about it by afternoon. But if an Eskimo is angry with you he'll never speak to you again."

Niqi's anger was like that of the kapluna in this comment. It is the other, the long-lasting, anger that really frightens people, containing, as it does, implications that the angry person is brooding one's destruction. Of such a person, at the opposite pole from Niqi, it is not said that he is short of sense *(ihumakit-tuq)*, like Niqi, but that he has too much mind *(ihumaquqtuuq)*. In Eskimo belief angry thoughts long fostered can harm others simply by the force of their own festering; the wish to harm has the same effect as a physical attack.

In any case, though Niqi's bad temper seemed to be a central cause of her being disliked, the dislike had such repercussions that there was hardly an aspect of her behavior that was not criticized. When she was cheerful, she "laughed too much," people said. When she went fishing or trapping, went for a walk or to visit neighbors, people said she "couldn't sit still," or "never stayed home." When she sat at home they said she was "lazy" or "sulking *(qiquq)*." They criticized her housekeeping, saying that her sewing and cooking were laughable, that she tended the household lamp so carelessly that it smoked up the whole iglu, and that because she was never home the dogs were always getting in and stealing from her iglu or tent. Even Nilak complained publicly of her domestic defects, and I expect this was one of the reasons the neighbors judged he did not love his wife. In any case his habit of criticizing was considered to be in extremely poor taste and earned *him* much criticism.

Niqi's physical characteristics were also the butt of private humor. The neighbors, both men and women, secretly parodied her mannerisms: her occasionally confused speech, her embarrassed laugh and jerky, hasty, often clumsy motions—the way she darted in and out of tents, tripping over intervening objects.

Niqi's sense of the appropriate seemed to be less highly developed than other people's, both with regard to emotional expression and with regard to mature feminine behavior. People laughed behind her back at a variety of things she did that were odd in a person of her age and sex: her fondness for playing with children (who, in turn, readily accepted her); the way she rough-housed with Tiguaq; rolled on the ground playfully with the puppies; or sat with binoculars on a hilltop, scanning the tundra for caribou as a man would do. I never heard anyone tease her concerning her predilection for child-companions, but when she returned from her expedition to the hilltop people did ask her jokingly: "Where's the caribou?"—to which Niqi responded with a characteristically self-conscious giggle.

In another respect, too, Niqi showed lack of judgment and control: she lacked patience and circumspection. Instead of waiting quietly as she should have done till the future, or other people, of themselves answered her private speculations about events, Niqi asked frequent questions, as a child would do: "Where are you going?" "What are you going to do?"

Again like a child, Niqi found it difficult to wait when some exciting event was anticipated. In July, when the Eskimos were daily expecting planes carrying sports fishermen to arrive at the Rapids, Niqi would hear the hum of a plane's motor in every passing sound and run out to search the sky. It was the same way in the winter when men who had gone to Gjoa Haven to trade were expected home again. The Eskimo estimates of how long the round trip would take were always more optimistic than mine by several days; but Niqi's estimates were optimistic to the point of absurdity, and every time a dog howled or even cocked an ear she was convinced the men were coming, though they could not possibly arrive for another week.

Pala one day vividly described the Eskimos' view of Niqi, though we were not talking about Niqi directly; he was telling me how one could recognize a person of little sense (*ihuma*). Mockingly groping from side to side with his hands and open mouth in a silly, aimless, wandering way he said: "A person who lacks sense knows nothing. He is always playing, always happy (*quvia*); he searches everywhere for caribou, for fish, for airplanes; he is always expecting and hoping; he laughs easily, is easily annoyed (*urulu*), and easily forgets."

II. Outsiders All: My Ambivalence toward the Disliked

Many of these criticisms of Niqi and of Nilak I heard only after I had been living with the Utku for some time; but enough of

Niqi's aberrance was immediately apparent to influence quite strongly, to my dishonor, my dealings with her and her family. Though I tried to maintain an impartial face, internally I adopted all too readily the attitudes of Pala's faction toward Nilak's household. When the morning after their return from the hunt, Nilak and Niqi came to invite me to become their daughter and to move my tent to their camp across the river, I refused, and though I justified my refusal to myself in terms of Nilak's social isolation, I am afraid my decision was unduly influenced by the distaste I felt for Niqi's half-witted giggle and by the difficulty I experienced in communicating with "the married couple," who lacked the extraordinary sensitivity that Pala's family showed in ferreting out my meanings and conveying theirs.

Maata, Amaaqtuq, and Pala came with Nilak and Niqi to my tent and explained to them the incoherent gestures and diagrams through which I tried to convey my desires: to stay where I was for the present and to postpone the decision on my winter quarters. In Nilak's presence Pala's people showed no reaction to my choice of camp, and Nilak himself said merely: "It can't be helped (ayuqnaq)." But as we watched Nilak's canoe receding across the river I was conscious again of a possessive quality in the smiles that surrounded me, an exclusiveness in the warmth with which Pala thanked me for remaining with *them*. The impression of Nilak's separateness that Pala's protectiveness had given me on the previous afternoon was strengthened. Inuttiaq was still two days' journey distant, yet in effect I was already adopted by his group. I was grateful and yet a trifle uneasy— doubtful that I had done the right thing to align myself with any group of families that might prove partisan. My discomfort increased when, several times in the next days, Amaaqtuq, with glee in her eyes and with full knowledge of my answer, asked me: "Is Nilak going to be your father?" Much later I discovered to my consternation that I had had good reason to feel uneasy; Pala's faction had correctly interpreted my decision not to join Nilak, either because my private motives were more apparent than I had flattered myself they were, or because the Eskimos' perceptions were colored by their own malicious tendency to cast others' behavior in the worst possible terms, a quality that often disconcerted me later. In any case, when I returned to

Gjoa Haven for a visit three months after I had first gone down to Back River, I learned that "somebody" from Back River (I suspected Amaaqtuq) had written that I had chosen to live with Inuttiaq because I disliked Nilak.

Communication continued to be a major problem in my relationship with Nilak and Niqi (though not with their daughter Tiguaq) throughout my sojourn in Chantrey Inlet. I am still not sure why this should have been so. Certainly Niqi's lack of intelligence was a factor, and perhaps Nilak, too, lacked some of the intelligence and imagination that characterized Pala's family. Instead of adapting the speed and complexity of his speech to my limited comprehension, Nilak habitually raised his voice, bending his head toward my ear, as people so often do when speaking to foreigners. Niqi made no adjustment in her speech at all.

I suspect, however, that emotions, both the married couple's and mine, may explain more than intelligence. Many times, tangled in Nilak's cobweb phrases, I felt my mind closing in irritation, a feeling compounded by my resentment at the couple's long, difficult visits and by their frequent oblique references to tea and tobacco. Nilak and his wife, too, had grounds for resentment and frustration in my obstinate lack of comprehension, and in my preference for Pala's camp, which they must jealously (and mistakenly) have imagined to be flowing with the tea and tobacco that I gave *them* in meagre driblets. Their shyness of me undoubtedly also complicated communication. Months later, when Tiguaq had become my most helpful linguistic informant, she proved as imaginative in her teaching methods as Pala's family had formerly been. "She is not afraid *(ilira)* of you any more," Niqi confided to me. And my mother, Allaq, gave me another clue when she maliciously said: "If you had lived with Niqi you would never have learned to speak Eskimo, because she would always have agreed with you when she didn't understand what you said." People who are afraid *(ilira)* of you agree with you.

As time went on my initial dislike of Niqi was tempered by warmer feelings, though I am afraid she never knew it. She was a friendly soul and when she, like Tiguaq, had lost her fear of me, her friendliness had at times an almost puppylike quality;

if we were out walking together she would run ahead and crouch, grinning at me as if inviting playful pursuit. I never responded to her childlike antics, because they embarrassed me and because I feared to augment the rather considerable reputation for childishness that I myself had acquired. But for the very reason that I, like Niqi, *was* "childish" in Eskimo eyes, I eventually developed quite a kindred feeling for her. We were, in a sense, children together, neither of us able to maintain the behavior proper to an Eskimo adult: Niqi because she lacked the wits, I because I had been brought up in a different world. And both of us were subject to the same disapproval from the rest of society on account of our reprehensible volatility. When, toward the end of my stay, I was punished for a series of blunders by being ostracized, Niqi, darting from iglu to iglu as was her wont, occasionally looked in on me, too, in my solitude. "My, it's cold in here," she remarked on one such visit; "you have even fewer visitors than we do." I pitied her as I pitied myself at that time, but her fate was worse than mine. I could eventually go back to a world that accepted me, but isolation was Niqi's permanent lot.

Another bond between us was the fact that I found Niqi's impulsive actions reassuring and refreshing in face of the tremendous pressure to self-control that oppressed me, a volatile alien in Eskimo society. It was because her actions were "familiar" to me that I liked them; in my world, too, people sulk or shout when they are angry, ask questions when they are curious, cry when their feelings are hurt—so I empathized with Niqi when she did these things; it was as though I were witnessing a fragment of my own culture, and it gave me relief.

But my later liking for Niqi was always qualified by my awareness of the dislike with which the other Eskimos regarded her and by my resultant need to dissociate myself from her. Moreover, the fact that she was disliked by other people made it appallingly easy to make a scapegoat of her, in thought; the hostile atmosphere seemed to give me tacit permission to snarl at her mentally when things went wrong between me and other members of the group. Thus, when Niqi came to visit me during my period of ostracism, gratitude was never, alas, my sole reaction; I also felt threatened: aware of how low I had sunk in the eyes of the community, that Niqi should be my only visitor, and anxious that she should leave before my irritation at her presence took visible shape.

Another factor that complicated my relationship with Niqi, and with Nilak, too, was that they invariably took advantage of any friendliness on my part to ask for things (food, tobacco, pieces of clothing hide), and their requests were invariably for items that were in critically short supply. I hated to refuse but equally I hated to give. I felt more obligated to share with Inuttiaq, who fed me, and at the same time I felt an un-Eskimo but very kapluna pressure to be "impartial" to all families—not to mention a selfish urge to hoard the precious, rapidly dwindling supplies that linked me with my own world. The resultant tensions made it all too easy to accept in private thought the opinion of Pala's group that the married couple were leeches, "always jealous (*tuhuu*), always wanting, wanting (*piyuma*)."

III. Loneliness and Isolation

There was no plaintiveness in Niqi's voice when she remarked that there were even fewer visitors in my iglu than in hers, but I wondered to what extent Nilak's family shared my feeling that their isolation was lonely. I saw Tiguaq stroll by herself along the edge of the rapids or sit at home, cutting a jigsaw puzzle out of cardboard while the girls of Pala's and Inuttiaq's families went berry picking on the tundra. I saw Niqi wander by herself in the dry gully under the bluff Itimnaaqjuk, searching for a bit of soapstone to work into a pipe bowl, or bring a solitary load of twigs into camp while the other women went fuel gathering together in the opposite direction. Nilak, too, was most often alone when I saw him setting off on trapping or trading trips, unlike the other men, who traveled together in twos and threes.

Perhaps Nilak and his family were people of independent tastes, to whom periods of solitude were welcome interludes in the constant sociability of Utku life. I think it unlikely, however, that this was so. The absence of people is synonymous with loneliness for Utku, and loneliness, for them as for other Eskimos, is a central concern. There is a word, *hujuujaqnaqtuq(hujuujaq)*, which covers a multitude of unpleasant feelings and actions. If a man is prevented by lack of dogfeed from making a trip he has looked forward to: *hujuujaqnaqtuq*. If there is not enough to eat one day: *hujuujaqnaqtuq*. If a woman cannot make up her mind whether she prefers to sew or fish one morning, or if someone who is disliked comes to visit: *hujuujaqnaqtuq*. People who lie, steal, scold, or laugh too much are *hujuujaqnaqtuq*. Damp, windy weather, mosquitoes, autumn darkness, the dropping of the water in the rapids after the exciting turbulence of spring, all are *hujuujaqnaqtuq*. But if I asked the meaning of the word *hujuujaqnaqtuq* I was always told: "It is a feeling one has when one is alone and wishes for other people." Loneliness seems somehow the essence of unpleasantness. It is a feeling often complained of and one that people are solicitous, by visiting, to prevent those they care for from suffering.

I think that Nilak's family were not different from other Utku. There was a one-sidedness, a lack of reciprocity, in the pattern of their associations, which said that their solitude was not entirely of their own choosing. They sought company but were not sought in turn. Niqi and Nilak, especially, spent a great deal of time visiting at Pala's and at Inuttiaq's while these others visited them much more rarely. Tiguaq's company was sometimes sought by Pala's daughters Amaaqtuq and Akla, but the extent to which this was so depended on what alternative companionship was available to Amaaqtuq and Akla. During the summer, when Pala's granddaughter Kamik was home from school, she and Amaaqtuq were inseparable; and when another of Pala's granddaughters, Ipuituq's thirteen-year-old stepdaughter, Mitqut, was in camp, she and Akla were equally inseparable. At these times more than at others, Tiguaq was often alone.

There were other signs, too, that Nilak's family was lonely. Nilak had once expressed his loneliness, as Utku do, by building a cairn, up-ending a stubby thumb of granite on a boulder on the bluff above his usual summer tentsite. Cairns provide company for people.

Children provide company, too, and the married couple had more than once tried to compensate for their own lack of children by adopting the children of others, but Tiguaq was the only one who had remained with them. Two attempts to adopt daughters of Inuttiaq had aborted. One of these children, an infant twin of Raigili's, had died in the married couple's care. Perhaps Allaq had not been able to nurse both twins. When Allaq's most recent child, Qayaq, was born, Niqi had asked again if she might adopt the child, but this time Inuttiaq and Allaq had refused, saying the baby was too lovable (*naklik*) to part with. An orphaned niece and nephew had also lived with Nilak for short periods during their adolescence, but neither of these considered himself more than a visitor in the household. It was their other uncle, Nilak's brother, Nattiq, whom they considered their adopted father and with whom they lived except when he was hospitalized. So they said, and Nattiq and his wife, and Tiguaq too, confirmed that view. Only Nilak and Niqi saw it differently. In their view, the young people were their own adopted children; they lived with Nattiq merely as visitors.

The married couple's misperception spoke much, and so did the tenderness they showed to small creatures other than children. If children could not be adopted, baby birds and puppies could. Utku children showed toward baby birds a mixture of tenderness and callousness that I found hard to understand. Charmed by the littleness of the creatures, the children often sought them as pets, but a bird rarely survived the first few hours in the home of its tender captor, and when it was dead or dying, it was cast aside with seeming indifference. On occasion a child might even kill the bird deliberately, as Raigili squeezed the heart out of her captured longspur. Adults, like children, enjoyed stoning small birds, and Nilak and Niqi were no exception. Indeed, I once saw Niqi, like Raigili, gradually choke a longspur to death, as if absentmindedly, while her glance and her conversation were elsewhere, then toss it to a dog, who gulped it down. But tenderness toward birds seemed rarer among adults than among children. Was it an accident that it was in Nilak's family I saw the only signs of it? Nilak himself one day showed me a striking sight. He had stunned a longspur with a well-aimed pebble, but then instead of tossing it to the dogs, he picked it up, stroked its head gently for a few minutes and let it go, only to attack it again as it sat, still half-unconscious, on the gravel. It was Nilak's household, too, that once succeeded in keeping a pet ptarmigan alive for more than a week in a corner of the tent, carefully nourished with grass and flower stalks that Tiguaq and her mother collected.

There was a clearer difference between Nilak's family and others in the way they treated puppies. Ordinarily, puppies were ignored, except by the children, who played with them. They were fed, to be sure, until they were old enough to fend for themselves; they were protected from frost and from hungry dogs; but except in the first weeks of life, when they were still too young to steal, they were not allowed indoors. When they broke in, as they often did to scavenge, they were sent flying. The shrill yipping of beaten pups was a familiar sound in Utku camps, and the animals soon learned to run, cowering, from adults even when the latter had no aggressive intent at the moment. By contrast, the puppy in Nilak's household led a cozy life. Snuffed and caressed by all the members of the family until its head reached nearly to Tiguaq's knee, it slept on the family ikliq or in Tiguaq's lap and ate fish scraps from the family larder, which Niqi or Tiguaq cut into convenient morsels. It rode on Tiguaq's shoulders and romped with Niqi. Only when it was nearly old enough to be harnessed did Nilak chain it with the rest of his team to the dog line behind the camp. Once when Allaq and I were talking about the difference between the two words *naklingnaqtuq (naklik)* and *niviuqnaqtuq (niviuq)*, which describe warm feelings, I asked her whether either word applied to puppies. "Yes," she said, "puppies are *naklingnaqtuq*, to be taken care of, but they are not usually *niviuqnaqtuq*, caressable. Only people who have no small children are sometimes tender *(niviuq)* to puppies."

Tiguaq herself may have received more affection than usual, and it may have been more openly expressed, too, because she was all that her parents had. Nilak said as much one day. He was sitting in my tent, watching Tiguaq help me to transcribe some anecdotes she had recorded for me. I was playing the tape, phrase by phrase, while Tiguaq with crystal diction repeated each word so that I could write it down. Saarak was puttering around the tent, too, probably in search of raisins, as she usually was; I hid them in a different place every day. Nilak, who had been silently smoking, suddenly removed his pipe and said in a tender voice *(aqaq):* "She's very lovable *(naklik)*." I thought he meant

Saarak; people often said that about her as they watched her trotting around the camp. But he did not mean Saarak; he meant his own daughter, Tiguaq. I must have looked surprised. I had never before heard affection so openly expressed to a grown child. Nilak explained: "Because she's my only child I love *(naklik)* her." Nilak had thought one autumn of sending Tiguaq to the school at Inuvik where a few of the children, one from each of the other families, went to learn English. He had had poor success with the autumn caribou hunt, so clothing hides for the winter were scarce. At Inuvik the government would clothe Tiguaq. But when the time came she stayed at home. "We would miss *(unga)* her too much," said Niqi.

Tiguaq's reactions to her parents' isolation were never clear to me. Though she became one of my best language teachers and we spent many hours together, recording and writing out the stories she told of her experiences, she never spoke to me about people, either her own family or others. The stories were all about events: a caribou hunt (where they camped, what they ate); the coming of kapluna fishermen in an airplane (how many there were, how the Eskimos visited them, what they were given as presents); the famine (again, where they hunted, what they ate). Occasionally she would remark that an occurrence was funny *(tiphi)*, or unpleasant *(hujuujaq)*, or made one want to cry, but these observations, especially the unpleasant or sad ones, rarely had to do with the relationships of people with one another; they concerned bad weather, or hunger, or a caribou that escaped. The same was true of the stories told by other Utku; the people described in anecdotes often did amusing things, but they seldom made one unhappy. It was in ordinary conversation and in gossip that one heard about people's personal qualities and the reactions to them. And Tiguaq, unlike other Utku, never gossiped to me. Neither did she express pleasure in people, as others occasionally did. Perhaps because I belonged to the Other set of families, not to hers, she was moved, by shyness or by loyalty, to be discreet. Perhaps her loyalties were divided because, strange as it seemed to me, given the uneasy state of peace between the two families, Tiguaq was betrothed, had been betrothed as an infant, to Pala's son Mannik. Nothing obvious either in Tiguaq's behavior or in Mannik's, neither unusual closeness nor shyness, betokened their status; I would not have guessed it had Allaq not told me of it. Nevertheless, it is possible that Tiguaq's knowledge of her future may have made her reluctant to talk against Pala's family. So complete was her discretion, however, that I can only speculate on its causes.

Tiguaq was never, to my knowledge, the subject of gossip, either. From the distance at which I saw her she seemed a pleasant girl, evenly agreeable to everybody as she came and went, making tea, fetching fuel and water, helping to harness or unharness her father's team, or playing ball with the rest of the camp. It is difficult to find any vivid words to describe her; she was not colorless, yet there was nothing remarkable, nothing idiosyncratic about her to fasten on, either in disposition or in appearance—except that she was big and her mother little. I was relaxed, perhaps naïvely so, by this quality in her. Even during the period when I was ostracized by the community I never worried what Tiguaq thought of me. She was not actively friendly, but neither did I feel her actively hostile. On the other hand, I never felt I knew her. Perhaps it was partly this same evenness of temper that was responsible for the seeming absence of hostility toward her. Although she shared in her parents' isolation, yet I wondered, in her case more than in theirs, whether some of her solitude was of her own choosing. One thing was certain: she made much less effort to remedy her solitary condition than her parents did. Whereas Nilak and Niqi responded to the absence of visitors in their home by going visiting themselves, Tiguaq many times occupied herself at home instead of following, when Amaaqtuq went off somewhere with Kamik. Sometimes she sacrificed quite tangible gratifications for solitude. In the summer, when the clink of cups signaled to the camp that Allaq or Amaaqtuq or I was serving tea, Nilak and Niqi almost always appeared. Tiguaq appeared much less often. Even when her mother called to her where she sat alone in the tent to ask if she did not want to come and drink with the rest of us on the beach, her pleasant voice replied: "I don't feel like tea."

Why did she do this? It was unusual for anyone to refuse food or drink; indeed, the day's comforts were counted in cups of tea. Did she really not feel like tea, or was her withdrawal in part a response to her parents' situation: a proud refusal to eat, as her parents so often did, from the larder of those who shared grudg-ingly?

In other ways Tiguaq, though she sought out Pala's family less than her parents did, did not dissociate herself from her own fam-ily. She seemed to have a most friendly relationship with her mother. If a trip was sighted, returning from Gjoa Haven, while Niqi was sitting unaware at home, Tiguaq ran to give her the news. If Niqi was alone at home, which happened once or twice when severe laryngitis made her, for once, disinclined to visit, Tiguaq curtailed her own visits on the grounds that her mother would be lonely (*hujuujaq*) without company. When Nilak was away on trips Tiguaq even shared her mother's quilts.

Tiguaq also seemed to have more diversions in common with her mother than other grown daughters had with their mothers. I often found the pair occupied together when I went to visit: playing cards, coloring a picture book, sewing doll clothes. Once in a while, as I have said, they even tussled together, play-fully. Perhaps Niqi shared more of her daughter's frivolities because she was more childish than other women. Although in leisure moments there was a playfulness in most men and women that seemed childlike to my eyes and that combined oddly with their more serious qualities, certainly in some re-spects Niqi's playfulness was more extreme: I never saw another woman of her age romp with puppyish abandon, crouching and tugging at her opponent, as Niqi did with her daughter. Having such a small family to sew for and no little children to care for, she had almost as much leisure as a girl. I often thought that this might have been a truer, as well as a kinder, explanation for the inactivity that Pala's family called "Niqi's laziness." But it seems to me there could well have been a third strand in the bond between the two. Whether Tiguaq felt the exclusiveness of Pala's family directed against herself and, in response, withdrew, or whether she simply took it upon herself to share the emptiness surrounding Niqi, I do not know, but in some measure, surely, mother and daughter owed their intimacy to the isolation that they shared.

IV. Stinginess and Greed

The existence of ill feeling between Pala's extended family on the one hand and Nilak's household on the other seemed to be little affected by the proximity of the two. Regardless of whether or not they were camped together, the tension between them existed, on our side often emerging secretly into nasty jokes and murmured comments uttered with hostilely narrowed eyes. I assumed that Nilak's family privately returned all our compliments in kind, but as Inuttiaq's adopted daughter I was in a poor position to find out, since, I think, daughterly loyalties were ascribed to me.

Though the specific sources of tension varied with the seasons, nevertheless, generally speaking, almost all the complaints directed against the married couple were concerned with their unhelpfulness, greed (*piyuma, tuhuu*), and bad temper (*ningaq, urulu, huaq, qiquq*). Bad temper the couple were certainly guilty of on occasion; but I was never sure whether Nilak's so-called "unhelpfulness" and "greed" were really greater than other people's or whether he merely acted as anyone else, especially as anyone who lacked close kin, would have done toward people outside his own extended family.

Although the ideal says that "everybody" should be helped, in reality, help is extended much more willingly to close relatives than to others, and people, knowing this, sometimes prefer to do without, rather than appeal to outsiders, if what they need cannot be provided by close kinsmen. The reluctance to ask from people outside the extended family is phrased as a fear of being unkindly refused. (Refusals are almost always construed as unkind (*quya*).) Similarly, a major motivation for giving to people in the larger group is the fear of being thought unkind. Thus, I was always reassured when I hesitated to ask a favor: "Don't be afraid (*ilira*) to ask us; we are kind (*quya*); we won't refuse." These "reassurances," to be sure, intensified rather than lessened my hesitant feelings, which were of exactly opposite order to those the Eskimos imagined, deriving, as they did, from the fear that the person would *fail* to refuse in the event that my request proved an imposition.

So great is the embarrassment of refusing and being refused

that requests are, as a rule, made most indirectly; if one wishes to ignore the hint one can do so. But in my own experience when requests were made they were usually of such modest proportions: a handful of tea, a lampful of kerosene, half a cup of sugar, that I, at least, found it impossible to refuse without feeling ashamed. Perhaps this was the petitioner's intent. Very frequently, moreover, the responsibility for requests is attributed to someone else. One may say, "So-and-so told me to ask" (assuming a cloak of docility—a Good quality), or: "I ask because so-and-so is cold" or "hungry" (presenting oneself as generous and thoughtful). Appeal on behalf of a small child is particularly effective. Inuttiaq frequently used concern for *me* as his excuse for making a request, a maneuver whose true character it took me some time to recognize. Being himself cold, he would say to me, "You are cold; make yourself some soup." He knew well that when I made it he would be offered some, but as the soup was mine, and I at best a pseudo-daughter, he was reluctant to ask directly.

Actually, it very rarely happens that a person refuses a request outright. Instead of saying "no," he may say "I don't know" or "maybe," smiling warmly the while; he may deny that he has the item requested, or he may pass the responsibility for the refusal to someone else, as Tiguaq did one day. Seeing that she had become restless, apparently bored after an hour or two of tape-recording words for me, I asked her if she wanted to play ball with the others, whose laughing shouts were audible outside the tent. "Who knows," said she, looking embarrassed; "I don't know." Then turning to Amaaqtuq, who opportunely appeared in the doorway at that moment: "Are you going to tell me to go play ball?" "Yes," said Amaaqtuq, and off went Tiguaq, her problem solved.

However, it sometimes happens that even when there has been no request, a failure to *offer* assistance spontaneously will be interpreted as deliberate unkindness. And when people, whoever they may be, are slow to offer help, or show themselves jealous and greedy (*tuhuu*), the wider values, "people should be good to everybody," are invoked against them—not, by and large, in direct accusations, but in private gossip or in the moral generalities of Sunday sermons. I expect that these wider values are traditional ones, as the fear of refusing and being refused seems profoundly ingrained; but nowadays they are phrased in Christian terms: "Jesus says we should help everybody; we should be kind *(quya)* to everybody and love *(naklik)* them because they are our brothers—kaplunas, too."

Nilak's "unkindness *(quya)*" and "unhelpfulness" often took the form of a failure to offer spontaneous assistance. And the Christian values were often invoked against him, as he in turn invoked them against Qavvik, and no doubt against Inuttiaq and Pala when I was not around to hear. I never knew Nilak to refuse to lend a tool when asked, or to refuse to carry goods from Gjoa Haven for the other men (though they accused him often enough of not wanting to do it); but there were occasions on which he failed to offer food that the others felt he should have offered.

One instance of this occurred during the springtime, the season of greatest food scarcity. For a month or more, Inuttiaq, Pala, and Nilak had been camped together near the Rapids, living off the fish caches that they had each made in that general area during the previous autumn. Then one morning Nilak and his family packed up their sled and, as is customary, departed without saying a word of their intention or of farewell to the rest of us. They set up their tent on a point of land two or three miles away, just visible in the distance from where the rest of us remained. They may have moved because the new campsite was closer to their caches (which it was), or because they were tired of our company, or perhaps (as I suspected at the time) because they wanted to eat their bacon, newly arrived from Gjoa Haven, in solitary peace. I do not know; they did not offer a reason and we did not ask for one. We simply peeked out of our tents to watch them packing and remarked to one another: "Nilak seems to be leaving."

It was soon after the two groups had parted company that Pala's and Inuttiaq's families ran out of dog food. The autumn fish caches were used up, and whereas it was possible to shoot enough birds to feed the human beings in camp from day to day, the dogs were another matter. The men of our camp went to pay a friendly call at Nilak's camp one day and returned home with most of the contents of a cache of fish roe, which Nilak had given them. It was enough for one meal for the two teams of dogs.

But it was not long after the receipt of that gift that Pala remarked to me in the colorless, conversational voice in which people mask their annoyance: "Nilak doesn't offer us any dog food. It can't be helped *(ayuqnaq).*" I asked how many caches Nilak had left. "Two," said Pala. He did not mention a cache of roe that I next day discovered we still had, ourselves.

I felt quite in sympathy with Nilak's unwillingness to share his limited food supplies. It would be several weeks yet before the fish would begin to run and food would become plentiful again. Inuttiaq and Pala planned to try their luck at Kajat, north at the river bend, when the fish caches at Itimnaaqjuk were exhausted; there were sometimes a few large fish at Kajat in the springtime, and birds were more plentiful there than at the Rapids. After the ice went out in July, we would return to the Rapids to spear the migrating salmon trout. But Nilak's family had no canoe in which to travel after the ice broke up (except for a leaky old rowboat that Pala had lent them), and they were apparently unwilling to make the long trip on foot, as people had done before the government gave them canoes. So they planned to stay by themselves at Itimnaaqjuk, eking out their caches until the fish began to migrate. Under these circumstances two caches would hardly provide a luxurious diet for three people and ten dogs, I thought.

I was in sympathy also, on the whole, with the provident spirit that resulted in Nilak's having proportionately more caches than Pala's group had to begin with. Not only had he cached fish during the autumn, as we had; he had also checked his fishnets nearly every day all winter instead of going jigging for trout, as the rest of us did. The others criticized Nilak for not going jigging: "He has fine warm fur clothes, but he never goes fishing." (That is, he had not the excuse of being cold for staying at home.) But though trout make better eating than the disagreeable little whitefish that are caught in the nets, far fewer of them are caught in a day's fishing; and as a result of Nilak's conscientious net-checking he still had a plentiful store of whitefish to carry with him to his spring camp in March. Inuttiaq and Pala had none; they had to begin using their autumn caches at once.

Inuttiaq's and Pala's households were not in sympathy with Nilak's providence. Allaq expressed their attitude one summer day when she explained to me why Niqi never boiled fish for the camp to eat, as we did. Allaq said: "They are like children: fearful *(kappia);* they're afraid there will be a food shortage." Nilak always cached everything he caught, and every day he and his family shared our meal. They were never penalized for their failure to contribute but were given equal portions with us, as is proper in camps where all camp members eat together.

Allaq was scornful, but I wondered whether Nilak's prudence might not be a natural result of his isolated social position. Perhaps he feared—with some justification—that, in case of a real food shortage, he would receive minimal aid from the other households. His failure to contribute to the common pot could also have been a form of retaliation, however unthinking, against the treatment that he and his family received at the hands of the others. To be sure, it might have been true, as Allaq claimed, that he had been just as ungenerous with his own brothers. But had he been? A lack of concern for others might well have been heightened in Nilak's household by the rejecting attitudes of Pala's kin.

I speculated, too, on whether the "greed" *(piyuma, tuhuu)* of which Nilak was accused behind his back might also have its roots in his social isolation. Having no close kin from whom to make requests when he needed something, Nilak was forced more frequently than were the members of Pala's kin group to ask favors from outsiders, who resented it and called it greedy. "Nilak is jealous *(tuhuu),*" they said; "he's always *wanting* things *(piyuma)."* And they secretly laughed at him when he walked along the river shores after the kapluna sportsmen had left in the autumn, looking for fishhooks that they might have dropped.

"Wanting" was not a trait peculiar to Nilak, no matter what others might claim. Inuttiaq and Pala were nothing loath to join Nilak in a minute inspection of the kaplunas' rubbish dump as soon as the latter had left. And when, one day as Inuttiaq was sorting his fishhooks, I remarked on their quantity, he said with feeling: "*I* don't have a lot; *they* do"—pointing toward Pala's and Nilak's tents.

But, as usual, Nilak's behavior was judged by a standard different from the one applied to Inuttiaq and Pala. Allaq one day expressed more fully than usual the feeling she shared with her family. "Nilak always tells everybody when he succeeds in trapping a fox; he wants people to be jealous *(tuhuu)* of him. He himself is jealous when other people have things. He is jealous of households whose men have just come back from trading and of people who have fish when fish are scarce. Nakliguhuktuq says we ought not to be jealous, we ought to love *(naklik)* everybody. *"We* (the households of Pala, Ipuituq, and Inuttiaq) are not very jealous; *we're good."* Curious to know how Allaq would react, I replied tactlessly: "All of you tell everybody when you acquire things, too." "Yes," Allaq said, "but *we're* not jealous; *we're* just talking sociably."

V. Ostracism and Confrontation

None of the criticisms that Pala's kin made of Nilak were ever thrown directly at him. Even his tendency to scold *(huaq)* Niqi and Tiguaq, which was, from his critics' point of view, one of Nilak's worst faults, was never remarked on to his face. If his scolding was overheard at a distance, people listened with narrowed eyes and murmured disapprovingly to each other, "Mmmmm," and that was all. Later, in the intimacy of the family, someone might observe in a cheerful tone, followed by a little laugh: "Nilak is angry *(urulu)* with his wife; it's annoying *(urulu)."* There would be no answering comment.

Niqi was never directly criticized, either. She might be teased if she went to the hilltop to seek caribou or if she clumsily fell off the edge of the ikliq and spilled the fish boiling on the primus stove. But her more serious aberrancies were greeted with silence, and were mocked or commented on only when she and the other members of her family were absent.

Only once did I see a positive attempt made to direct Niqi's behavior into more socially appropriate channels. By far the more usual technique for coping with her was to ignore her. Not only did people fail to comment on Niqi's peculiarities within her hearing; they also ignored her presence—not openly and dramatically, but so subtly that I did not notice they ostracized her until I had been living with Inuttiaq's family for three months or more. The treatment simply consisted in letting all initiative for interaction come from Niqi. Pala's womenfolk almost never visited her unless there was no one else in camp to visit, or unless Nilak's household happened to have something particularly delectable in the larder that day, such as caribou or dried fish, which could only be tasted by visiting there. But it was more than that. People were completely passive toward her. If she smiled or spoke to others, they smiled or spoke to her in return; her visits were impassively accepted by her neighbors; and if she was present among a group of visitors when tea or food was served, she received tea or·food with the others. But that was all. I rarely heard anyone except her child-companions initiate a conversation with her, or respond meaningfully to her giggling remarks. The usual reply was an indifferent "yes," or "who knows?" which left a residue of chill perhaps all the heavier for the deceptively warm tone in which it was uttered.

Perhaps the fact that Niqi and the others rarely addressed one another by kin terms might also be seen as a subtle form of ostracism. Almost all other Utku, including Nilak and Tiguaq, did address one another by kin terms, real or putative. Niqi may have been differently treated in this respect, however, only because of her witlessness; though the others knew how to address Niqi as a kinswoman, Niqi herself did not know most of the terms that would have been proper for her to use. The basic principle governing the behavior of Pala's group toward the married couple seemed to be that the surface smoothness of camp life should not be ruffled, and the latter did their part, too, in maintaining a facade of friendliness. No relationships were broken outright, and no one saw occasion to blame himself for unkindness. On the other hand, every occasion was taken to blame the other faction, in secret, and tangible evidence of friendship was hard to find.

The quality of the relationship as I saw it between the two kin groups was especially apparent in our summer and autumn camps at the start of my second year at Back River. I am not sure that the interaction between the families then was typical of their summer camps; perhaps an unusual heightening of hostility for some reason made feelings that were often successfully submerged more visible. In any case, that season, relations, unexpectedly smooth at first, gradually deteriorated until, by autumn, comments on the defects of Nilak's household were daily fare in the other qaqmaqs, and the remarks were accompanied by acts, too, that signaled that the air was highly charged.

It was mid-July when Pala and Inuttiaq and their households rejoined Nilak at the Rapids after the spring separation that I described earlier. This time, unlike the previous summer, we all camped beside Nilak on one small gravel beach by the rapids; and here in August we were joined by Ipuituq and his family. So the camp was ultimately composed of the four households of Pala, his two sons-in-law, Inuttiaq and Ipuituq, and Nilak.

Nilak's family, who had been living alone at the Rapids since late in May, greeted us on our arrival with as much apparent pleasure as they themselves had been greeted on their return from caribou hunting the year before. Niqi, sitting with her binoculars on the hilltop beside the camp, had spotted us approaching in the distance, and tea was hot on the fire when we arrived. There was much to talk about over tea: the height of the river in the spring floods, the campsites where we had stayed on our peregrinations along the river, the weather, the food situation, the measles epidemic that had been brought by the returning school children in June. Nilak's family had had measles, as we had; all of us had run very short of food during the worst of the epidemic; and several young dogs in both Pala's and Nilak's teams had died of illness (distemper, perhaps). But now the trout were running well, and Nilak already had a great number hung up to dry on lines behind the camp. Inuttiaq and Pala's son Mannik had shot two caribou on the way back to the Rapids. Allaq brought out some of the meat, and Niqi boiled it for a festive dinner for us all.

For the first few days after our arrival, relations between the two family groups were more convivial than I had yet seen them. Inuttiaq, Mannik, and Nilak were absorbed in their fishing. Balancing on boulders around the edges of a foaming pool, they stabbed dramatically at the leaping trout with their long tridents, shouting, posturing aggressively, and, especially if the fish escaped, uttering streams of vigorous remarks for the amusement of their companions. Pala watched them through his telescope from the top of the bluff above the pool, and sometimes, taking a throwline, he went down to fish alongside the spearmen. The women, when they had time, often wandered over to watch with Pala, or to cast a throwline; but most of their day was spent in splitting the fish for drying and hanging them from lines, where their orange flesh flamed in the sunlight against the blue river.

Fish drying was one job that the women of each kin group did separately. Pala's and Inuttiaq's women worked together, and Nilak's worked apart, since their fish would be dried and stored separately from those of the other families. But when dry lichen was to be gathered for the campfires we combined forces. All of the six women and girls went together up into the hills behind the camp to pull the lichen and to help pack it home; and sometimes the smaller children also followed, not so much to help as to find berries to eat and small birds to stone.

Almost every evening one of Pala's daughters, Amaaqtuq or Allaq, boiled a tub full of fresh trout heads from Inuttiaq's or Mannik's catch, and when the cry of "patau (boiled fish)!" went up, the whole camp gathered on the gravel beach before the tents to eat, the men from one tray and the women from another, while the children ran back and forth among the adults, looking for choice morsels. Afterwards, as we lay on the beach, smoking in the cool evening sunlight, one of the men, belching comfortably, would observe to the circling gulls that he felt like drinking tea; whereupon his daughter or his wife would slowly rise, fetch a kettle of water from the river, and take it to one of the blackened stone fireplaces that lined the edge of our gravel strip. Usually one of the other women decided that one kettle was too little for so many people, and she would start a second kettle brewing. Soon there would be a cluster of women and children gathered sociably around the fireplaces while the tea heated and the men, hooded against the mosquitoes, lay smoking together on the gravel higher up by the tents.

In the first days after we joined Nilak at the summer site, Allaq sometimes joined Niqi at the fireplace when the latter was brewing tea, and chatted with her in a friendly manner, behavior that was in striking contrast to her treatment of Niqi in other camps where I had seen them together. Sometimes she even visited Niqi in her tent, as she very rarely had during the winter and spring. My surprise at this change was the greater because, as we made our way back down the river toward the summer camp, Allaq had predicted that when we first arrived Niqi would be even more unpleasantly *(hujuujaq)* volatile than usual: "She will smile too broadly and get angry *(urulu)* easily." Perhaps Niqi did not fulfill the spiteful prediction. Or perhaps Allaq's own euphoria at being with people again was stronger than her dislike of volatility. In any case, only friendliness showed in her behavior.

Bit by bit, however, the first conviviality ceased. Inuttiaq, Mannik, and Nilak still fished in the same pool, but after the first day, Nilak fished on one side of it while the other two, and Pala, when he joined them, fished from the other side. Conversations, which had continued until midnight the first two or three nights after our arrival, stopped earlier; people were often in bed by 9:30. Allaq again drew away from Niqi, only smiling at the latter's overtures in order to preserve the surface equilibrium of camp life. And soon it seemed to me that, not consistently but fairly often, when people lay in front of the tents in the evenings, I had to choose which of two kin groups to join: Nilak's or the other, which comprised the families of Pala, Inuttiaq, and, in August, Ipuituq. In the days of wider sociability or when the women formed their own circle apart from the men, there had been no problem of choice.

I had become accustomed in earlier camps to this social cliquishness and to the simmering dislike that underlay it, so that I accepted it as a matter of course when Allaq, feeling lonely or wanting to soothe the cranky baby with a change of scene, took her sewing to her sister's tent instead of to Niqi's, where Niqi and Tiguaq always sewed by themselves. However, toward the end of the summer the situation deteriorated to such a point, especially between Niqi and the others, that I began to wonder if something out of the ordinary was the matter. I do not know what brought about the change. A number of factors may have contributed: the cumulative effect over the weeks of the strains engendered by summer life, when shared activities drew the families together for many more hours in the day than during the winter; autumnal vissicitudes, the dark, chill days coinciding with increased pressure of work in preparation for winter; some injury, real or imaginary, that rankled more than usually in Niqi;

tensions that I myself caused at this time—all of these may have been irritants, which were reflected in increased friction between the family factions. In part, too, though I think not wholly, the increase in hostility that I felt in the camp may have been an artifact of my perception, which no doubt became increasingly sensitive to expressions of dislike as a result of my own strained position in the group. In any case, I began to see hostility in a variety of acts, and later, words. I noticed Niqi's behavior first. She stopped accompanying the women of Pala's kin when they went to collect plants to feed the cooking fires. She preferred to bring in her contributions separately, or in company with Tiguaq. And one day when the autumn winds had scattered the fires from the summer fireplaces that all had used together on the beach in front of the tents, two new fireplaces appeared in sheltered nooks on opposite sides of the camp: one for Niqi, the other for Pala's women. Nobody commented on these developments in my hearing so, as discreetly as possible, I sought explanations. When Niqi returned one day with a load of lichen, I observed: "You're all alone." "Yes," she said, "I want to be alone." Again, I remarked to one of Pala's daughters: "Niqi seems to have built a new fireplace of her own," and the reply came: "She wants to."

But not all of Niqi's independent actions received the same tolerance. As autumn wore on, even behavior that had passed uncriticized during the summer began to incur the wrath of Pala's womenfolk. During the summer the fact that Nilak's family regularly stored their own fish catch against future emergencies while as regularly partaking of Inuttiaq's, Ipuituq's, and Mannik's catch, and the fact that, as a natural consequence, Niqi never helped cook the patau, did not seem to be a *major* source of strain between the two groups. Pala's group gossiped about Nilak's "fearfulness *(kappia),*" of course, but they seemed resigned to it, simply remarking that "Niqi never makes patau; it's very laughable *(tiphi).*"

But Niqi's failure to help with the work of cooking in the autumn camp *was* increasingly censured. The wrath derived some of its force from the fact that autumn is the busy season of sewing winter furs, and the two seamstresses in Pala's group, Allaq and Amaruq, had a much heavier load of sewing than Niqi, with her tiny family, did. Under these circumstances Niqi's irresponsible behavior was one straw too many. It takes about two hours to boil a five-gallon drum of frozen fish heads, and two hours of a short autumn day is a long time to devote to cooking when men are waiting for their winter clothing. They are uncomfortable hours, too, as the cook shivers outdoors over a tiny blaze, coaxing it every few seconds with fresh twigs; protected from the worst winds, but not from the cold, by a high encircling wall of snow, and forced by that wall to suffer choking clouds of smoke. Indeed, the job is so unpleasant during these autumn months that only mature women are entrusted with it. "Girls would be too cold to cook the fish well," they say. But Niqi, all unheeding, went fishing with Nilak and Tiguaq. So busy were the three with fishing that they even gave up collecting a share of the fuel, and as before, they usually failed to contribute fish to the pot from which they ate.

Allaq and Amaruq, the unfortunate cooks, murmured mightily behind Niqi's back about her failure to cook, when they had so much sewing to do. Lazy, they called her, though I was not so sure that was the proper explanation. She kept busy enough, fishing, and, later in the season, trapping, often walking considerable distances in these pursuits. But none of her activity was for benefit of the community—only for benefit of Niqi and family.

Dissatisfaction with Niqi's failure to share in the work of the camp grew in intensity, becoming a consistent theme in the pattern of hostile feeling that enmeshed the two family groups. Other hateful remarks, directed not only at Niqi but also at her husband, were also heard with increasing frequency. It was as though the annoyance at Niqi's frivolity had activated and focused all the hostility that festered under the smooth exterior of camp life. Some of the remarks were utterly without point, like the one Allaq made when she caught sight of Nilak's family, fishing in the distance along a route she had to travel on her morning's errand: "It will be unpleasant (hujuujaq) to pass them." Other comments rang the familiar notes: "Nilak's family is stingy; they are jealous (tuhuu); they never want to help."

It was at this time, too, that hostility broke the surface in other petty acts, especially acts of stinginess. Autumn is the season in which kapluna goods are naturally scarcest, since people by that time have been cut off from their source of supply in Gjoa Haven for several months. Although trout are plentiful and actual starvation is not ordinarily feared then, people do feel pinched by the lack of tobacco, tea, and bannock. For me, these needs assumed additional importance in the fall, because life at that season offered such a small variety of comforts, and also because the time at which these things would become available again was nearing but had not yet arrived. I do not know whether the Utku shared these more intense autumn cravings, but tensions did seem to focus increasingly around possessions as the season wore on. Nilak's family requested one of our last six teaspoonfuls of tea. It was given, but resentful comments followed: "They shouldn't have asked; they knew there was only a little left." It was the same with the chocolate from my emergency supplies, which we drank, weak and bitter without milk or sugar, after the tea was gone. And then there was the salt. Nilak's household still had salt, it was reported; so did I. Although it was never used in the cooking itself, it gave a welcome tang to the broth that was drunk after the fish itself had been eaten. I was indifferent to the taste and seldom bothered to hunt out the salt at broth time, preferring to drink quickly, before the icy air had had a chance to dissipate the comforting heat of the liquid, and also before the possibility of a second cup had vanished into the stomachs of the fast-drinking Eskimos. Allaq knew this, as did the others, but such was her hostility toward Nilak's family that when Niqi demurred at replenishing the supply for the communal patau, saying, "Yiini never uses hers," Allaq lied to her: "Yes, she does." So Niqi was forced to supply the salt.

There were two days when Allaq made bannock out of the remains of my supply for the households of her own kin group, while Nilak's family was away, fishing. On one of these occasions they came back, from our point of view, a few minutes too soon: just as the finished bannock was being distributed. When Niqi popped expectantly into our qaqmaq and stood there, giggling, Allaq, who had been cutting the bannocks into halves, one half per person, silently cut off a third of one of the bannocks for Nilak's household. She smiled with apologetic warmth as she handed it to her visitor: "I didn't know you were going to be here." On the other occasion Nilak's family got none at all. They arrived as we were eating; the bannock was already divided. Nilak himself looked in this time, smiling handsomely, as always. We smiled back, as always, and went on eating. It would have been proper to offer a small share, but nobody said anything. When Nilak had gone on his way to Pala's qaqmaq, Allaq whispered: "He wanted to eat bannock."

There was also an incident involving a caribou legskin. I knew nothing of the matter until one afternoon Allaq, followed immediately by Niqi, came into our qaqmaq, carrying an enamel cup of the sort that everybody owned. She went over to her place on the ikliq and drew out of the piled household goods the bundle of legskins that she was saving for winter mitten material. One of these she handed to Niqi with her usual warm smile. Niqi beamed, giggled, and said: "A fine skin." Allaq replied graciously: "A fine cup," and Niqi darted out. When Niqi had gone, Allaq said to me with lowered voice and narrowed eyes: "All the time, all the time she kept saying she wanted a legskin. They have mitten material, but she kept saying she wanted a legskin. She was so noisy about it, I had to give her one. Always wanting, wanting (*piyuma*), those people. I gave her the worst one; the fur is all coming out of it. Very funny (*tiphi*)." And she laughed. She repeated the story of that trade several times, later, both to her own sisters and to a neighbor woman in the winter camp: "I gave her a bad one; it was funny."

Niqi finally did make patau one day about this time, and on the same day she and her family also brought in a sled load of birch twigs for the fire. It was the only such gesture they made during the six weeks in which we lived side by side in autumn qaqmaqs; and to bring it about took an attack which, though subtle to my ear, was nevertheless far more than usually direct. The technique used was hinting, and the hints began some days before they took effect. The first one I heard was ostensibly a joke. Allaq's brother Putuguk was visiting in camp one day. Because he lived with his adoptive father, Qavvik, the head of the third Utku kin group, we seldom saw him except in winter, but he still considered Pala's children his brothers and sisters and was treated by them, too, as a brother. On this particular day he had stopped off in our camp on his way to fetch some of Qavvik's fish from a cache nearby, and visiting in Pala's qaqmaq he had no doubt heard the story of Niqi's delinquency. Later, he came to drink tea with us, as well, and found his sisters Allaq and Amaruq there, discussing which of them was going to make the patau that afternoon. Niqi was also there, saying nothing. "Niqi is going to make patau," said Putuguk with a genial laugh. Allaq also added in a joking tone a comment whose substance I did not catch. Niqi giggled. Allaq made the patau. Ten days later the subject was brought up again in my hearing. This time Allaq's sister Amaaqtuq said something to Allaq about the latter's making the patau that afternoon. Allaq had earlier asked Amaaqtuq if she would pack the baby, Qayaq, while she, Allaq, cooked, so I was startled when Allaq, instead of responding to her sister, turned to Niqi and said in a tone that to my ear rang with surprised innocence: "I thought *you* were going to make the patau." Niqi, mumbling something about having "told Tiguaq to make it, no joke," giggled and ran out. That day we finally did eat patau cooked by Niqi. Some of the fish she took from her own supply; the rest she solicited from the other households, and she heaped a five-gallon tub as full as Pala's women ever did. Several times that night after Niqi had gone home, Allaq remarked on the painfully empty state of her stomach, and the next afternoon when she was preparing to take her turn at the cooking pot, she remarked: "Today *I'm* going to make patau because yesterday I didn't have enough to eat."

6

Kapluna Daughter

There was never any end to the mutual dislike with which Nilak's and Pala's kin regarded each other. Though its expression waxed and waned, it rarely, if ever, disappeared altogether. It made no difference whether Niqi made patau or not; if one excuse for hostility failed, another was found, and so a steady round of incidents provided opportunities for watching how the Utku handled the irritations engendered by, or expressed in, bad temper, stinginess, and unhelpfulness.

My own relationship with the Utku gave me even richer opportunities to observe the handling of difficult social situations, because the differences between my behavior and that of the Utku could not help but create difficulties, on occasion, for the latter. On the whole, the situations that created tension between me and my Utku hosts were different from those that disturbed the peace between Pala's kin and Nilak's, because the nature of my aberrancy was different from that of Nilak and Niqi. The married couple were, perhaps, not very good Eskimos in the eyes of Pala's kin, but I was not Eskimo at all. It was not only the strangeness of my face and tongue that made me different. I was incongruous in other ways as well. I was an adult, yet as ignorant of simple skills as a child. I was a woman, yet I lacked the usual womanly attributes of husband and children; a "daughter," yet independently wealthy and accustomed to organizing my own life. This last incongruity, especially, gave rise to tensions that were different from those in which the married couple were involved. Another difference between my situation and theirs was that whereas the standard to which their behavior should have conformed was clear, it may not always have been so clear in my case. Since I was a foreigner, more tolerance may have been felt for my peculiarities than for theirs.

In one respect, however, there was real similarity between Niqi and myself, namely in the degree of our volatility and in the demand, which applied equally to us both, that the volatility be controlled. Toward the end of my stay I learned much about the way in which I was regarded from the resemblance between the treatment accorded to Niqi on the one hand and to me on the other. It was only by degrees, however, that the way in which I was treated became similar to the way in which Niqi was treated, and the evolution of that similarity was instructive in itself.

I. Stranger and Guest: Graciousness

In retrospect, my relationship with the Utku seems to divide approximately into three phases, in which from the Utku point of view I was first a stranger and curiosity, then a recalcitrant child, and finally a confirmed irritant. This does not mean that I was never liked. I was, at times. Days and weeks passed very harmoniously, but I want to describe here the less harmonious aspects of the relationship, which illuminate the ways in which the Utku handled the problems created by my presence.

The initial phase of the relationship I have already described in part. In this period I was treated with all the solicitude that is accorded an honored guest. When I visited in the Eskimo tents, I was given the softest seat, often a seat on the family ikliq, and, like the always privileged children, I was offered milk and sugar in my tea. My interests were tended equally in my own tent. When I offered food to my visitors, they never took advantage of my ignorance of an owner's prerogatives; I was always urged to serve myself first, the largest pieces of the bannock that I hospitably fried were always urged upon me, and if I offered to share a meal with a visitor, the latter never failed to ask whether I had finished eating, before he took the pot I held out to him. My fish supply was always replenished before I felt the need, and often even the usual division of labor between men and women stood in abeyance as men offered to fetch me water from the river or to refuel my primus.

To be sure, such solicitous acts were not wholly altruistic. Neither did they necessarily signify that I was liked. They were, not surprisingly, motivated in part by fear *(ilira)*, which was admitted only months later, and by a desire for profit, if a word of such exploitative connotations can be used of the very moderate requests that Utku make of their wealthy kapluna visitors. My hosts expected to be rewarded for their solicitude, both by my goodwill in a broad sense and by the tangible expression of that goodwill: a share in my kapluna supplies. As Inuttiaq put it once when I thanked a young man for repairing a tear in my tent wall: "If you are grateful, make tea." In the early days, before I was integrated into Utku life to the point where I might reasonably be expected to share my goods as a participating member of the community, people did not often ask for gifts; however, in addition to the services they performed for me, they besieged me daily with small bone and wood objects, nearly all the crude result of an hour or two of work: miniature models of fishhooks, fishing jigs, fish spears, seals, airplanes, and sleds, which their makers wished to trade for "a little bit" of tobacco, tea, sugar, milk, flour, or oats. Generous at first, I quickly became alarmed when I saw how quickly and in what quantity these trade goods were manufactured; but each request was so modest, and the Utku set such a precedent for generosity in their treatment of me that it was difficult—as I am sure they hoped it would be—to refuse them.

So in this early period of my stay, I was both guest and provider; and I played another role, as well, that of comedian. My curious appearance and manner were closely, though covertly, observed and gave the community endless amusement. The unpronounceable plant names that I was required to repeat for entertainment on my first meeting with the married couple were brought out on other occasions, too, together with other known tongue-twisters, like the intensifying form "-hlkha," which I could never pronounce except as "-lzga." "Yiini," someone would observe, with a twinkle, "Niptaihlkha (it's terribly foggy)." And when I, knowing full well the nature of the game, obligingly agreed: "Eee, yes, indeed, it's terribly foggy: niptailzga," then my audience would be overcome with laughter, in which I was expected to join. Amaaqtuq once remarked to me: "You're nice (*quvia*) because you're comical (*tiphi*)."

So convivial was the laughter of the Utku and so gracious their attempts to smooth the unknown ground for me that I am chagrined to remember how thorny this first period was. Of course it could not have been otherwise. In such a new and strange situation it was impossible even to simulate the composure that the Eskimos would have approved of and that would have made the relationship between us comfortable and harmonious. I was afraid in those first weeks: afraid of freezing to death, of going hungry, of being seriously ill and unable to reach help. All of these fears, natural enough in anyone who undertakes to isolate himself in a completely foreign environment, were aggravated in my case by the exaggerated warnings with which I had been bombarded before setting out on my venture. I had been at pains to conceal from my well-wishers that their anxieties had borne fruit, but they had. By the time I arrived at Back River I was not at all convinced that my undertaking was rational and feasible. Long before the temperature reached zero, I had acquired three frost-reddened toes and twelve chilblains on my hands, which convinced me that I would never be able to survive the winter temperatures of thirty to seventy degrees below zero. The fear itself, of course, added to my chill, lowering my body temperature perceptibly and causing me to curse futilely at my anxiety.

My fear of food shortage was not quite as realistic, in a material sense, as the fear of cold. Though I had been alarmed in Ottawa by reports of "recurrent famines" at Back River, that myth had been exploded by a sensible priest in Gjoa Haven, who had experience of the region. The value that my kapluna food supplies had for me, therefore, was primarily symbolic. It was hard to accustom myself to a diet of raw fish, eaten skin, scales, and all. I never did succeed in mastering the skin, but at first I tried, valiantly, though the scales stuck in my throat and the slime made me retch. Fish were usually plentiful, and I was rarely really hungry; nevertheless I craved the solace of oatmeal, dates, boiled rice, and bannock, and much of the time my secret thoughts crept guiltily around one problem: how best to create opportunities for gorging myself on these familiar foods without having to share them with the visitors who were so generous with their own food. It is hard for anyone who has not experienced isolation from his familiar world to conceive the vital importance of maintaining symbolic ties with that world and the sense of deprivation that results from their absence. One can be driven to lengths that seem ludicrous once one is safely back on home ground. Unpacking on my return, I was amazed to find eight sesame seeds that I had hoarded, carefully wrapped in tinfoil, for an emergency: a time of emotional starvation. Food provided many comforts beyond the fundamental satisfaction of a full stomach. Whenever anything went awry; whenever I failed to make myself understood; when Saarak wailed at the sight of me; or when the cries of the seagulls reminded me of home, my solace was food. Though I did not know it at the time, my dependence on food as a solace was very Eskimo; the problems were that I preferred my kapluna foods to the plentiful fish, and that the demand of the Eskimos for my limited supplies was great.

Frightened as I was of cold and hunger, mishaps seemed to occur constantly, and the smallest one assumed momentous proportions in my imagination. When I discovered that I had left my gun on the plane that brought me in; when I found that I had bought all the accoutrements of a fishnet but had neglected to buy the net itself; when I learned that I had been misinformed about the date at which the Utku normally move to their winter campsite and that as a consequence I had brought too little kerosene to the autumn site; when I understood Allaq to tell me that the caribou hides I had brought were not suitable for my winter clothing, ridiculous as it seems to me now, I was filled with panic. I had no realistic image of what the winter would be like, no idea whether the Utku would deal with it in ways that I could tolerate, and, worse, no way of allaying my apprehension, since I could not speak Eskimo.

Equally appalling, however, was the thought of giving up and going home, after having stubbornly resisted all those well-meant warnings. "I told you so"s rang in my imagination and hardened my resolve. Nevertheless, the conflicting wishes and fears hammered for expression and, on occasion, made it difficult to smile in proper Eskimo fashion.

My spontaneous reaction to any sort of strain is tearfulness. I tried to suppress that reaction, knowing from previous experience with Eskimos that equanimity in the face of difficulty is a high virtue and that tearfulness is not to be countenanced; nevertheless I am certain that all too frequently I was unsuccessful in concealing my distress. The first such incident that I remember occurred on a Sunday morning, shortly after the return of the caribou hunters to the camp at the Rapids. A number of Pala's kin, including Inuttiaq, were drinking tea in my tent at eight in the morning when Nilak and his family appeared in the entrance. Nilak was oddly dressed: from underneath his short parka a plaid wool bathrobe flowed over his trousers. It was a costume that he affected every Sunday at that time, but I had not seen it before. He and his wife and daughter each carried a small calico bag containing, as I later found, a Bible and a prayerbook. I was puzzled, both by the bathrobe and by the mysterious calico bags, but no one volunteered an explanation. People sat and drank tea, and every hour or half-hour one of the men asked me: "What time is it?" I suspected that a church service was in the offing; it was, after all, the first Sunday since Inuttiaq's return from the caribou hunt. It was a dismal day in my private world, I can no longer remember why, and my anticipation of the forthcoming service did little to cheer me. On the contrary, the reticence of my visitors intensified my depression and made me feel altogether isolated. Though I very much wanted the opportunity to observe the religious behavior of the camp, I was sure they would not invite me to join them. So when I pronounced the time to be 10:30, and Inuttiaq confirmed my suspicion—"we are going to pray at 11"—I asked if I might come. Inuttiaq's face and Pala's went blank. The words of their reply were incomprehensible to me, but their reluctance, their hesitation, were evident enough. I felt a spasm cross my face. Nothing was said on either side, but when the company rose to leave at eleven, Inuttiaq turned to me: "We are going to pray. You, too." And so, restored to cheer, I accompanied the others.

Tactful compliance was the characteristic response of the Utku in those early days, whenever resentment, fatigue, or anxiety brought the tears close to the surface or made my voice sharp. Such breaches of emotional decorum occurred fairly frequently, too, all precipitated by the fear of cold and hunger, and by the difficulty of communicating with my Eskimo hosts. Concerned about the effects of my untoward behavior, I recorded a number of these incidents even though at the time I had no idea how right I was to worry about Utku reactions. Now that I know how strongly they disapproved of volatility, I am astonished that they continued to respond with graciousness and, instead of withdrawing from me, continued to court me in a friendly manner when I was in a mood to permit it.

My moodiness in the early days, and the reactions of the Utku to it, are exemplified by my relationship with Pala, who subsequently became my grandfather. For various reasons, Pala attracted more of my impatience than did the rest of his kin in those first days. Nevertheless, Pala, like his kin, gave no sign that he was offended by my snappishness. Perhaps it would be more accurate to say that neither he nor the others showed offense in any way that was recognizable to me at that time.

In part, the friction between Pala and me arose from my unpleasant suspicion that he cast a covetous eye on my possessions. Though it never occurred to me that he might actually take something of mine (and neither he nor anyone else ever did), nevertheless I did not find his attitude attractive. There was a game he used to play with me, in which he pretended to steal from me, always ostentatiously showing me his action: "Yiini, watch!" or in which he pretended to reach for an object I was holding: a boot, a spoon, a piece of bannock. "Mine? Mine?" he would inquire, extending his hands with fingers curled in mock aggressiveness, his eyes and mouth wide in simulation of greed. And when I, entering into the comedy, made a great show of pulling the "stolen" object back, or hiding the object reached for, with exaggerated exclamations of alarm or umbrage, Pala and the others present laughed with the greatest merriment. Others, taking their cue from Pala, used occasionally to play the same game with me, but Pala was its creator and chief actor, and it seemed clear to me that his real wishes were being expressed under cover of a joke.

Of all my possessions, tobacco was what Pala most craved, and it was tobacco that created the greatest tension between us. It was not necessarily that he craved it more than other people, but his wish to have it was certainly more clearly expressed. His visits were more conspicuously correlated than were other people's with the state of my tobacco supply; he was the only person who ever made the performance of a service *contingent* on receiving tobacco, and he was the only one who ever demanded, "More!" when, on request, I filled the men's tobacco pouches of a morning. His "greediness," for such I felt it to be, contrasted with Inuttiaq's attitude; Inuttiaq more than once stopped me when his pouch was half full: "That's enough; more later today or tomorrow."

In retrospect, I am not sure why I resented so heartily Pala's inroads on my tobacco supply. I do not smoke; he was not depriving me of a commodity that I cherished. But so constant were his demands that, imposing my kapluna sense of fairness on the situation, I feared he would manage to acquire more than his "share" of my limited supply. In particular, I feared that he would acquire more than Nilak and Niqi who, camped on the other side of the river, could not so readily "visit to smoke." Actually, from the Utku point of view, Pala probably should have received somewhat more than Nilak, since I was living in his camp and being fed by the members of his family; and even if Pala's share *was* disproportionately large I should not, in their view, have attempted to interfere. Nilak would have seethed quietly on his side of the river, and that would have been that. But I tried, in my kapluna fashion, to regulate the situation, which meant giving to Pala with obvious reluctance and in the smallest quantities that he would accept. I will never know how much of my unwillingness he sensed. I expect that his occasional demands for "more" are a sign that it *was* noticed, but he continued to visit, to smile, to joke with me, and to offer words and fish, as Nakliguhuktuq had said the Utku should do.

Unfortunately, Pala's attempts to teach me words irritated me, also. Whereas the rest of his kin quickly saw the need to pronounce words in slow and complete syllables so that I might write them down, Pala failed to understand what I wanted of him. The difficulty was caused by the nature of the syllabic system of writing, in which one symbol may represent more than one sound, and the final consonant of every syllable is omitted. Thus, a word that is pronounced approximately *a-ngil-zraq-tuq* is written *a-gi-ga-tu*. When Pala obligingly dictated words for me to write down, he always pronounced them as they were written, with all the distortions imposed by the script, and as a consequence, especially before I had discovered the reason why my written versions of words never coincided with the spoken versions, I sometimes lost patience. I would ask Pala to say a word—*angilzraqtuq*—slowly. He would oblige: "A-gi-ga-tu." I would repeat it back to him: "Agigatu." He would wrinkle his nose. "No, a-gi-ga-tu." And so it would go, around and around, with complete lack of comprehension on both sides, until impatience sharpened my voice, whereupon Allaq, Inuttiaq, or Amaaqtuq, all of whom saw at once where the difficulty lay, would interpose quietly: "A-ngil-zraq-tuq." These impasses never seemed to discourage Pala from continuing patiently to repeat, "A-gi-ga-tu," nor was there ever a change in the even quality of his voice.

Occasionally, Pala was the innocent recipient of ire that was really directed at other individuals, or at the Utku in general. There was the day, for instance, when Inuttiaq had brought me a delectable fresh char, the choicest of fish, for my day's eating, and then, with my other visitors, had proceeded to devour it entirely, leaving me nothing to eat. With each mouthful that disappeared, my anxiety mounted, and the cheer instilled by Inuttiaq's gift faded. And when I looked down at the untidy, dismembered skeleton on the gravel floor, resentment and depression choked me. My visitors also surveyed the bones, and Pala, as he left, remarked in a tone that, to my ear, held just a trace of chagrin: "We've eaten it all. But tomorrow, if it's calm enough to fish, we'll bring you some more." Unable to muster the proper cheerful gratitude, I querulously inquired: "What am I going to eat TONIGHT?" My visitors said nothing, only smiled, but very shortly Pala reappeared with a large piece of rotted fish from the caches. It was what the Eskimos themselves were eating; it was all there was. "For tonight," he said, holding it out to me, "but it tastes awful." Still angry, I accepted his offering with a mutter of thanks, whose ungraciousness he gave no sign of noticing.

Pala was, to be sure, not the only person who encountered my moodiness in those autumn weeks before I moved into Inuttiaq's qaqmaq. My most egregiously hostile act was directed at Nilak and Niqi. Overcome with irritation at one of their prolonged visits, I simply turned my back on them, lay down, and pretended to sleep. They sat on for a while, quietly, occasionally speaking to one another in low voices so considerate-sounding that I, lying buried in my parka, was stabbed with remorse. Then, with a final murmur, they rose and left, tying the tent flaps behind them and carefully weighting the entrance with rocks to prevent the roaming pups from breaking in to steal from me while I slept.

The overt response of the Utku on each of these occasions was always the same: they humored me, complied with my apparent wishes, and seemed to ignore my ungraciousness. But now I wonder just how blind I was to the real feelings of people faced with my eccentricities. It is possible that in that early period they were watching, weighing, not yet confirming unpleasant judgments but puzzling how to interpret my strange behavior, just as I puzzled how to interpret theirs. The letters they wrote in the first two or three months to Ikayuqtuq in Gjoa Haven were not critical of my behavior. On the contrary; they said I was pleasant (quvia), kind (quya), and amusing (tiphi), and that they were helping me because they felt protective (naklik) toward me. Knowing as I do now, however, the intensity of their aversion to hostile expressions, I think it unlikely that critical judgment was wholly in abeyance. There was fear (ilira) in their early feeling for me, too, as they later confessed, and I wonder if perhaps it was partly this fear, as well as their kindlier feelings, that made them continue to court me as they did, in spite or even because of the rudeness that came and went so unpredictably. Perhaps they were not sure how dangerous my moods really were and wanted to prove themselves unthreatening in order that I should treat them kindly in turn; I later had opportunity to see exactly that reasoning in their treatment of other kapluna visitors. In any case, I think it likely that these early incidents planted the first seeds of resentment toward me, resentment that, I fear, in Pala's case at least, ultimately hardened into firm dislike.

II. Family Living: Covert Conflicts

A week or two after my arrival, after Inuttiaq had adopted me as a daughter, my relationship with his family began to take on a different quality from my relationships with the other households. Nilak's family, and to a lesser extent, the families of the brothers Pala and Piuvkaq continued to refer to me as the "kapluna"; to treat me with ceremony; and to trade with me, rather than simply asking for small amounts of my supplies; but Allaq, and especially Inuttiaq, began to treat me as a daughter. Some of these changes I have described already. They were very warming. I enjoyed the fact that I was expected to participate, as far as I was able, in the daily work of the camp, and I basked in the approval that met my efforts. I was grateful for the family-sized chunks of caribou tallow that fell to my share, even though I had not yet learned really to enjoy the waxy stuff. I was grateful, too, that Inuttiaq took it upon himself to keep me supplied with the staple fish, insofar as the weather permitted, and that Allaq sometimes brought her breakfast or her sewing to my tent, to keep me company as she ate or worked. Most gratifying of all, perhaps, were the efforts that people made, had made from the beginning, to teach me the Eskimo skills that Ikayuqtuq had told them I wished to learn; and again, after my adoption, it was Inuttiaq and Allaq who took the primary responsibility for instructing, for encouraging, and for protecting me from too burdensome tasks. In all of these ways and more, I was made to feel that I belonged to Inuttiaq's family.

Of course, my daughterly status entailed responsibilities, too, and inevitably there were times when I failed to fulfill them graciously. The first occasion on which I recall feeling that being a daughter might have its drawbacks was the morning I was awakened at dawn by a light touch on my shoulder and looked up to find Allaq standing beside my bed. "Daughter, your father feels like drinking tea." It was apologetically said, but I seethed inwardly at the disturbance. Though Utku are ordinarily considerate of sleepers—I never saw one waked carelessly or as a prank—nevertheless they do not hold sleep inviolable, and any need, however small, is reason enough to wake a person on whom one has a claim. To me, on the other hand, sleep is sacred. I cherish it, and in those days it was even more precious than usual, protecting me, as it did, for all too short periods, from the vicissitudes of the day: the icy breezes that attacked my fingers and toes, the raw fish, the incomprehensible words, the giggles, and above all, the necessity to hold myself in check. I found it exhausting to play an unfamiliar role all day long, constantly to try to react in ways that would be acceptable to my hosts, instead of in ways that came naturally to me, and constantly to keep alert to cues that would tell me whether or not I had succeeded. I buried myself thankfully in sleep at night and in the morning withdrew myself reluctantly from its shelter. So resentment roughened my voice when I replied to Allaq: "Help yourself!" and caused me to turn over sharply toward the wall and pull the sleeping bag over my head. The tea can was in evidence beside the entrance; Allaq could have helped herself by extending a hand, without even entering the tent, and I testily asked myself why she had not done so. She may have sensed my thought; in any case she answered it: "I could have taken *your* tea by the door," she said, "but I wanted to take the tea that you gave your father last night and that he forgot to take home." Permission granted, she silently filled her palm with tea and withdrew, tying the tent flaps behind her and rearranging the stone barricade that kept the dogs out, considerate acts well calculated to make me repent my abruptness.

By calling me daughter, Allaq had justified waking me. However, there was nothing in her request for tea that distinguished it from requests made by other members of the community for small amounts of my supplies. Neither was there anything different in Allaq's impassive reaction to my snarl. In early October, however, when I moved from my solitary tent into Inuttiaq's qaqmaq, the parental nature of Inuttiaq's and Allaq's relationship with me became much more evident, and the conflict between Inuttiaq's definition of the daughter role and mine began to create problems of a new order. The first such problem was occasioned by the move itself. I had been anticipating the move for a month, but when the time came, I was taken by surprise.

The nightly snow flurries were no longer melting in the morning air, and the inlet had lain silent under ice for several days when I woke one morning in my tent to hear unaccustomed sounds of chopping. Rummaging for the several pairs of wool and duffel socks that always lost themselves in my sleeping bag, where I dried them as I slept, I pulled myself, reluctantly as always, out into the cold air. My boots, hung from the ridge pole, were festooned with feathers of frost, and as I drew them down, prickles of snow showered my neck. Shivering and cursing, I pulled on the frozen boots and, still in my longjohns, crunched across the gravel floor to peer between the entrance flaps. Almost all the men of the three households in our camp were out on the ice of the inlet. The old man Piuvkaq was chopping rectangular blocks, like huge dominoes, out of the ice. A dark oblong of water showed where other blocks had already been cut and removed. Pala was knotting a rope around one of these blocks, while other people stood in readiness to pull. I had not a clue to the meaning of the scene I was witnessing, and when Amaaqtuq, seeing my protruding head, came to pay her morning call, her explanation did not enlighten me: "They are making a qaqmaq." It was only as I saw the walls taking shape, the ice dominoes set up side by side in a circle and mortared with slush, that I realized what a qaqmaq was. "Qaqmaqs are warm," Amaaqtuq told me. "Not in winter but in autumn. They are much pleasanter (*quvia*) than tents. You will see. Are you going to live in a qaqmaq?"

I did not know, in truth, whether I was going to live in a qaqmaq or not; I did not even know whether I wanted to. Warmed and protected as I had felt on the evening, a month earlier, when Inuttiaq, with the offer of a cup of tea, had welcomed me as his daughter, I found myself filled with trepidation now that the move into Inuttiaq's dwelling was imminent. Could I tolerate the company of others for twenty-four hours a day? In the past month my tent had become a refuge, into which I withdrew every evening after the rest of the camp was in bed, to repair ravages to my spirit with the help of bannock and peanut butter, boiled rice, frozen dates, and Henry James. So reviving were those hours of self-indulgence that I dreaded their loss. I prayed that Inuttiaq would not invite me to join them until he built an iglu in November.

My prayer was not granted. It was Allaq who issued the first invitation to join the qaqmaq household. She had brought her sewing to my tent, as she often did in those early days. She was making the body of Saarak's fawnskin winter suit while Amaaqtuq, at her sister's request, sewed the sleeves, and I, unable to assist in such useful preparations for winter, copied vocabulary notes. From the shore came sounds of qaqmaq construction; Pala's was nearly finished. "In a little while we are going to build a qaqmaq, too," Allaq said. "Would you like to move in with us then?" I hesitated. "I don't know; it's difficult; after a while I'll tell you."

"Eeee." She smiled, and nothing further was said. But soon after she had gone home, Inuttiaq came to visit: "Would you like to move in with us when we build a qaqmaq, or would you rather have a separate one for yourself?"

Again I hesitated; then in my halting Eskimo I tried to explain that I thought it might be difficult to live with others, especially at times when I wanted to work. Inuttiaq, in turn, insisted that I would be cold if I lived alone. The conversation grew increasingly confused, each of us uncertain what the other was trying to say—uncertain, too, how to extricate ourselves from the impasse. Finally, I thought Inuttiaq suggested that I sleep in his qaqmaq, for warmth, but that my tent be left standing as a retreat: "If you get tired." I was relieved at this compromise, and I accepted it gladly. Unfortunately, either my understanding was deficient, or Inuttiaq changed his mind, or both. I still do not understand precisely the chain of events that led to my finding myself four days later ensconced without refuge in Inuttiaq's qaqmaq.

It was when Inuttiaq started to build that I began to wonder whether I had understood aright. He began his qaqmaq, as Piuvkaq did, on the morning after Pala had built and moved into his. All three dwellings were to be clustered tightly together, as the tents had been, at the head of the inlet. But Inuttiaq's wall, unlike the other two, for some reason refused to hold properly.

When the first block fell, and the second broke at a touch, Inuttiaq decided the ice was still too thin for building. He turned to me as I stood nearby, watching. "I'll go fishing today," he said, "and when the ice is better, I will build another qaqmaq, for you (he used the singular pronoun), over there," and he gestured in the direction of my tent, some distance away. I assented, surprised at this development but vastly relieved at the thought that, after all, I should have a home of my own, and yet not be obliged to live in a windy tent.

When Inuttiaq appeared at my tent entrance three mornings later to ask if I planned to come and help with the chinking of "my" qaqmaq, I went with alacrity. The circle that Inuttiaq had drawn on the gravel was large, and when the walls were up, the building was, indeed, larger than either Pala's or Piuvkaq's. Inuttiaq asked me if it would be big enough for me, and when I assented, he sent me back to my tent to stuff my loose belongings into sacks for moving. Curiously, Allaq, over in *her* tent, was also packing. I wondered what for, but only when I saw the goods of Inuttiaq's household being moved into "my" qaqmaq did it dawn on me that "my" qaqmaq was, in fact, "our" qaqmaq. I tried hastily to reconcile myself; this, after all, was the plan to which I had originally agreed. It was when Inuttiaq informed me that my tent was to be used as the qaqmaq's roof, since his tent was not large enough, that dismay overcame me. I tried to control it with the thought that I could set up my double-walled winter tent as a refuge instead; but it was small and dark; it was not the cosily familiar summer tent in which I had been living, and I could not prevent myself from demurring at the sudden loss of the latter. I told Inuttiaq that, although I did have another tent, a warm tent, that I could put up, I would like to use the summer tent, folded up, as a seat therein. It was a ridiculous notion, born of an alarm that must have been completely incomprehensible to Inuttiaq, if he was aware of it at all. He must have recognized the folly of the demand at once, but he handled it with the indirectness characteristic of his people. Pointing out again that his own tent was too small to roof the qaqmaq, he offered to let me use that for a seat instead. Then outdoors, next to the qaqmaq wall, he stacked all the household goods that were not to be used immediately, both his things and mine for which there was no room in the qaqmaq, and he covered the cache with his tent.

What could I do? I was helpless to protest, and the very helplessness made me panic. I looked at the square of gravel that had been my home for more than a month and felt its emptiness unbearable. I *had* to have a tent. Inuttiaq and Allaq were busy, setting a wooden door into the wall of our qaqmaq, mortaring the frame to the ice block with slush, and chopping away the ice inside the frame to make an entrance. Everyone else in camp was indoors, visiting or drinking tea after the day's work. There was no one to offer assistance when I took my winter tent from the household cache where Inuttiaq had laid it and carried it up to my old gravel patch on the bluff. It was a pyramid tent with four built-in aluminum corner poles attached together at the top. In order to erect the tent it was necessary to spread these poles as far as possible at the base, then weight down the canvas between them with stones. It seemed simple, but I had never tried it before, and a strong breeze, which swelled the canvas, did not help. I struggled to spread the poles, first on one side, then on another, while the wind continually undid my work.

"What are you doing?" Inuttiaq stood at my side. I tried to explain that if I was tired or wanted to type I would use this tent. "You can write in the qaqmaq," he said; "the tent will be cold." I tried to explain that this was a different sort of tent and that, heated with a primus stove, it would be warm. "I will write sometimes in the qaqmaq and sometimes here," I said, feebly trying to be pliant. But Inuttiaq, after pulling two of the poles apart for me in a half-gesture of helping, departed without further comment to drink tea in the tent of the newly arrived Qavvik, and left me to struggle by myself. It was the first time since I had been with the Utku that I had been left to cope with a difficult activity by myself. People came and went around the qaqmaqs at the base of the bluff, but no one else came up to inquire what I was doing or whether I needed help. And no criticism could have made me feel more vividly than this disregard the antisocial nature of my act.

The tent stood there, empty and unused, for two weeks, until we took it down in preparation for moving to the winter camp in Amujat. In those two weeks I had never felt the need of a refuge.

I basked in the warm protectiveness of Inuttiaq's household. What solitude I needed I found on the river in the mornings when I went fishing with Inuttiaq or, to my surprise, in the qaqmaq itself, in the afternoons when the room was full of visitors and I retired into myself, lulled and shielded by the flow of quiet, incomprehensible speech. No one ever mentioned the folly of my tent, even when they helped to take it down.

In many ways life in Inuttiaq's household was easier for me than life in my solitary tent had been. For one thing it was no longer necessary for me to play hostess. The fact that I could sit quietly in my corner and let Inuttiaq and Allaq entertain our visitors gave me privacy without the chill of isolation. Then too, Inuttiaq and Allaq did their utmost to make me feel welcome. I felt it in the parental responsibility that they assumed for my welfare, more than ever teaching me how to do things, feeding me, and protecting me from the dangerous effects of my ignorance of the land and climate. I felt it also in the many considerate allowances that they made on my behalf in the ordering of household life, assuring me from the first that, if I wished, I might type, or keep my lamp lit later than they at night, or "sometimes" eat kapluna food without offering it to them, "because you are a kapluna." They even said they were lonely when I spent an evening visiting in another qaqmaq. That was the most heartwarming of all.

Occasionally, to be sure, I wondered whether my parents' considerateness was a response to remembered snarls, an attempt to forestall any recurrence of such behavior. When Allaq, on my first evening, asked whether it would wake me if she opened and closed the squeaking door or made tea while I slept in the morning, I had uncomfortable memories of a morning past, when I had growled, "Help yourself" and pulled the sleeping bag over my head. Similarly discomfiting was the stormy day on which the qaqmaq, full of visitors, was kept hushed all day because I was asleep. Allaq even refrained from making tea once during the morning for fear of waking me. I was sleeping off an attack of indigestion, but she did not know that. She assumed that I was tired from getting up at dawn the day before to accompany Inuttiaq on a fishing trip.

It is possible that this assumption that I tired easily accounted for a good deal of the leniency and consideration that was shown me during these weeks. Often, if I walked far, or tried to carry a full load of twigs, or worked hard at scraping a hide, people cautioned me that I would be tired; often they silently took my work on themselves, switching my load for a lighter one when we stopped to rest, or taking a turn at the scraping. On a number of occasions, too, people interpreted my withdrawal from company as a sign of fatigue, whether I had gone to bed early to conceal depression and to ease my cold toes, or whether I merely walked silently a little behind the others to enjoy the view and think my own thoughts.

I am not sure whether this interpretation of my behavior was owing to a perception that I was, indeed, tired, emotionally, if not physically, or whether it was owing to preconceptions about the feebleness of white women unaccustomed to Eskimo ways; both, perhaps. At the time, I did not question the solicitude; I was grateful, but I took it for granted. Only now am I impressed by the tolerant view that was taken of my unsocial behavior. Among the Utku themselves, fatigue is called on to explain lethargy and weakness that are produced by a variety of causes. Thus, a person who is mildly ill will describe himself as "not sick, only tired"; old people are also described as "tired"; and I suspected that depression might also be expressed as fatigue, as it is in our own society. But there are less kind ways of describing lethargic, unsocial behavior, too. If an Utku were lethargic or withdrawn as frequently and as unpredictably as I was in those days, his neighbors would have murmured in disapproval: "He is upset *(hujuujaq, huqu)"*; and in later months the Utku became as intolerant of my variations in mood as they were of one another's.

To some extent Inuttiaq's, and especially Allaq's, initial consideration of me may have been due to shyness, too. I had the feeling that Allaq, more than Inuttiaq, was afraid *(ilira)* of me in the first weeks after I moved into their home, and much later she admitted that she had been. Her shyness *(ilira)* was most noticeable as a reluctance to use my goods unless I expressly gave permission—and more, unless I volunteered that permission; she rarely brought herself to ask whether she might use a little of my tea or heat the water on my primus instead of over the weak tallow flame in the hollow rock that served her in the autumn as a lamp. Her nearest approach to a request was a smiling statement: "While you were out fishing I didn't make tea, although my hands were too cold to sew." Sometimes she said nothing at all; it was Amaaqtuq who told me: "While you were out fishing this morning my sister made tea on the lamp instead of on the primus." Such reports were very effective; it did not take me long to learn that when I left in the morning I should leave instructions for Allaq: "Be sure to make tea if you get cold, and be sure to use the primus."

Inuttiaq had no such reluctance to use my goods, and this fact was a source of considerable tension between us in the first weeks after I joined his household. Already, before moving in with him, I had worried about the effect the move would have on the distribution of my property. The anxiety had several conflicting facets. I wanted to conform to Utku ideas of justice, but at the same time I was pressured by my American prejudice in favor of equality, and the latter was the stronger because I was still uncertain what the Utku ideas were. I was afraid that Inuttiaq might acquire a larger share of my wealth than was strictly proper, either in terms of his own code or in terms of mine. Moreover, questions of justice aside, I was also selfishly concerned about the almost certain increase in the rate of depletion that membership in a larger household would entail.

The one possibility that had not occurred to me was that Inuttiaq would take it upon himself to distribute my goods to the rest of the camp. In view of my concern for equalization of my kapluna benefits, I suppose I should have been relieved the first time I saw Inuttiaq generously hand a can of my tobacco to a smiling neighbor. I confess that I was not relieved; I was alarmed. If my goods were to be distributed, I wanted the credit for generosity; I did not want Inuttiaq to use my goods to increase his own prestige in the community, and noting the fact that our qaqmaq had suddenly become the social center of the camp, I was afraid that this was precisely what was happening. My alarm was the greater because, ludicrous as it seems to me now, I had the idea then that I ought to do my utmost to avoid disturbing the social balance of the community, the patterns of friendship and of interdependence, so that I could study those patterns in their natural state. I said nothing to Inuttiaq, but tried to repair whatever damage was occurring by anticipating him. I offered supplies to our visitors, myself, before he had a chance to do so; but then, on occasion, he would instruct me, in the visitor's presence, to give more than I had done: "If you want to." In recording this now, I wonder whether perhaps he was attempting to teach me Utku generosity, but at the time I only imagined that he was trying to accumulate credit for himself, and though I smiled at the visitor, I do not believe I smiled at Inuttiaq. On occasion, my response to this situation was even more hostile. There was one time, for instance, when I had not been quick enough to offer first. Our visitor was Itqiliq, a young Netsilingmiutaq, who had been to school for four or five years and spoke some English. Inuttiaq had turned to me: "Itqiliq wants some tobacco." I smiled at Itqiliq and filled his pouch. Itqiliq smiled at Inuttiaq and thanked him. I smiled at Itqiliq and said in English, "You're welcome."

Neither Inuttiaq nor I, however, recognized the conflict overtly, though I am sure he must have been aware of my displeasure, and antagonism generated on this score may well have fed the other conflicts that developed during the winter. In any case, ultimately, without a word being said—really, without my being aware that it was happening at all—we reached a modus vivendi. One can of tobacco, one pound of tea, or one bag of sugar was always open and available on Allaq's side of the ikliq, and from that supply my parents offered, or gave on request, small amounts to our visitors; but the storeroom was in my charge. When the household supply, the open can or bag, was gone, I was informed, and I brought out a replacement. When neighbors wished larger amounts of anything than were forthcoming from our household supply, they approached me. During the winter, when Inuttiaq traded foxes, he had supplies of his own. These were in Allaq's charge; she dispensed them to me as she did to the other members of the family, and while they lasted, neither she nor Inuttiaq ever drew on mine.

The only time that Inuttiaq openly recognized my feelings concerning the distribution of my supplies was on one occasion when he had traded with my property, as distinct from giving it away. A Netsilik trapper who was camping in the neighborhood had asked him for several cans of my powdered milk and had offered in exchange shells to fit Inuttiaq's gun. Inuttiaq had traded as asked, then, scrupulously honest as always, had told me what he had done. I recall my displeasure, and I am sure he saw it in my face. He said immediately: "I shouldn't trade with your property." I agreed, but added: "This time it's all right." Inuttiaq continued: "I don't really need those shells. I'll give them back. I can get some in Gjoa Haven." And though I urged him to keep them, he reported several days later that he had returned them to the trapper.

So the covert struggle for control over my supplies was ultimately resolved, at least as far as the larger community's use of them was concerned. On one occasion, later, a conflict over Inuttiaq's own use of my primus stove broke the peaceful surface of our relationship, as I shall shortly describe. But apart from any questions of use, there was still another way in which, without my being fully aware of it, my wealth strained the relationship between me and my foster parents: it was heavy. Minimal by kapluna standards, my gear was mountainous from the point of view of the man responsible for transporting it. Too heavy to carry on foot, cumbersome to haul by canoe or dogsled, impossible to leave behind, my possessions were a nuisance from start to finish. I do not like to recall Inuttiaq's expressionless face as he surveyed the contents of my tent one day in June, and asked which of my belongings I was planning to leave on the hilltop when we moved that night to a new campsite, and his silent acceptance when I said it would be impossible to leave more than half. I lack the optimism and the seasonal attitude toward possessions, which are so useful to the nomadic Utku.

The Utku take with them during wandering seasons an absolute minimum of goods and leave the remainder scattered hither and yon on convenient hilltop boulders or, if perishable, in one of the large orange oil drums that mark the most frequented campsites. In one series of spring moves we left on the various hilltops near our camps the following articles, which the advancing season had rendered temporarily unnecessary or useless: our *qulliq* (the flat semilunar blubber, or in the Utku case, fish-oil, lamp that is a characteristic Eskimo possession), our foxtraps, a kerosene storm lantern, a dogsled, ice chisels, winter bedding and fur clothing, an empty fuel drum, a urine pot, and a primus stove, temporarily out of order. Nobody would touch any of these possessions until their owners came for them, which they would do as the season demanded or as circumstances permitted.[1]

I found it disturbing to leave a wake of belongings behind me as I moved. I like to provide for contingencies: to take my rain clothes in case it rains and my warm clothes in case it turns cold; and I was very unwilling indeed to leave my precious fieldnotes and tape recorder under a quilt on the summit of a little hillock shortly before the river was expected to flood. Inuttiaq said: "It isn't going to rain, at least, not much." And: "Summer is coming; it will get warm soon." And: "The flood isn't going to reach the top of that knoll." I was unconvinced. My caribou clothing was irreplaceable; so were my fieldnotes and other equipment. And even greater than any practical worth was the symbolic value that my kapluna possessions, like kapluna food, had acquired. When I first set out for Utku country, a country judged by kapluna and Eskimo alike as dangerous and difficult for a kapluna woman to survive in, I had no means of assessing, rationally, my ability to cope with that unknown and, as I have said, my ignorance of the language prevented me from even questioning the alien judgments of those on whom I had to depend. I clung to my belongings with the strength of fear; and, to a degree, I continued to do so until one full cycle of seasons had passed, and I knew, through having lived them, what to expect of the seasons, of myself, and of the Utku.

When Allaq, under Inuttiaq's direction, sorted the goods of their household into piles to be taken or cached, Inuttiaq, especially in the first months, usually tried to give me instructions, too. But when I demurred, as I almost always did, he never complained. Perhaps it was because of this silence that I was slow to realize how burdensome my dependence on my gear must have been to him. To be sure, I was aware that when we

1. Rasmussen (1931), who saw the Utku in their spring camps where they were burning melted tallow in concave rocks, was under the impression that these Eskimos never used the traditional blubber lamps. I also saw concave rocks used as makeshift qulliqs in the autumn camp, and I shared Rasmussen's misconception until we arrived at the winter campsite and the real qulliqs were brought down from the hilltop.

moved short distances, Inuttiaq usually made two sled trips, one to move his own household goods and one to move mine. I noticed, too, that sometimes when we were preparing for longer trips, I was instructed to carry some of my things to Pala's sled or canoe, rather than to Inuttiaq's. But it was only after I had returned to my own country that I saw, in my photographs of a spring move, the contrast between Inuttiaq's sled load and Ipuituq's, the latter little over knee high, the former shoulder high. At the time, I was blind.

On one occasion this blindness led me to make a most misguided gesture of generosity. Knowing how fond the Utku were of the kapluna foods they ordinarily enjoyed only in the winter, I tried to furnish them to the camp (and to myself) during the summer, as well. I caused the community, and Inuttiaq in particular, only consternation. The food arrived by plane in early June, as we were about to set off on our month-long series of spring moves downriver, not to return until after the river flooded. There was no place to store the food, and it was far too heavy to transport. We stacked it on the summit of a knoll, erected my winter tent over it, and left. In August and September, when we happened to be camped near that cache, we enjoyed the food. Nevertheless, Inuttiaq's expressionless face when he looked at the boxes being unloaded from the plane in June, and his immediate decision to abandon them, made an impression even on my kapluna mind. I began to realize that it is not just "improvidence" or "poverty," as some kaplunas think, that makes the Utku buy "insufficient" flour to carry them through the summer when they are cut off from Gjoa Haven; they just do not want the bother of carrying it around with them. The following January, when I was on my way home, Inuttiaq said to me: "If you come back again, bring only a cup, a pan, a teakettle, and food. And if you have lots of money, bring a few ready-made cigarettes."

The problems created by my material possessions were not the only ones that complicated my relationship with my Utku parents. There was another sense, too, in which I must have weighed on them. At times I tried, as best I might, to help with the household tasks that were within my ability. I fetched water from the river, made tea, brought in fresh snow to spread on the iglu floor and gravel to fill the concavities of the ikliq, jigged through the ice with Inuttiaq or hauled the day's take of whitefish in from the nets with Allaq and cut out the bellies (often a hundred or more of them) for oil. Nevertheless, I could by no means assist as a grown daughter should. For one thing, I was constantly torn between the needs of the household and the demands of my own work: to observe, preferably without interfering, and to record. Frequently, when Saarak shrieked with rage and the rest of the family and visitors were absorbed in appeasing her, instead of helping, I watched to see what would happen. After our breakfast tea, when Allaq knelt on her hands and knees to hack away the grimy surface of the iglu floor, I lay in bed and wrote, so that I would not forget the events of the early morning. Allaq never commented or criticized, unless the amused remark that she and others sometimes made—"always writing!"—was a criticism. I never knew; the voices were always cheerful. Still, I wonder whether at times Allaq did not contrast my sporadic and awkward assistance unfavorably with the help that Kamik must have given her before she went away to boarding school. Though Allaq, like the others, explicitly excused me from helping when I lacked the skill, her judgment may have been less tolerant on the occasions when I failed to offer assistance that she knew me capable of rendering. Then she may have considered me unkind and lazy: "Not wanting to help"; and such judgments, if she made them, would have contained a kernel of truth. It was not always my work that kept me from helping; it was sometimes simple lack of perception. I was, to my dishonor, by no means as careful to anticipate her needs as she was to anticipate mine; and, unlike Inuttiaq, she was loath to ask outright for my assistance, as she would have asked her own daughter. She usually waited for me to volunteer my aid.

But worse than my failure to provide Inuttiaq and Allaq with the services that they should have received from an adult daughter was the fact that they were forced to serve *me*. In many ways I was as unskilled as my small sister Saarak, less skilled then six-year-old Raigili. Allaq had to make and mend my fur clothing, chew my boots in the morning to stretch and soften them after the night's drying, and even, for the first month or two, turn my fur mittens right side out when they were dried. She had to fillet my fish when it was frozen; and she thought she had to do it when it was thawed, too, but that was owing to a misunderstanding. True, I was inept at circumventing the lateral bone, and both my parents knew it, but then, I did not find it so very dreadful to eat bony fish. It was for other reasons that, when I was left to cope with my own fish, I sometimes failed to join the others at their frequent meals: either I was not hungry for a raw fish snack, or I was busy writing and was reluctant to chill my fingers with the wet fish. Inuttiaq or Allaq then would ask me if I did not feel like eating, too, and I, in order to avoid the rudely direct "no," would say, "in a while," a gentle form of refusal that was often used by Utku themselves. They would wait a while; and Inuttiaq might reassure me: "Whenever you feel hungry, eat; help yourself." But if I continued to work, sooner or later, Allaq would cut a piece of fish and lay it beside me, saying: "For you, if you come to feel like eating." Then, to show my appreciation, I ate, and so, inadvertently, perpetuated the service.

I have mentioned the mixture of gratitude and irritation that characterized my reaction to these services: gratitude that I was taken care of and irritation that I was thereby placed under obligation. There was another side to my reaction, too: the service was more seductive than I cared to admit. I came, after a time, to feel it my due and to resent it if, by chance, the usual courtesies were not forthcoming. At the same time, I was ashamed of allowing myself to be seduced in this way, ashamed that I enjoyed the solicitude of my Utku parents and my own childlike dependence. I did not realize how very natural it is for a person to feel childish, to enjoy being taken care of, when he is isolated from everything familiar, and especially when he lacks the skills requisite for existence in his new environment. Instead, I carried over the values of independence and reciprocity that had been appropriate in my own world, and often an inner voice reminded me that the services I enjoyed were not in any sense my "due"; that, on the contrary, it was time I recognized my obligations, behaved as much like a self-sufficient adult as possible, and showed my parents the same consideration they showed me.

This moral voice was supported, too, by the part of me that resented being treated as an incompetent—for that was one implication of the rendering of service. The Utku considered me even more incompetent than I considered myself. They saw most kaplunas in the same light, and though there was a measure of justice in their view, nevertheless the naïve arrogance of the image, the extreme to which it was carried, offended me as much as similar prejudices offend me in my own culture. None of the adult skills, domestic or scholarly, for which I was accustomed to receive recognition in my own world had value in the Utku view—if the Utku were aware of their existence at all. Inuttiaq, and probably others, even took for granted that Eskimos learn English much faster than kaplunas learn Eskimo. There was, as usual, some truth in his perception; nevertheless, he had little awareness of the effort involved in learning a foreign language. People more than once asked when I recorded the same word twice, six months or a year apart: "Do all kaplunas forget as easily as you do?"

One result of the low expectations the Utku had of me was that it became more difficult than ever for me to improve my skills. Somebody was always at my elbow to do the difficult job for me. On numerous occasions I tried to subvert the tendency to treat me as a prima donna or a child by taking it upon myself to do things that were usually done for me and by refusing the help that was always quietly proffered. Once in midwinter I wrote to Ikayuqtuq in Gjoa Haven, describing how very good the Utku were to me—so good and helpful that I was not learning how to do anything for myself. The word was duly repeated to Inuttiaq, when he was in Gjoa Haven on a trading trip, and one day shortly after his return, he said to me: "Ikayuqtuq says you want to cut your own fish—that you want to learn." I agreed that I did, and for a day or two after that, beyond reminding me that if I were hungry I should help myself, neither Inuttiaq nor Allaq made a move to feed me. But when meals came and went, ignored by me, fillets began appearing again on my plate.

More often than not, I fear, in my efforts to acquire skill I manifested a petulant stubbornness which, I am sure, my parents regarded as more childish than the dependence from which I was trying to escape. There was the time I tried to improve the soles of my boots. It had been Ikayuqtuq's idea. She had noted, when I was in Gjoa Haven on holiday, that my boots had soles of caribou, which is warm but wears out easily. She had suggested that an outer sole of horsehide (obtainable at the Hudson Bay Company store) would make the caribou last much longer; and she had described to me the stitch appropriate for attaching the patches.

Allaq looked over at me questioningly when I took out the horsehide and the boots, then, seeing what I was about, she came over without a word and cut the patches for me. "After I smoke a cigarette," she said, "I'll sew them for you." I thanked her, but, wanting to practice, myself, I took up the second boot and began to sew it while she was occupied with the first. Under any circumstances, sewing leather is harder than sewing cloth, and this was my first experience of it. Moreover, though I did not yet realize it, I had not understood Ikayuqtuq's instructions as well as I had thought. Allaq had finished with her patch before I had properly begun on mine. "Shall I sew it?" she asked. But by this time hackles of independence had risen. I smiled, appreciatively, I hoped: "I'll do it."

Allaq smiled, too, and silently rolled another cigarette. The horsehide patch slithered over the smooth caribou sole, boggled, puckered, and refused to be sewn. Allaq, occupied on her side of the ikliq, seemed to notice nothing, but the second time I ripped the patch out, she appeared beside me. "I sewed it this way," she said, quietly, and she showed me a technique that I immediately recognized as the one Ikayuqtuq had described. I tried again, and ripped it off again. "Tack it," said Allaq, "here and here and here and here," and she showed me: on the center of the toe and the center of the heel and in the middle of each side. I did it again, and this time managed to sew all the way around the patch. True, the horsehide meandered in a most inelegant manner onto the upper part of the boot, making it appear that I was walking on the side of the boot, rather than on the proper sole. Still, the job was so much better than my past attempts that I decided to leave it. I showed it to Allaq.

"It's finished," she observed.

"It's not well done," I admitted.

She neither agreed nor disagreed. "Is it good enough?" she asked.

"I don't know; *is* it good enough?"

"I don't know; are *you* satisfied with it?"

I said I was, and nothing further was said. But one day, weeks afterwards, when I put my boots on, I noticed that no longer did one sole meander onto the upper boot; both soles were equally neatly in place. I wondered: had I disgraced Allaq as a mother by walking around in a tipsy boot? Was she sorry for my unkempt state or did it offend her sense of craftsmanship? Allaq never said a word.

On the whole, my helplessness seemed to be accepted as a matter of course by everybody, and it was consistently treated with tactful solicitude *(naklik)*, the same solicitude that characterizes Utku reactions to other helpless creatures, like puppies, children, and sick people: "Because you don't know how to do things, you are one to be taken care of *(naklik)*." If by chance I did succeed in acquiring some simple skill I was rewarded, as a child would have been, by the knowledge that the fact had been observed. "You are beginning to be less incapable *(ayuq)*," someone would say. It was what people said about babies when they began to smile, to speak, to grasp. Or: "You are becoming an Eskimo," a "person"; the word *inuk* has both meanings.

Inuttiaq and Allaq said these flattering things to me less often than others did, or such was my impression. I thought that perhaps they were more aware than others exactly how insignificant my growth in capability was, how little I was really becoming a "person." But perhaps there was just less need to be formally polite to a "daughter." Inuttiaq did reward me occasionally. More than once, when we were out fishing or checking the nets, I was happily startled to hear him say to a neighbor, gesturing in my direction: "She helps a lot, that one."

III. Recalcitrant Child: Open Conflict and Attempts to Educate

The innocent arrogance that I heard in the derogatory queries about kaplunas' memories was usually suppressed in my presence. Whatever Inuttiaq and Allaq may privately have felt, they never deliberately made me feel that my helplessness was either ludicrous or reprehensible. It was my own embarrassment that convicted me and made me suspect that this was a source of strain. A more obvious cause of antagonism than my helpless dependence was the reverse: my mutinous independence. And perhaps worse than the independence itself was my obvious irritation when Inuttiaq, asserting his fatherly prerogatives, ignored my wishes. In these situations, where we clashed as openly as I ever saw Utku do, Inuttiaq mustered his strongest weapons. Ultimately, the entire community made me suffer for my intractability and my temper.

Trouble was forecast already by the rebellious raising of the pyramid tent that marked my entry into Inuttiaq's household in October. From that time on, the atmosphere was never entirely peaceful, but the conflict between Inuttiaq and myself did not become acute until midwinter. I am not sure why it was so slow in developing. Perhaps in the early days there was still too much formality in our relationship, too much desire on both sides to create a happy situation. Warmed by the family life that I enjoyed so much more than my isolated tent and by the willingness of Inuttiaq and Allaq to take me into their midst, I often obeyed gratefully when Inuttiaq told me to make tea or bannock. And if I hesitated from a desire to finish what I was writing, Inuttiaq met me more than halfway. "Shall Allaq do it?" he would ask, and sometimes: "Shall *I* do it?" Had I been a good daughter, I should not have agreed to these suggestions, but I was innocent of that fact at the time. I always did agree, grateful that Inuttiaq was so obliging, and only now do I wonder whether he was trying, by shaming me, to teach me my daughterly duties. Certainly Allaq was taken aback when I agreed once to Inuttiaq's making bannock. Her laugh had an embarrassed ring to my ear, and though she was bootless on the ikliq, she hastily offered to do it herself if Inuttiaq would hand her the ingredients and the stove. But nobody seemed annoyed with me, and nobody informed me that my behavior was out of order; only the quality of Allaq's laugh and the hastiness of her reparation gave me a clue.

In other ways, too, Inuttiaq was more than considerate of me in those early days. One day, I recall, we had been caught by a fierce snow-driving wind in the midst of our move from the Rapids to the winter campsite in Amujat, and had taken shelter for the night in an empty wooden shack built, I think, as a fishing camp by the Catholic mission in Gjoa Haven. It was warm, and I was warm for the first time in more than a month, and I seized so eagerly on the unexpected opportunity to type that for some time I forgot the rest of the family. Then, in changing my paper, I happened to look up. It was late in the evening. Inuttiaq's eyelids drooped as he smoked beside me. "Are you sleepy?" I asked. "No," he said, "but I will be when you finish typing." This time I stopped typing.

Perhaps if Inuttiaq had not been so extremely gracious to me at first, his everyday manner, when he reverted to it, would not have struck me so unpleasantly. I was disconcerted when he began to address me in the imperative form of speech sometimes used to women and young people, instead of continuing to use the more permissive forms. And I was jolted by the assumption he seemed to make that I would obey him unquestioningly, even when he gave me no reason for his order. Though his expectation was appropriate to my status as daughter, it seemed doubly arbitrary by contrast with his earlier anticipation of, and compliance with, *my* wishes. Perhaps it was partly these feelings—of which I am not proud—that made me susceptible to the remarks I heard in Gjoa Haven about Inuttiaq's reputation as a "showoff." In any case, the suspicion implanted there that Inuttiaq was ordering me around for his own enjoyment decidedly heightened my perception of his assertiveness and sharpened my resistance to it.

Another factor in the development of our conflict was Inuttiaq's moodiness, a quality that I saw, I think, only after I had been living with his family for some time. Although Inuttiaq was usually the most energetic member of our household, there were hours, and occasionally whole days, when he lay silently on the ikliq, so aloof that he seemed insensible of our presence—working, talking, and playing around him. His very position on the ikliq expressed aloofness. When properly in bed one lies with one's head toward the center of the dwelling and one's feet to the wall, and during the day one sits in one's sleeping place facing the center of the dwelling, where one can converse with the visitors who stand or sit around the edges of the floor space by the entrance. A man sometimes sprawls on the ikliq if he is relaxing in his own home, his booted feet dangling over the ikliq edge out of consideration for the bedding; but he lies with his body curved, so that his torso is still oriented toward the social center of the dwelling. By contrast, Inuttiaq in an aloof mood turned his back to society, his head, and sometimes his face, toward the wall as he smoked or read the Bible.

He was not, in fact, as unconscious of his surroundings as he appeared; he was simply inert, torpid. He would hear if I asked him a question, but instead of answering, he would wrinkle his nose in the Eskimo gesture of refusal. In such moods, his helpfulness with small domestic problems was minimal, too. Ordinarily, if Allaq were not immediately available when Saarak began to bounce up and down in an agony of impatience for the urine can, Inuttiaq would reach for the can, which was always within arm's length, and place Saarak on it. In a passive mood, however, he would not move a muscle. Instead, he would shout for Allaq, who might be gutting fish in the storeroom. "Allaaq! She's going to pee!" Allaq always came running, with never a reproach, wiping her fishy hands as she ran.

It was only in the privacy of his family, or when women and children visited, that Inuttiaq would maintain a mood like this. If Mannik or Pala, Qavvik or Nilak came to visit, he sat up at once and entered into conversation with his usual geniality. At other times he ended his self-isolation by telling Allaq to brew tea or make bannock, or by jumping up suddenly and going out to visit somewhere, with never a word to us as he departed.

Whether Inuttiaq's moodiness was greater than other people's I do not know. He was not the only person who sometimes lay silently on his ikliq, resting, thinking, or perhaps merely being. There was often a companionable silence also among people who sat together, working or visiting. But Inuttiaq's nose-wrinkling refusal to communicate, his unhelpfulness in small domestic crises, and his physical position with his back to his audience all made his withdrawal seem different from others'. The quality of it was reminiscent of the passivity into which Allaq sank once during Inuttiaq's midwinter absence in Gjoa Haven, but it was not identical. Though Allaq, like Inuttiaq, was completely inactive during her period of hibernation, nevertheless, unlike him, she remained responsive to her children and to me. Moreover, her passivity was so striking only on that one occasion, whereas Inuttiaq was frequently moody. Of course, it is possible that I was simply in a better position to observe Inuttiaq's withdrawals, and that when I entered other iglus their inmates roused themselves to greet me, as Inuttiaq did to greet his guests. But even when we lived jointly with Pala's family I never was aware of withdrawal like Inuttiaq's on the part of any of the members of Pala's household.

I could never guess Allaq's reaction to these moods as she sat quietly sewing, or smoking, or playing with Saarak in her corner of the ikliq. Her surface equanimity was never ruffled. As long as Inuttiaq ignored the rest of us, she ignored him. I found his aloof moods depressing, the more so because Inuttiaq and his family provided most of the warmth in my life. When I turned to Inuttiaq, expecting a friendly laugh or an answer to a question, and was met instead by a solid back or a silently wrinkled nose, I was more unpleasantly startled than if he had always been so withdrawn. His moods triggered mine; I sulked, and my resentment fed my insurgency.

It was in the middle of the first winter that conflicts between Inuttiaq and myself began to emerge into the open. The first one I recorded occurred only ten days after I had returned from Gjoa Haven in December. It was precipitated, as were others, by an act that must have seemed incredibly insignificant to Inuttiaq and Allaq, though it was by no means insignificant in its consequences for my work. The morning's net-checking and fish-gutting were finished, and Allaq had brewed the usual kettle of tea to warm us after our work. I planned to spend the rest of the day typing up some of the notes that had fallen into arrears during the Gjoa Haven trip, and to that end I was eager to warm the iglu up to the thirty degrees necessary to make my fingers flexible and the carbon paper printable. Unfortunately, as the chill began to dissipate and my project began to seem realizable, Inuttiaq appeared in the doorway. He had come for a cup of tea, but since he had not yet finished his outdoor work, instead of shedding his furs, as usual, and ensconcing himself on the ikliq, he sat down in the open doorway to drink his tea, sociably but coolly. The subzero draft that cut through the iglu from the storeroom in which Inuttiaq was sitting threatened to undo in minutes the work of an hour. I asked him: "May I shut the door?" Inuttiaq looked at me in silence, his face expressionless; he did not move. Allaq hastily intervened: "Wait a while." I tried to explain the reason behind my apparently rude request: when the iglu was cold I could not write easily. But irritation devoured my still feeble vocabulary; I could not find the words. I stood up. "I want to go out," I said curtly, and Inuttiaq, moving slowly, as if to acknowledge my rudeness, moved aside just enough to let me pass.

I walked until nearly dark on the empty snowfields behind the camp, thinking kapluna thoughts, and feeling my anger still itself in the cold silence. The iglus were dim humps on the slope below me when I returned to camp. Raigili and Qijuk ran to meet me at the top of the hill: "Where have you been?" "Over there," I gestured, "walking." Raigili accompanied me back to the iglu and immediately reported to Inuttiaq, who was now in his place on the ikliq: "She was over there, walking." Inuttiaq repeated his daughter's question: "Where were you?" I told him. The wooden box on which I was accustomed to type had been placed in readiness in front of my place on the ikliq. Neither of us mentioned it.

That evening, after Inuttiaq had read a short passage aloud from the Gospels, ostensibly to himself, he gave me a lecture on Christianity, while Allaq hushed Saarak so that I should not lose a word. "God is Three," Inuttiaq said; "Father, Son, and Spirit. God made the world, and there is just one God for Eskimos and kaplunas. The Bible says so. God loves (naklik) us and wants us to belong to him. Satan also wants us. He takes people who get angry (urulu, ningaq) easily and puts them in a fiery place. If anyone here gets angry with other people, I will write immediately to Nakliguhuktuq, and he will come and scold (huaq) that person. If you get angry with me, or if I get angry with you, Nakliguhuktuq will come and scold the angry person." Allaq giggled at these illustrations, and Inuttiaq added: "We don't get angry here. If Nakliguhuktuq comes and scolds it's very frightening (kappia)."

Inuttiaq's lecture left its mark. Though I was not as awed by

visions of Nakliguhuktuq's righteous wrath as Inuttiaq undoubtedly hoped I would be, nevertheless I was reminded afresh
of the urgent necessity for restraint, not only in my relationship
with Inuttiaq, but in all other relationships, as well. I was
acutely aware of the high level of control valued, and to a large
extent achieved, by Utku, and with secret discomfort I contrasted
that control with my own tempery reactions to minor misfortunes.
Though my reactions were well within the bounds set by my
own culture, in an Utku setting they did not seem so harmless.
Innumerable instances of Utku control were filed in my mind as
models to emulate. When Putuguk tripped against our primus
and knocked the kettle of boiling tea to the iglu floor, no one,
including Putuguk, expressed startle; I felt no unusual intensity
even in the general murmur of laughter. "Too bad," he said
quietly, refilled the kettle, and repaired the floor. When the
sinew fishline that Allaq had spent days in braiding for Inuttiaq
broke under his first experimental pull, Allaq laughed a little,
and Inuttiaq handed the line back to his wife with no sign of
reproach: "Sew it together." There were also times when people
failed to control themselves, and so minute did these lapses seem
to me that I was astonished at the criticism they drew. Once
when Inuttiaq shot impulsively at a bird, which had flown as he
aimed, Allaq, watching at a distance, had observed in amusement: "Like a child (nutaraqpaluktuq)." When the old man
Piuvkaq prepared himself to be taken to hospital on the government plane, perhaps not to return, a tear had run down the nose
of his fourteen-year-old son, and this incontinence was reported
as amusing (tiphi) by the boy's older sister on her visits to the
neighbors.

Applying Utku standards to my behavior, I felt each of these
incidents as a personal reproach; but all too often my resolve
to act in a way that Utku would consider exemplary was unequal
to the situation. It was inevitable that it should be so. The control required was much greater than that to which I was accustomed to discipline myself. At the same time, I was under
considerably greater strain than I was used to, and the resulting
tensions pressed for expression. Though I did my best to express
them through laughter, as Utku did, laughter did not come
naturally. Discouragingly often after hours, or even days, of

calm, when I was congratulating myself on having finally achieved a semblance of the proper equanimity, the suddenness or the intensity of a feeling betrayed me. There was the coldness in my voice, which concealed a desire to weep with fatigue or frustration when I had to say for the thousandth time: "I don't understand." There was the time when, hurrying to leave the iglu, I unthinkingly moved Raigili aside with my hand instead of quietly telling her to move. There were the critical remarks I made in murmured English when the narrowed eyes and malicious whispers of Allaq and her sister, absorbed in a gossip session, irritated me beyond endurance. There was the burst of profanity (also in English) that I uttered when a lump of slush from the overheated dome fell for the third time in as many days into my typewriter and ended my work for the day.

The silence that met these transgressions seemed pregnant with disapproval, sensible as I was of my mistake. Conversation caught its breath for a second before flowing smoothly on again as if nothing had happened. Other transgressions were met with even more visible withdrawal. One day, in a fit of pique after my typewriter had received another bath of slush, I tossed a knife, too vigorously, into the pile of frozen fish by the door. It rebounded, knocking onto the floor one of the cups of tea that was cooling on a box nearby. "Iq!" somebody murmured, and within a few moments the iglu was empty of visitors.

A similar incident occurred one day when I was alone in the iglu, trying unsuccessfully to skin and cut up a hard-frozen whitefish. I had thought a little chowder might allay the mild depression that afflicted me, and I thanked providence that I was alone for once and could eat the soup by myself without having to share. Unfortunately, the fish, the first I had ever tried to skin in a frozen state, proved unexpectedly difficult to handle. I tugged and fumed while my fingers froze, and my knife refused even to dent the surface. In the midst of my frustration, the door burst open and I turned to meet the eyes of two young neighbor boys, Pamiuq and Ukhuk. The two were constant companions, drawn together perhaps not only by their common age and sex, but also by shared experiences in the kapluna boarding school that they had both attended for several years. The two moved in a private English-speaking world of their own, their conversation a mystery to all except two or three other half-schooled boys. Charming as I thought them, they were the bane of my existence, because they knew (or professed to know) too little English to help me in my linguistic crises, yet enough to read (upside down as easily as right side up) the notes whose contents I did not wish to reveal. On this particular occasion, the sight of the boys released the guilt that I was trying to stifle with regard to my selfish activity; and the resulting outrage provoked a vehement outburst in English: "I HATE fish! And I hope when I go home I never see another fish." Ukhuk said, "Hunh?" in a voice of surprise, and I assured him again, with no less vehemence, that I regarded fish in a most unfriendly light. He murmured to Pamiuq: "Let's go out," and they departed precipitately, leaving me overcome with chagrin, to wonder which neighbors would be regaled first with that story.

I thought I had seen the last of them for the day, but in an hour or two, to my surprise, they reappeared, smiling and friendly, as if nothing had happened. I welcomed them gratefully, with pieces of the Christmas fruitcake that I was hoarding, and tried to explain that I did not really dislike fish; it was simply difficult to skin. We had, I thought, a delightful visit, and when, as the boys left, they told me how kind (*quya*) I was, I felt much reassured.

No repercussions from that incident ever came to my attention, but in general, as I later discovered, I was too easily reassured concerning the effects of my irritable lapses. When I succeeded in catching myself up, as I sometimes did after the first aggressive impulse had spent itself, if I recounted the incident afterwards with amusement and heard others laugh with me, or if people seemed to accept the generous gestures with which I tried to dispel the chill that followed my transgression, then I was persuaded that no damage had been done. How wrong I was I learned only a year later when, on my return to Gjoa Haven, Ikayuqtuq told me of the reports that Utku had made of me that first winter, the letters they had written to her, and the things they had told her and Nakliguhuktuq when they went to Gjoa Haven to trade. I had taken pains to conceal from Ikayuqtuq and Nakliguhuktuq the vexatious aspects of my life, wanting neither to arouse doubts concerning my adaptation to iglu life nor to appear dissatisfied with the treatment afforded me by my beneficent hosts. Nakliguhuktuq, however, reading the cheerful letter that I had sent with Inuttiaq in January when he went to Gjoa Haven to trade, had marveled aloud at my seeming happiness despite the coldness of the winter, whereupon Inuttiaq had observed: "She is lying. She is not happy. She gets angry very easily, and I don't think she likes us any more." Amaaqtuq had written in a similar vein to Ikayuqtuq. Instead of reporting, as she had in November, that I was kind and fun to be with, she described how annoyed I became whenever I failed to understand. Ikayuqtuq, concerned lest she make matters worse, did not let me know how people felt about me. Instead, she wrote a letter of advice to Amaaqtuq: "Kaplunas, and some Eskimos, too, get angry at themselves, sometimes, rather than at other people. If Yiini is angry, leave her alone. If an Eskimo gets angry it's something to remember, but a kaluna can get angry in the morning and be over it by afternoon." "I tried to make her think," Ikayuqtuq explained to me. "I thought maybe if she thought about it, she would understand." [2]

As I listened to Ikayuqtuq's story, gratitude at her unknown intervention and surprise at the accuracy of her intuition concerning the nature of my anger mingled with dismay: dismay that my volatility had so damaged my relationships with the Utku, and dismay, also, that my own intuition of danger had completely failed me.

My relationship with Inuttiaq must have suffered more than most. Though my irritability overflowed in other directions at times, it was he who bore the brunt of it, because of the frequency with which our wills collided. The time I objected to Inuttiaq's sitting in the open door was the first of several occasions when anger was openly recognized between us. The most memorable of these storms occurred that first January, shortly after Inuttiaq's return from Gjoa Haven. The two weeks of his absence had been an especially trying period for me. Having looked forward to a long and peaceful interlude in which to work, free from the interference of Inuttiaq's demands, I had

2. Note that the very similar comparison between Eskimo and kaluna tempers that was quoted in Chapter 5, section II, was made by a different informant from a different Eskimo group.

found myself instead faced with an iglu so frigid and a mother so passive that I could accomplish nothing at all. Silently, I fretted and fumed over the swelling pile of penciled scrawls, which there was no way to type. Obviously, nothing could be done until Inuttiaq returned, but I determined that when he did come, I would take drastic steps to improve my working conditions. I debated with myself whether perhaps I might go to live by myself for a week, or for a few days at a time, in the government building a few miles from our camp. The place was an empty wooden shell, built as a nursing station but never used except by me as a cache for my useless belongings. It had a kerosene stove, which would make it luxuriously comfortable. Or perhaps, I thought, Inuttiaq might build me a tiny iglu near our own, which I could use as an "office." It could be built small enough so that I could heat it with a primus stove. As a third alternative, perhaps I might set up the winter tent again; it had lain untouched in the nursing station ever since we had moved to Amujat in November. *Something* would have to be done, that was clear. The decision itself markedly lightened my inner gloom.

I broached the subject to Inuttiaq a few days after his return to camp. He listened attentively to my explanation: I needed a place to work; it was difficult in the iglu; either my fingers froze or the dome dripped or people wanted to sleep and I did not like to bother them. I said I had thought about going to live for a while in the nursing station, but that I was a little afraid the stove might not work well. It might go out, as a similar stove in a similar nursing station in Gjoa Haven had done once in December when I slept there. When I woke the following morning the temperature in the building had been thirty below zero. Inuttiaq agreed that the stove was unpredictable. Instead, he suggested that he take me to the nursing station every morning and fetch me again at night, so that I would not freeze. As so often before, he reassured me: "Because you are alone here, you are someone to be taken care of *(naklik)*." And as so often before, his solicitude warmed me. "Taking me to the nursing station every day will be a lot of work for you," I said. The round trip took an hour and a half by dogsled, not counting the time and effort involved in harnessing and unharnessing the team. He agreed that it would be a lot of work. "Could you perhaps build me a small iglu?" I asked, thinking that this would be by far the least taxing alternative for him. It would take only an hour or two to build the tiny iglu that I had in mind, and then he need concern himself no further. Lulled by the assurance he had just given me of his desire to take care of me, and by the knowledge that the request I made was not time-consuming, I was the more disagreeably startled when he replied with unusual vigor: "I build no iglus. I have to check the nets."

The rage of frustration seized me. He had not given me the true reason for his refusal. It took only two hours to check the nets, every second or third day. On the other days, Inuttiaq did nothing at all except eat, drink, visit, and repair an occasional tool. He was offended—but why? I could not imagine. Perhaps he objected to my substituting for his suggestion one of my own, however considerately intended. Whether Inuttiaq read my face I do not know, but he softened his refusal immediately: "Shall Ipuituq or Tutaq"—he named two of the younger men— "build an iglu for you?" Perhaps it would be demeaning for a man of Inuttiaq's status, a mature householder, to build an iglu for a mere daughter. There was something in Inuttiaq's reaction that I did not understand, and a cautioning voice told me to contain my ethnocentric judgment and my anger. I mentioned my tent: "I hear it is very warm in winter." Inuttiaq smoked silently. I struggled for a semblance of calm. After a while, he asked: "Shall they build you an iglu tomorrow?" My voice shook with exasperation: "Who knows?" I turned my head, rummaging— for nothing—in the knapsack that I kept beside my sleeping bag, until the internal storm should subside.

Later, when Inuttiaq was smoking his last pipe in bed, I raised the subject again, my manner, I hoped, a successful facsimile of cheerfulness and firmness. "I want to try the tent and see whether it's warm, as I have heard. We can bring it here, and then if it's not warm, I won't freeze; I'll come indoors." Allaq laughed, Inuttiaq accepted my suggestion, and I relaxed with relief, restored to real cheer by Inuttiaq's offer to fetch the tent from the nursing station next day—if it stormed so that he could not go on the trapping trip he had planned.

My cheer was premature. Next day Inuttiaq did not go trapping, and he did not fetch the tent; he checked the nets. I helped without comment. The tent was not mentioned that day or the next, until in the evening, unable to contain myself longer, I asked Inuttiaq, in the most gracious voice I could muster, when he thought he might get my tent. "Tomorrow," he said. "You and Allaq will do it while I check the nets."

Morning arrived; the tent was mentioned in the breakfast conversation between Inuttiaq and Allaq. I could not catch the gist of the exchange, but when Inuttiaq inquired of a neighbor child who came in whether any of the young men of the camp were going near the nursing station that day, and was told they were not, I realized that once more the tent would not be brought. As usual, I was not informed of the decision. Had I been a good daughter I would have trusted Inuttiaq to keep my interests in mind and to fetch my tent in his own time, when convenient opportunity arose. Unfortunately, I did not trust Inuttiaq to do any such thing. The repeated delays had convinced me, whether rightly or wrongly I do not know, that he had no intention of bringing me my tent. I imagined that he had no faith in my assertions that it was a warm tent, that he could not conceive of a tent being warm in winter, and that he did not believe I would really use it. I had not used it, after all, when I had set it up as a refuge at the Rapids in October.

My voice taut with exasperated resolve, I asked what the weather was like outside. I said nothing of my intention; nevertheless, I was surprised when Inuttiaq asked why I wanted to know. "Why?" was ordinarily a rude question; I was forced to ask it frequently, myself, in the course of my investigations, since I had not yet discovered the more polite ways of asking for reasons; but I did not expect to be asked in turn. "Who knows why?" I replied. It was a rude evasion, and Inuttiaq said nothing, but went out to check the nets. When I began to put on my fur clothing, Allaq, too, asked what I planned to do; I never wore my furs in the vicinity of camp. "I'm going to walk," I said, more gently. I thought her inquiry was probably prompted by concern lest I wander off by myself and come to harm. I was too angry with Inuttiaq to consider that his inquiry might have been similarly motivated. I never felt as hostile toward Allaq as I did toward Inuttiaq.

Like Inuttiaq, Allaq was silent when I evaded her question, and silently she set off for the nets, dragging the sled on which she would haul home the netted fish. Watching her move away, coughing with the effort, her shoulders set against the harness rope, I felt a pang of remorse. The sled was not really so very heavy; it slid easily over the hard surface of the river snow; but it was my custom to help her pull, and it suddenly seemed unduly hostile not to do so now. I ran after her and picked up my half of the rope. But when we reached the nets, the sight of Inuttiaq enraged me again, and instead of staying, as usual, to shovel the drifted snow away from the holes, to help collect the fish and haul them home again, I set off without a word in the direction of the nursing station, invisible on the horizon. I had no intention of fetching the tent myself; it would have been impossible; but I needed a few hours alone, and vaguely I knew that the direction of my walk would be to Inuttiaq a sign, however futile, that I was in earnest about my tent.

I knew it would be a sign, but I did not dream that he would respond as charitably as he did. I had just arrived at the nursing station and was searching among my books for a novel to comfort me in my frustration, when I heard the squeak of sled runners on the snow outside and a familiar voice speaking to the dogs: "Hooooo (whoa)." Inuttiaq appeared in the doorway. I smiled. He smiled. "Will you want your tent?"

Gratitude and relief erased my anger as Inuttiaq picked up the tent and carried it to the sled. "You were walking," he said, in answer to my thanks; "I felt protective (naklik) toward you."

It was a truce we had reached, however, not a peace, though I did not realize it at once. It was nearly dark when we reached camp, so Inuttiaq laid the tent on top of the iglu for the night to keep it from the dogs. Next morning I went with Inuttiaq to jig for trout upriver, and when we returned I thought that finally the time was ripe for setting up the tent. Not wanting to push Inuttiaq's benevolence too far, and remembering the force of his response to my query about iglu building, I asked: "Shall I ask Ipuituq to help me put up my tent?" "Yes," said Inuttiaq. There was no warmth in his face; he did not smile, though he did tell me to keep my fur trousers on for warmth while I put up the tent. I obeyed, but the wind had risen while we drank our homecoming tea, so that even in fur trousers tent-raising was not feasible that day or the next.

When the wind died, two days later, Inuttiaq and I went fishing again, most companionably. Relations seemed so amicable, in fact, that this time, on our return, I was emboldened to say directly, without mention of Ipuituq: "I would like to put up my tent."

Naïvely, I thought that Inuttiaq would offer to help. He did not. His face was again unsmiling as he said: "Put it up."

My anger was triggered again. "By myself?" I inquired rudely.

"Yes," said Inuttiaq, also rudely.

"Thank you very much." I heard the coldness in my voice but did not try to soften it.

Inuttiaq looked at me for a moment, then summoned two young men who were nearby and who came, with a cheer that was in marked contrast to his own manner, to help me set up the tent.

Inuttiaq's attitude toward the raising of the tent puzzled me. I failed to understand why he resisted it, unless he thought it ridiculous to set up a tent in winter. I think now that he did consider it foolish, not only because of the frigid temperatures but because of the winds, which can have relentless force in January. There was a storm the very day after the tent had been raised, and afterwards, when Mannik dug out our entrance and came in to visit, Inuttiaq's first question concerned the tent: "Is it still standing?" It was; and I thought I heard a note of surprise in the "mmmm" of his acknowledgment.

But it seems to me now that more was at stake than the feasibility of the project: Inuttiaq was personally affronted by my request. One clue to his reaction I find in a question that I hardly heard at the time. He had wanted to know, after the tent was up, whether I planned to sleep in it or only to work there, and I think he may have felt that my demand for a tent was a sign that I was dissatisfied with him as a father, with his concern for my welfare. He may also have considered an offense against his dignity the suggestion that he himself set up the tent. The thought crossed my mind even at the time, when he substituted younger assistants for himself; but in other seasons, when moving was the order of the day, Inuttiaq readily helped to raise my tent.

I cannot know Inuttiaq's thought, but in retrospect I see so many reasons why he might have opposed my wish that I am no longer astonished that he did resist it. I am surprised only by the extent to which he remained protective (naklik) throughout the whole episode, while obviously intensely opposed to my wish. Perhaps, in part, the protective actions were a shield for the hostile feelings, making it possible for Inuttiaq to convince himself that he was conforming to Utku values of helpfulness and obligingness. Or perhaps, as I believe, he really did feel both protective (naklik) and hostile toward me, simultaneously. It is possible that his outrage at my exorbitant demand was owing, in part, precisely to the fact that he was a good (naklik) father to me and he knew it. In any case, his behavior was a curious blend of opposites. He chose the site for my tent with care, correcting my own choice with a more practiced eye to prowling dogs and the prevailing wind. He offered advice on heating the tent, and filled my primus so that it would be ready for me to use when my two assistants and I had finished setting the tent up. And when I moved my writing things out, he told me that if I liked I might write instead of going fishing. "If I catch a fish you will eat," he assured me. But he turned his back on the actual raising of the tent and went home to eat and drink tea. And next day I saw his displeasure in another form.

It was Sunday morning and storming; our entrance was buried under drifting snow. Since there could be no church service, Inuttiaq and Allaq had each, separately, in a mumbling undertone, read a passage from the Bible. Then Inuttiaq began to read from the prayerbook the story of creation, and he asked if I would like to learn. I agreed, the more eagerly because I feared that he had perceived my skepticism and that this was another hidden source of conflict between us. He lectured me at length. The story of creation was followed by the story of Adam and Eve (whose sin was responsible for the division of mankind into kaplunas and Eskimos), and this story was in turn followed by an exposition of proper Christian behavior: the keeping of the Sabbath—and of one's temper. "God is loving (naklik)," said Inuttiaq, "but only to believers. Satan is angry. People will go to heaven only if they do not get angry, or answer back when they are scolded (huaq)." He said further: "If a kapluna policeman kills me, I won't be afraid, because we'll both go to the sky and stand before God. I will go to heaven and live forever, but God will kill *him*." He told me that one should not be attached to earthly belongings, as I was: "One should devote oneself only to God's word." Most striking of all was the way Inuttiaq ended his sermon to me. "Nakliguhuktuq made me king of the Utku," he said. "He wrote that to me. He told me that if people, including you, don't want to believe what I tell them, and don't want to learn about Christianity, then I should write to him, and he will come quickly and scold *(huaq)* them. If people don't want to believe Nakliguhuktuq either, then Nakliguhuktuq will write to Cambridge Bay and a bigger leader, the kapluna king in Cambridge Bay, will come in a plane with a big and well-made whip and will whip people. It will hurt a lot."

Much of this I had heard before, but this version was more dramatic than previous ones. It renewed my sense of Inuttiaq's inner fires and made me see, more clearly than I had before, something of the way he viewed kaplunas, generally. I heard the hostility directed against myself, as well, but again he had softened the latter by blending it with warmth, in the manner that I found so confusing. He knew *I* believed in God, he said, because I helped people, I gave things to people—not just to one or two, which God doesn't want, but to everybody.

In view of that commendation, it seems particularly unfortunate that my next graceless gesture, that very night, was to refuse a request that Inuttiaq made of me: to borrow one of my two primus stoves to take on an overnight trip he planned. "Request" is perhaps the wrong word; his manner was peremptory, and that was partly the trouble. "You can use that one in your tent," he said, "and I will borrow this one." He pointed to the one that I had contributed to the iglu household. He had not neglected to make provision for my welfare but, still raw from recent events, I was in a mood to run my own affairs. And, most important, I knew that if any accident befell that second primus, my hard-won tent would be useless to me. In other words, any systematic work would be impossible for the rest of the winter. To me, that was reason enough for refusal. To Inuttiaq, however, my attitude must have been neither comprehensible nor justified. I had two primuses; he had none, as his own was cached in his overnight trapping shelter, a day's journey distant; and therefore it was right that he should borrow mine. I said I did not see why he could not share the primus that Putuguk and Mannik, his two young traveling companions, planned to take; it was standard practice to share traveling equipment in that way. Worse, instead of mentioning the anxiety that I felt for the safety of the stove, I phrased my refusal as a concern for Allaq's warmth. "She will be cold in the iglu without the primus," I said, "if I am using the other primus in the tent." It was a tactic that I had learned from the Utku, but behind the charitable words lay the knowledge that I would be troubled by guilt if I monopolized the only available stove in my tent while Allaq sat blowing on her hands in the iglu. (I knew by then how cold iglus could be when men, and stoves, were absent.)

It is just possible that Inuttiaq wished in some recess of his mind that the absence of that household stove might make it difficult for me to use my tent in peace, and that my refusal to lend the stove foiled that wish. But he had more obvious cause, as well, to demur at my resistance. After all, he, not I, was Allaq's "leader" and, in principle, he was mine, as well. I was interfering with his jurisdiction over both of us. "She won't be cold," he said.

When I remained silent, a sign that I did not acquiesce, Inuttiaq dropped the subject, and it was not until next morning, Monday, that I discovered how extremely angry he was with me. He did not plan to leave on his trip until Tuesday; on Monday he planned to fish, and I was, as usual, going with him. He had gone out to ice the sled runners, and I was pulling on my fur trousers when he reappeared, snow knife in hand, and announced in a ringing voice: "The tent is ruined!" So tense was the atmosphere at that moment that I was sure he had hacked the tent to pieces with his knife. He had not, of course; the dogs had torn the sleeve entrance off, and after Inuttiaq had left— alone—to fish, Allaq volunteered to help me sew it on again, sitting on the snow outside at ten degrees below zero. But as I sewed, racing against the freezing breeze and singing "Yankee Doodle" loudly with hastily composed English lyrics concerning the worthlessness of humanity in general and Eskimos and dogs in particular, I still mentally accused Inuttiaq of feeling satisfaction at the damage to my tent.

His displeasure was, in fact, expressed more overtly that day than it ever was again, but he did not attack my property. Just the reverse: he refused to touch it. In lieu of the primus that I declined to lend, he had decided to take on his trip a feeble kerosene heater that he owned: "In case I get separated from the others in blowing snow," he said. It was unlike him to prepare for unpleasant contingencies in this way. Perhaps he did not wish to depend on the younger men, or perhaps he wished to assert himself against the conditions that my refusal imposed on him. I do not know his reason for deciding to take the heater, but when, on his return from fishing, he set about preparing his equipment for the next day's trip, I saw how I had alienated him. He picked up the two-gallon can in which he carried kerosene, and bypassing my ten-gallon drum, which stood in the iglu, open and accessible for household use, he took the can outdoors, pried his own, still unopened drum out of the snow where it stood in reserve, waiting for my drum to be emptied, and filled his can there on the slope, where the wind took toll of the precious fuel.

Surprised, and not a little remorseful, I followed him out, intending to reassure him that I would be glad to have him use my oil. But my choice of words was not felicitous. "Why are you using *your* drum?" He raised his head sharply from the drum, whose frozen cap he was trying to disengage with the hatchet, and with sharpness in his tone, too, he replied: "It is my will!"

The rest of the winter, for a wonder, passed more peacefully, at least on the surface. Partly, I think, this was because I spent a great deal of time closeted in my tent, typing up the notes that had accumulated during the months when conditions in the qaqmaq and in the iglu had prohibited typing. Partly, too, it was because Inuttiaq almost never again permitted his own hostility to emerge so overtly against me. In a flash of the eye; in a silence; in a comment unintelligible to me, at which Allaq laughed; in a surreptitious glance toward Pala or toward Mannik, who remained expressionless, I saw, or imagined I saw, irritation or disapproval; but the explosions, which still occasionally occurred, were all mine, and Inuttiaq's restraint in the face of them was extraordinary. Most often he was silent, sometimes he offered me something to eat, occasionally he reassured me that I was cared for *(naklik)*, and occasionally, too, he lectured me.

The most notable of these lectures was delivered one day in March, when I was disturbed because Inuttiaq had refused to repeat to me a conversation he had had with the husband of a woman, Pukiq, who was very ill. I thought the two men had been discussing whether or not Pukiq should send to Gjoa Haven for medical help, as she had so far refused to do for fear of being taken out to hospital. I was alarmed for her life, and conscience-torn, because at her request I had promised not to notify the priest in Gjoa Haven of her illness; and I thought, when I overheard a fragment of the conversation between Inuttiaq and Uyuqpa, that I could still help by explaining that Pukiq would not necessarily be sent to hospital if she asked for help; the priest might be able to contact the nursing station in Cambridge Bay and get medicine that would help her here at home.

But Inuttiaq replied to my question that Uyuqpa had said nothing at all; and he went off to attend to the far end of the fishnet, which he and I were checking. I began to shovel snow from my end with more than usual vigor, and when Inuttiaq was, I fear, not quite out of earshot, I said loudly in Eskimo: "You're lying."

Inuttiaq did not turn around, but later when, temper restored to resignation, I joined him at his end of the net, he looked up from his work: "Are you angry *(ningaq)?*" I blushed and hesitated, gesturing "no" and "yes" simultaneously. Inuttiaq laughed and said with surprising directness: "You get angry *(ningaq)* easily. It's nothing to get angry about. Uyuqpa was talking to me alone."

Inuttiaq was right, of course, which did not lessen my frustration. I had neither the desire nor the ability, however, to describe the complexities of my conscience, so I sought an explanation that would make sense to him and, more important, one that would reassure him that my temper was harmless. "I'm a little bit angry *(ningaq)* from fear *(kappia)* that the kapluna leaders will be angry with me, because I didn't tell them that Pukiq was ill."

Inuttiaq nodded: "I, too, fear the anger *(ningaq)* of the kapluna leaders." But then his tone changed suddenly. "The kapluna leaders are not frightening *(kappia),*" he said. "They are not to be feared. Only God is to be feared. Nakliguhuktuq isn't afraid of the kaplunas and neither am I. You, too, should be neither afraid nor angry. You get angry easily. I don't get angry. If you keep on getting angry, I'll write to Nakliguhuktuq." There was no anger or disturbance in his tone, though his voice and his words were strong.

As I was about to reply, Allaq came from the iglu to join us, and the subject was dropped. Inuttiaq was exceptionally cheerful and solicitous of my welfare while we three finished checking the net, more than once asking me whether I were warm enough and not too tired. And when we returned home, he took special pains to see that I had a choice piece of fish to eat.

It seems to me now that my controversial tent proved more of a blessing in preventing the development of conflicts between Inuttiaq and me than I had any idea it would when I insisted on setting it up. I was astonished at the relief I felt during those hours in the tent. I expanded in the warmth that thawed my fingers and the carbon paper, and that on still days even made it possible to remove my parka, which I otherwise never did except at night in bed. The solitude, too, was more of a blessing than I had anticipated. Though quite aware of the irritations that beset me daily in the iglu: the murmuring voices, the giggles, the chill air, Inuttiaq's presence, nevertheless I had not felt the cumulative weight of these small strains until it was lifted.

I had only two regrets as I sat happily typing. One was that I was unable to see out of my shelter. I could hear footsteps coming and going among the iglus and voices calling, but the sounds gave me few clues to what was happening. I never knew what anthropologically interesting events I might be missing. I could not go outside to check, either, without turning off the primus that warmed the tent, and when the primus was off, my papers and typewriter all had to be put away, because within a very few minutes after the primus had stopped, the tent would return to outdoor temperature, which might be anything from twenty to sixty below zero, and frost crystals would begin to fall on all exposed surfaces when the temperature dropped. For the same reason, I could not go home to eat during the day, and this was my second regret. However, a week or so after I had begun to work in the tent, I happened to mention my hunger, in a casual fashion, to Allaq, and that afternoon the squeaking footsteps to which I listened approached my tent instead of going by, and Allaq's voice said, "Yiini, here is tea for you." She had brought me a small kettleful of hot tea, already sugared and milked, and a lump of caribou stomach fat, as well. From that day on, either Allaq or Raigili regularly brought me tea and food when they were eating at home. Sometimes, Allaq said, it was at Inuttiaq's suggestion that she did this.

I was touched by this attention; and in the weeks following the January crisis, Inuttiaq made other gestures, too, that soothed and warmed me. Only a few days after he returned from the trip for which I had refused to lend my primus, he sent my kapluna father a message, the tone of which startled me by contrast with the events just passed. "Tell him," said Inuttiaq, "that because I am very grateful *(hatuq)* indeed for the help you are giving us with kerosene, I am feeding you with the caribou meat that I have fetched." A month later, when one of Raigili's two dogs was about to whelp, Inuttiaq asked me if I would like to "own" one of the pups for the duration of my stay, and the neighbors pointed out the significance of his offer: all members of a family, adopted or otherwise, own dogs belonging to that family's team.

Such gestures, as well as the more even flow of daily life, lulled me into believing that the hostile feelings that had infected the air earlier in the winter had been forgotten, and convinced me that the tensions that I continued to spark from time to time were momentary flashes without lasting effect. I am no longer sure that my peace of mind was justified. In retrospect, it seems to me possible that these warm acts were neither rewards for improved behavior on my part nor evidence of a generous willingness to accept me in spite of my thorny qualities, but were, rather, attempts to extract or blunt some of the thorns. I think my Utku parents may have hoped that the same techniques of pacification and reassurance that throughout the winter had soothed crises away might also serve to prevent difficulties from arising. If I knew I was cared for *(naklik)*, I might not get angry so easily. I thought I heard similar logic in the admonition Inuttiaq once in a while gave his sulky daughter, Raigili: "Stop crying, you are loved *(naklik)*." Another possible motive may have been a desire to shame me, by virtuous example, into reforming. Perhaps these kind acts even had the effect of nullifying Inuttiaq's and Allaq's own prickly feelings, permitting them to prove to themselves that, as Inuttiaq had said, *they* didn't get angry, only *I* did.

IV. The Fishermen: Crisis

Whatever the interpretation of these particular incidents, it is clear to me now that there remained more of an undercurrent of tension in my relationship with Inuttiaq and Allaq than I perceived at the time. I had come to accept the everyday vicissitudes of the relationship as matter-of-course; consciously, I felt the rewards far greater than the strains. The same was not true, I think, of Inuttiaq and Allaq; but I saw their feelings only at the end of April, when our iglu melted and Inuttiaq ordered a move into tents. Then he decided (as usual, without telling me) that I should return to my own tent, rather than joining the rest of the family in theirs. And during the five months in which I lived in my tent before moving back into Inuttiaq's qaqmaq in the following October, Allaq almost never visited me, as she had done in the first days after my arrival.

To be sure, during the last two months of that period almost no one else visited me, either. Short of murder, the ultimate sanction against the display of aggression in Utku society is, as I have said, ostracism. Niqi, Nilak's overly volatile wife, lived her life in its vacuum, and for a period of three months during my second summer and autumn at Back River, I experienced it, too. It was precipitated, in my case, by a misunderstanding that occurred in August, at the start of my second year. I am sure, however, that the tensions of the preceding winter added their residue of hostility, as well, to create a situation in which the kapluna member of the community ceased to be treated as an educable child and was instead treated as an incorrigible offender who had, unfortunately, to be endured but who could not be incorporated into the social life of the group. The misunderstanding came about as follows.

At the time I went to live with the Utku, Chantrey Inlet was becoming increasingly known among sports fishermen in the provinces of Canada and in the United States. Every year in July and August small charter airlines in Ontario and Manitoba, which cater to sportsmen, flew men in, for a price incredible to me, to spend two or three or five days fishing for arctic char and salmon trout at the Rapids. Until a year or so before my arrival only a few had come each summer, perhaps five or six, but then they had begun to come in numbers. Fifteen or twenty, the Utku calculated, had come in 1963, and in 1964, when I was there, forty came, not all at once but in groups ranging in size from two or three to approximately fifteen. One or more of these groups was with us constantly from July 26 until August 23. They camped across the river from us, out of sight behind a point of land, and their outboard motors sputtered up and down the river from dawn to dark.

Some of these fishermen and their guide, a Canadian named Ray, kept to themselves on their side of the river. They traded generously with the Eskimos when the latter went to offer bone toys in exchange for tea, tobacco, and fishhooks, but otherwise they largely ignored the native inhabitants of the Inlet. The Utku—it was Nilak, Pala, Inuttiaq, and, later, Ipuituq, who were camped by the rapids that summer—liked Ray. He was a mild-mannered man, who had been bringing fishing parties to the Inlet for several years and who treated the Eskimos with dignity.

Individuals in other groups were less innocuous. Hard drinking, cigar smoking, and gruff-voiced, lacking in gentleness and sensitivity, they were the antithesis of everything Eskimo. They stared at the Eskimos; visited the Eskimo camp and photographed people without asking permission; peered into the tents; and when the Eskimos tried to trade for the coveted tea, tobacco, and fishhooks, one or two of these kaplunas offered instead strings of pink beads and other useless items, which the Eskimos were too timorous and too polite to refuse. The Eskimo women were particularly afraid *(kappia, iqhi)* of one of the plane pilots who, they said, had "wanted a woman" the previous year and had made his wishes known distinctly.

The Utku did not fail to notice differences among the fishermen and to judge some of them kinder (*quya*) than others, but whatever dislike they felt showed neither in avoidance nor, of course, in aggressive acts. The Eskimos looked forward with excitement to the coming of the kaplunas in July. As soon as the ice left the river, they began to listen for planes and, as they sat together on the gravel in front of the tents, they filed away at bits of caribou antler, shaping them into miniature replicas of fishhooks, pipes, knives, and other objects to trade to the kaplunas. Their talk was of tea and tobacco and of other things—food and clothing—which they had received from the fishermen in the past in very generous amounts, and which they hoped to receive again. When a plane was heard they hurried with one accord to the other side of the river in order to be present when the kaplunas landed, to help with the unloading of the plane, and to watch the strangers. Regardless of the quality of the men who had arrived, regardless of how the Utku felt about them, they treated all alike with the same obliging acquiescence with which they had treated me on my arrival. Their courtesy did not fail even when the kaplunas took advantage of their mildness to treat them in ways that I considered most humiliating. One champion wrestler picked up Mannik and held him horizontally, by shoulder and thigh, over his head: for a television ad, he explained to me. Mannik, who knew nothing of what was happening until he found himself in the air, giggled. On another occasion a loud-voiced man staggered off the plane, steeped in champagne, and wove his way over to Pala, whom he had singled out as the Eskimo "chief." Hugging Pala warmly, he inquired what his name was and invited him in incoherent English to be his friend. Pala, to my astonishment, understood the man to ask his name and replied "Peeterosi" (Peter, his Christian name). "Ha ha, Peeterosi!" roared the drunken kapluna. "Ha ha, Peeterosi! Le's be frens, I like Eskimos, nice Eskimos," and he stroked Pala's head, while Pala laughed mildly and resisted not at all. The other Utku watched, expressionless, in the background.

When we returned to our camp, later, I discovered that the Utku did have a way of retaliating against the kaplunas' condescending behavior; they made fun of it. They taught Saarak to imitate the drunken fisherman, and for months she ran from person to person, on request, stroking their heads and laughing with kapluna boisterousness in her piping voice: "Ha ha ha, Peeterosi, ha ha ha!" But even when I saw this mockery, my feelings were not relieved. I was ashamed of being a kapluna among such kaplunas, and I was humiliated on behalf of the Eskimos who watched, smiled, nodded, and submitted.

Yet I did not identify entirely with the Eskimos, and this fact made the situation even more painful. In spite of myself, I was drawn to the men camped across the river. Except for an exasperatingly brief conversation with a passing police officer in May, I had seen no member of my own culture and heard no English since the previous November. Neither had I tasted any kapluna food other than the few items: bannock, tea, rice, raisins, and chocolate, that I stocked in meagre quantities. Most trying of all, perhaps, I had had no mail since March, except for a few pitiful items, mostly bills and advertisements for camping equipment, which the police officer had brought in May. I deplored the insensitive ways of the men, and yet I was starved for the sights and sounds of my own world that they represented and for the familiar food that symbolized that world and that they had brought in enormous quantities.

But more detrimental to my peace of mind than the sudden sharp awareness of my deprivations was the fact that, since I was the only bilingual present, the members of each camp expected me to mediate with the other on their behalf. I often tangled the two languages hopelessly in my distress, unable to muster a coherent sentence in either one. It was not too hard to help the Utku in their attempts to trade with the kaplunas, since I almost always felt the Eskimos' requests reasonable. Difficulty arose only if a fisherman countered with beads a request for tea. Then I was tempted to demur on behalf of the unresisting Eskimo. Far more awkward were the requests that the kaplunas made of me. I was supposed to explain to Mannik why he had been so summarily hoisted skyward; to ask Nilak for his braided boot laces, though I knew no wool was to be had for replacements; and to negotiate with Allaq and with Niqi for the manufacture of fur mittens, though I knew that hides suitable for mittens were scarce and that our own winter mitten material would be used. The Eskimos would never refuse.

Most painful of all the transactions that I was expected to mediate were negotiations for the loan of the two Eskimo canoes. Once, each Utku family had owned a kapluna-style canoe of wood and painted canvas. The Canadian government had provided them after the famine of 1958, in order to encourage the Utku to depend more heavily on their rich fish resources than they had formerly done. One by one the canoes had been damaged and now either lay beached for lack of repair material or had been burned for firewood. Inuttiaq's and Pala's were the only two usable canoes remaining to our camp. During the spring, the canoes were used to transport the household goods up and down the river in the long series of moves, and during the summer and early autumn the men anchored them in midriver at the foot of the rapids and fished from them more efficiently than they could have fished from the shore. The canoes were used also to set and check the nets in the open river before freeze-up, and to ferry people back and forth across the river on various errands: to fetch birch twigs, which grew more plentifully on the far side of the river, to bring in needed possessions from caches, and to visit other families camped nearer the mouth of the river. The canoes had innumerable uses; without them Utku life would have been greatly constricted. Just how constricted I discovered when the kaplunas asked to borrow the boats.

All the groups, both the pleasanter ones and the less pleasant ones, wanted the use of these canoes. The kaplunas had two aluminum boats of their own, but these were not large enough to enable all of the men to go fishing at once. The ins and outs of the negotiations that I was forced to conduct are too complicated to record here, but the result was that from July 26, when the first plane arrived, until August 15, when the last large party of fishermen left, we seldom had the use of both of our canoes and sometimes we had the use of neither. The kaplunas suggested that to compensate us for the loan of the canoes, which prevented us from fishing as we would have done, they would bring us the fish that *they* caught during the day; Ray also offered to feed us a meal of kapluna food every evening. Of course, it was impossible to know what Inuttiaq and Pala thought of this plan when it was proposed, but they agreed to it with alacrity. I myself thought it sounded like a reasonable solution to the conflict of interests, one that would involve minimal discomfort for the Utku. In fact, however, the effects of the arrangement were more inconvenient than I had foreseen.

It was worst for the Utku, of course, when the kaplunas used both of our canoes. Then we were stranded on our shore and in many little ways were made dependent on the kaplunas. The days were spent not in fishing but in craftwork, as the men made toy after toy to trade to the kaplunas. Once Mannik went out to cast a throwline from the boulders along the edge of the rapids, but the hook, caught by the still swollen midsummer current, snagged under a stone and could not be retrieved until the kaplunas came to fetch us for our evening meal. Then they lent Mannik his canoe so he could paddle out to disentangle the hook. Once Inuttiaq shot a gull that was swimming near the camp. An occasional bird made welcome variety in our diet, but we could not fetch this one; we had to wait until it drifted to shore of its own accord. We ran out of sugar one morning, but the supply was cached on an island, so we had to drink bitter tea that day until, again, the kaplunas came to fetch us in the evening; then they took us out to the island in one of their outboards. We were deprived of our daily patau because we no longer had fresh fish to boil. The fish that the kaplunas brought us faithfully every evening were, inexplicably, fed to the dogs, and we ourselves ate the fish we had been drying for autumn and winter use. Not the least of the constrictions was our inability to visit the kaplunas freely. On the evenings when Ray was in the Inlet, if the wind had not whipped up the river too much, he came for us after the kaplunas had finished their supper and ferried us across to their camp for a meal, and after we had eaten, he ferried us home again. But often there was no visiting at all.

I do not know how strongly the Utku felt about the absence of their canoes and their dependence on the foreign visitors. Perhaps none of the alterations in the daily patterns troubled them as much as they did me. Characteristically, the Utku kept well under control whatever negative feelings they may have had. Gratitude was the feeling they expressed openly. Every week they thanked God in their prayers for the help the kaplunas were giving them with food, clothing, and equipment, and, indeed, the kaplunas were incredibly generous with their supplies; the leader of one party even brought boxes of discarded wool clothing to distribute among the Eskimos. I chafed against our enforced dependence on the kaplunas, against the loss of our patau, and perhaps most of all against the restrictions imposed on our visits to the kapluna camp, starved as I was for the sound of English and the taste of American food. From my point of view, it was most painful when we had one canoe. When we had none at all, no one went to visit except when the kaplunas fetched us, but when we had one, the men went, frequently and at length, leaving the women and children at home. When they returned, after hours of visiting, their pockets were filled with candy and gum for the children, and they regaled us with detailed accounts of all the good things they had eaten in the kapluna camp: canned pears, and steak, and potatoes, and oranges. Oranges! I would have sold my soul for an orange. Inwardly frantic with frustration and envy, I tried to conceal my feelings and to reason with myself: I was being treated the way the Eskimo women were treated; but the feelings remained and may have caused me to read more covert resentment into the Utkus' own behavior than was actually there.

Nevertheless, a change was clearly evident in the atmosphere of the Utku camp during the period of the kaplunas' sojourn, a change that indicated to me that feelings other than gratitude toward the kaplunas lay under the surface. Though I have no way of knowing whether the Utkus' feelings coincided in detail with mine, there was evidence that the loan of the canoes was to them, as it was to me, a source of strain.

The Utku were as fascinated with the kaplunas as I was. As they sat about on the gravel beach, filing bits of antler and soapstone into pipestems and knives for trade, they watched the kaplunas trolling up and down the river in their borrowed canoes and laughed at the odd cant of the boats, weighted down by the outboard motors that the kaplunas had attached. "It would be nice to have a kika (an outboard)," Inuttiaq joked; "paddling is no fun (hujuujaq)." The others laughed. Talk was all of the strangers, their personal and collective peculiarities: this one has a big nose; that one is frightening *(kappia, iqhi)*, he doesn't smile, just stares; they are all disgustingly furry (that is, hairy); they drink liquor, and that is frightening *(kappia, iqhi)*, too; they never eat fish, just catch them and throw them back or give them away. Most of all, talk centered on the bounties that the kaplunas would probably leave for the Eskimos when they departed, as they had done last year. And when the kaplunas disappeared at noon and in the evening into the cove where they were camped and their motors were silenced, the Utkus' thoughts followed them. "I wonder what they are eating?" someone would muse with a little laugh.

Given such absorption in the fishermen and their activities, it would have been strange had the Utku not felt regret at being unable to visit them at will. The year before, when the Utku were camped on the other side of the Rapids, when no water separated them from the kapluna campsite, they had spent many hours standing in a silent cluster on the slope just above the kapluna camp, watching the comings and goings below them, and accepting the food and tobacco they were offered.

There were several signs that something was, indeed, amiss in the Utku camp. For one thing, people were afflicted with a most unusual lethargy. They yawned, complaining of sleepiness in midday, something I had never seen at any other season. Inuttiaq and Allaq once fell sound asleep at noon. I remembered that lethargy one autumn day after the kaplunas had gone, when Amaaqtuq was describing to me how one could recognize that a person was upset *(huqu)*. "He will sleep long hours during the summertime when people usually stay up late," she said, "and he'll sit idle instead of working."

Another puzzling phenomenon was the waste of the salmon trout that the kaplunas gave us. The fish were larger and fatter and more numerous than those we caught ourselves. In every obvious way they were desirable, and yet the Utku, who had accepted with such alacrity when the kaplunas offered us their catch, let the fish lie until they rotted on the beach where the kaplunas threw them; then they gave them to the dogs. Before the arrival of the kaplunas, the women had spent hours every day filleting the catches of their men and hanging them to dry in the sun. The dogs had been fed only the bones and heads. The kaplunas, good conservationists all, remarked on the cavalier way in which the Utku treated their gifts of fish, whereupon, wanting to justify to the kaplunas the apparently reprehensible behavior of the Eskimos, I tried to inquire into the latters' reasons for neglecting the fish. I was not satisfied with the replies I received. "The women feel too lazy to cut them up," said Inuttiaq. "Not at all," replied Allaq, "the fish are unpleasantly soft from having lain too long in the sun." The truth was, however, that even when the fishermen brought us fish caught only moments before, as they sometimes did after I had informed them of the Eskimos' dislike of sun-softened fish, the Utku still let most of them lie.

To be sure, neither the Utkus' lethargy nor their neglect of the kaplunas' fish was clearly attributable to the absence of the canoes. It was, characteristically, Inuttiaq who gave me the clearest evidence that the thoughts of the Utku did dwell on their canoes. One morning, two days after the kaplunas had borrowed both canoes, he asked me: "Are the kaplunas leaving tomorrow?" When I replied that those who had his canoe would be gone in two more days, he said with feeling: "That makes one grateful *(hatuq)*." The following day, he inquired again whether the kaplunas who had his boat would be leaving the next day, and when I assured him that they would, he went so far as to tell the guide of that party, through me, that "tomorrow" he would want his boat to fish in.

Curiously, though other Utku men, too, occasionally remarked as they sat stranded on the beach: "One feels like going fishing," or "One feels like eating fresh fish," nevertheless when the departing kaplunas returned the two canoes, nobody went fishing. The remaining kaplunas, covetously eyeing the beached canoes, commented on this inconsistency, too, and again I felt it incumbent on me to explain the Eskimos to the kaplunas. But when I tried, cautiously, to sound the Utkus' reasons for not fishing, telling them, truthfully, that the kaplunas had inquired, Pala replied: "When the kaplunas leave, we'll go fishing again"; and indeed, the day the last plane disappeared, the men sat and fished from their canoes all day in midriver. Not only that, they also set the nets for the first time since spring. What they did use the canoes for, as soon as they became available, was to cross the river to visit the kapluna camp, frequently and at length.

The strength of Inuttiaq's desire to retain his canoe, for whatever reason, appeared a few days after the first group had returned it. We were expecting another group of fishermen to arrive as soon as the clouds lifted. Knowing this, and knowing that Inuttiaq had been restless without his canoe, I tried to assure him that the kaplunas would not take it amiss if he refused to lend it again. If he wished, I said, I would tell them; and I warned him that if they used the boat when they were drunk, they might break it. Inuttiaq responded strongly. "I don't want to lend my canoe," he said. "I want to fish in it. If those kaplunas ask to borrow my canoe tell them they can't. The kapluna leader gave us those canoes because he cares for (naklik) us. It's Eskimos he cares for, not kaplunas, because we live under more difficult conditions (ayuq), and he said that if any harm came to those canoes, the people who damaged them would be stabbed with something metal—I forget exactly what—something metal, yes? It will hurt." He made a stabbing gesture in the air and turned to Allaq for confirmation, which she silently gave. Little did I suspect how much trouble my literal interpretation of Inuttiaq's instruction that day was to cause me.

The fishermen arrived in due course, and shortly thereafter they came for a canoe. Trouble began almost at once, but I was not aware of it. The Utku did not lend their best canoe, Inuttiaq's; they lent Pala's, which was slightly leaky; but even so, I was annoyed at their compliance. I wished they had refused to lend either and, in my irritation, when the kapluna guide asked me for assurance that the Eskimos would really use the fish he offered as rental payment for the canoe, I replied that the Eskimos had not used the kapluna fish before when they were given, and probably would not do so now. Pala's fourteen-year-old son, Ukpik, freshly arrived in camp after a winter at school in Inuvik, listened, expressionless, to my remarks.

The rest of the day passed uneventfully. As usual when they had the use of a canoe, the men spent a large part of their time at the kapluna camp, but they returned with less booty than sometimes; this trip leader did not believe in "spoiling the natives." Next morning early, I woke to hear the sound of an outboard approaching, and kapluna voices down at the shore. Anxious not to lose an opportunity to use my native tongue, I dressed and joined the men, Eskimo and white, who clustered at the edge of the beach. Inuttiaq and Pala approached me as I went toward the group. "The kaplunas are going to borrow the other canoe," they told me. "They say they will return it when they are through with it."

The kapluna trip leader corroborated what Pala had said. "That first canoe is no good," he said; "it has a hole in it, so we have to borrow this other one." There was, indeed, a sizeable rent in the canvas, which had certainly not been there when we loaned it and which made the canoe unusable. The two men who had come with the guide were already attaching the outboard to Inuttiaq's canoe, as Inuttiaq and the other Utku men watched.

I exploded. Unsmilingly and in a cold voice I told the kapluna leader a variety of things that I thought he should know: that if he borrowed the second canoe we would be without a fishing boat, that if this boat also was damaged we would be in a very difficult position, since a previous guide had forgotten to bring on his return trip the repair materials that Inuttiaq had traded for, and that we would be unable to buy materials ourselves until the strait froze in November. I also pointed out the island where our supplies of tea, sugar, and kerosene were cached and mentioned our inability to reach it except by canoe. Then, armed with my memory of Inuttiaq's earlier instructions, I told the guide that the owner of that second canoe did not wish to lend it.

The guide was not unreasonable; he agreed at once that if the owner did not wish to lend his canoe, that was his option: "It's his canoe, after all." Slightly soothed, I turned to Inuttiaq, who stood nearby, expressionless like the other Utku. "Do you want me to tell him you don't want to lend your canoe?" I asked in Eskimo. "He will not borrow it if you say no."

Inuttiaq's expression dismayed me, but I did not know how to read it; I knew only that it registered strong feeling, as did his voice, which was unusually loud: "Let him have his will!"

I hoped my voice was calm when I replied to Inuttiaq: "As you like," but I was filled with fury at kapluna and Inuttiaq alike, as well as at myself for having undertaken the futile role of mediator, and my tone was icy when I said to the guide: "He says you can have it." Turning abruptly, I strode back to my tent, went to bed, and wept in silence.

V. Persona Non Grata: Ostracism

That incident, bringing to a head, as it did, months of uneasiness concerning my volatility, marked the beginning of a new phase in my relationship with the Utku. Some days passed, however, before I became aware that I was ostracized. My work seemed somehow more difficult than usual, I felt tired and depressed; "bushed," perhaps, I thought, in need of a vacation. There was certainly reason enough why I should be tired; the strain of the summer, the long isolation without mail, and the frustrations engendered by the presence of unlikeable kapluna men, my impossible role as mediator—all had taken their toll. Now that the men were gone, I spent a great deal of time alone in my tent, typing notes, writing letters, and trying to analyze my linguistic data. I felt little desire for company and was grateful when the smiling faces that appeared from time to time between the flaps of my tent entrance withdrew again without entering. I noticed nothing unusual in the behavior of anyone toward me.

Realization came suddenly and from an unexpected source. Autumn was upon us. The kaplunas, fearing to be weathered in for the winter, had departed precipitously in a sudden snow squall the day after my outburst—an unfortunate coincidence, I am afraid—and the able-bodied members of our camp, released from their fascinated vigil around the kapluna camp, had gone off to hunt caribou, leaving, as usual, only the infirm, the immature, and the school children behind in camp. Pala, his daughter Amaaqtuq, and I were the only adults who remained. Knowing that the school plane was expected imminently, I wrote letter after letter to send out. There might be no opportunity to send out mail again until November.

Pala also wrote a letter to be sent—to Nakliguhuktuq—and, smiling warmly, he gave it to me to keep until the plane should come: "So I won't forget to send it," he said. The letter was in syllabics, of course, and, moved by I know not what amoral spirit, I decided to read it—to test my skill in reading Eskimo. It had been written ten days earlier, the day the kaplunas left. It began, more or less as I had expected, by describing the bounty of the kaplunas and how much they had helped the Eskimos. Then it continued in a vein that I had not anticipated: "Yiini is a liar. She lied to the kaplunas. She gets angry *(ningaq)* very easily. She ought not to be here studying Eskimos. She is very annoying *(urulu),* because she scolds *(huaq)* and one is tempted to scold her. She gets angry easily. Because she is so annoying, we wish more and more that she would leave."

I pored over the crudely formed syllables for some time, unwilling to believe that I was reading them correctly. Perhaps I was inserting the wrong consonants at the ends of the syllables; the script does not provide them. But I was not. There was only one way to read the characters. So there was a reason why my work was going poorly! And my depression was not all due to the fatiguing summer. What shocked me most was that, in thinking back over the ten days since I had spoken to the kapluna guide, I could recall no change in the habitually warm, friendly, considerate behavior of the Utku. Though I had had few visitors, I had attributed that fact to my obvious preoccupation with typing; I had assumed that it was I who was withdrawing from the Eskimos, not they from me. Whenever I joined the group sitting on the beach in front of the tents, I was welcomed with smiles, as always, and every morning when tea was brewed for the camp, the kettle was brought to my tent so that I might share. Indeed, care was always taken to provide me with two cups, a matter that required special attention, since I drank much more slowly than other people. Generosity was shown me in other ways, too. When the kaplunas departed, leaving behind them a boatload of food for the Eskimos, Inuttiaq had taken it upon himself to distribute it among the households. There were tea bags, potatoes, onions, powdered milk . . . Pala's household acquired a thirty-pound tub of jam. To me, Inuttiaq gave one of two large roast turkeys and ten boxes (a disproportionate share) of lard. When I protested at the latter gift, saying that I still had some lard in my cache on the island, Inuttiaq insisted that I take it: "Because you help people so much."

I think now that Inuttiaq's gifts were probably telling me that in addition to my other defects I was considered stingy, but at the time that explanation did not occur to me, and I could not reconcile his generosity and the considerate behavior of the other Utku with Pala's letter.[3] Perhaps, I thought, the letter had been written in umbrage, which the passage of time had soothed. Or perhaps it was only Pala who felt so hostile toward me. Unfortunately for such consoling hypotheses, a day or two after I had read Pala's letter, Amaaqtuq paid one of her rare visits to my tent. Asking if she might have a piece of paper and a pencil, she wrote a letter to Ikayuqtuq, and delivered it into my keeping until the plane should come. With no moral qualms at all this time, I read it, praying that her sentiments were friendlier than her father's; certainly her smile had been of the warmest and her manner as a visitor had been most appreciative. But her letter matched Pala's, word for word, only elaborating somewhat on my obnoxious characteristics and on the gentle virtue of the Utku in dealing with me. She told Ikayuqtuq again, as she had the previous January, that I became angry (*qiquq*) every time I failed to understand something, in spite of the fact that linguistic difficulties were unavoidable (*ayuq*). "Because she is the only kapluna here and a woman as well, we have tried to be good (*pittiaq*) to her, but even though we try to help her she gets angry (*qiquq*) very easily without cause. It's sometimes very annoying (*urulu*) and makes one lose patience . . . She keeps doing what she shouldn't, even when she's told not to." As Pala

3. I have suggested elsewhere in this chapter that Utku may sometimes use obligingness and generosity to shame a person into better behavior, or perhaps just to express hostility in an inverted way—to say, in effect: "I am a better person than you are." Strategies of this kind have been noted by other observers of Eskimos, too; it is not unusual to find a social offender treated with exaggerated consideration and concern. Freuchen (1961:155–160) illustrates this in a delightful story about his Greenlandic Eskimo wife, Navarana. Navarana, outraged by the smallness of a gift of meat she had received, responded with exaggerated gratitude. She loaded down the unhappy donor with all of the rarest kapluna foodstuffs in her own larder, and sent her away wailing with shame. Conversations with Jonathan Jenness (1966) concerning Alaskan Eskimos from the Bethel area, and with Milton Freeman (1967) concerning the Canadian community of Grise Fiord also support the observation. With regard to both Grise Fiord and James Bay Eskimos, Milton Freeman mentioned the reverse kind of inversion, as well: if A is scolding B, and C feels sympathetic with the victim, B, he (C) will appear to take A's side and scold B even harder than A does. This indicates to B and to the rest of the world that C is really on his side. However, I did not notice this kind of behavior among the Utku, perhaps because scolding so rarely occurred.

had done, Amaaqtuq accused me of lying (I assumed this was a reference to my telling the kaplunas that the Utku were wasting the fish the kaplunas gave them, and I found later that I was right) and she said that people wished increasingly that I would go home. The letter ended, however, on a more cheering note: "Now she's becoming very nice *(pittau)*, thank goodness *(quya)*. Sometimes she's pleasant *(quvia)* and amusing *(tiphi)*. She has been kind *(quya)* tonight during my visit."

Pala was not alone, then, in his condemnation of my behavior, and the disapproval was not an ephemeral thing; people still wanted me to go home. On the other hand, that last sentence gave me hope. Perhaps if I exerted all my will to maintain a semblance of the equanimity I could not feel, there was a possibility that the situation might be repaired. I began to watch more closely the way Pala and Amaaqtuq treated me, trying to discover signs, however minute, that would tell me how I was regarded. And I did see things that had escaped me before. Not only was I visited very seldom and very briefly (now I put a new construction on this fact); I was also, in subtle ways, encouraged to stay in my tent. By faithfully bringing me tea every time it was brewed, Pala and Amaaqtuq forestalled my coming to drink it with them outdoors or in their tent, and they did not invite me to join them as they used to do. When I did visit in Pala's tent, I perceived no difference in the welcoming warmth of my hosts, but now and then I thought a smile seemed slightly dimmer than usual; and when I asked questions, as I often did on various subjects, the answers, though rendered smilingly, were usually brief or evasive. More often than formerly, the answers seemed to be "unknown," and I later discovered that Pala had lied to me during this period, "because," as Inuttiaq told me, "he didn't want to talk to you."

I did my utmost to appear unperturbed, to appear not to notice. And so covert were these small withdrawals that at times I succeeded in persuading myself that they existed only in my depressed imagination. The illusion that all was well, however, never lasted for long. I felt myself in limbo, and I fumbled for a way to break out. I wanted to confront my punishers with my knowledge of their feelings toward me, and to explain why I had acted as I had toward the kaplunas, but I feared I would only shock them the more by my directness. I considered the advisability of leaving on the school plane when it came; it was expected any day. I had not intended to leave for several more months, but since my work had come to a standstill anyway, perhaps there was no use in staying on. There were other inner voices, however, which told me to stay. I feared I had not gathered adequate data for the dissertation that was supposed to result from this field trip; and I did not wish to admit defeat before those who had said at the outset that Chantrey Inlet was too difficult a place for a white woman to live.

I buoyed myself stubbornly with the last sentence of Amaaqtuq's letter, and I thought I did see signs that disapproval might evaporate if my behavior warranted it. The isolation in which I found myself was not wholly consistent. After several days during which only smiles and tea had passed between me and the Eskimos, suddenly, for no apparent reason, an overture would be made: Amaaqtuq would bring her sewing to my tent and sit with me while I worked; Pala would respond in detail to one of my questions or would call me to tea in his tent. Relief and joy would dissolve the oppression and convince me that I had done right to decide to stay. Unfortunately, however, such moments of joy were rare. I was unable to maintain the flawless equanimity that the situation seemed to demand. As Amaaqtuq quite justly observed, I was upset when I did not understand, and if I showed so much as a glimmer of discomposure, if I said, "Too bad!" with feeling, instead of laughing, when she confessed to being confused by my speech, it was enough to drive her away immediately, pleading, with a warm smile, that she was sleepy or needed to urinate.

Such incidents occurred all too frequently, and each time I sank back into gloom. As I tried in self-protection to maintain a clinical distance from my difficulty, it struck me that my gloom itself aggravated the situation. It seemed to me that at times Pala and Amaaqtuq withdrew less from my irritability than from the depression that instantly resulted when I became aware of my lapse. One such incident occurred when the school plane came at the end of August without the autumn supplies of food and fuel that I had expected, and worse, without the mail that I had hoped for. There was still a possibility that the Catholic missionaries in Gjoa Haven would send their fishing boat down to Chantrey Inlet, as they sometimes did in September, in which case supplies might yet come; but the chance was remote, and if the boat did not come, there would be no outside contact until the end of November. My disappointment was intense, and my control, I congratulated myself, was herculean; but again it was not perfect. I joked with the pilot in a tone so aggressive that, hearing myself, I was sure the listening Eskimos, attuned to the tone but not to the words, could not help but hear the anger while the attempt at humor must escape them. Again, I felt, I had failed, I had alienated people, and before Pala and Amaaqtuq had a chance to show their displeasure, I walked away from them. When I withdrew, so did they, and so a vicious circle was created. I reproached myself for being unable to reassure people with a show of warmth, but I felt none. Both the Eskimos and I became increasingly sensitive to my acts. I grew more and more discouraged; the others grew more and more intolerant.

Matters did not improve when the caribou hunters and their families returned to camp. Inuttiaq and Ipuituq and the members of their households seemed to feel just as strongly as did the members of Pala's household that my behavior was reprehensible. They wrote no letters to Gjoa Haven—they could not; the plane had come and gone—but in all the same hardly perceptible ways they isolated me. Indeed, I felt more isolated than I had been before they returned, since now the group whose periphery I circled was so much larger.

The only people who treated me with favor at any time during this period were Nilak, his wife, and his daughter. All summer while we were camped together at the Rapids they had courted me more than they had done at any time since my arrival at Back River a year earlier, but toward the end of the summer this behavior was intensified. They brought me offerings of tea, bannock, and fish, and even asked if I would like to come to their tent to eat, rather than being served in my tent. Niqi invited me to go with her and Tiguaq to gather plants for fuel, and Nilak offered me tidbits of information on the private life of Qavvik.

My reactions to this attention were mixed. To Tiguaq, who continued patiently to help me with my linguistic work, I was grateful, but I suspected her parents of their usual ulterior motives: a desire for material gain. They seemed, in my jaundiced view, to be pressing the advantage that my social isolation gave them to ingratiate themselves with me. After the departure of the kaplunas, who had replenished in some small degree our supplies of tea, sugar, and bannock ingredients, these goods dwindled rapidly, until by early September there was almost nothing left. Nilak's goods diminished even faster than those of the other households, because both Inuttiaq, as an assertive trader, and I, as a kapluna, had received more than he had in the first place. As autumn wore on, therefore, Niqi more and more frequently came with a cup and a hesitant smile to ask for a "tiny bit" of my last bag of tea or sugar, or to offer me bone toys, which I valued less than food, in exchange for one of my last few boxes of rice. Nilak and Niqi must, justifiably, have felt they had earned these bits of food by treating me kindly. Nonetheless, I begrudged them; at this point whatever remnants of cheer I felt were contained in those grains of sugar, rice, and tea.

I resisted the kindness of Nilak and his wife for another reason, too. I sensed in it a recognition, perhaps shared by both Pala's faction and Nilak's, that now I was aligned with Nilak's family as a pariah among pariahs. Perhaps that feeling was a figment of my depressed imagination; perhaps not; I do not know. In any case, I began to notice parallels between the way in which Pala's people treated Niqi and the way they treated me. Her isolation was similar in quality to mine and, paradoxically, the more akin to her I felt, the more need I felt to dissociate myself from her.

VI. A Vicious Circle: Depression and Hostility

I am not sure whether the silence that surrounded me gradually increased in intensity as the autumn advanced, or whether the new manifestations of hostility that developed were simply a result of qaqmaq living. In any case, it was in October, after the qaqmaqs were built, that I became most sensible of my isolation. I was not at all sure that Inuttiaq would invite me to move into his qaqmaq again, as I had done the year before. I was not even told that the dwellings were under construction on a point of land out of sight a quarter of a mile from the summer camp. It was Niqi who informed me, when I asked why the tent camp was empty that day. So the relief I felt was the more grateful when, after the dwellings had been built, Allaq came and told me to pack my belongings so that she could help me move—into their qaqmaq.

The difference in my situation from that of the previous year, however, was quickly apparent. Indeed, it was partly the contrast with the previous year that made my isolation so striking. The year before, Inuttiaq's qaqmaq had been the social center of the camp, always filled with family and visitors. Enclosed in protective warmth, I had suffered only when people impinged on me too much: when Inuttiaq told me to make tea or to give Itqiliq some tobacco, or when the laughing conversation had gone on, uninterrupted, for too many hours. This year, Pala's qaqmaq was the social center. Inuttiaq, Allaq, and the children, too, spent the better part of every day at Pala's. Even Nilak and Niqi stopped courting me and spent their time either at home or at Pala's. Too conscious of the meaning of this change to enjoy visiting, myself, I sat at home most of the time in our empty qaqmaq, took detailed notes on the way my camp fellows and I handled our hostility, wrote virulent twenty-page letters which could not be mailed until November, and read Jane Austen. And when the other members of the camp were served their daily patau in Pala's qaqmaq, I brought mine home to eat, because there never seemed to be a corner for me to sit in, in the other qaqmaq. On better days, the two little girls Raigili and Akla, and the two older ones Amaaqtuq and Tiguaq, ate in our qaqmaq, too, since Pala's really was crowded, but they sat in a huddle over their tray in the middle of the ikliq, giggling with each other, and I was not included in the conversation. On particularly bad days, they did not come at all but preferred to squeeze into Pala's qaqmaq. It was at this season that Niqi, popping in on one of her flighty visits, remarked that our qaqmaq was even colder and emptier than theirs.

Even in the early mornings when the family woke and at night when we were preparing for bed, I was isolated. It was as though I were not there. If I made a remark to Inuttiaq or Allaq, the person addressed responded with his usual smile, but I, like Niqi, had to initiate almost all communication. As a rule, if I did not speak, no one spoke to me. If I offered to fetch water or make tea (which I seldom did), my offer was usually accepted, but no one ever asked me to perform these services. I did not realize how pointed this avoidance was until one day when we were cooking something. I do not recall what was being made or who had initiated the cooking; I think it likely that I had done so, since the primus stood on the floor in front of me, instead of in its usual place near Allaq. Nevertheless, when the pressure began to run down, unnoticed by me, Inuttiaq turned not to me but to Allaq: "Pump up the primus." And she had to get up and come over to my side of the qaqmaq to pump up the primus. Had he spoken to me, I would only have had to lean over to do it.

Inuttiaq did not consult me when he was hungry for kapluna food, either, as he had done the previous year. My supplies were almost gone, but I still had a bag of oatmeal, two or three boxes of rice, some raisins, and a little powdered chocolate, which we drank thin and sugarless (a tablespoonful dissolved in twenty cups of hot water). Instead of asking me, as he had before, "Shall we make rice?" he said to Allaq, "Make rice!" And she obeyed with alacrity, as I sat silent in my corner.

Too late I realized the dignity inherent in the Utku pattern of authority, in which the woman is obedient to the man. I envied Allaq the satisfaction of knowing that she was appreciated because she did well and docilely what Inuttiaq told her to do. And sealed off, as I felt, from the life of the camp, watching it around me as if through glass, I realized, too, with a force I had never felt before, how vitally necessary society is to men. If I could have gained acceptance then by abandoning my own ways and transforming myself, emotionally, intellectually, and physically into an Utku, I would have done so. But I still had objectivity enough to know that the idea of "going native" was ludicrous, that such a metamorphosis was impossible; after all, it was my inability to be Utku in important ways that had created my difficulties in the first place.

Invisible as I felt in the qaqmaq, the other occupants gave evidence that they found my presence, however walled off by their silence and mine, extremely irritating. One day about a week after we had moved into qaqmaqs, Inuttiaq even suggested that when we moved into iglus later on I should be physically walled off, to a degree. Often when Utku build their permanent winter iglus they attach to one side a small chamber called a *hiqluaq* in which to store the fish they net. The hiqluaq opens into the interior of the iglu by way of a hole just big enough to crawl through. Inuttiaq's idea was to build such a hiqluaq for me to live in; after I left, he would use it in the orthodox manner, for fish storage.

To be sure, it was not always my mere presence that was irritating. No matter how hard I tried to prevent it, every now and then, small hostile acts slipped past the barriers I set against them. Such an incident occurred one day when Saarak was crying for raisins. Instead of handing the box to Inuttiaq, who was sitting beside me, so that he might pass it to Allaq on his far side, I tossed it, in an ungracious spirit, directly to Allaq. Allaq took a cupful of raisins and tossed the box back to my side of the ikliq. Inuttiaq had given no sign of noticing my gesture, but when the box landed beside me again, to my immense surprise, he asked loudly and with distinct annoyance: "Was that tossed?" Allaq admitted that it had been. "Like a kapluna in the house!" said Inuttiaq in the same loud tone. I had never heard him raise his voice to Allaq before, and I never heard him do so again. I could count on one hand the times I had heard him speak with such undisguised annoyance to any human being; he had done so once to me during the midwinter upheavals, and once to Kamik, after having endured in silence all summer long the torments she inflicted on her sister Saarak. He must have been hard pressed to have scolded Allaq then.

Another of the incidents that awakened me to the intensity of the irritation I aroused also involved raisins. On this occasion I actually knocked Saarak's head with the box, which I held in my hand. I had intended only to call her attention to the raisins she was screaming for, since she was so absorbed in tearing Amaaqtuq's cloth parka with her teeth that she had ignored several verbal offers, but, tired and impatient, I hit her too hard, and she wept. Up to that moment, the day had been an unusually cheering one. Allaq had offered to mend my boots, and both Amaaqtuq and Tiguaq, to my astonishment, had stayed to visit with me, following the afternoon patau. Now, when Saarak burst into tears at my impulsive gesture, depression washed over me again. Tiguaq, Amaaqtuq, and Allaq all soothed her tenderly. I should have soothed her, too, but instead, my voice cold with discouragement at my impulsiveness, I said: "You're not hurt; have some raisins." Allaq silently took some raisins and handed the box back to me with a smile. Tiguaq very shortly excused herself and went home, and neither Allaq nor Amaaqtuq looked at me or spoke to me for the rest of the evening. Instead, they brought out some religious comic books and pored over them together, while Amaaqtuq, in pious tones, described the scenes portrayed and discoursed on moral subjects. "Niqi gets angry (*urulu*) easily," she observed. "She doesn't listen to what the missionaries tell us: that we should love (*naklik*) others." And she coached Saarak in the Lord's Prayer.

In spite of all these tensions I was still treated with the most impeccable semblance of solicitude. I was amazed that it should be so—that although my company was anathema, nevertheless people still took care to give me plentiful amounts of the foods I liked best, to warn me away from thin ice, and to caution me when my nose began to freeze. Allaq one day made explicit the ethos of concern. Our tea was all gone, and so was our cocoa; we were drinking infusions of dead weeds, which we scraped with ulus from under the shallow snow and boiled in the tea-kettle. Bilberry bushes were my favorite; their essence tasted a little like an exotic Chinese tea; other plants tasted more like clean earth, but the brew was hot, and not unenjoyable. I had asked Allaq whether in the old days, before the Utku had access to commercial tea, they had brewed teas from these plants, as they did now. "Very little," she said; "only once in a while. The only reason we do it every day now is that you are here; we do it for you." That was not strictly true, of course; the other households also brewed such teas every day for their own consumption. But the factual falsity of her statement made its message all the more forceful: the Utku saw themselves, and wanted me to see them, as virtuously solicitous, no matter what provocations I might give them to be otherwise.

Nevertheless, the tensions could not help but poison even the most courteous gestures. I wanted to go ice fishing, as I had done the previous year with Inuttiaq. The solitude of the open river refreshed and soothed me after the very different solitude of the qaqmaq. Jogging from foot to foot for warmth in rhythm with the rise and fall of the jig in my hand, I rested my eyes on the snowy hills and my thoughts on the kapluna world to which I would be returning soon—as soon as the strait froze, I promised myself. Last year Inuttiaq had seemed to acquiesce willingly in my desire to fish. He had located and cut my fishing holes and adjusted my line with as much care as he did his own, and when I had caught a fish, as I frequently did, his smile had been pleased and his words approving: "You fish well." I had wanted to learn to cut my own fishing holes, but so willing had Inuttiaq been to do the job for me that I had been embarrassed to persist stubbornly and ineptly while he stood silently by, offering now and then to help; so I had never learned.

This year Inuttiaq was not pleased to have me accompany him on his fishing trips. Sometimes, if I asked to come, he would assent, but the gesture was empty. Instead of selecting a virgin fishing spot for me and cutting a fresh hole through the whole thickness of the ice, he reopened a hole that somebody had used the day before. It was easier, there was less ice to cut through, but it was also, in his view, well-nigh useless. In Utku belief, fish do not readily come to the same hole twice. Similarly, instead of supplying me with a fresh sliver of white-fish tail, such as he himself used for bait, he might, on occasion, hand me a piece that had been cut the day before and was therefore less efficacious. Possibly he knew that I was unlikely to catch anything, anyway, since the sinew fishline that Allaq had braided for me at my request was too short for use in many of the usual fishing spots. When Allaq had handed the half-made line to Inuttiaq to measure in arm-lengths, as he measured his own, he had judged it completed, though it measured only five arm spans, as compared with the seven that he required for his own line. On the other hand, he may have forgotten the length of my line. He certainly had forgotten it by midwinter, by which time the unpleasantness of the autumn was past. Concealing in a joke his wish to have my line, he suggested that he might steal it when I left, as I was about to do. Half-jokingly, too, I reminded him that it was only five arms long. Inuttiaq looked at me with surprise, denied it, measured the line to check my assertion, and laughed in acknowledgment.

In any case, that October I was convinced that Inuttiaq had not the slightest interest in my catching a fish, that he took me along only because it was difficult to refuse my direct request. When he planned distant trips he did refuse to take me. "I am going overland today," he would say; "you will hurt yourself on the sharp rocks when the sled hits them." And he arranged for Niqi, the other pariah, to take me with her when she went to fish near camp.

One incident I find hard to explain, however. I feel in it a more genuine solicitude than I felt in many of the other formal gestures of concern that were my lot that autumn. Yet, since the incident was never mentioned in my presence and explanations were never given, I will never know. The morning was unusually windy, even for October. The ice was black glass, and snow snaked, hissing, over its surface. Inuttiaq, Allaq, and I had been fishing together at the edge of the rapids, close to camp. The rapids were never solidly frozen at any season, and this early in the autumn there was still a large expanse of open water in the vicinity of our fishing holes. The water was so close to us, in fact, that had I been alone I should never have trusted the ice. As it was, I relied on my companions' judgment and paid no attention. After an hour or two I was roused from my daydream by Inuttiaq's voice: "Yiini! You're going to get wet!" Sure enough, the wind, stronger all the time, was blowing a rapid stream of water directly toward us. In another minute it would reach my feet. Inuttiaq and Allaq had already wound up their fishlines and were picking up their tools in preparation for moving to another, safer fishing spot, farther from the rapids. I wound up my own line in haste and started after them; they were already some distance away, walking with the swift, shuffling slide with which Utku make their way across the bare autumn ice. I, too, had learned never to raise my feet from the ice as I walked, and ordinarily I managed quite well to keep up with my Utku companions. Today, however, the fates were against me. Perhaps the wind was unusually strong, or perhaps I was unusually tired; my depression did consume considerable energy. In any case, Inuttiaq and Allaq, shuffling along with no apparent difficulty, were growing smaller and smaller in the distance, while I was blown three feet off course for every few steps I took forward.

I had struggled in this way for perhaps a quarter of a mile; camp was just opposite me to the right, and Inuttiaq and Allaq were, I judged, another quarter of a mile ahead of me, still moving. Suddenly, something in me gave up. I had no will to struggle further. Dropping to my knees and lowering my head to the ice, I crawled toward home, seething with humiliation and rage but totally unable to stand up. Shielded by the parka hood that fell over my face, I wept at my ignominy. After I had gone some distance, I looked up to gauge my direction. The camp was straight ahead, several hundred yards away, and in front of Pala's qaqmaq stood every member of the community who was at home that morning. My face, my whole body, burned, in spite of the freezing wind. I dropped my head again and stubbornly pursued my four-legged way toward the watching group. When I looked up again in a few minutes, not a soul was visible. Only the dogs lay curled asleep on their chains.

I went straight to our empty qaqmaq and busied myself with irrelevant domesticities. I was fastening a long-damp washcloth to the outside of the qaqmaq roof, hoping that the wind would finally dry it, when the door of Pala's qaqmaq creaked and Allaq emerged. But how did she get there! She had been following Inuttiaq to a new fishing spot far down the river when last I had seen her. She looked at me—questioningly, I thought —as she approached, but did not mention what she had seen. I laughed, hoping the laugh did not sound as forced as it felt. "I almost got blown away." Allaq laughed, too, then, and replied: "The wind makes one feel like blowing away." I asked how it was that she was not out fishing with Inuttiaq. "He sent me home to make bannock," she said. "Too bad (hujuujaq) I couldn't keep on fishing." I wondered. Had Inuttiaq really been struck by a sudden craving for bannock? Or was he responding to my mishap in the way he knew best?

Unfortunately, I forced myself to laugh all too seldom. The vicious circle that I thought I perceived in September remained unbroken throughout October and into November. Looking back at my notes for that period, I am impressed not only by the careful way in which the Utku preserved the face of our relationship but also by their occasional tentative attempts to approach me. Some of these overtures I saw at the time, as I have said, and they gave me hope. Others I failed to see, and I fear that my blindness was mistaken for conscious rejection. Inuttiaq, within a few days of our moving into the qaqmaq, gave me two such opportunities to participate in family life, and I was oblivious to both of them until too late. In the first instance, he hummed quietly, as if to himself, a tune that in other days I had often played on the recorder. Inuttiaq had loved to have me play the recorder, and this tune, "The Tavern in the Town," had been one of his favorites. I paid no attention to his invitation. He never hummed recorder tunes again. On the second occasion his overture consisted in saying the Lord's Prayer exceptionally slowly one evening. The family often repeated it at bedtime, but usually Inuttiaq led it at top speed, mumbling the words under his breath so that they were doubly incomprehensible. This time every word was distinct. It was the first time Inuttiaq had conducted bedtime prayers since we had moved into the qaqmaq. Five months had passed since I had last heard him; consequently the unusual quality of his enunciation failed to register until he had reached the last sentence. I resolved that on the next evening I would join in. But next evening, and on all succeeding evenings, he recited the prayer in his usual rapid mumble.

VII. Reconciliation

October dragged into November, bringing no change in my situation. The men were waiting for the strait to freeze so that they could go to replenish our long-exhausted supplies of tea, flour, and tobacco. I waited for mail: mail from home, and perhaps even more important, mail from Gjoa Haven. After reading the letters written by Pala and Amaaqtuq to Nakliguhuktuq and Ikayuqtuq in August, I had written to Ikayuqtuq, myself. Though I did not confess the source of my information, I told her that I was afraid she would hear unpleasant reports of me from the Utku, and that I wanted her to know my version of the story. I told her, in brief, that my attempts to protect the Utku from

the inroads of insensitive kaplunas had, I thought, been misinterpreted by the Eskimos, and that the latter were unhappy
to have me stay longer with them. I said I hoped that she, knowing the ways of kaplunas better than the Utku did, would be
able to explain my irascible behavior to them. There had been
no reply from Ikayuqtuq; the Catholic boat had failed to appear
in Chantrey Inlet in September, just as I had feared. Now,
however, finally, there would be word from Gjoa Haven, and I
had confidence that Ikayuqtuq and Nakliguhuktuq, already so
understanding, would help me again.

There was another reason, too, why I waited impatiently for
the strait to freeze. Buoyed as I was by the hope of Ikayuqtuq's
intervention, I had nevertheless decided that as soon as a plane
could reach us I would leave. I had planned to stay until January
or March, but the exhaustion that had grown in me as a result
of the autumn's events made me fear for the winter, the more
so as the strain was beginning to take physical toll. And my
resolve to leave had been strengthened by the cheerfulness
of Inuttiaq's acquiescence. I had therefore written a letter to
send out with the men to the priest in Gjoa Haven, asking him
to arrange by radio for the government plane to come and pick
me up.

For all these reasons, when finally one frozen dawn I stood
outside the qaqmaq and watched Inuttiaq's and Mannik's sleds
disappear into the north, my spirits leapt. A physical weight
was lifted; I could breathe freely, knowing that within two weeks
(Niqi said six days, but she was foolish) the men would return
with reassurance and that within a month (two at the most) I
would be on my way back to the kapluna world where a person
could snarl a little without disastrous consequences. I was ebullient. Had I dared, I would have hugged Allaq, who stood beside
me. As it was, I channeled the joy into generosity. "Shall I
make some oatmeal? Shall I help you sew Raigili's new parka?
Do we need some water?" I had not felt such good will for
months. The effect of my new cheer on the others, moreover,
confirmed my suspicion that my depression had created a vicious
circle. Allaq, and others, too, responded, it seemed to me, with
much more warmth than at any time in recent weeks, and I was

too euphoric to notice whether or not it continued to be necessary for me to initiate our conversations.

Inuttiaq and Mannik returned ten days later. They had lost their route in bad weather on the way home and had bypassed the fifty-pound flour sack *full* (Inuttiaq emphasized "full") of my mail, which had been left for them to pick up on a certain promontory two-days' travel north of our camp. "It can be fetched later this winter if the foxes don't destroy it," said Inuttiaq reassuringly. But the response the men brought from Ikayuqtuq and from Nakliguhuktuq surpassed my most sanguine expectations; it made even the missing mail seem, for the moment, a paltry disappointment. Inuttiaq reported: "Nakliguhuktuq says that the kaplunas almost shot us when Yiini was not there." He turned to me: "Did you write that to Nakliguhuktuq?" I denied it; and later in Gjoa Haven Nakliguhuktuq denied having made such a lurid statement to Inuttiaq. But I did confirm the gist of Inuttiaq's report.

The effect was magical. That night after Inuttiaq and the children were asleep, Allaq's voice came out of the dark. "The kaplunas almost shot us?" Again I denied it, but exulting in the long-denied opportunity to explain my behavior, I told her what I had written to Ikayuqtuq and something of the reasons for my anger at the kaplunas. Allaq's response was a laugh of surprise: "So *that* was it!"

She must have repeated to Inuttiaq what I had told her, because at midday next day, when I came home from fishing with the children, Inuttiaq immediately began to interrogate me on the moral qualities of the various fishing guides who had brought parties to the Inlet during the summer, and for two days, off and on, he and other members of the camp continued to ask me for information about them. The wall of ice that had stood between me and the community dissolved. People talked to me voluntarily, offered me vocabulary, included me in their jokes and in their anecdotes of the day's activities—and Inuttiaq informed me that next day he and I were going fishing together.

With a suddenness and a completeness that astonished me, I was renewed. I expanded in social approval and regretted only that it was improper to hug these people who had accepted me once more. Still, one fear laid a sobering hand on my joy—the fear that a misunderstanding might occur again. It cautioned me not to ask too many of the questions that Utku found so impertinent; it adjured me not to relax such control as I had over my volatility; and it caused me to tense with trepidation when I asked Inuttiaq if I might, after all, stay until after Christmas. Would it make them unhappy *(hujuujaq)*?

My fear was not eased when I saw Inuttiaq's odd expression. Was it only the untoward directness of the question, or did he have reservations? He hedged: "Why?"

"I think sometimes I'm difficult *(ayuqnaq)*."

"In what way?"

"Am I inconvenient *(ihluit)* in the iglu?"

Inuttiaq was hard pressed, I think, but he replied nobly: "You are not very inconvenient *(ihluit)*. You are not inconvenient. You may stay because you help people a great deal with kerosene."

That Inuttiaq was not wholly happy to have me stay seemed clear. Being father to a kapluna was difficult, I knew it, and his tactful reply could not conceal it. I had other evidence of his feeling, too. There was the remark he made, suddenly, when we were both sitting, silently working, on the ikliq: "I think you're a leader in your country." The remark had no obvious context; it must mean, I thought, that Inuttiaq had never reconciled himself to my intractable behavior. There was the slightly wild look that I caught in his eye when I said I thought that I might someday return to Back River. The look vanished when Allaq explained that I meant to return after I had been to my own country, not merely to Gjoa Haven. "Eeee," he said then, "we will adopt you again—or others may want to: Nilak, perhaps" —he laughed—"or Mannik, if he marries."

But there were more positive feelings, too. I still remember with happiness one afternoon in late November, shortly after we had joined the rest of the Utku at the winter camp in Amujat. The iglu was filled with visitors, and the hum of the primus, on which tea was brewing, mingled with the low voices of Inuttiaq and his guests. I knew every detail of the scene even as I bent over my writing, and I paid no attention until suddenly my mind caught on the sound of my name: "I consider Yiini a member of my family again." Was that what Inuttiaq had said? I looked up, inquiring. "I consider you a family member again," he repeated. His diction was clear, as it only was when he wanted to be sure that I understood. And he called me "daughter," as he had not done since August. "Eeeeee." It was little enough to reply, but perhaps he heard the gratitude in my tone.

There is another memory, too. Inuttiaq and Allaq and I were alone in the iglu. Inuttiaq had asked me whether other "learners," like me, might someday come to Back River. I asked whether they would be unhappy if others came. Inuttiaq replied: "We would be happier to have a woman come than a man— a woman like you, who doesn't want to be a wife. Maybe *you* are the only acceptable kapluna."

Allaq's feelings about me as the time of my departure neared were not so clear. When I repeated to her the question I had asked Inuttiaq, whether it would be inconvenient if I stayed, she reassured me: "You're only inconvenient when we move." And when Inuttiaq one day heard me inquire the meaning of a very simple word and asked me whether I had learned the Eskimo language imperfectly, Allaq salved the discomfiture that I had tried not to show. "You know other words," she said. And next day, when she and I were sitting alone in the iglu, she repeated to me a complimentary remark that she had heard the previous winter about my ability to speak Eskimo. She talked with me on subjects that no one else felt free to discuss, laughed about her former shyness (*ilira*) of me, and shared jokes and reminiscences with me in a way that seemed quite in accord with my own affection for her. In all ways, she seemed more at ease with me than were any other members of the community, except perhaps Inuttiaq and Saarak. Still, it was a remark of Allaq's that precipitated my departure.

Since December I had been trying to decide whether to leave in January or in March. Inuttiaq advised March, because there would be less danger of my freezing on the long dogsled trip (I had given up the idea of summoning a plane to take me out). There was another reason for his preference, too, namely that my heavy load of gear would be less burdensome in March, because the lengthened days would shorten the trip, but he did not stress this thought. "If you prefer to leave in January," he said, "we will take care of you then, as well as in March, and we will try to keep you from freezing."

I was torn with indecision, and when neighbors asked me my plans I always put them off: I was waiting for a letter about money; I was going to take a long walk in the winter air to test my resistance to frostbite before I decided; or I simply did not know. People stopped asking, but they did not stop watching for the little signs that would indicate the way my thoughts were tending. They read my mind before I knew it myself. Allaq was particularly acute. I caused hearty laughter one day in Pala's iglu by remarking, as I entered, that the entrance passage stank. "That's because you're going home soon," said Allaq. "You didn't used to think it stank." A little disconcerted, I hastily explained: it was only because one of the pups had had diarrhea there. Allaq noted also that my aversion to raw whitefish seemed greater than the previous winter. Whitefish was a noxious fish in almost everybody's view, but it was the winter staple, and the year before I had eaten it as stoically as others did. This second winter I lacked appetite unless there was salmon trout, caribou, or fox in the larder, and Allaq explained this phenomenon the same way: "It's because you're going home soon."

A voice told me that Allaq was right, that I was, indeed, releasing my hold, little by little, on Eskimo things and drawing my own ways of life around me again, as the kapluna world began to seem real and attainable once more. True, in some ways the arctic world also seemed to have acquired an added vividness. I savored, even more than I had before, the gentle Eskimo voices, the peacefulness of the iglus on their moonlit slope, the wolf-howl of huskies, and the intensity of the winter silence; but the very poignancy of my perception seemed to confirm Allaq's impression that my departure was nearing.

On the other hand, I suspected that Allaq's vision might be sharpened by her own wish that I should leave. To this day, I am not sure which of us made the decision that I would leave in January. It came about in the following way.

Inuttiaq and Mannik were planning a trading trip to Gjoa Haven in early January to replenish the kerosene supply. The fuel was almost gone, and we were eking out the last gallons by burning papers, stray bits of wood, and expendable clothing in a stove made from an oil drum sawed in half. The men said they would leave as soon as we finished eating a caribou that had been fetched from one of the autumn caches. I had still not decided whether I would accompany the men, when one day I noticed that both Allaq and her sister Amaruq were absorbed in sewing. "Your traveling furs," they explained. "So they will be ready for you."

At this news, the fear that had never quite died—the fear of another change in the emotional climate—was reawakened. Did Allaq perceive that I was eager to leave, more eager than I myself knew, or was it she who wished me to leave? Watching her with the suspicious alertness of anxiety, I could not be sure. Once in a while I thought I caught a glimmer of hostility. On one or two occasions, in pouring tea for the family, Allaq forgot to fill *my* cup, and her laughter, when I remarked on the omission, seemed to my ear as excessively hearty as her laughter on another occasion when she had caught herself neglecting to offer Niqi a cigarette. I heard an unaccustomed stridence in her laughter also on another occasion, when I castigated myself, jokingly, as a "bad kapluna" for cutting the back instead of the belly out of a fish I was gutting. On the other hand, her friendliness disarmed me, so that I chided myself for letting imagination run wild. I puzzled, until one day a remark that Allaq made to Niqi tipped the balance, and I resolved, finally, to leave. Allaq and I were alone in the iglu when Niqi popped in on one of her brief visits. Allaq, standing on an oil drum by the door, was scraping the night's accumulation of frost feathers off the ice window, a morning routine, while I sat, writing as usual, on my corner of the ikliq across the way. Niqi, making conversation with me, remarked, as people occasionally did, that Utku would be unhappy (*hujuujaq*) after I had gone. Such remarks were delightful to hear, and though I reminded myself that the words were probably more gracious than sincere, still I somewhat shamefacedly allowed myself to be flattered. I was taken aback, therefore, when Allaq, perched on her oil drum above Niqi, murmured: "I don't think we'll be very unhappy." After Niqi had gone, I asked Allaq, in a general way, how people felt when others went away: ought people to remain happy (*quvia*)? Allaq laughed. "No," she said. "People are usually unhappy (*hujuujaq*) when others go away, especially if they know they are not going to see them again. Of course, they are sadder at first than they are, later." I pressed the question, then, indiscreetly focusing it again on myself. "You just told Niqi that people wouldn't be unhappy when I left." Allaq covered herself beautifully, as I might have known she would do. "I was joking. It's only because you are eager to leave that we won't be sad (*hujuujaq*); because you are growing unhappy here." She laughed. "Are you growing unhappy?" She laughed again, a merry laugh in which I joined, cooperating with her effort to assure me that she was joking. Then she continued, seriously: "We *will* be unhappy when you leave—more at first than later. I speak truly. And I think Saarak will be more unhappy than Raigili."

We left a week later: Inuttiaq, Mannik, Ipuituq, Qavvik, and I; it took that many to carry my several hundred pounds of gear. Allaq proffered last tidbits of data even as she helped carry my things out to the sled. And when Inuttiaq's team was harnessed and the other sleds were already sliding out across the river, she came and silently, in a most unusual gesture of farewell, clasped my hand. My mind went back to the only other farewell handshake I had seen. It was the parting of the old man Piuvkaq with his adopted son when Piuvkaq had mistakenly thought the government plane was taking him away to the hospital, probably to die. I, too, might never return, though I had said I would like to, if I could.

Pala also gave explicit recognition to my departure and, doing so, sharpened my sense of separation. "So you are going to Gjoa Haven," he said. "If you don't freeze, you should be all right (*naamak*)." And Niqi echoed him: "Don't freeze or be cold." The other women who stood on the slope were silent. Inuttiaq motioned me to the sled and with a tug at the anchor and a sharp-breathed "ai!" released the team. We slid down the slope in the wake of the other sleds, Inuttiaq running alongside to steer with pulls and shouts. I looked back. Pala, Allaq, and the others were black shapes on the dog-stained slope with its domes of snow—motionless, still watching. "The neighbors," said Inuttiaq. He waved, and I waved, too.

The last parting of all was with Inuttiaq. He and Ipuituq had come to visit me on their last evening in Gjoa Haven. I had just moved into one of the small stone iglus that had been built by a former priest for the use of his Eskimo parishioners. The temperature inside was still close to sixty below zero, and my primuses were both solidly frozen. Inwardly cursing at them, at my ineptitude, at the temperature, at life in general, I was struggling to discover what ailed the stoves when the door creaked open and Inuttiaq's head appeared; Ipuituq's smiling face was close behind. "Cooooold!" Inuttiaq observed. "Shall I do that?" Not waiting for my answer, he took the icy primus out of my hands and showed me how to hold it over a storm lantern until it thawed. I was astonished at the strength of the love and gratitude that I felt for him at that moment—grief, too, that next morning he was leaving. I would have left Gjoa Haven before he came back to trade again. "Eat!" I said. "Are you hungry?" They were, of course, and Inuttiaq offered Ipuituq's services in heating up the various cans of kapluna meat that I had bought. My gratitude overflowed into words, too. "I will be sad (*hu-juujaq*), I think, when you two leave, because you have helped me very much." The two men ate in silence, but after we had finished and we were drinking tea, Inuttiaq said: "I, too, will be sad (*hujuujaq*), I think, when I first leave here. The iglu is going to be wide." "I, too," said Ipuituq. They recounted the purchases they had made that day and recalled the homes they had visited and what they had eaten. The teakettle was empty. "I have to pee," said Inuttiaq. "I'm going out. I'm going out, and in the morning I'm leaving." Ipuituq followed him out without a word or glance.

I had letters from Back River twice before I left Gjoa Haven in March. Allaq said: "Saarak asks where you are and mistakenly thinks you will come soon." She and Inuttiaq both said: "I didn't think I'd care (*huqu, naklik*) when you left, but I did (*naklik*)."

Appendixes   Glossaries   References

Appendix I. Emotion Concepts

The preceding narrative has illustrated some of the ways in which Utku communicate affection and hostility and the ways in which they attempt to control the improper expression of such feelings in themselves and in others. In this appendix I shall draw together more systematically the kinds of behavior that are classified under the various emotion terms that have occurred in the text.

The narrative makes it clear that Utku do not classify emotions exactly as English speakers do; their words for various feelings cannot in every case be tidily subsumed under our words: affection, fear, hostility, and so on. Nevertheless, in order to make it easier for the kapluna reader to locate the various kinds of emotion to be discussed, in several cases I have clustered the Eskimo emotion terms under rubrics that correspond to our English categories of emotion, at risk of doing violence to the Eskimo ways of conceptualizing feelings. Nine emotions or emotional syndromes ("syndromes" at least in the view of an English speaker) are described: affection; kindness and gratitude; happiness; ill temper and jealousy; humor; fear; anxiety; shyness; and loneliness. In addition to these emotional concepts, several other terms that occur in the text are described. Three of these are evaluative terms, expressions with a wide range of meaning, which occur in the narrative. The last term to be discussed is the concept of *reason* and its various ramifications. This is included, because it is of major importance in understanding the emotional reactions of the Utku. In each case the relevant Eskimo words or concepts are presented, and insofar as data are available, the discussion of each term includes:

1. a verbal definition of the term, that is, what I was told when I asked what the term meant;

2. behavioral definitions of the term, that is, the behavioral contexts in which the term occurs in spontaneous speech;

3. an indication of the classes of people to whom the term applies—who expresses a particular emotion and toward whom—where variation was observed;

4. attitudes toward the emotion and its various expressions;

5. some of the ways in which the emotions are conceptually interrelated.

My aim is to define, in a preliminary way, a situation for future study, and it should be emphasized that the glossary presented here is tentative and incomplete. The data were not obtained systematically, but rather experientially, since my problem was not clearly formulated until after I returned from the field. No attempt was made to record a complete emotional vocabulary, and there are gaps in the data regarding the terms I do have, as well. In a few cases I do not have verbal definitions for the terms, and where I do have them, in most instances they are derived from statements of only one or two informants; I did not systematically sample to find out how much consensus there was. Moreover, my informants may have tailored their definitions to my limited vocabulary more than I was aware at the time. It may be owing in part to these circumstances that the verbal definitions I recorded tend to be narrower than the ranges of meaning found in spontaneous speech. Although I think verbal definitions do naturally tend to be narrower than behavioral ones, since one is not normally aware simultaneously of all the situations in which one uses a word, nevertheless it is quite possible that some of the distinctions I have drawn between the verbal and behavioral definitions of a term would not be sustained, given more systematic data.

With regard to the situational contexts in which the terms occurred, the data are also uneven. Since I heard some terms used far more commonly than others, I had more opportunities to record behavior associated with these terms than with others. And it is an open question whether the kinds of behavior associated with a term vary according to the class of person who is acting. Do children express unhappiness (*hujuujaq*), for example, or the wish to be with a loved person (*unga*) differently from adults? In sum, the complete behavioral and conceptual meanings of the terms—the distinctions and interrelationships among them—have yet to be determined.

A word needs to be said, also, about the way in which my point of view and the Utku point of view are mingled in the presentation in this appendix, as compared with the narrative. In the narrative I presented both points of view. When the Utku explicitly labeled an act with an emotion term, I stated in the text what that label was; but I sometimes wrote of an act as expressing "affection," "hostility," or some other emotion, when I intuitively understood it as such, even though I did not know how the Utku would classify the act. Though oversights are unavoidable, I tried throughout to make clear whether a statement was made from my point of view or that of the Utku.

In this appendix I have limited the discussion to situations in which an Utku term and a certain behavior were *explicitly* associated as, for example, when Saarak hit her mother with a spoon and Allaq asked her: "Are you angry *(ningaq)?*" However, even here, my point of view is mingled with the Utku view not only in the way I have clustered the terms but also in the way I have categorized the contexts in which a given term occurs. For example, when I say below, in the section on Loneliness, that "unpleasant physical conditions" or "being thwarted in one's intentions" make one feel *hujuujaq,* I am making judgments about the cues to which Utku react in becoming *hujuujaq,* and these judgments have not been checked against Utku statements. However, when I say that the absence of a person one loves makes one *hujuujaq,* this *is* based on Utku statements. Here, as in the narrative, I have tried to state explicitly the sources of my statements. To find out in every case precisely what aspects of a situation Utku are reacting to when they label it with one emotion term or another is a project for the future.

Finally, the picture presented here should be investigated comparatively. I do not yet know to what extent Utku patterns of emotional expression are also characteristic of other Eskimo groups. On the basis of anecdotal accounts to be found in Eskimo literature, which ranges geographically from Alaska to Greenland and historically from first contact with European culture to the present, one gains the impression that, broadly speaking, considerable consistency is to be found. But pending more systematic research, the reader must suspend judgment, or measure what I write against his own knowledge of the behavior of other Eskimos. Discussion of emotion terms follows.

Affection

The first feelings to be discussed are those comprised, more or less, by the English concept of affection. I recorded six terms that bear on what I call "affection." These can be glossed briefly as follows:

unga: to wish or to arouse the wish to be with another person;
niviuq: to wish or to arouse the wish to kiss or touch another affectionately;

aqaq: to communicate tenderly with another by speech or by gesture (other than touch);

iva: to lie next to someone in bed, with connotations of affectionate cuddling;

huqu: in certain contexts, to heed; to respond, with nurturant connotations, but see also the section concerning Anxiety;

naklik: to feel or to arouse concern for another's physical or emotional welfare; to wish or to arouse the wish to be with another. (Of the terms commonly used to express positive emotion, this one is used in the widest range of situations.)[1]

As indicated by this terminology, the Utku distinguish at least three different aspects of feeling within what *we* call "affection,"[2] namely (1) the desire to be with a loved person; (2) demonstrativeness: the desire to kiss, touch, or express tenderness verbally; (3) protectiveness: the desire to take care of the physical and emotional needs of another. For the reader's convenience, I will cluster the terms to be discussed under these rubrics. However, it should not be assumed that the terms fit tidily under these headings. *Naklik* has connotations of "wanting to be with" as well as of "protectiveness"; and *niviuq* may also connote "wanting to be near another person" as well as wanting to touch or kiss; and the terms for demonstrative

1. Most of the terms discussed here are not, properly speaking, words; they are not units that stand alone in speech; they are combining forms, most of which occur as bases of verbs: *niviuqtuq:* "he/she expresses the desire to kiss or touch"; *niviuqnaqtuq:* "he/she/it arouses the desire to kiss or touch"; and so on. I have treated these bases as words so that they might be more easily incorporated into English sentences; and sometimes I have attached English elements to them *(aqaqs, aqaqing),* for the same reason. Three exceptions to the above statement are: *nutaraqpaluktuq:* "he/she seems a child"; *ihuma:* "mind, thought, reason"; and *ayuqnaq:* "it is difficult or impossible." These three constitute words in themselves, though they may also appear as elements in other words.

2. Let me stress here, as in the beginning of this appendix, in referring to these Utku concepts as "aspects" of the overarching concept of "affection" I am grouping them according to the scheme imposed by English speakers. My data on the interrelationships that the Utku themselves see among these concepts are still fragmentary. Moreover, it is possible that more than three "components" will emerge when a complete emotional vocabulary has been obtained from the Utku.

behavior (*aqaq* and *iva*) can express *naklik,* and perhaps *unga,* as well as *niviuq* feelings.

(a) The desire to be with a loved person (*unga*)

The verbal definition of the term *unga* and its spontaneous usage coincide. When Saarak cried in the absence of her mother or father; when Ukpik decided to stay at home instead of returning to boarding school; when Raigili, after her baby sister's birth, refused to sleep by herself—next to her father, as before, but under separate quilts—they were said to feel *unga.* And when Uyuqpa stayed in bed beside his seriously ill wife instead of going about his ordinary business, he explained his behavior to me, saying: "A wife makes one feel *unga.*" But *unga* is not necessarily a response to the *absence* or threat of absence of a loved person. Inuttiaq's children were said to *unga* him, to want to be with him, because he was never annoyed (*urulu*) with them; in this context his absence was not at issue.

It was almost always in the context of relationships within the extended family, the *ilammarigiit,* that I heard the term *unga,* and most often it referred to feelings between parents and children.[3] I do not know whether *unga* feelings are considered a natural ingredient in a marital relationship; nor do I know how many husbands would admit to having such feelings, as Uyuqpa did. Uyuqpa was an unusually expressive man and, like Niqi, was disliked for this characteristic. In reference to the parent-child relationship, however, people spoke openly of *unga* feelings on the part of both parent and child. And such feelings may remain extremely strong even when a child is

---

3. On one occasion I heard a pious adolescent girl say, with feeling, that the deacon, Nakliguhuktuq, "made one feel *unga*"; but she added quickly: "One feels that way only about his teachings."

David Damas (1963:48–51) has glossed the term *unga* as "affection" in the Iglulik dialect; it is one of the two key concepts that he uses in his analysis of the logic of the Iglulik kinship system, the other being "obedience (*nalar*)." According to the Iglulik, relationships among certain categories of kin, such as siblings and cousins, are characterized primarily by *unga* feelings, and the relationships between other kinds of kin, especially certain classes of affine, are characterized by *nalar* feelings. It is possible that if I had inquired systematically along these lines, I might have found a similar pattern among the Utku, although, partly because of different marriage customs, I do not believe that the distribution of *unga* and *nalar* feelings among the specific categories of kin would be identical with that found in Iglulik.

grown. Pala, speaking of his half-grown and adult children, remarked: "They *unga*'d their mother more than me when she was alive, but now it's only me they *unga*." After my departure, when Tiguaq married her betrothed, Mannik, and moved with him to Gjoa Haven, Nilak planned to follow: "Because he *unga*s his adopted daughter."

(b) Demonstrativeness (*niviuq, aqaq, iva*)

When I asked what *niviuq* meant, I was given the synonym: "to want to kiss." As used in spontaneous speech, the concept also seems to include the wish to touch or to be physically near someone. For example, the day Raigili tried repeatedly to join her family on the cliffside, Inuttiaq said, "If we send her on any more errands she'll think we don't *niviuq* her." Raigili was past the age of being kissed; Inuttiaq meant that she would imagine her family did not want her to be near them.

In general, it is children under the age of three or four who inspire *niviuq* feelings: when they first respond with smiles and gurgles to social overtures, and when they first begin to imitate adult behavior, walking, talking, and "performing" on demand the other motions that adults teach them. *Littleness* seems to be a central characteristic of objects that are considered *niviuqnaqtuq*. In addition to babies, a great variety of small things, both live and inanimate, may produce *niviuq* feelings; newborn puppies (especially when there are no small children in the household), baby birds, a doll's dress, even the inch-long slips of paper on which I recorded vocabulary— people used the term *niviuq* in connection with all these things. Old people, on the other hand, explicitly do *not* make one feel *niviuq*. Allaq occasionally used to tease the very charming (*niviuq*) Saarak by saying to her: "You don't make me feel *niviuq*; you're an old lady."

Infants tend to be *niviuq*'d, to be treated with affectionate attention, by everyone, regardless of degree of kinship, though close relatives may be more demonstrative than others. Children past infancy tend to receive such attention primarily from members of their *ilammarigiit*: parents and grandparents, aunts and uncles, siblings and cousins. Of my acquaintances only one old man, Qavvik, was demonstrative to *all* small children, regardless of how distantly they were related to him. Pretty children are said to be more charming (*niviuq*) than others are, and people are more demonstrative to them than to others. In the absence of prettiness, however, other infant characteristics may arouse *niviuq* feelings. Thus, Allaq, speaking of a neighbor's baby, who had a large nose, large, protruding eyes, and a bad case of cradle cap, remarked: "He doesn't make one feel very *niviuq;* only his little voice makes one feel *niviuq.*" The tape-recorded sounds of my newborn kapluna nephew, drinking a bottle, were also described as *niviuq* by the listening Utku.

Utku consider that it is in the nature of a child to wish to elicit demonstrative attention, to be *niviuq*'d. When a small child behaves self-consciously, bouncing coquettishly, making "cute" faces, or "showing off" (as *we* would call it) in other ways, people remark: "He is being a child; he wants us to show him affection *(niviuq).*" Adults sympathize with this wish, encourage and indulge it for the first few years of a child's life. The rationale is that the child lacks reason *(ihuma).* But as a child grows older and loses its baby ways, it stops making other people feel *niviuq.* And ultimately it stops wanting to be *niviuq*'d, a development that I think the Utku view as concomitant with the growth of *ihuma,* but my data on this last point are scanty.

An interesting point concerning the demonstrativeness shown to children who are at the *niviuq* age is that in spite of its unrestrained quality it is highly patterned. I have mentioned that children at this age are kissed, cuddled, and cooed at by everyone. The Utku word for this cooing is *aqaq;* and *aqaq*ing takes several characteristic forms. Two of these are common to all Utku; any Utku *aqaq*ing a baby may nod repeatedly at it or may say tenderly: "Ee eee!" or "Vaaaa!" People are quite conscious of these *aqaq*ing patterns, and I was once asked: "What do kaplunas do when *they* aqaq a child?" a question to which I could not give a satisfactory general answer. There are also other forms of *aqaq*ing which are strictly dyadic. These consist of phrases, each of which is characteristic exclusively of the relationship between two people, the person *aqaq*ing and the person *aqaq*'d and expresses the affectionate bond between them. Mannik, for example, when *aqaq*ing Saarak, repeats one endearing phrase again and again: "Niviuqnaqtujuuuulli (you are kissable)"; the vowel is drawn out tenderly. But when he *aqaq*'d Raigili as a baby, he used a different phrase: "Oooo Raigili oo Raigili oo Raigili," sung to the tune of "The Farmer in the Dell." Other aunts and uncles use different endearments when addressing the same children, but each always uses the same endearment to the same child. And the individual nature of each endearment is enhanced by the fact that it is always said in the same tone of voice. If one heard only the tone reproduced, say, on a tape, deleting the syllables themselves, one could tell which phrase was being "said."

Utku are as consciously sensitive to these dyadic *aqaq*s as they are to the more general ones: the nods and the "ee eee"s. Allaq showed me this when she taught Saarak to repeat, with proper words and tones, the endearments by which the latter was addressed, just as she taught her to recognize the kinship terms appropriate to the various people around her. Occasionally, such endearments may even replace a kinship term as a way of addressing or referring to a person. Thus Raigili refers to Qavvik as "my nonni-nonni," because his endearing phrase for her is: "Nonni nonni; nonni nonni." And the phrases that have been used as *aqaq*s are remembered for years after the children concerned have outgrown *aqaq*ing. Allaq told me what her brother Mannik's *aqaq*ing phrases had been for each of their younger siblings, ten to fifteen years earlier.

Often *aqaq*ing is, as I have said, an expression of *niviuq* feelings. In fact, *aqaqtuq* (he/she *aqaq*s) was given me as a synonym for *niviuqtuq* (he/she *niviuq*s). And it is the children who are most charming *(niviuq)*, as described above, who are most *aqaq*'d. Everything I have said above about who *niviuq*s whom applies to *aqaq*ing. However, small children are *aqaq*'d not only when they are behaving in the self-conscious ways that I have described as wanting to be *niviuq*'d, but also in other circumstances. Saarak was sometimes *aqaq*'d when she had screamed herself into a frenzy; when she first showed signs of developing sulky behavior; and when she was lying in bed, fast asleep. Moreover, the term *aqaq*ing is also applied sometimes to the matter-of-fact-sounding expressions of approval that are addressed to older children. Allaq, for example, remarked one day to Raigili, who was chattering away on the ikliq: "Raigili talks a lot; it's nice *(ihluaq)*"; and when I asked Allaq what she had said, she replied: "I *aqaq*'d her." But whether all expressions of approval and liking are labeled *aqaq*ing I do not know.

In the last cases described, I am not sure what Utku term would be used for the feelings expressed by the *aqaq*ing behavior. There are still other cases in which I think that *aqaq*ing is an expression of *naklik* feelings, but my evidence for this is ambiguous. It consists partly in the fact that the word "naaaaaklingnaqtuq" *(naklik)* was often said in a voice that sounded to my ear like an *aqaq*ing voice, an affectionate, cooing voice. Twice, people associated *aqaq*ing behavior with the word *naklik*, but both instances admit of other interpretations. One was the occasion on which Nilak nodded *aqaq*ingly at his adolescent daughter, Tiguaq, in the distance. His wife, Niqi, watching him, said to me, "He feels *naklik*." But the simple-minded Niqi was often "confused" or "mistaken," as others told me; she tended to make causal connections that were laughable to her neighbors. In the other instance, I had been trying to explain to Inuttiaq the meaning of the word "comfort" in the Bible. I said, "If you help up a child that has fallen and *aqaq* it, that is 'comforting' him." "Oh," said Inuttiaq, "it must mean 'feeling *naklik*'." But he may have been responding to the "helping up," rather than to the "*aqaq*ing," when he defined the situation as *naklik*.

The last term to be discussed under the heading of demonstrativeness is *iva*. I do not have a verbal definition for this term. As used in spontaneous speech, *iva* means to lie next to someone in bed under the same covers, and it almost always connotes a gesture of affection *(naklik, niviuq, unga)*. Small children are *iva*'d (cuddled) by their parents and usually by most other close relatives, as well, being carried from iglu to iglu or from tent to tent in the mornings, to be tucked into bed with aunts, uncles, grandparents, and cousins. Sometimes when a child is displaced from its mother's side by a younger brother or sister the father may continue to *iva* the child, as Inuttiaq did for Saarak on the birth of Qayaq. Often, however, some other older member of the household: an older sibling, an uncle, or an aunt, may take over the role of cuddler. In some cases, it is said that the person who *iva*s a child as a substitute parent "adopts" him, that is, the *iva* relationship itself constitutes a sort of "adoption," developing into an especially close bond, which persists into adulthood, beyond the period when the actual *iva*ing occurs. Ordinarily, the cuddling itself gradually comes to an end as the child loses its *niviuq* (kissable) qualities. The youngest child in the family may lie under the same covers with its elders for a much longer period than other children. Pala's ten-year-old daughter, Akla, as I have said, still slept under her father's quilt. Whether this was defined as *iva*ing, however, I do not know.

As might be anticipated, a small child's desire to be *iva*'d is treated warmly and indulgently, and I think to *iva* a child is considered good, *naklik* (protective) behavior. Even quite small children may cry to *iva* their baby brothers and sisters. When Saarak cried to *iva* Qayaq, Allaq, though reluctant to comply from fear for Qayaq's safety, nevertheless remarked with apparent pleasure that Saarak was behaving "like an older sister," that is, feeling *naklik* toward her baby sister.

Most of the talk about *iva*ing concerns children. However, when husbands and wives lie together under one cover, as they usually do, that is also called *iva*ing.

(c) Protectiveness *(naklik, huqu)*

The most important of all the aspects of affection is that of protective concern. I recorded two terms that denote such concern: *huqu* and *naklik*.[4] *Huqu* will be discussed in the section on Anxiety.

The term *naklik*, as I have said, seems to have the widest ramifications of any of the terms used for positive emotions. The central meaning of *naklik* appears to be "protectiveness." I judge this partly because when I *asked* people what the term meant, I was always told that it referred to the desire to feed someone who was hungry, warm someone who was cold, and protect someone who was in danger of physical injury. I judge it also on the basis of the fact that the term seems to occur spontaneously in protective contexts more frequently than it occurs in other contexts. Often the protectiveness referred to is of the physical sort elicited in the verbal definitions of the term. Sometimes one hears the term used in reference to an ear or a hand—a part of a person—that is in danger of freezing. More often, however, it is an individual as such who arouses *naklik* feelings. During my first winter, people responding to my annoyances or explaining why they performed services for me often said: "Because you are alone here and a woman, you

4. I had originally included also a third term, *kama*, under the rubric of protectiveness. In the intransitive form, *kamahuktuq*, the word means to respond physically: to hear, to be alert. When a dog pricks up its ears to listen, it is said to *kama(huktuq)*. In the transitive form, *kamagijaa*, the word, like *huqu*, can be glossed as: to heed, to respond, with nurturant connotations. However, since I heard this transitive form only in a religious context, and therefore only in the Baffin Island dialect that is used for religious speech, I have decided to omit it until I find out whether it has been incorporated into the Utku dialect, or whether, like some other religious words, it is used with little knowledge of its meaning.

are someone to be *naklik*'d"; or: "Because you lack skill *(ayuq)*, you are someone to be *naklik*'d." Allaq, watching from a distance while Saarak struggled to put on her sock, or while Raigili tried to carry a heavy kettle of water up the beach, said: "She makes one feel *naklik*." *Naklik* feelings are given as reasons for taking care of the ill, for adopting orphans, and for marrying widows, all categories of people who are in need of physical assistance. And the term was chosen by missionaries to translate the Biblical "love," a protective concept. As the Utku say: "Because God *nakliks* us, if we do what he wishes, he will save us from Satan and from burning in hell."

The verbal definition of the term is limited to physical pro-tectiveness. Imaginary and social dangers, for example, a child's fear of strangers who, in the parents' judgment, have no intention of attacking, are explicitly excluded. But in spontaneous speech protectiveness in a broader sense may be referred to, too. If a child who is perceived as being still small enough to lack rea-son *(ihuma)* cries or mopes in the absence of someone he loves *(unga)*; if he screams or swats at people when his wishes are interfered with; or if he is distressed for any reason whatsoever, people say: "Naklingnaqtuq (he makes one feel *naklik*)." And Pala used the word in this larger sense when he said of his daughter Akla: "She makes one feel *naklik*; she *ungas* me very much." Here the *naklik* response seems to be a reaction to emotional rather than physical need.

In the contexts so far described, both physical and emotional, it may be that "pity" is the appropriate gloss for *naklik*. Indeed, when I told Ikayuqtuq about the incident I have just recounted, she translated as "poor little thing" the word *naklingnaqtuq*, which I have translated as: "She makes one feel *naklik* (pro-tective)."

The term also occurs in situations in which protective con-notations of any sort are obscure, as, for example, where *naklik* feelings are adduced in explanation of name-avoidance prac-tices.[5] In still other cases, protectiveness may be a part of the

5. Name avoidance refers to the practice of habitually avoiding the names of certain individuals, instead addressing or referring to the latter by kinship terms or by circumlocutions: "the old man," "my cousin," "that one." In the Utku case, as the text makes clear, the motive is said to be a feeling of affection *(naklik)* or shyness *(kanngu)* toward the person whose name one avoids. In Utku ideology there are no particular kin relationships in which this behavior occurs more regularly than in others; people do it toward "anyone, if they feel like

feeling that is expressed but, it seems to me, by no means the whole of it. Inuttiaq, for example, listening to a tape-recorded story told by his absent daughter, Kamik, said, "She makes one feel *naklik*." Allaq named her baby for one of her younger brothers who had drowned, "Because I *naklik*'d him very much." She had "adopted" this brother, had cuddled *(iva)* him in bed after the birth of his younger sibling, and this fact was associated with *naklik* feelings toward him, which lasted throughout his life and beyond. In these situations it seems to me that *naklik*, in addition to the protective connotation, also has connotations of "wanting to be with." The latter aspect of the *naklik* concept is most clearly seen in the idea of "loving *(naklik)* too much *(-pallaaq-)*," which was described in the narrative (Chapter 1, section V). As Inuttiaq put it: "I love *(naklik)* Saarak and Kamik a little bit more than I love Raigili and Qayaq. I love them too much. When I am away on trips, hunting or trading, I want to see them. I sleep badly. When Kamik is away at school I miss her; it makes me feel uncomfortable *(ihluit, naamangngit)* ... People don't like to feel uncomfortable. If one doesn't love *(naklik)* too much it is good."

The ramifications of the *naklik* concept become more evident when *naklik* is seen in relation to other emotion terms, as in the last example and in those that follow. *Naklik* occurs in some of the same contexts as *niviuq:* "to want to kiss." I have mentioned, for example, that the endearments *(aqaq)* that are cooed at small children who arouse *niviuq* feelings sometimes contain references to the *naklik*, as well as to the *niviuq*, qualities of the children. And once when Amaaqtuq and I were walking the dogs of our respective households to a new camp, and one of her dogs persisted in running close beside her, now and then rubbing against her and looking up at her, she kicked him away and laughed: "He thinks, mistakenly, that he arouses *naklik* feelings." This situation, too, seems to me similar to a situation in which *niviuq* was the term used: when mosquitoes lit on Allaq's arm, and she laughed, "They feel *niviuq* toward me." I do not know yet, however, whether Utku consider these situations parallel, or whether they make distinctions among them that are invisible to me. *Niviuq* and *naklik* are sometimes clearly distinguished. Small children, Allaq told me, are both *niviuq*

_____

it." I do not rule out the possibility that there are regularities, indeed, it seems to me probable that there are such, but in my small sample I could observe none.

(kissable) and *naklik* (one wants to nurture them), but, in general, puppies are only *naklik,* not *niviuq.* Only in households where there are no small children are puppies sometimes *niviuq*'d (kissed and cuddled).

Naklik often occurs in opposition to terms expressing anti-social feelings and behavior. In fact, almost any antisocial behavior or any offender may be described as *naklingnangngittuq* (not *naklik),* or, with characteristic euphemism, *naklingnaq-luangngittuq* (not very *naklik).*[6] Acts that are particularly liable to be so labeled are those of stinginess, greed, a reluctance to help or to share with others, and expressions of bad temper, ranging from silent sulkiness to violent outbursts, as we shall see in the discussion of ill temper and jealousy, below. In other words, *naklik* behavior is a major criterion of human goodness, and in this sense it is a central value of Utku culture.

Ideally, in the Utku view, a good person, that is, a person whose behavior is characterized by protectiveness, who is helpful, generous, and even-tempered, will demonstrate these qualities to all people, even to strangers, kaplunas, and so on, not just to his close kin. In this sense protectiveness is a universal value. It is universal also in that everybody—not Utku alone, but any human being except the youngest of children—is judged by the extent to which his behavior measures up to this ideal. Small children are thought to feel *unga,* to want to be with people they love, but they only gradually begin to love in a nurturant *(naklik)* way, a development that I think the Utku associate with the growth of *ihuma* (reason).

In the universality of its applicability, protectiveness *(naklik)* differs from the other aspects of affection: wanting to be with a person (which, as we have seen, may also be expressed by *naklik* or by *unga),* and wanting to kiss or cuddle a person *(niviuq).* These latter aspects of affection are expressed and, I think, felt primarily within the *ilammarigiit.* To be sure, in the details of its expression there are differences between the way the protective ideal is applied to people in general and the

6. It is possible that such condemnations on occasion refer to the feelings of the observer, rather than to the undesirable behavior or its perpetrator. In other words, the meaning of *naklingnangngittuq* may sometimes be not "that behavior is unprotective," but rather "that behavior doesn't make me feel protective." Often, however, the meaning is unambiguous, as, for instance, when a person says: "The missionary says we should behave protectively, should love *(naklik)* one another, but 'those people' (for example, the neighbors) don't do that *(nak-lingnangngittut)."*

way it is applied to one's own *ilammarigiit*. I have described some of these differences in Chapter 4. The only *naklik* quality that one must express with rigorous universality in order to avoid criticism is even temper. One should be mild and sociable with everyone, and never under any circumstances angry or resentful. With regard to sharing with and helping others, the ideal, stated in its broadest form, is also universalistic. No distinction is made between *ilammarigiit* and others; one should help everyone. As Inuttiaq once said to me: "I know you believe in God, because you help everybody, not just a few people, but everybody." However, a person is not expected to help or share with everyone equally. All that seems to be required in relations with people outside one's *ilammarigiit* is that one never refuse a request (requests made of people outside one's *ilammarigiit* are always modest in the extreme) and that one volunteer a *little* help, as needed, or a *small* share of whatever one has that others have not. In reality, the universality of the sharing-and-helping ideal is diluted still further by the tendency for relations between *ilammarigiit* to be unfriendly. By and large, the ideal of even temper is not strictly achieved in reality, either. Though, as the narrative has shown, Utku tend to be far more restrained than kaplunas in their expressions of hostility, they do gossip a good deal about members of *ilammarigiit* other than their own. The gossip mostly focuses on the un-*naklik* qualities of those families: their jealousy, greed, stinginess, unhelpfulness, or bad temper, while confidently asserting the *naklik* virtues of one's own kin.

The high value that is placed on loving *(naklik*ing*)* and being loved *(naklik*'d*)* makes the ambivalence toward these situations, to which I referred earlier, particularly interesting. I have mentioned the feelings of loneliness experienced by the person who loves "too much." The discomfort of the person who *is* loved may be more closely related to the protective aspect of the *naklik* concept, more precisely, to the conflict between nurturant *(naklik)* feelings and behavior on the one hand and the value placed on self-sufficiency and independence on the other hand. In theory, as I have said, the people who are most to be protected are the helpless *(ayuqtut)*: small children, sick people, the elderly, and others who are unable to cope by themselves, either through lack of material means or through lack of knowledge of the environment (like lone female anthropologists). Small children, and even infants too young to understand, may be soothed when they cry or sulk by being assured that they are "someone to be taken care of *(naklingnaqtut)*." But as a child grows he becomes, in theory, "a little less someone to be *naklik*'d." And Utku adults are not, I think, as often reassured explicitly that they are *naklik*'d, perhaps for fear of embarrassing them. Utku do seem to recognize that adults, too, have a wish to be *naklik*'d. Inuttiaq, away from camp on a two-week trading trip, expressed this in the note that he sent back to his family: "You who remain behind *(pai)* are people to be *naklik*'d." On the whole, however, it is discomfort about being *naklik*'d that is uppermost in discussions on the subject with adult Utku. Various Utku agreed explicitly and strongly that an adult does not wish to be an object of concern to others, does not wish to be *naklik*'d. Allaq blushed when I asked whether wives were *naklik*'d by their husbands. "A little bit," she said, and then added quickly, "but mostly it's the children who are *naklik*'d." She blushed also when she told me that her father had *naklik*'d her very much even after she had grown up, and again she added quickly, "But it's all right now; he has stopped *naklik*ing me so much."

Such feelings about being *naklik*'d may partially explain why Utku often deny or minimize physical and emotional pain, with a smile and an assurance that they are "all right."[7] It was Ikayuqtuq who gave me some insight into the dynamics of this stoicism, but I think her reasoning may be similar to that of Utku. She told me that one of several reasons why Eskimos in hospital do not like to tell the medical staff that they are in pain is that "they are grateful to the staff who are helping them to get over their sickness. They know the staff are worried enough about it; why let them know they are unhappy and have a pain, and make them still more worried." And on another occasion, explaining why she had not talked to me about the death of her baby son, she said: "I used to get lonesome when I was a little girl and used to cry when I went to bed without letting my grandparents [with whom she lived] know, because I loved them so much . . . If they found out I was unhappy they might get sad and . . . pity me, and lots of Eskimos don't like to be pitied . . . If I knew I made you sad . . . I was going to be sadder still and sorry for myself . . ."[8] Here it appears that a person who does not wish

7. See also the section on Reason, below.
8. These quotations are taken from letters written in English; the Eskimo terms are not available. The relationship between the concepts of "pity" and

to be *naklik*'d, with all that this implies of dependence and pity, may switch the situation around so that he becomes the nurturant *(naklik*ing*)* person, protecting others from the sadness that they would feel if he allowed them to feel nurturant *(naklik)* toward him. The same kind of reasoning, I think, explains, in part, the remarks my Utku friends made when talking about my departure: "We will miss *(hujuujaq)* you when you first leave, but it will be all right *(naamak);* only Saarak will be unhappy *(naamangngit),* poor dear *(naklingnaqtuq).*" I think people may have been reassuring me that I need not feel protectively concerned *(naklik)* for them when I left, thereby transforming into concern *(naklik)* for the three-year-old Saarak and for me their own wish not to be an object of concern.

Kindness and Gratitude

The concepts of kindness and gratitude are related to the concept of nurturance or protectiveness *(naklik),* which we have been discussing, in that one of the qualities of a person who is nurturant *(naklik)* is kindness. Put in other words: he inspires gratitude. The Utku express both of our English concepts of gratitude and kindness by one term: *hatuq*,[9] which in the form *hatuqnaq* can be rendered by the one gloss: "inspires gratitude."

I do not have a verbal definition for the term *hatuqnaq,* but the word occurs frequently in everyday speech, referring sometimes to a quality of a situation and sometimes to a quality of a person. Many different kinds of situation make one feel grateful *(hatuq).* One is grateful *(hatuq)* when one is materially helped, or when a difficult interpersonal or physical situation in which one is involved is eased. When one has good luck in hunting, when one is given food, fuel, clothing, tool materials, or any other object that is desirable or necessary; when sleds run easily over smooth snow or ice, instead of having to be tugged and

---

naklik in Ikayuqtuq's thinking, however, is indicated by her translation of the word *naklingnaqtuq* as "poor little thing" (page 321 above).

9. Another term, *quya,* is also in frequent use, but the Utku consider this a Netsilik term. In my data, the Utku use *quya* in all the same contexts as *hatuq,* and the two terms appear to be close, if not complete, synonyms. One datum seems to indicate that the Netsilik, who also use both terms, consider *hatuq* a stronger expression than *quya.* When the weather is good, or when one catches a fish, one says in Netsilik, "Quyanaq (it makes one grateful)," whereas if a loved relative comes home safely from the hospital, one says, "Hatuqnaq (it makes one grateful)." But the Utku do not appear to make this distinction.

hauled through soft snow or jagged ice; when people whose presence is undesirable leave, or when a loved person returns; when people who have behaved badly mend their ways or make amends, one feels grateful *(hatuq)*.

The connection between nurturance *(naklik)* and gratitude *(hatuq)*, which was mentioned above, lies in the nature of the personal qualities that "inspire gratitude." In order to be considered kind or as "one who inspires gratitude" a person must not only respond freely to requests, but must also offer help spontaneously, on occasion, in the form of goods or services. And in addition it is important that he be even-tempered, thereby demonstrating that he is not frightening *(kappia, iqhi, ilira)*, so that one need not hesitate to ask help from him. It is apparent that the Utku concept of "kindness" is considerably broader than our own, and that the label is more difficult to earn.

Often the feeling of gratitude will be expressed verbally. "Hatuqnaq (it makes one feel grateful)!" one will exclaim. But the Utku, like other Eskimos, place a high value on reciprocity, so when it is a person who has inspired gratitude, the latter feeling is very often given material as well as verbal expression. The person who is grateful *(hatuqtuq)* will give a gift to the person who has helped him or will offer to perform some service for him.

Happiness

The last emotion to be considered in this complex of highly valued feelings is happiness *(quvia)*. Happy feelings are not only pleasanter to entertain than are unhappy ones, they are also a moral good in a sense that, I think, is not true for us. I shall elaborate on this point below.

I did not obtain a verbal definition for the term *quvia* but have glossed it as "happiness"; it occurs as a translation for this word in the Eskimo religious literature. The term occurs frequently in spontaneous speech, both as an expression of a person's own feeling and as a judgment on other people's behavior. People who laugh, smile, joke, and enjoy telling stories are judged to feel *quvia*, and they are said to rouse *quvia* feelings in others. Enjoyable experiences as diverse as listening to music, dancing, playing, fishing, chasing lemmings or stoning ptarmigans, traveling (under good conditions), visiting with pleasant company or being with a loved person, being physically warm, and eating are all described as "making one feel happy *(quvia-naqtuq)*." It is interesting that in one instance happy *(quvia)* feelings were expressed, smilingly, as a "wish to cry." The reference was to a tape of opera music that I sometimes played. Inuttiaq and Amaaqtuq enjoyed the tape very much and requested it often: "Play the music that makes one want to cry." Ordinarily, crying is defined as angry *(qiquq)* behavior.

Happy *(quvia)* feelings contrast with the unpleasant feeling of loneliness *(hujuujaq)* and with disapproved feelings such as hostility *(ningaq, urulu, huaq, qiquq)*. Happy *(quvia)* behavior: smiling, joking, a liking for sociable conversation and story-telling, is a sign to others that a person is not angry. It is in this sense that happiness is a moral good.[10] I was told that if a person feels happy *(quvia) all* the time he lacks reason *(ihuma)*, but in general a person who feels *quvia* is a good person; he is safe, not frightening; one need not feel *kappia, iqhi,* or *ilira* with him. By the same token, the person is probably kind *(quya)*; the two terms, *quvia* and *quya*—together with two others: *tiphi* (amusing) and *pittau* (good)—very often occur in conjunction in descriptions of liked people. On the other hand, a person who is kind *(quya)*, who makes one grateful, is not necessarily one who makes one happy *(quvia)*. This distinction was made in the case of the kapluna fishermen who visited us. They were said to be kind *(quya)* because they gave us clothes, food, and trade goods, but they did not make the Utku feel very *quvia*, because their company was not very agreeable.

Ill Temper and Jealousy

Having discussed some of the highly valued emotions in Utku culture, I now turn to one of the most disapproved feelings: hostility. As a warm, protective, nurturant, even-tempered person represents the essence of goodness, so an unkind, bad-tempered person represents the opposite. Expressions of ill temper toward human beings (as distinct from dogs) are never considered justified in anyone over the age of three or four; and even when one expresses hostility toward dogs one must defend it as a disciplinary action. The Utku, moreover, define unkindness and bad temper more broadly than we do, and condemn it far more stringently, with the result that bad temper

10. "He is a happy person" is an expression of approval among the Alaskan Eskimos of my acquaintance, too.

and aggressiveness are two of the first qualities that they notice about us, as indicated, for example, by the stories that children bring back from boarding school. In the Utku view, kaplunas are about as bad-tempered as the dogs from which they consider we are descended.[11]

I recorded five terms that refer to aspects of bad temper[12] and one term that has hostile meanings among a wide variety of others. These terms I have glossed as follows:

huaq: to aggress verbally against another; to scold;

ningaq: to aggress physically against another; to feel or express hostility;[13]

qiquq: literally, to be clogged up with foreign matter; metaphorically, to be on the point of tears; to feel hostile;

urulu: to feel, express, or arouse hostility or annoyance. The term may also be used as an expression of sympathy at the misfortunes of others;

piyuma: to want something, often with connotations of jealousy, envy, or greed;

tuhuu: to want for oneself a possession or a skill belonging to someone else; to want to participate in another's activities or life situation; or to rouse such wishes;

hujuujaq: to be unhappy because of the absence of other people, or to rouse such unhappiness; to feel or provoke other unpleasant feelings, including hostility. This term will be discussed in the section on Loneliness.

11. In this connection it is interesting to compare the opinion obtained by Rasmussen (1931:128) from an old Netsilik Eskimo: "It is generally believed that white men have quite the same minds as small children. Therefore one should always give way to them. They are easily angered, and when they cannot get their will they are moody and, like children, have the strangest ideas and fancies."

12. Again I am creating an overarching category, "bad temper," which may be foreign to the Utku; I have not recorded an Eskimo term that subsumes the others recorded here.

13. As indicated earlier in the footnote to Chapter 1, I discovered on my second visit to the Utku that *ningaq* really means only: to aggress physically against another. There is another base, *ningngak*, which means: to feel or express hostility. At the time this book was written, I did not realize that there were two words. Consequently, the reader should bear in mind that wherever the base *ningaq* occurs in the text it may represent either the word *ningaqtuq* (he fights) or the word *ningngaktuq* (he is angry). In no instance do I know which word was actually used by the Utku speaker.

As the terms indicate, the condemnation of bad temper applies to a variety of behaviors, ranging from physical aggression *(ningaq)* to silent withdrawal *(qiquq)*. I will discuss the behaviors associated with each term in turn.

(a) Verbal abuse *(huaq)*

The term *huaq* refers to verbal abuse, which may be directed either against people or against dogs. I lack a verbal definition for the term, but in practice it is used quite broadly; almost any sort of criticism, other than that which is expressed explicitly as a joke, is labeled "verbal abuse *(huaq)*." Rasmussen (1931: 461) gives "scolds" as the intransitive meaning of the verb *huaq*-(suäk- in his orthography) and "shouts commandingly to him to do this or that" as the transitive meaning. My experience agrees with Rasmussen's intransitive meaning, but I found no difference between the transitive and intransitive senses of the term. The term can be used transitively, as well as intransitively, to refer to criticism rather than to commands. And the voice is by no means always raised. Sometimes it is, and a raised voice is almost always taken as an indication that the speaker is *huaq*ing, but on the other hand, criticism expressed in a conversational tone of voice will also be considered *huaq*ing, if it is addressed to the person who is being criticized and if annoyance is assumed to motivate the criticism.

*Huaq*ing behavior is, on the whole, frowned on; it makes other people feel unhappy *(hujuujaq)*, annoyed *(urulu)*, and sometimes frightened *(kappia, iqhi)*, because the *huaq*ing is considered to express feelings of annoyance *(urulu)*. Occasionally, however, the word is used in a positive, disciplinary context. It is all right to *huaq* dogs. "Everybody does it," people said, "it makes them behave." And Inuttiaq warned me in one or more of his lectures that if people did bad things, like losing their tempers or not obeying him, then Nakliguhuktuq would come and *huaq*: "It will be frightening." In the same context, he told me that people who answer back when they are *huaq*'d don't go to heaven. But I was not actually given a scolding. No reference to my own behavior was made in the lecture; I was free to make my own inferences. The wish to "scold," that is, to criticize *directly*, was attributed to a third person who was 150 miles away in Gjoa Haven and who was not really very likely to appear.

Positive attitudes toward scolding *(huaq)* appear rather infrequently. Even in a disciplinary context, people tend to feel negatively toward the idea of scolding. Thus, for example, when Nakliguhuktuq baptizes an Utku child he tells the parents that they should "teach *(ilihaq)* the child; don't scold *(huaq)* him." To be sure, Nakliguhuktuq is not an Utku, but Inuttiaq and Allaq repeated his words with approval. And the Utku very rarely do seem to *huaq* children. I make this statement tentatively, because I do not know whether the annoyed tone of voice that I have called a "moo," which is often addressed to children, is considered *huaq*ing. I do not know, either, whether remarks intended to shame children into self-control are defined as *huaq*ing. In any case, only a few disciplinary incidents that I *knew* to be labeled *huaq*ing occurred. In Inuttiaq's household I heard only two scoldings that I knew to be so labeled. One was delivered by Inuttiaq to his daughter Kamik during the summer after her return from Inuvik. As I have said, she appeared to be intensely unhappy at home on her return in the spring, and she showed it in a number of antisocial ways: [14] she consistently pretended to be deaf, so that she could not hear the requests her parents made of her; she was as sulky and demanding of her mother as a small child; and worst of all, she tormented her sister Saarak by grabbing her toys, stepping on her foot till she screamed, and so on: unheard-of behavior toward a small child. Her parents had overtly ignored much of this, only occasionally teasing Kamik about her deafness or mooing at her when she made Saarak cry. But finally, one day toward the end of the summer, when she had made her sister scream with rage, her father *huaq*'d her, telling her that she was unfeminine and out of her mind.

The only other instance of scolding *(huaq)* that I observed in Inuttiaq's household was administered to Raigili. She too had offended by being annoyed with Saarak, whereupon Inuttiaq told her, in a firm but not loud voice, that she should not continually get annoyed *(urulu)* at her little sister. The family's discomfort about this incident was evidenced later when I tried to find out the exact words used in the scolding, some of which I had missed. Allaq (with whom I was alone) refused, with apparent embarrassment, to tell me exactly what Inuttiaq had said to Raigili. I noted embarrassment about *huaq*ing also one day when I was being given a lecture on the Bible. The story was that of the money changers who were driven out of the temple.

14. This case is described in more detail in my appendix to Hobart (1965).

"Jesus *huaq*'d them," said Inuttiaq; then he added immediately: "But he only did that once. The money changers were being very bad, *very bad,* and refusing to listen to him." One of Jesus's godly virtues is that he never scolds *(huaq),* never gets angry *(ningaq, urulu). Huaq*ing is antithetical to the protective *(naklik)* behavior that is so highly valued—and that is also one of Jesus's central virtues, as seen by the Utku. Ordinarily, the only people who *huaq*'d other people (as opposed to dogs) were the ones who were known and disliked for their bad tempers: Nilak, Niqi, Uyuqpa, and myself. My impression is that even when people shout at dogs "to make them behave" some discomfort is felt. I judge this from the defensive way in which such behavior is explained: *"Every*body does it. *Every*body."

(b) Physical aggression *(ningaq)*

As the term *huaq* expresses the idea of verbal aggression, so *ningaq* expresses the idea of physical aggression, fighting. The term is applied to a variety of such behaviors: angry flailing on the part of a small child; a physical fight observed between two kaplunas; Jesus whipping the money changers; and, in the most violent of all contexts: "If God ever *ningaq*s, he will destroy the world."

The term occurs also in situations in which no actual physical aggression has taken place, but in which it is clear that anger is felt. For example, when Rosi screeched in response to her grandmother's teasing pokes, the latter asked her, "Are you *ningaq?*" When I angrily accused Inuttiaq of lying one day during our midwinter upheavals, he asked me whether I was *ningaq.* And one of the complaints that Pala and Amaaqtuq made of me the next summer in their letters to Gjoa Haven was that I *ningaq*'d easily [though I had never attacked anyone physically]. On one occasion, Allaq used the term *ningaq* to denote a feeling, rather than a form of behavior, a feeling whose presence explained *qiquq* ("clogged") behavior: "Whenever people are *ningaq,* they *qiquq.*" Possibly the implicit assumption is that a person who feels *ningaq* will sooner or later show it in aggressive acts—a likely assumption considering the Utku belief that angry thoughts can kill, simply of their own force. The *wish* to harm, in other words, is as real, as potentially lethal, an attack as a physical assault.

It is no wonder that Utku heartily fear and condemn angry *(ningaq)* feelings and behavior. Anger is not only incompatible with affection and nurturance, the highest values; it can also kill. As I have said, among adults there are no situations that justify *ningaq* feelings or behavior, no people, Utku or other, toward whom it is permissible to express them. The Utku distinguish, however, between two kinds of anger *(ningaq)* in terms of their causes. If a person is frequently angry *(ningaq)* but gets over it easily, this is a sign that he has very little reason *(ihuma);* he is like a child. A child's frequent tempers are a sign that his *ihuma* is still not developed. In the smallest children, *ningaq* may be greeted with amusement, or even, on occasion, jokingly encouraged, as in the case of the mock "hitting" game that Rosi and her grandmother played. On the other hand, if a person is angry *(ningaq)* for long periods of time, if he nurses *ningaq* thoughts "every day, every day," as Allaq said, this is owing to his having too much *ihuma*. My impression is that this latter type of *ningaq* is more frightening, and that it is primarily the latter that is thought to cause death.[15]

(c)   Being clogged up *(qiquq)*

The terms *qiquq* (to be clogged up) and *urulu* (to feel annoyed) seem somewhat vaguer in their scope than the two so far discussed, though perhaps this vagueness is only a sign of insufficient data. *Qiquq* in its physical sense is applied to objects such as iglu ventilators, fishing holes, and primus nipples, which get, quite literally, clogged up and have to be cleaned out. In its emotional sense, the behavior most often labeled *qiquq* in my experience was sulky, silent withdrawal: sitting with head lowered or turned away from company; ignoring or rejecting friendly overtures; refusing to answer questions; leaving a gathering precipitately. Signs of imminent tears are also labeled *qiquq*. Whether openly aggressive behavior may also be defined as *qiquq* I do not yet know. The verbal definitions that I obtained for the term in its emotional sense were "very *urulu*" and "*ningaq*."

As I have said, *qiquq* behavior is thought to be motivated by angry *(ningaq)* feelings, but my hunch is that it is associated very largely with childish anger, that is, with anger caused by

15. My impression is that the other concepts that have to do with ill temper: *huaq, qiquq, urulu,* are all associated with too little *ihuma,* rather than with too much; but my data are not adequate on this point. For further discussion of attitudes toward anger associated with various states of *ihuma,* see the section on Reason, below.

having too little, rather than too much, reason (*ihuma*), and that it is therefore less feared than some other kinds of behavior associated with anger. The word was applied frequently to the behavior of children and of Niqi, who was like a child. It was also applied to my behavior, as I learned when I read the letters Pala and Amaaqtuq wrote at the time I was ostracized. People refer to *qiquq* behavior as *urulu* (annoying, or too bad), *tiphi* (funny), *hujuujaq* (unpleasant), and not-*quvia* (also, unpleasant); I never heard it called *kappia* or *iqhi* (frightening).

(d)   Annoyance *(urulu)*

Urulu is the hardest to define of all the terms I recorded for ill temper. Whenever I tried to elicit a definition I was consistently told: "It means 'unsmiling'." The exclamation "Urulunaq (it's annoying; it's too bad)!" is very frequently heard and can be a response to a great variety of situations, including unpleasant physical conditions (bad weather, tiring work), and being thwarted in one's wishes or activities (losing a knife, spilling one's tea). The tone of the exclamation belies any hostility or irritation implicit in the verbal content. If the reference is to an untoward event in one's own life the tone will probably be cheerfully matter-of-fact; if the reference is to events in another's life it will be sympathetic or, again, matter-of-fact. Even when it is a third person's misbehavior that draws the comment, the person commenting—always behind the offender's back— usually appears to express regret, rather than genuine annoyance, when he says, "Urulunaq!" He may in fact *be* annoyed, but annoyance does not show in the conversational manner with which he says, "Urulunaq!" and I am intuitively convinced that the exclamation is viewed neither by the speaker nor by his audience as an admission of ill temper. My reason for this assumption will be clearer in a moment.

The base *urulu-* occurs also in another word: *urulujuq*, which I translate as "he/she is annoyed," as distinct from the more impersonal *urulunaq:* "it is annoying." " Urulujuq," in contrast to the exclamation "Urulunaq!" is an accusation, a description of another's behavior, rather than a comment on the speaker's feelings about the situation; it may be uttered in a disapproving tone, with eyes narrowed in a gesture of criticism, always, of course, in the absence of the offender. The accusation seems to be sparked by behavior that is classified under all three of the terms for ill temper so far discussed, that is, by both verbal and physical aggression and by withdrawal. When Nilak scolded his wife; when Raigili sulked or when she surreptitiously pinched Saarak and made her cry; when Niqi made a separate kettle of tea for herself instead of joining her neighbors when they drank theirs; or when she gave Amaaqtuq (of whom she was jealous) an inferior portion of the boiled fish she was distributing, people whispered behind the offender's back: "He/she is annoyed (*urulujuq*)."

The exact nature of the conceptual difference between the term *urulu* on the one hand and the terms *huaq, ningaq, qiquq,* and *hujuujaq* on the other is still unclear to me. Next to *hujuujaq* (which will be described in the section on Loneliness) *urulu* seems to be the broadest of the terms I recorded for negative emotions. It is possible that *urulu* refers to an *emotion,* which is thought to underlie the *behavior* described as "scolding (*huaq*)" and "clogging (*qiquq*)." And in contrast to *ningaq,* which may refer either to a feeling or to behavior, my intuitive impression is that *urulu* is a milder word. But all of these possibilities need to be explored further.

One fact that is clear is that Utku tend to deny to others and, I think, often to themselves the existence of their ill-tempered feelings. And we will see in the section on Humor that denial of *urulu* feelings is explicitly taught to children. *Urulu* feelings and behavior, like the other manifestations of ill temper that have been discussed, are opposed to affectionate feelings (*naklik, unga,* and *niviuq*). Allaq once in a while used to tease Saarak, saying: "You don't make one feel *niviuq,* you make one feel *urulu.*" Inuttiaq's children were said to *unga* him because he felt *naklik* toward them and never *urulu.* Niqi, on the other hand, "gets *urulu* easily; she doesn't listen to what the missionaries tell us, that we should *naklik* others." It is significant that among adults I recorded the expressions *urulu(juq)* and *qiquq-(tuq)* only in the third person: he/she is annoyed/clogged. I never heard it in the first person, and never in the second person either, except when an adult was lecturing a child who was out of sorts. *Ningaq(tuq)* (he/she is angry) was also recorded almost entirely in the third person. The one exception was the midwinter crisis mentioned earlier, when Inuttiaq asked me whether *I* was *ningaq.* The question, normal enough in my own culture, struck me as extraordinarily bald after months of living with Utku indirection, and I read it as a sign of Inuttiaq's desperation in the difficult situation I had created.

It is the contrast between this unwillingness to admit genuine annoyance and the apparent ease with which people exclaim, "Urulunaq (too bad; it is annoying)!" that makes me think the exclamation is not viewed as a real expression of annoyance. The same form, *urulunaq(tuq)*, may, however, occur without being an exclamation, in which case it does refer to real annoyance, and the discomfort about expressing such feelings is again in evidence. I quote again, more fully this time, the statement that Allaq once made when I asked her which of her children she loved more, Saarak or Raigili: "Sometimes they're both lovable *(naklingnaqtuk)* and sometimes they're both annoying *(urulunaqtuk)*: *Every*body gets annoyed at children sometimes, and *every*body: Maata, and I, and *every*body—except Inuttiaq." Her defensiveness was notable.

(e) Jealousy and greed *(piyuma, tuhuu)*

I have included a discussion of jealousy, envy, or greed *(piyuma, tuhuu)* with my discussion of terms denoting bad temper, because greed and envy are forms of aggression, and in the Utku scheme of things jealousy, like bad temper, is antithetical to the protective, nurturant *(naklik)* behavior that is so highly valued, and like bad temper its presence is denied in oneself and in one's close kin. One hears remarks like the following, always referring to members of *ilammarigiit other* than one's own: "He feels *tuhuu;* he doesn't listen to the missionary; the missionary says we should feel *naklik. We* don't feel *tuhuu; we're* all right."

Piyuma means, literally, to want a thing or an act. The expression occurs sometimes in a neutral sense: "Do you want to trade?" "Would you like some tea?" and sometimes in a positive moral context: "God doesn't want us to do that." Sometimes, however, it appears in the sense of greed or jealousy: "Nilak is always wanting, wanting, wanting, because he's jealous *(tuhuu)* of what *we* have."

I do not have a verbal definition of *tuhuu*. The term occurs in a variety of situations in which a person wants something that belongs to somebody else: his skill (for instance, his knowledge of English), or his possessions (his fishhooks, his food, or his wife). It refers also to the wish to participate in another's activities: a hunting trip or a game. It is mostly adults outside one's own *ilammarigiit* who are accused (as always, behind their backs) of feeling *tuhuu*. I am not sure whether children are thought to feel *tuhuu* sometimes, too; my data on this are contradictory. In any case, among adults two kinds of behavior are especially likely to evoke *tuhuu* accusations. If a person asks too often to trade or to be given small gifts, others outside his family will gossip that the demanding person feels *tuhuu*. Or if a person derogates the possessions of another, the same accusation may be made. Actually, it rarely happens that a person makes derogatory remarks except when gossiping within the shelter of the *ilammarigiit*, whose members will *not* accuse him of feeling *tuhuu* toward the person he gossips about.

Tuhuu feelings are a major source of tension among the Utku; or at least the tensions that exist are very often expressed as accusations of *tuhuu* feelings. As I have said, to feel *tuhuu:* envious, jealous, and greedy, is considered very bad indeed, and people are at pains to deny that they do have such feelings. Nevertheless, I judge that *tuhuu* feelings are quite widespread. Sermons denouncing them in general terms are frequent, and more specific accusations are rife in gossip. Jokes on the subject are also very common. There was the game that Pala and others played of pretending to steal food or other goods from the watching owner. And "I'm envious, no joke *(tuhuu, takhaa)!*" was a standard response when a visitor or family member reported a pleasant event, a new acquisition, or a good meal. Such preoccupation with the subject of *tuhuu* feelings certainly is evidence for their prevalence, it seems to me. So is the fact that people occasionally accuse others not of *feeling tuhuu* but of wanting to *be tuhuu*'d, that is, envied. I interpret this to mean either that the accuser feels *tuhuu* and is projecting his feelings onto the other person, or that people want to be *tuhuu*'d and, again, are projecting their feelings onto the other.

Humor

Humor in any culture probably serves a variety of uses,[16] and the Utku culture is no exception. In fact, in certain respects

16. There is a very sizeable body of literature on the nature and functions of humor in western society. Two classic contributions to the subject are those of Freud (1922) and Bergson (1911), but many other philosophers, beginning with Plato and Aristotle, have also dealt with the subject. Recently sociologists and social psychologists have discussed the social functions of humor, its use in maintaining and restructuring social situations (e.g., Coser 1959, 1960; Duncan

humor may be a more important expressive device for them than it is for us, a point on which I shall elaborate below. I have chosen to discuss humor at this point in my exposition because of its importance in the expression of the hostile feelings we have just been considering.

The most common of the Utku terms that refer to humor is *tiphi*. It can be glossed as "to provoke laughter" (in the form *tiphinaq*) or "to feel like laughing" (in the form *tiphihuk-*). These are the verbal definitions I was given. The behaviors that are conducive to laughter are very diverse; indeed, at first I had the impression that people laughed all the time at everything. Easy laughter is a trait that has been noted by most other observers of Eskimos, too, and it is one that I think has been subject to a good deal of misinterpretation, or at least oversimplification, on the part of kaplunas. In the following pages I shall roughly categorize the commonest circumstances in which people tend to laugh, but I must emphasize that these categories are my own; I do not always know whether I have classed a bit of behavior according to the aspects that are salient to the Utku themselves. The categories shade into one another, and any one humorous event may fall into more than one category.

1. When behavior, either one's own or other people's, is unexpected, unusual, or incongruous, though not necessarily either socially inappropriate or morally disapproved, people refer to it as *tiphi* and laugh. Allaq sitting ding-toed; my writing every day (and even before I was out of bed in the morning); the fact that Niqi is shorter than her adolescent adopted daughter; the sound of foreign Eskimo dialects, not to mention foreign languages; unusual tones of voice, facial expressions, and physical antics, all are cause for laughter. Amaruq laughed when she heard some of her father's genealogy for the first time, "because she'd never heard it before," Allaq explained to me.

2. People also laugh at behavior that is socially inappropriate or morally disapproved. I am not sure that *all* such behavior is seen as *tiphi*, but much of it is. Excessive expression of emotion is a form of inappropriate behavior that is often laughed

---

1962; Olesen and Whittaker 1966; Pitchford 1961; Victoroff 1953). A good summary of some of the major theories of laughter is found in Monro (1951). In most respects the classification of Utku humor that I give here and the functions that I suggest it serves are similar to those outlined by Monro (1951:34, 40) and by the sociological authors cited.

at, whether the emotion concerned is grief, amusement, or ill temper of a "childish *(nutaraqpaluktuq)*" sort. Thus when the fourteen-year-old Pamiuq cried (hardly perceptibly) at the thought that his adoptive father was going away and might not return; when Niqi giggled excessively or was "clogged *(qiquq)*"; when Saarak hit her mother with a spoon; or when Raigili shrieked in anger, people laughed. And excessive emotionality is not the only form of inappropriate behavior that is considered amusing. People laughed at the fear of famine (exaggerated, in their view) that made Nilak cache all of the fish he caught during the summer instead of eating some of it as others did theirs. And they laughed when Kanayuq defecated near the waterhole, though at the same time they called it "disgusting."[17]

3. People very often express amusement at errors, stupidities, misfortunes, and minor pains, both their own and those of others. When I picked up the wrong pot lid by mistake, mispronounced a word, or accidentally cut the back instead of the belly out of a fish I was gutting; when one day Allaq, having set out to check the nets, turned around in midstream and went trapping, because her "feet were too cold to check the nets"; when Maata tripped on a hummock with her three-year-old daughter on her back and sent herself and the child flying into a puddle of muddy water; when one of the children accidentally knocked her tooth out while playing in a ball game; when a puppy fell off Mannik's sled unnoticed during a long move and Mannik had to turn back after several arduous miles to find him; and when Allaq unwittingly rubbed caustic insect repellent over her raw mosquito bites, both the victim and their audiences laughed and called the incidents *tiphi*. Indeed, the incidents became comical anecdotes, which were retold again and again for several days, and sometimes longer.

4. Similarly, when the actions of other people interfere with one, it is, or should be, considered *tiphi*, not *hujuujaq* (unpleasant) or *urulu* (annoying). This opposition of emotions was explicitly phrased both by Ikayuqtuq and by Amaaqtuq.

17. The term glossed here as "disgusting" is *quinak;* I have not included it in this discussion of emotional terms, since it only occurs once in the book. The relationship between *tiphi* and such other emotions as displeasure *(hujuujaq)*, annoyance *(urulu)*, fear *(kappia, iqhi)*, and disgust *(quinak)* is not yet clear to me. Sometimes they appear explicitly in opposition, but sometimes they appear together, in reference to the same unpleasant person or event. More systematic data are needed here, as elsewhere.

Ikayuqtuq had been telling me a story (in English) about a kapluna who had prevented Nakliguhuktuq from getting something he, apparently, had very much wanted. Since I thought I sensed indignation or irritation in Ikayuqtuq's voice, I sympathized, saying that she must have felt very annoyed. "Oh no," she corrected me, quickly, "it wasn't annoying, it was funny." The other incident is particularly interesting, because it illustrates how children are explicitly *taught* to substitute feelings of amusement for the feelings of annoyance that are so condemned. Raigili was annoyed at Saarak. Amaaqtuq asked her: "Is your little sister annoying *(urulu)?*" Raigili agreed that she was. "She's not annoying *(urulu)*," said Amaaqtuq, "she's funny *(tiphi)*."

5. Feelings of amusement *(tiphi)* can also be a reaction to fear *(kappia, iqhi)*, or to being startled *(tupak)*. In some instances it may be that the amusement serves to convert the unwelcome feeling of fear into a more acceptable one. We have just discussed a similar mechanism with regard to annoyance. In the case of startle the amusement is, at least sometimes, a reaction to the prior fear reaction. A person who is startled will jump, laugh, and later describe as funny *(tiphi)* the way he (she) jumped *(tupak)*. At other times, however, the two feelings of fear and amusement are described as coexisting. Once, for example, one of the kapluna fishermen who had had a little too much to drink went around to all the "pretty girls," as he called them, offering them gifts of towels and soap. This incident was afterwards spoken of as both frightening *(iqhi)* and funny *(tiphi)*. In this case the amusement seemed to be directed at the fisherman's behavior itself, rather than at the Eskimos' fear; and if conversion from the one feeling into the other was attempted, it didn't quite succeed.

6. Finally, amusement *(tiphi)* can be a reaction to experiences defined as happy or pleasant *(quvia)*. Once Amaaqtuq laughed as she listened to her favorite opera tape (the one that "made one feel like crying"). She explained: "I feel *tiphi* because the music makes me happy *(quvia)*." On another occasion, Inuttiaq had just returned from Gjoa Haven, where he had bought bannock ingredients, milk, gum, and the other foods that delighted the children. Allaq, listening to Raigili giggle at her games, said to her: "You won't feel so *tiphi* when the kapluna food is all gone." One of the giddiest of the women's and children's pastimes is chasing lemming and ermine to stone

them. Here, too, *quvia* and *tiphi* feelings are associated. "Quvianaq; tiphinaq (pleasant and amusing)!" say the women with satisfaction as they come back, panting, from the chase. "Happy, kind, and amusing *(quvia, quya,* and *tiphi)*" is an often-heard trilogy of praise for a person, too.

It would be hard to overstate the pervasiveness of *tiphi* reactions in the daily life of the Utku. "Tiiiiiphinaq (funny)!" was one of the first words that Saarak was taught when she began to learn to talk, and the word punctuated the remarks of her elders, as well. Most of the anecdotes that interlard Utku conversations seem to be told for their *tiphi* quality. Even when the events reported in the anecdotes—bad weather, bad luck in hunting, a runaway dog—are "unpleasant *(hujuujaq),*" "annoying *(urulu),*" or "tiring" the raconteur often ends by saying, "Tiiiiiphinaq!" with the vowel drawn out for emphasis, and the response of the audience is laughter.

Though too great ebullience in the expression of *tiphi* feelings is discouraged as childish *(nutaraqpaluktuq),* unpleasant to see *(hujuujaq),* and conducive to nightmares on the part of the volatile person, nevertheless most Utku do laugh easily. Laughter and joking, *tiphi* feelings and behavior, are important to the Utku in several ways, I think. First, they indicate that a person is happy *(quvia)* and, as we have seen, happiness is a moral good. "We Utku joke a lot," said Inuttiaq. "People who joke a lot are not frightening *(kappia, iqhi).*" Secondly, *tiphi* feelings and expressions can be cathartic. The embodiment of misfortunes and fears in humorous anecdotes, to be told and retold to appreciative audiences, probably constitutes a cathartic use of amusement. Thirdly, *tiphi* reactions serve as a way of expressing, and simultaneously denying, hostility. We have seen this mechanism at work in the Utku habit of viewing inappropriate (annoying or frightening) behavior as "funny."

My impression, based on my own surprise at the situations in which Utku laugh, is that Utku tend to rely more heavily on laughter than we do in all three of these contexts: to relieve the strain that results from misfortune; to convey reassurance that a person is unfrightening, that is, not hostile; and to express subtly one's own hostility.

Analysis of the situations in which people use the word *takhaungngittuq* or, more briefly, *takhaa,* may provide clues to several of the functions of humor among the Utku. *Takhaa* indicates that the speaker is joking, though I am not sure that in all cases the statements to which *takhaa* is attached are defined as *tiphi*. *Takhaa* follows any comment that might possibly be construed as critical, hostile, plaintive *(hujuujaq)*, or jealous *(tuhuu)*: "The girls aren't rowing very hard—*takhaa*." "As soon as Yiini goes home we'll make tea—*takhaungngittuq*." "Terrible weather today—*hujuuuuujaq, takhaa*." "I wish that fish you caught were *my* fish—*takhaa*." The *takhaa* form is often used even when a speaker is gossiping, making hostile remarks behind someone's back. Possibly to whiten the sin of gossiping? I often made the mistake of omitting *"takhaa"* when I was joking with Utku. I thought that my smile and laugh would be sufficient signs of my benevolent intent, but they were not. It occurred to me, then, that perhaps it was necessary to express reassurance so explicitly, because when almost every statement is made in the same even, cheerful voice, it is difficult to distinguish serious from joking remarks on the basis of tone of voice or facial expression.[18]

To tell a person that he makes one feel *tiphi* is a compliment. But since amusement has so many meanings for the Utku, it follows that a person who makes one feel *tiphi* is not always a good or likeable person. In the latter case, one does not *tell* the person he is *tiphi*; one says it behind his back. Ideally, none of the hostile expressions of *tiphi* ever come to the notice of their victims. Children may be laughed at as a form of discipline, but adults are nowadays never laughed at directly, except in good spirits.[19]

18. *Takhaa* also occurs sometimes with statements that refer to the future: "I'm going fishing tomorrow," "Soon the ice will come," and I think here the intent is to protect oneself from being shown a fool when events do not turn out as anticipated. Utku, like the North Alaskan Eskimos of my acquaintance, tend to be reluctant to predict the course of events. Children are laughed at when they ask questions about future events or make statements about the future that are too flat and unqualified. This cautious attitude toward the future finds linguistic expression also in the use of a conditional form, "if," in future statements: "If the ice comes," not *"When* the ice comes." English-speaking Eskimos often express this respect for unknown contingencies by the very frequent use of "maybe." This attitude is further discussed in the section on Reason.

19. Eskimo groups in Alaska and Greenland (see, e.g., Birket-Smith 1953 and Holm 1914) as well as in the Central regions (Rasmussen 1929, 1931, 1932) used to settle disputes and punish social offenders by a form of public ridicule in which caustic lampoons were sung in the presence of the offender. Such ridicule often took the form of "song duels" in which the object was to outdo

Considering the disciplinary use of humor in dealing with children and the sensitivity to criticism, which seems to be expressed in the reassuring use of *takhaa,* one wonders to what extent people are sensitive to being laughed at, even in good spirits. Perhaps they are not sensitive. Being the butt of a joke may make a person feel as though he "belongs" and is accepted by the group; it had that effect on me, very often, when I was openly laughed at, especially after the difficult period when I was excluded from the circle of laughter. The cathartic effect of laughter, too, may obtain even when one is, oneself, the object of amusement, especially if one laughs at oneself first, as Utku often do. Then one can persuade oneself that others are sharing one's own amusement, rather than laughing at one's downfall and humiliation. Nevertheless, it seemed to me that children and even adolescents had to *learn* to appreciate humor that was directed at them. Small children, aged four to seven or thereabouts, were likely to shriek if teased, and older children would listen with an expressionless face, then leave the scene precipitately, followed by the giggles of their elders. Inuttiaq still showed some of this lack of appreciation when laughed at. If he had initiated the joke deliberately, he loved being laughed at, but not otherwise. When his dogs ran away with his sled and dragged him along on the ground behind in sitting position he was not amused, nor was he amused when I laughed at the odd appearance of his newly cut hair, though on the occasion of an earlier haircut he himself had observed jokingly that his hair looked like birch shrubbery. Other adults, however, appeared to share fully, if sometimes a trifle sheepishly at first, in humor that was directed at them.

Fear

The kinds of things that Utku fear and their manner of expressing fear is quite in keeping with the patterns we have seen emerging in the discussions of other emotional concepts. I recorded four terms for fear:

---

one's opponent in mocking verse while the community applauded. The man who received the most applause won the dispute; his opponent's reputation was destroyed. The Utku, whose culture is in many ways very close to that of the Netsilik Eskimos, seem to have had a similar practice in the past. One of the song duels recorded by Rasmussen is between an Utku and a Netsilik Eskimo (1931:345–349 and 515–516).

kappia:	to fear or to rouse the fear of physical injury;
iqhi:	the same as *kappia;*
ilira:	to fear or to rouse the fear of being unkindly treated;
tupak:	to wake from sleep; to startle or to be startled.

I shall deal with the last of these terms first, because I have least to say about it. *Tupak* is commonly heard in two contexts, and both of these were elicited when I asked for a verbal definition of the term. First, it describes a person waking from sleep, and secondly, it describes a person who is startled by a noise or by a sudden unexpected event: a sneeze; the sudden entrance of a visitor; the teakettle boiling over. In the case of dreams that make one *tupak,* the two contexts merge: the dreamer is startled into wakefulness.

A person who is startled *(tupak)* may jump slightly, look around quickly toward the disturbance, or utter half under his breath an exclamation: "Iq (no)!" or "Ee heee!" or "Kahla!" (an expression of caution or warning). Then he will probably laugh and remark, "Tupangnaq (startling)!" I never heard anyone utter a *loud* exclamation when startled; when *I* did so on occasion, I felt very conspicuous and, I think, startled others more than I had been startled. Their response was to laugh at me.

The other three terms recorded refer to fears that I think, on the whole, the Utku consider more serious than momentary startles. At least they tend to be longer lasting. *Kappia* and *iqhi* appear in almost all the same contexts in my data, and Utku, in defining the terms for me, specified that they are "genuinely the same *(atauhimmarik),*" and that both alike apply to fear of dangerous animals, evil spirits *(tunngait),* natural hazards such as thin ice or a rough sea, angry *(urulu, ningaq)* people, and an angry God.[20] I was told that the term *ilira,* on the other hand, refers only to fear of people, not to animals (except dogs, according to one informant), and not to evil spirits, or other hazards. I was not given explicit information on the specific nature of these two kinds of fear: *kappia* and *iqhi* on the one hand and *ilira* on the other. The qualitative difference that I have incorporated in the glosses above (physical fear *vs.* fear of unkind-

20. Information obtained on my second field trip indicates that *kappia* and *iqhi* are not *quite* the same, though my informants had difficulty in defining the difference. My impression to date is that *iqhi* refers to real and immediate dangers, whereas *kappia* refers to imaginary and future dangers, but my data are not yet fully analyzed.

ness) was derived not from Utku statements but from observation of the contexts in which the terms occurred. A comparison of situations in which it is human beings who are frightening is especially illuminating. For instance, when Inuttiaq described a fight he had once watched between two kapluna workmen, he said it had made him *iqhi,* not *ilira;* and when the women talked about drunken kapluna sportsmen who made sexual advances to Utku women, they said the men made them feel *iqhi, kappia;* they did not use the term *ilira.* The latter term, on the other hand, is used in situations in which a person fears that his request will be refused, or that he will be scolded or criticized *(huaq).*[21]

Ilira feelings appear to be very widespread among the Utku. Everybody has such feelings, and quite often, judging from the frequency with which the term occurs in daily speech. Children are said to feel *ilira* toward their parents, that is, their "leaders *(ataniq)."* Whether wives are said to *ilira their* "leaders," that is, their husbands, I do not know. Strangers, especially, both Eskimo and kapluna, are *ilira'*d by everyone, and people of uncertain temper are also *ilira'*d, I think, whether or not they are strangers. Thus, Inuttiaq told me: "People who joke frequently are not frightening *(iliranaittut),"* implying that people who do *not* appear happy *are* frightening.

I have the impression that references to fear of physical danger *(kappia, iqhi)* occur less frequently in everyday speech, whether because incidents provoking such fear occur less frequently, or because these fears are less readily acknowledged, I do not know. Children and other people of little sense *(ihuma)* are thought to frighten *(kappia, iqhi)* easily under circumstances that would not seem dangerous or frightening to a more sensible person. Children more than adults, for example, are said to fear harm from people *(kappia, iqhi),* as distinct from feeling *ilira* toward them. I would expect that the reverse might

21. In the main, the occurrence of these "fear" words in Rasmussen's Netsilik texts (1931 *passim*) bears out the distinctions I have tentatively made here, but not entirely. Instances of *kappia* and *iqhi (Ersi,* in Rasmussen's orthography) support my glosses, but the case of *ilira (ilEra)* is a little more complicated. Rasmussen defines the term as: "is afraid of him, takes heed of him" (1931:455). And four out of five occurrences of the term in his texts refer to fear of people, which supports my data. The nature of the fear, however, is not clear. And in the fifth case (1931:278–279) the fear is one of not knowing how to hunt in a strange country, and here Rasmussen glosses the term as "anxious and perplexed."

be true of *ilira* feelings: that is, they might be associated with the *presence* of *ihuma* and therefore might be thought more characteristic of adults than of children. But the relationship between *ilira* and *ihuma* is a still uninvestigated question.

The following kinds of behavior are all noted on occasion as signs that a person feels *ilira:* silence and constraint; a loss of appetite (or at least an unwillingness to eat) in the presence of the *ilira*'d person; a tendency to smile and agree, if the latter speaks, and a reluctance to disagree or to admit that one does not understand what the feared person says. If a person who feels *ilira* has done something that he thinks will annoy the person he fears—if, for example, he has damaged or lost an object belonging to that person—he may not tell him, even though such secrecy is defined as "lying" and contravenes the strong Utku value of honesty. On the other hand, when a person is very careful to ask permission before acting, such behavior is also sometimes explained as due to *ilira* feelings. In Pala's family, for example, the children always asked their father before helping themselves to the scarce kapluna foods (though not to the commoner Eskimo foods) in the household larder, because they *ilira*'d him: they feared he might not want them to take the food. In this context, the *ilira* feeling was conducive to a socially approved obedience: "Because they feel *ilira* they want to obey." Pala was obviously pleased that his children behaved in this way, and for his part, he never failed to comply with the children's requests—behavior that is recognized as conducive to reassuring a person who feels *ilira*.

Feelings of *ilira* may make a person unwilling to ask favors. Allaq said that her early *ilira* feelings about me had made her reluctant to use my primus without express permission, and reluctant also to ask for food from my supplies. And throughout my stay, whenever I hesitated to ask a favor of someone, for example, when I was uncertain whether to ask a man to bring back flour or oil for me from Gjoa Haven along with his own goods, I was always reassured in the same words: "Don't be afraid *(ilira)* to ask; we are kind *(quya)*; we won't refuse." It may be worth noting that the phrasing of this reassurance is exactly opposite to the phrasing a kapluna might use to a person who hesitates to ask a favor: "Don't be afraid to ask; if it's inconvenient, I'll tell you." Both the Eskimo and the kapluna are afraid that the person of whom the favor is requested will find the request an imposition, but the Eskimo is more afraid than the kapluna of a refusal per se, which he views, more consistently, I think, than the kapluna, as a form of "unkindness (*quyanaittuq*)."

Another way of reassuring others that one is not a person to be *ilira*'d is, as I have said, to smile, laugh, and joke a lot, that is, to convey the impression that one is a happy *(quvia)* person. The desire to communicate such reassurance is, I think, an important reason for the warm and obliging public face that the Utku present.[22]

Since fear of physical injury *(kappia, iqhi)* was less frequently referred to in ordinary conversation, and since I did not make a point of discussing the expression of these feelings with Utku, I have fewer data on the forms that such expression takes. Children who feel *iqhi* or *kappia* sometimes cry and sometimes become silent and motionless or fall asleep. All these signs are recognized by adults. One of the few cases I observed personally in which I knew through their own admission that the Utku adults involved had felt *iqhi* or *kappia* was the meeting between the Eskimo women and the drunken kapluna fishermen to which I have referred. In this case, the women were silent and stood apart, as they always did in the presence of strangers, whether the latter were perceived as people to be *ilira*'d or *iqhi*'d. Perhaps these two kinds of fear are mingled in Utku perceptions of strangers. In any event, I would guess that *iqhi* behavior is quite similar to *ilira* behavior, that both kinds of fear are expressed in withdrawal and, if extreme enough, even in disappearance from the scene.

Anxiety

I recorded two other terms, *huqu* and *ujjiq,* that seem related to the English concept of "fear," but my data on the ranges of meaning of these terms are more than usually scanty. Though I discuss them both here under the rubric of "anxiety," this classification is only a temporary expedient and, moreover, is only partly accurate. The second term, *ujjiq,* was recorded only once in spontaneous speech, and I neglected to ask Utku informants about it, afterwards. The other term, *huqu,* occurred more frequently in ordinary speech, but was exceptionally difficult to elicit by questioning, possibly because of some error in the

22. See the section on Affection concerning other aspects of this obligingness.

phrasing, or unacceptability in the context, of my questions. I include the terms here, nevertheless, because I think they may prove to be important concepts to watch for in future research.

Huqu has both a good and a bad sense. It was the latter that I had difficulty in eliciting. In both senses the term can be glossed broadly as "to respond" or "to pay attention," but the acceptability of the response seems to depend on whether the person one responds to is oneself or someone else. In the latter case, to *huqu* is good. Thus, I was told: "If you ask me to pass you the sugar, and I hear and obey you, I *huqu* you." And again: "If we pray to God to save us from famine and he sends us caribou, he *huqu*s us." Conversely: "If you ask for the sugar and I sit here and ignore you, I don't *huqu* you," and "If God sends us no caribou he doesn't *huqu* us." In this *good* sense, the responsiveness, the *huqu* behavior, results from the protective, nurturant *(naklik)* feelings that are so highly valued. For example, Allaq once, reminiscing about how frightened Saarak had been of me when I first arrived in Chantrey Inlet, said to me: "Did you mistakenly think I *naklik*'d her because of her fear? When she cries from fear [of people] I don't *huqu* it, because there's no real danger." And a letter that I had from Allaq after I left Back River said: "I didn't think I would *huqu* you when you left, but when you set out for Gjoa Haven I did *naklik* you."

But the term also occurs in reference to unpleasant events in one's own life, and in this context to *huqu*, to respond, is unacceptable. This sense of the term I have glossed as "to be upset"; and in this sense it occurs mainly in the negative forms, *huqutikhalaittuq* and *huqutigilaitara* (not to be upset). The unacceptable meaning of the positive forms, *huqutikhaqtuq* and *huqutigijara* (to be upset) was, in fact, so difficult to elicit on questioning that I am not sure the words are really used in this sense, even though I thought I heard them so used, now and then, in spontaneous speech. A description of the first occasion on which I heard a positive form of the word will serve as an example of my difficulties and also, I think, as an example of attitudes toward "being upset." Inuttiaq, talking to Allaq about some chronic pains he suffered, and not realizing that I was listening, said: "I *huqu* them." I asked him to repeat what he had said, so that I could learn the word, but while I was speaking, Pala came in, and Inuttiaq said firmly: "I don't *huqu* them."

And when I tried to elicit the word in a more neutral context, independent of Inuttiaq and his pains, he insisted that there was no such word as the one I thought I had heard him use.

On most occasions when I asked about the term *huqu*, I was given the beneficent meaning: "God hears us when we pray" or "I pass you the knife when you ask for it." Just once when I was struggling to find some way to elicit the unacceptable meaning, Inuttiaq obliged me by giving me two of the "fear" terms (*ilira* and *iqhi*) as synonyms for *huqu*, and he said: "A person who *huqu*s does not make one feel grateful (*hatuq*; that is, he is unpleasant). Children *huqu* often because they have no reason (*ihuma*)." At the time, I suspected that he might be obliging me to the point of inventing the meaning that he knew I wanted to hear, since Allaq demurred, saying, "That's not a very correct word." However, once later when I used the word in this undesirable sense in conversation with Amaaqtuq, I was understood. We were waiting for the plane that was to take the school children away to Inuvik for the winter. I knew that Mitqut, a thirteen-year-old girl who was going for the first time, had had a chronic stomach ache during the last week or so of waiting, so I asked Amaaqtuq whether Mitqut was upset (*huqu*) about going away to school. "I don't think she is very upset (*huqu*)," said Amaaqtuq; "she minds (*huqu*s) less than Kamik did when *she* went for the first time." And when I then asked Amaaqtuq how people who were upset (*huqu*) could be recognized, she had no hesitation in telling me the symptom: lethargy. "People who *huqu* sleep longer hours than others, don't work, and don't play."

The anxiety denoted by the term *ujjiq* is associated with disturbances in nurturant situations, or was so on the occasion in which I heard the word. It was at the time of Qayaq's birth. Saarak had just seen Qayaq nursed for the first time and had cried herself to sleep. Inuttiaq, looking at Saarak's tear-stained face, remarked: "Ujjiqtuq." And when I asked the meaning of the word, he gave as a synonym *tumak(tuq)*, which can be glossed as depression, sometimes associated with loneliness. Later I asked Ikayuqtuq about the word, and she explained: "Saarak realized that she was not the only baby any more and she started to worry: 'What will become of me if they start to look after the baby alone? Maybe they won't have any more time to look after me, now.' *Ujjiqtuq* means something like that: to worry over something and wonder about it, when you have never thought about or realized it before." From this description I judge that, in this instance at least, the "worry" was a fear of no longer being nurtured (naklik'd). However, Ikayuqtuq's explanation was in English, so I cannot be sure that the term naklik would have been used in this context. Much more remains to be investigated, also, concerning other contexts in which the anxiety denoted by the term ujjiq may occur.

Shyness

To a kapluna observer one of the most striking characteristics of Utku and, I think, of other Eskimos, is an absence of self-assertiveness. In contrast to many kaplunas, most Utku adults and children over the age of three or so (except for those who have been exposed to kapluna schooling) seem to blend un-obtrusively into the social background. This quietness may be partly due to a dislike of volatility and noise; children are told to go out when they play too noisily in the vicinity of adults; or they are warned that their exuberance may give them night-mares. It may be due partly to the sanctions on aggressiveness, and to the habit of withdrawal in the face of fear (ilira), which have been discussed above. But there is another factor involved, too, a wish to avoid displaying or exposing oneself before others, which the Utku call kanngu. When I asked what kanngu meant, I was told of several contexts in which the feeling may occur: one may wish to prevent others from seeing one's flesh, one's person, or one's accomplishments (or lack of accomplishments). The term occurred in all of these contexts in spontaneous speech, as well. If Saarak stayed quietly on the ikliq near Allaq and refused to run around conspicuously on the floor when there were many people present she was said to feel kanngu. When Nilak refused to join the other men in acrobatic games during the Christmas festivities, he was said to feel kanngu. "He knows how to somersault," I was told; "he just doesn't want people to see him." When Pamiuq refused to speak English with me, though he knew the words, people said it was because he felt kanngu. And when Allaq took a dislike (hujuujaq) to the boot trim she was embroidering, she said: "I feel kanngu about it; I'm not going to work on it any more until there is no one around to see." In addition, I once heard kanngu feelings, like naklik feelings, cited as a motive for avoiding the use of a person's name.

Nilak one day surprised me by asking me, without any context that I could discover, how *kanngu* feelings are expressed in my country. I told him that people who feel *kanngu* are sometimes silent and refuse to talk, they blush, avoid others' eyes, and do not like to be seen. "It's the same here," he said.

The development of reason *(ihuma)* is, I think, considered to be a prerequisite for the growth of *kanngu* feelings, and in Chapter 3 I have suggested some of the means by which children may learn to feel *kanngu*. The first signs of the feeling in children are noted with interest. One day when Saarak was wrestling with me in fun, she slipped on the iglu floor and fell. Picking herself up, she ran into Pala's iglu (it was the second winter, when our iglus opened into each other), and then after a moment, she ran back again into her own iglu and resumed wrestling with one person and another, making "cute," self-conscious grimaces the while. Her mother watched her. "She's beginning to feel *kanngu*," she said. "If she hadn't felt *kanngu*, she would have stayed in her grandfather's iglu and visited, instead of coming back here and making faces. She wouldn't have minded falling."

I am not sure what people's attitudes toward *kanngu* feelings are. If my impression is correct that such feelings are considered a concomitant of *ihuma*, which is valued, this might indicate that they are favorably regarded, but whether the absence of *kanngu* feelings is unfavorably regarded, I do not know. The feelings may simply be considered natural, without moral connotations. The absence of *kanngu* is occasionally remarked on. When one of the kapluna fishermen showed Pala a magazine picture of a scantily clad lady, Pala said: "She doesn't feel very *kanngu*." But I could not tell whether the remark was critical or neutral.

Loneliness

I recorded three terms associated with the idea of loneliness and have tentatively glossed these as follows:

hujuujaq: to be unhappy because of the absence of other people, or to rouse such unhappiness; to feel or provoke a variety of other unpleasant feelings, including hostility;

pai: to be or feel left behind; to miss a person who has gone;

tumak: to be silent and withdrawn in unhappiness, especially because of the absence of other people.

Of these three, the term *hujuujaq* is the most complex. The "central" meaning of the term, that is, the meaning one is given when one asks for a definition, is loneliness. Utku say that *hujuujaq* is the way one feels in the absence of people whose company one desires. One feels *hujuujaq* when someone one loves *(naklik, unga)* leaves, or when one is left behind or is all alone.

In spontaneous usage, however, *hujuujaq* has a range of meaning much broader than the English "loneliness," so that it is difficult to find an appropriate gloss. One alternative might be to use an inclusive term like "unhappiness," "depression," or "distress." But because of the incompleteness of my present data, I have preferred not to assign an Eskimo gloss corresponding to a single English concept, but have simply classified the contexts in which the term occurs in spontaneous speech and drawn no firm conclusions regarding the nature of the emotional common denominator. Even the classification that I present here must be provisional, however, as was my classification of the functions of humor, above. Like the latter, this classification is based on the understanding of the ethnographer, an outsider, rather than on the understanding of the Utku themselves, and the two views may not coincide. That is, if an Utku were asked to state exactly what it is that makes him feel *hujuujaq* in the situations in which he uses that term, I do not know whether he would select the same defining characteristics that I have selected.

1. First and most important of the contexts in which the term *hujuujaq* appears is, of course, the one described above: the absence of loved people. The salience of loneliness as an experience not only for Utku but for other Eskimos will be discussed further, below.

2. Shifting to the hostile contexts, the term occurs as a rejecting comment on disapproved behavior or on people who engage in such behavior, for example, lying, stealing, getting angry, engaging in un-Christian sexual activity.

3. It occurs also as a rejecting comment on the physical appearance, behavior (however intrinsically neutral), or mere

presence of people one dislikes. Thus in our camp *hujuujaq* comments tended to focus on the unpleasantly volatile Niqi. It seemed to make no difference whether she laughed and smiled, or was silent and still, whether she visited or sat at home, people said her behavior made them *hujuujaq*. If she made flabby oatmeal or let the lamp flare so that it sooted up the iglu, it made people *hujuujaq*. Just having to pass her where she fished on the way to one's own fishing hole made one feel *hujuujaq*.

4. *Hujuujaq* feelings may also arise when a person feels himself inappropriately placed in a social situation, even though he may like and approve of the other people present. Thus, a single man alone in a group of women, or a woman alone among men will feel *hujuujaq*: "Not shy *(kanngu)* but *hujuujaq*," I was told.

5. Unpleasant physical conditions and tasks are also often described as conducive to *hujuujaq* feelings. Cold, wet, or windy weather; the approach of autumn darkness; the presence of mosquitoes; hunger; the recession of the water in the rapids after the exciting spring torrents all make one *hujuujaq*. Inuttiaq, watching the kaplunas skim around with their outboards, remarked that paddling a canoe made one *hujuujaq*; and Allaq said the same of having to scrape the iglu floor when she was tired.

6. Being thwarted in one's intentions or one's wishes, or being unable to make a decision can also make one *hujuujaq*. When a man had bad luck in hunting; when Inuttiaq told Allaq to go home from fishing, which she enjoyed, to make bread; and when Saarak, by refusing to get dressed, prevented her mother from going to check the fishnets: *hujuujaq*. The frustrating agent can be located within the person, too. Allaq one day described as *hujuujaq* her uncertainty as to whether she wanted to sew or fish; and on another occasion she called a boot she was embroidering *hujuujaq*, before she discarded it in dissatisfaction with the design she was creating.

Hujuujaq feelings in all of the above contexts are frequently expressed,[23] but very often only in the form of matter-of-fact

23. It is interesting, and somewhat curious, considering the frequency with which *hujuujaq* feelings are expressed in everyday conversation, that the word does not occur even once in Rasmussen's Netsilik texts (1931 *passim*), unless it has escaped me, owing to his orthography.

comment. People do not complain; they remark, often with a little laugh that seems to deny the seriousness of the condition: "One is made to feel *hujuujaq (hujuujaqnaqtuq)!*" In tone, and in the ease with which it is expressed, the exclamation "Hujuujaqnaqtuq!" is similar to the exclamation "Urulunaq!" which was discussed above.

People say that when they feel *hujuujaq* they do not feel very much like laughing and joking, and they recognize *hujuujaq* feelings, like *huqu* feelings, in lethargy and droopiness. Once when I yawned in the presence of a visitor, the visitor joked that I must be feeling *hujuujaq* (as I was). And once a sagging pole that was supposed to be supporting the dome of our thawing iglu was jokingly called both *hujuujaq* and "sleepy." Children are more likely than adults to express *hujuujaq* feelings in visible lethargy, and I think therefore that such unsocial behavior is less acceptable than mere neutral comment. But lethargy may sometimes be felt by adults, too, even though it was not perceptible to me. I judge this because adults occasionally say they are not hungry when they are alone and feeling *hujuujaq*, when traveling by themselves, for instance, and because one cure for *hujuujaq* feelings is activity. Allaq told me that children, when they feel *hujuujaq*, are sent outdoors to play, and that adults usually occupy themselves with work. Once, jokingly perhaps, she referred to her sewing as her "activity for making me stop feeling *hujuujaq*." Sometimes, too, an adult counters *hujuujaq* feelings by indulging himself with a special food: making bannock or putting milk in his tea during a season when it is scarce and therefore usually reserved for children. But the commonest cure that I observed for *hujuujaq* feelings was to seek out company. Children, too, are sent out to visit even more often than to play when they feel *hujuujaq*. Occasionally, a man moves camp in order to be with a person he misses, and once in a while, too, when real company is not available, people build cairns that "look like people" to keep them company.

Both my own experience in Alaska and the reports of anthropologists working with other Eskimo groups [24] indicate that loneliness (I am speaking for the moment of the English concept, not of the *hujuujaq* concept which includes loneliness) is a salient experience for Eskimos generally. Both North Alaskan

24. E.g., Derek Smith, conversation re: Aklavik, 1965; Norman Chance (1966: 78–79); and my own field experience in North Alaska, 1961 and 1962.

and Aklavik Eskimos talk frequently about loneliness. They are solicitous to prevent others from feeling lonely, and often give their own or others' loneliness as a reason for going visiting. In general, the frequency and openness with which loneliness is mentioned by English-speaking Eskimos contrasts strikingly with the absence of reference to other emotions in their English speech. It is clear from what has been said that the salience of *hujuujaq* feelings among the Utku and the ways in which these feelings are expressed are similar to the Eskimo pattern observed elsewhere. Utku, like other Eskimos, are often solic-itous to prevent or to counter *hujuujaq* feelings in a person who is temporarily left alone. Thus a woman whose menfolk are away on a trip will tend to have many more visitors than usual, because "she must be lonely *(hujuujaq).*" I observed occasions, however, when a person's expression of *hujuujaq* feelings aroused covert amusement *(tiphi)*, rather than solic-itude, and I think this may have been because the *hujuujaq* feeling was overexpressed in these cases. This is only a guess, however, as I do not know what specific aspects of the situation inspired the amusement. I know only that the amusement was directed at Niqi and at children, who shared a tendency to withdraw visibly into lethargy when they felt *hujuujaq*, re-gardless of the cause.

I am not sure that *hujuujaq* feelings are all of a piece: that lethargy, for example, results from the *hujuujaq* aroused by a person's lying or stealing, as it does from the *hujuujaq* aroused by the absence of a loved person. As I have mentioned, I see two dimensions in the concept: hostility or rejection, on the one hand, and loneliness (possibly a feeling of being rejected?), on the other; and I think that lethargy and its cures: working, eating, visiting, are associated primarily with the feeling of loneliness. I suggest also that the latter meaning of the word may explain why the hostile feelings that are labeled *hujuujaq* are more readily acknowledged than are those that are labeled *ningaq, qiquq,* and *urulu*. Since *hujuujaq* feelings, when they refer to loneliness, are pro, rather than antisocial, and are curable by prosocial actions, one need not be reluctant to ex-press these feelings; and this socially acceptable sense of the word may mask its more hostile meanings. It is possible, how-ever, that these "two dimensions" that I see do not exist for the Utku.

The other two terms that I have included in this section,

pai and *tumak,* seem to be partial synonyms of *hujuujaq.* Unfortunately, my data on both are sparse, as they occurred far less frequently than *hujuujaq* in everyday speech.

The term *pai* occurs in two senses, both of which I obtained in verbal definitions. In the form *paijuq, pai* has a purely factual sense; it refers to the state of being left behind when other people leave the iglu, the camp, the resting place on the trail, or any other place where one happens to be. In the form *painngujuq,* on the other hand, *pai* has an emotive meaning; it refers to the feeling engendered by being left behind. Like most other negative feelings the *pai* feeling is most commonly expressed in a matter-of-fact comment: "One feels left behind." It was difficult for me to recognize other kinds of behavior indicative of the feeling, but I suspect that, as in the case of *hujuujaq,* depression invisible to me was sometimes there. One day, for instance, I had come back from a visit to a neighbor woman, Pukiq, whose husband was away on a trip to Gjoa Haven. Allaq asked me: "Does Pukiq feel left behind?" When I said I did not know, Allaq asked what Pukiq was doing. I said she was sitting alone in her iglu, drinking tea, whereupon Allaq said: "Yes, she feels left behind."

I have suggested that *pai* in this emotive sense seems similar to *hujuujaq,* and we shall see that it also resembles *tumak.* I was, in fact, given both of the latter terms in explanation of *pai.* A third synonym I was given is *unga,* which I have glossed as "the wish to be with someone one loves." I lack data regarding the people in whose absence one is most likely to feel *pai,* but such data as I do have support my impression that it is primarily members of one's *ilammarigiit* that one misses: mothers miss children, wives miss husbands, one branch of the family misses another with which it usually camps, and so on.

The term *tumak* I first noted in October, two months after my arrival at Back River, when Inuttiaq was speaking to me about the vacation trip I proposed making to Gjoa Haven. The plan was that I would travel to Gjoa Haven with two of the younger men when they went in to trade in early November and that Inuttiaq would pick me up there when he came to trade, later in the month or perhaps in December. Since he had changed his mind several times about the date of his trip, I began to fear that he might not go at all but would leave me in Gjoa Haven for the rest of the winter. I do not remember how I conveyed my apprehension to him, but he saw it. He said, "I'll come for you, as soon as we run out of tea and tobacco." And then, after a pause: "We'll miss *(tumak)* you." When I asked the meaning of the word, he dropped his head onto his chest and sagged his body as he sat on the ikliq.

On later occasions, I almost always recorded the term in the same context, that is, in response to a person's absence. The one exception was the occasion described in the section on Anxiety, when Saarak "worried *(ujjiq)*" about being supplanted at her mother's breast. Then, as I have said, Inuttiaq gave me *tumak* as a synonym for *ujjiq,* in explanation of the latter term. Here, perhaps, *tumak* refers to the loss of an established relationship, rather than to the physical absence of a loved person.

The behavior symptomatic of *tumak* feelings, which Inuttiaq demonstrated so graphically, seems very similar to the behavior characteristic of *hujuujaq* and, I think, also of *pai,* though, as I have said, my data on the latter emotion are sparse. The terms *pai* and *tumak,* however, differ in one important respect from *hujuujaq:* they do not seem to be used in situations where the feeling is hostile.

This concludes the discussion of terms that denote emotions and emotional behavior. It remains only to define three evaluative words that occur in the narrative and to discuss the concept of reason, which also has evaluative connotations and is of major importance in understanding the emotional reactions of the Utku.

Evaluative Words

The words to be defined here are: *ihluaq* and *ihluit; naamak;* and *pittau* or *pittiaq.*

The terms *ihluaq* and *ihluit* are used in a wide variety of contexts. I have glossed *ihluaq* as: "to be correct or convenient; to be or feel all right, good, proper, comfortable, or safe." *Ihluit* is the negative form of the base. If I perform a task correctly, it is *ihluaq;* if I make a mistake, it is *ihluit.* If I am typing busily when a would-be visitor looks in, or if I am obviously preparing to go out, the visitor may ask before entering: "Ihluittunga? Am I inconveniencing you?" If my host wants to make sure that I am comfortably seated, or if the weather is cold, windy, and wet, he may ask: "Ihluitpit? Are you uncomfortable?" If I love *(naklik)* someone so much that I cannot sleep well in his absense, I feel *ihluit.* If I love a bit less intensely, it is (or, I feel) *ihluaq*. If I refrain from stealing, losing my temper, and other immoral acts, I am *ihluaq*. If I have been ill and recover, I become *ihluaq* (well) again. If I am given what I ask for in trade, it is *ihluaq*.

These terms are very similar, perhaps identical, to *naamak* and its negative form, *naamangngit*. I am unable to say at this point whether there are any differences in their ranges of meaning.

Pittiaq and *pittau* are not word bases like most of the other terms that have been discussed. They are compound forms, consisting of a base, *pi-*, which can mean either "object" or "act," depending on whether the elements that follow convert the word into a noun or a verb, and a modifying postbase, *-ttiaq-* or *-ttau-*, which is used in a great variety of contexts to express liking or moral approval. So *pittiaq* and *pittau* can be glossed as references to a good or likeable object, person, or act. In the narrative, the terms appear in three contexts. In Chapter 3, section III, Allaq explains the fact that Raigili has brought in my urine can, unasked, by saying: "She likes *(pittiaq)* you, because you give her kapluna food to eat." In section VI of the same chapter, she asks me which of the two children, Raigili or Saarak, I like *(pittiaq)* better, and she describes which one her sister Amaruq likes better by illustrating how the latter used to kiss the one child more intensely than she now kisses the other. Finally, in Chapter 6, when Pala and Amaaqtuq write to Nakliguhuktuq about my poor behavior, they defend their own treatment of me by saying: "We have tried to be good *(pittiaq)* to her here." And when one evening Amaaqtuq finds me pleasant *(quvia)*, amusing *(tiphi)*, and kind *(quya)*, she notes in the letter she is writing: "Now she's becoming very nice *(pittau)*."

Reason

Reason *(ihuma)*, like nurturance *(naklik)*, holds a central place in the Utku system of values. The concept is central in two senses. First, it is invoked to explain many kinds of behavior and secondly, it is an important measure of the quality of a person. As nurturance *(naklik)* defines the *goodness* of a human being, so reason *(ihuma)* defines *adultness*. The sense in which this is so will, I hope, become clear below.

There are three terms to be discussed in this section on Reason:

ihuma:	refers to all functions that we think of as cerebral: mind, thought, memory, reason, sense, ideas, will;
nutaraqpaluktuq:	literally "resembles a child," a derogatory epithet applied to persons who evince a lack of *ihuma;*
ayuq:	to be difficult, unable, or impossible. In the form *ayuqnaq* this term means approximately "it cannot be helped" and is the classic expression of Eskimo "fatalism," a concept that I shall discuss further below.

(a) Mental functions (*ihuma*)

Ihuma, as the gloss indicates, is a broad term referring to abilities that we consider mental or intellectual. I do not know exactly how the Utku conceptualize *ihuma,* whether they think of it as a physical entity, locate it in the head, or associate it with the brain, as we do, but their view of the functions of this mental force are in many ways very similar to our views. It is the possession of *ihuma* that makes it possible for a person to respond to his surroundings, physical and social, and to conform to social expectations. *Ihuma* is, or should be, a governing force in an adult's life. Children are thought to be born without *ihuma,* and accordingly, as I have said, adults who show little evidence of possessing *ihuma* are spoken of as "childish *(nutaraqpaluktuq)."* The Utku believe that normally children acquire *ihuma* gradually as they grow. Child training consists very largely in providing the child with experience in the form of verbal instructions and models to imitate, which, as his *ihuma* grows, the child will remember, reflect on, and use. In the absence of *ihuma* no instruction is possible, and this is a major reason why parents do not discipline small children. Why bother? They will not remember.[25]

The growth of *ihuma* can be recognized in various kinds of behavior. When a child becomes conscious or aware *(qauji),* when he begins to recognize people and to remember, to understand speech and to talk, people remark that he is beginning to acquire *ihuma.* Later signs that *ihuma* is developing are the beginnings of self-consciousness *(kanngu),* the first spontane-

25. The beliefs of the North Alaskan Nunamiut concerning the nature and functions of *ihuma (ishuma)* are parallel in many respects to those of the Utku (Gubser 1965: 211–212, 221–222).

ous attempts to help with household tasks, the acquisition of skills, obedience to the directions of one's elders, voluntary conformity to religious proscriptions, such as not fishing or working on Sunday, and above all, the growth of emotional restraint. A person who has (or uses) *ihuma* is cheerful but not giddy. He is patient in the face of difficulties and accepts unpleasant but uncontrollable events with calmness; and he does not sulk *(qiquq)*, scold *(huaq)*, get annoyed *(urulu)*, or attack others physically *(ningaq)*. A person who lacks *ihuma*, on the other hand, whether adult or child, will be immoderately happy *(quvia)* and playful and will laugh too easily. He will be easily upset *(huqu)* and frightened *(kappia, iqhi)*, unable to distinguish between real physical danger and imaginary danger; and he will be easily angered or annoyed. He will cry, scold, and hit on slight provocation, but on the other hand, he will also forget his distresses quickly. His perception of his environment and his judgments concerning the future will be confused and unrealistic. When a child cries for a favorite food and fails to stop crying when told the food is gone, that is because he lacks *ihuma*. If a person grossly misjudges the length of a familiar trip, repeatedly sees imaginary caribou in the distance or hears nonexistent airplanes, as Niqi did, such errors are attributed to lack of *ihuma*. A baby's wish to be the center of affectionate attention is also attributed to a lack of *ihuma*, and I think that an adult who showed a similar wish would be defined as lacking *ihuma*, but this supposition needs to be checked.

(b) Childishness *(nutaraqpaluktuq)*

Most if not all of the kinds of behavior attributed to lack of *ihuma* are labeled "childish *(nutaraqpaluktuq)*," since in the Utku view, as we have seen, child nature is characterized by a lack of *ihuma*. Thus, for example, impulsiveness and excessive display of feeling often draw the epithet "childish." If a person is too ebullient, smiling too broadly, laughing too easily; if he gets "clogged up *(qiquq)*," or scolds *(huaq)*, he is said to be "childish." When Niqi moved with the quick, jerky motions that were characteristic of her, or when once Inuttiaq shot at a bird that had already flown as he aimed, people whispered, "Nutaraqpaluktuq (he/she is childish)."

Other kinds of devalued behavior are also defined as childish, and it is worth noting that in at least one such case the Utku point of view is the exact opposite of the kapluna viewpoint.

Kaplunas tend to consider Eskimos "childish" because the latter do not plan for the future with the elaborate caution characteristic of kaplunas. The Utku, on the other hand, labeled as childish the one man among them, Nilak, who was more provident than the others. When he and his family cached all the fish they caught during the summer instead of using some of them for patau, Allaq gossiped: "They are like children *(nutaraqpaluktut); they are afraid (kappia)* of a food shortage." And when Niqi's perceptions were confused, Allaq defined her, too, as childish. Thus, after I returned from my Gjoa Haven holiday, when I reported to Allaq that Niqi had said I seemed thinner than when I went away, Allaq said: "She's confused; she was lying; she is just like a child."

It is evident from the above that childishness *(nutaraqpaluktuq)* and simplemindedness *(ihumakittuq)* are in general considered unattractive traits. In a very small child, to be sure, the absence of *ihuma* arouses protective *(naklik)* feelings in older people. As we have seen, parents explain their reassurance and indulgence of a small child in terms of the latter's lack of *ihuma,* his inability to understand reality. But such tolerance lessens as the child grows older. After he has given evidence of possessing *ihuma,* he is expected to use *(atuq)* it, and if he does not, his parents may shame him by remarking that it seems as though he *has* no *ihuma.*

Adults who behave childishly or in a manner that shows lack of sense *(ihuma)* are also condemned, as we have seen, in gossip sessions. In spontaneous speech, childish *(nutaraqpaluktuq)* traits may be referred to as *tiphi* (funny), but twice when I asked whether a person who was *nutaraqpaluktuq* was *tiphi,* Allaq said, "No, not *tiphi; hujuujaq.*" The circumstances determining the choice of *tiphi* or *hujuujaq* are not yet clear to me. It is apparent, however, that all childish or simpleminded behavior is not condemned with equal vehemence. Allaq and I once talked about the way the Utku reacted to Niqi's brother and to another adult in the previous generation, who, according to Allaq, had been more defective than Niqi; they had been unable to talk correctly and had lacked adult skills. Since Allaq had characterized Niqi's "lack of sense *(ihuma)*" as *hujuujaq* (unpleasant), I asked her whether these other individuals had also made people feel *hujuujaq.* "No," said Allaq, "they were pleasant (made one feel *quvia); it's only when people get angry *(qiquq)* or annoyed *(urulu)* easily that they make one feel *hu-*

juujaq." Since one of the individuals under discussion had died and the other had moved away, I was unable to compare Allaq's statement with actual behavior, but it appears that in theory, at least, bad temper is more to be condemned than lack of skill *(ayuq).* Attitudes toward the latter will be discussed further, below.

(c) Other undesirable states of *ihuma (ihumaqaruiqtuq* and *ihumaquqtuuq)*

In addition to simplemindedness *(ihumakittuq,* literally: "insufficiency of *ihuma"),* there are in the Utku view two other undesirable states that are related to the concept of *ihuma.* One of these is the complete disappearance of *ihuma (ihumaqaruiqtuq);* the other, a superabundance of *ihuma (ihumaquqtuuq).*

In the category of people in whom *ihuma* has "disappeared," we find sick people who are unconscious or delirious, unaware of their surroundings, and insane people during psychotic episodes. Such loss of consciousness is thought to be caused by the intervention or intrusion of evil spirits and is, naturally, feared *(kappia, iqhi).*

Having "too much *ihuma"* also has unpleasant and sometimes dangerous implications, as Utku explained to me. Although it is obvious that one must have *ihuma* in order to be considered a fully competent member of society—the word *ihumataaq,* "wise person," denotes a leader in a community—nevertheless moderation is essential in this as in other matters; too much *ihuma* is as bad as too little. A person who has too much *ihuma* concentrates too much on one idea, one thought. In its most harmless form such concentration is viewed as "inconsiderate." [26] More than one anthropologist who has worked with Eskimos, very possibly including myself, has been characterized by his hosts as *ihumaquqtuuq,* because he put such pressure on them with his continual visits, questions, more visits, and more questions, when the Eskimos would have preferred to work, talk, eat, or sleep, unbothered by the anthropologist. In one case, the anthropologist was ultimately defined as "a little crazy," because he was too consistently interested in a single subject, but unfortunately, since my informant spoke in English, I do not know what Eskimo term was applied to the man.

26. This statement and those that follow in this paragraph were made not by an Utku but by a Netsilik informant, in English.

The more frightening *(kappia, iqhi)* implications of having "too much *ihuma*" have to do with the nature of such a person's anger. These implications have been mentioned already in the discussion of ill temper. When a person who has "too much *ihuma*" gets angry *(ningaq, urulu)* he gets *very* angry, and he stays angry. He does not recover easily, as does a person with "little *ihuma*"; he broods, and the angry thoughts can make the person who is brooded about fall ill or die. For this reason, people say they are careful not to arouse resentment in a person who has "too much *ihuma*." Old people, in particular, are thought to be *ihumaquqtuuq,* so when an old person is ill or housebound, people will take care to visit him and be kind to him, so that he will not begin to "think *(ihumagi-)*." It is quite possible that in some cases physical violence, as distinct from murderous brooding, may also be feared from a person who is *ihumaquqtuuq,* but I have no evidence of this.

An interesting question for future research concerns the nature of attitudes toward the various states of anger or violence that are attributed to different conditions of *ihuma.* The few data I have give me the impression that attitudes may vary in some respects, depending on whether the anger or the violence is attributed to too little *ihuma,* to its disappearance, or to too much of it. In the section on Ill Temper I mentioned the possibility that anger due to too much *ihuma (ihumaquqtuuq)* was more to be feared than anger due to too little *(ihumakittuq).* And earlier, I said that I thought attitudes toward ordinary *(ihumakittuq)* ill temper in adults seemed different from attitudes toward the violence *(ihumaqaruiqtuq)* of insanity. I said that the murderously insane woman, Ukalik, was feared *(kappia, iqhi)* when her *ihuma* disappeared, but that the tenor of remarks about her seemed to indicate that during her normal interludes she was as well regarded as anyone else, whereas the adults of "little sense *(ihumakittuq)*" who displayed bad temper might or might not be feared but were consistently disliked (aroused *hujuujaq* feelings). However, I do not know whether I would find these distinctions maintained in behavior if I had an opportunity to observe the insane Ukalik in the same camp with Niqi, Nilak, and Uyuqpa, the three people who were guilty of ordinary bad temper.

To sum up the discussion of *ihuma* so far: As I understand it, the Utku (and, I think, other Eskimos) consider intellectual faculties *(ihuma)* to be the sine qua non of socialization and of adult competence.[27] To its presence and use *in moderation* they attribute much if not all social behavior: the acquisition of practical skills and experience, the learning of values and precepts, and appropriate patterns of social and emotional responsiveness. And conversely, most inappropriate behavior is thought to be due either to an absence of *ihuma* or to too much *ihuma*. This view bears a marked resemblance to our own, though in the emphasis on moderation and in the concept of "too much *ihuma*," one does find some difference between the Eskimo and kapluna points of view. Both cultures believe that "brooding" and "worrying" are harmful,[28] but we tend to consider the *physical* effects of unhappy thoughts limited to the thinker himself, in the form of psychosomatic symptoms, whereas the Eskimos believe that such thoughts can do physical harm to the person brooded about as well as to the brooder himself.

(d) Fatalism *(ayuqnaq)*

One other attitude associated with *ihuma* deserves mention, because it is essential to an understanding of Utku responses to feelings. I refer to an attitude of resignation to the inevitable, which is expressed by the word *ayuqnaq*. The base of this word, *ayuq-*, refers to difficulty or impossibility inherent in situations and to inability in people. The form *ayuqnaq* means approximately "it cannot be helped" or, more precisely, "forces outside me make it impossible." The concept is often interpreted as expressive of a fatalistic inclination to give up in the face of adversity (see, for example, de Coccola and King 1955:9 and *passim*). It is the bane of many kaplunas who have dealt with Eskimos, because some of the actions it explains are so strikingly in contrast with kapluna ways. To the kapluna way of thinking, an Eskimo finds more difficulties "inevitable" than strictly necessary. Examples are cited in which an Eskimo lost in a snowstorm sits down and waits to die, instead of struggling to regain his bearings, or in which he fails to make the "all-out effort" that a kapluna would make to cache meat for a lean period, pre-

---

27. See, for example, Gubser (1965:211). And it is also significant, I think, that Damas (1963:54) says his Igluligmiut informants who disapproved of marriage between foster siblings applied the label "simpleminded *(ihumakittuq)*" to people who practiced this form of marriage.

28. Here, too, there seem to be parallels between Utku belief and the beliefs of other Eskimos. Gubser (1965:212 and 220), writing of modern Alaskan Eskimos, quotes Eskimo statements concerning the evils of "thinking too much."

ferring to live for the moment and let the future take care of it-self. In the first case it is a feeling of hopelessness that is implied: the goal is valued but striving for it is in vain. In the second case the feeling is one of insouciance: the value of the goal is denied; it is not worth striving for.

Both of these feelings can indeed be components of a fatalistic attitude and probably are characteristic of Eskimos under cer-tain circumstances. But in my own experience with the Utku it was a third sort of emotional overtone that seemed to me to be central to the *ayuqnaq* concept, namely a rational, pragmatic recognition of a situation that is seen as unpleasant but unavoid-able: the lost goal does matter but since wailing will not help, it is childish to fret. The person who says calmly, "Ayuqnaq," instead of flying into a dither is using his *ihuma;* he is behaving like an adult. Rasmussen (1931:190), speaking of the Netsiling-miut, puts it very well: "(I)t is a point of honour with them to preserve their equanimity... One might almost say that they have the happy gift of being able to rest content with the knowl-edge of sorrow; they know that they have suffered but do not become emotional, merely making some quiet utterance such as that it could not be otherwise."

One hears the word *ayuqnaq* all the time, in all sorts of situ-ations in which uncontrollable circumstances, including the will of others, interfere with one's own wishes or activities, and always it is said in a perfectly calm or mildly amused tone: when one spills one's only cup of tea or loses one's knife; when a sud-den thaw brings the iglu dome heavily down on one's head dur-ing a sound sleep; or when one's neighbor evades a request for assistance.

The word occurs also in contexts in which the source of dif-ficulty is one's own lack of skill or knowledge. People said it when they tried and failed to repeat English words that I pro-nounced for them; and the fourteen-year-old Ukpik said it when he failed to perform successfully in the men's acrobatic games at Christmas time.

The moral code, too, makes allowance for situations that are *ayuqnaq,* that "can't be helped." The rule says that a person who has food or fuel of his own should not take the supplies of another, but if one has none, that is, if food or fuel is *ayuqnaq,* unavail-able, then it is all right to take a little from another's cache, pro-vided one tells the owner one has done so. Similarly, although it is ordinarily forbidden to work, travel, hunt, or fish on Sunday under pain of hell fire, nevertheless, if someone is very ill, acutely hungry, or otherwise in extraordinary need, then the rule may be broken with impunity, because "it can't be helped (*ayuqnaq*)."

The excuse of *ayuqnaq* is rather extensively used in this moral context; people readily define situations as *ayuqnaq* when discomfort or inconvenience would result from scrupulous adherence to the rule. When the river froze on Sunday to the right depth for building qaqmaqs, qaqmaqs were built, "because it can't be helped." A woman who had been too tired to clean a fox on Saturday might do it on Sunday, in order not to delay the start of a trading trip that had been planned for Monday, "because it can't be helped." And one June Sunday when our kerosene supply was running low, Inuttiaq, thirsty for a cup of tea, gave me permission to go and collect lichen with which to make a fire, "because it can't be helped."

The base *ayuq-* does not occur only in the form *ayuqnaq,* which refers to difficulties inherent in situations. It also occurs in forms that refer to inability in persons. People who failed to pronounce English words, and Ukpik when he failed at somersaulting, instead of saying, "Ayuqnaq (it can't be helped)," might have said, "Ayuqhaktunga (I can't do it, or: I don't know how)." The most "unable (*ayuq*)" creature of all is, of course, a baby. Kaplunas in an Eskimo environment are also "unable (*ayuq*)" in many ways. A state of inability or ignorance (*ayuq*) is one of the qualities in a person that arouses feelings of protective concern (*naklik*) in others. I was several times assured: "You are someone to be taken care of (*naklik*'d), because you *ayuq*." And when Inuttiaq was explaining to me why the kapluna fishermen should not borrow his canoe, he said: "The kapluna leader gave us those canoes because he feels protective (*naklik*) toward us. He feels *naklik* toward us, and not toward kaplunas, because we are more *ayuq*." I think he meant that it is more difficult for the Utku than for the kaplunas to acquire the material goods necessary for survival.

Appendix II. Table of Seasonal Activities

November
Temperatures below freezing; hard snow. All move to winter campsite, Amujat; build iglus; net whitefish and jig a few salmon trout; trap fox; make first trading trips to Gjoa Haven.

December-January
Net whitefish; trap fox; make trips to Gjoa Haven.

February
Same as December; in addition, jigging for salmon trout begins again.

March
Families begin to move to spring campsites; take up whitefish nets; jig for salmon trout; trap fox; make trips to Gjoa Haven.

April
Warmer weather; softening snow. Remaining families move to spring campsites; some jig for salmon trout; others hunt seal; still others live on previous autumn's fish caches; fox trapping ends; make last trips to Gjoa Haven before break-up.

May
Snow melts. All move into tents; seal hunters live on seal; others continue to use previous autumn's fish caches; shoot birds; hunt birds' eggs.

June
River ice breaks up. Fish with reel or throwline for salmon trout and char; shoot birds; perhaps net a few whitefish.

July
Move to summer campsites; spear migrating salmon trout and char; dry much of the fish catch for late summer, autumn, winter use.

August
Jig or fish with reel and line for salmon trout and char; make toys to trade to kapluna fishermen.

September
Snow begins to stay on the ground. The able-bodied hunt caribou for one to three weeks;[1] others net whitefish to cache for
winter and spring; fish with reel and throwline for salmon trout
and char; women begin to sew caribou winter clothes and braid
winter fishlines of caribou sinew.

October
River freezes. Build qaqmaqs; jig for salmon trout; net whitefish
to cache; women sew and braid as in September.

---

1. Caribou are hunted sporadically at all other seasons, too, whenever their
tracks are seen near camp, but autumn is the only season in which caribou are
actively and vigorously sought.

Appendix III. Composition of Families

Chart I: Divisions between Extended Families (Ilammarigiit): Relationships among Household Heads

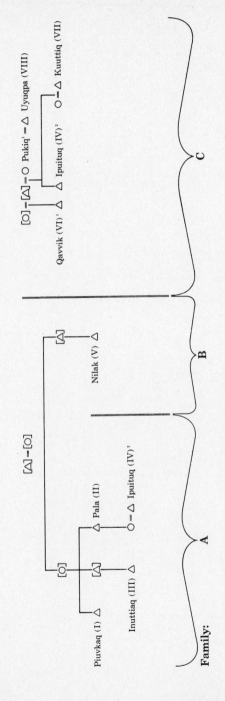

Key
△ means male.
○ means female.
[] means deceased.
= means married.
Vertical lines represent lines of descent.
Roman numerals refer to households in Chart II.

Notes
1. Qavvik (VI) and Pukiq were betrothed as children, but Pukiq was taken by Qavvik's father, instead.
2. Ipuituq (IV) is a member of two families: A and C.

Chart II: Household Composition of Extended Families: [1]

Key

△ means male.
○ means female.
[] means deceased.
= means married.
⚮ means betrothed.

Vertical lines indicate lines of descent.
Symbols in a vertical row *not* connected by a vertical line represent siblings.
⚮ means that the person whose name appears adjacent to the diagonal slash is an adopted child.
Capital letters associated with extended families refer to Chart I.

FAMILY A

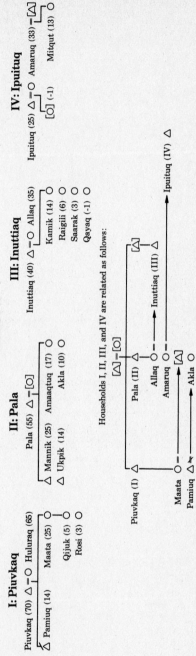

I: Piuvkaq

Piuvkaq (70) △ = ○ Huluraq (65)

Pamiuq (14) △ — Maata (25) ○ — ○
Qijuk (5) ○
Rosi (3) ○

II: Pala

Pala (55) △ = [○]

Mannik (25) △ — Amaaqtuq (17) ○
Ukpik (14) △ — Akla (10) ○

III: Inuttiaq

Inuttiaq (40) △ = ○ Allaq (35)

Kamik (14) ○
Raigili (6) ○
Saarak (3) ○
Qayaq (-1) ○

IV: Ipuituq

Ipuituq (25) △ = ○ Amaruq (33) = [△]

[○] (-1)   Mitqut (13) ○

Households I, II, III, and IV are related as follows:

[△] = [○]

Piuvkaq (I) △

Pala (II) △

Allaq ○ → Inuttiaq (III) △

Amaruq ○ → Ipuituq (IV) △

Maata ○

Pamiuq △⚮

Akla ○

FAMILY B²

V: Nilak

Nilak (40) △ = ○ Niqi (40)
└ Tiguaq (17) ○

VI: Qavvik

Qavvik (55) △ = [○]
└ Putuguk (22) = ○ Kanayuq (18)
　└ △ Qanak (-1)

FAMILY C³

VII: Kuuttiq

Kuuttiq (25) △ = ○ Uyaraq (23)
├ △ Nainnuaq (-1)　　Niaquq (4) ○

VIII: Uyuqpa

[○] = Uyuqpa (50) △ = ○ Pukiq (60)
├ △ Itqiliq (18)
├ △ Qingak (14)
└ △ Ukhuk (11)

1. The households shown here constituted independent dwelling units during much of the period between August 1963 and January 1965, but this was by no means a fixed situation. Households that sometimes combined into single dwelling units are: II, III, and/or IV; IV and VI; and VI and VII.

The ages given in parentheses are approximate.

Only family members whom I knew are listed. Those who were absent or deceased are not shown, except where necessary to show lines of descent or connection. The two young bachelors Tiriaq and Tutaq, who "floated" from household to household, are not shown.

Their residence patterns are described in the list of People at the front of the book.

2. This household does not constitute an extended family (*ilammarigiit*) B that remains in Chantrey Inlet.

3. Ipuituq's household (IV) also belongs to this *ilammarigiit*, but its composition is shown in the chart of Family A.

The interrelationships of households IV, VI, VII, and VIII appear on Chart I.

Glossary I. Eskimo Terms Other than Emotion Terms

hiqluaq: a fish storage chamber attached to an iglu or qaqmaq. It is built of snow blocks like a tiny iglu and opens into the living iglu by way of a hole just big enough to crawl through.

ikliq: the sleeping-and-living area of a dwelling. Every dwelling, whether iglu, qaqmaq, or tent, is divided into two sections: the *natiq* or floor (see below) and the *ikliq*. The ikliq is the rear half of the dwelling, that is, the half farthest from the entrance. It is where the family sit, eat, work, and sleep. In an iglu, the ikliq is a platform about two feet above floor level; in the other dwellings the ikliq is at ground level.

iglu (phonemically *iklu):* a dome-shaped snow house, the winter dwelling.

ila or *ilagiit:* family; associates. These terms refer to a category of people that has no precise limits. The base *ila* also occurs in the text in the forms *ilammarigiit* (real family), *ilammarilluangngittut* (less-real family), and *ilammaringngittut* (not-real family). The ilammarigiit is an extended family consisting of genealogical or adoptive siblings *(nukariit)* and the children of those siblings. These terms are discussed in section VI of the Introduction to the book.

kapluna: the Canadian Eskimo word for a white person. The Eskimo word is phonemically *qaplunaaq*. It is often anglicized in arctic literature as *kabloona*.

natiq: the floor space of an iglu, qaqmaq, or tent. This is the front half of the dwelling, the area by the doorway, where food is kept ready to cook or eat, and where visitors stand. Unlike the ikliq, the natiq is always at the level of the entrance.

patau: boiled fish steaks and heads.

qaqmaq: a circular dwelling, which has walls of ice or snow blocks (occasionally stone in the old days) and is roofed with a tent. It is used in autumn and occasionally in spring when the weather is not cold enough for iglu building but is too cold for tent living.

qulliq: a shallow, flat-bottomed, semi-circular lamp in which blubber or tallow or (in Chantrey Inlet) fish oil is burned for light and heat. The term is also applied sometimes to other oil-burning lamps and to the concave rocks that occasionally substitute for real qulliqs.

ulu: a semilunar all-purpose woman's knife.

uyautaut: a rope stretched taut between two points, for example, passed between the walls of an iglu, about six feet above the ground and used for acrobatics.

Glossary II. Emotion Terms

The following glosses are not to be understood as accurate and complete definitions. They are given only for quick reference, as an aid to memory. The terms are discussed more fully in Appendix I.

Where two or more terms are identically glossed this means that they are used in many of the same contexts and that I am ignorant of any contrast that may exist between them.

Two of the terms given here, *ayuq* and *ihuma,* do not denote emotions or behaviors associated with emotions, but an understanding of these concepts is essential to an understanding of Utku responses to feeling.

ayuq: to be difficult, unable, or impossible. In the form *ayuqnaq* it means approximately "it cannot be helped."

aqaq: to communicate tenderly with another by speech or by gesture (other than touch).

hatuq: to be grateful or to arouse gratitude; to be kind, unfrightening, helpful.

huaq: to aggress verbally against another; to scold.

huqu: to respond, to pay attention, either to the needs of others or to disturbing events in one's own life.

hujuujaq: to be unhappy because of the absence of other people, or to rouse such unhappiness. This term is also used in a wide variety of other situations that provoke unpleasant feelings, including hostility.

ihluaq: to be correct or convenient; to be or to feel all right, good, proper, comfortable, or safe.

ihluit: is the negative form of *ihluaq* (above).

ihuma: refers to all functions that we think of as cerebral: mind, thought, memory, reason, sense, ideas, will.

ilira: to fear or to rouse the fear of being unkindly treated; to respect, with overtones of fear.

iqhi: to fear or to rouse the fear of physical injury.

iva: to lie next to someone else in bed, with connotations of affectionate cuddling.

kanngu: to wish to avoid displaying or exposing oneself before others.

kappia: to fear or to rouse the fear of physical injury.

naamak: to be correct or convenient; to be or to feel all right, good, proper, comfortable, or safe.

naamangngit: is the negative form of *naamak.*

naklik: to feel or to arouse concern for another's physical or emotional welfare; to wish or to arouse the wish to be with another. Of the terms commonly used to express positive emotion, this one is used in the widest range of situations.

ningaq: to aggress physically against another; to feel or to express hostility.

niviuq: to wish or to arouse the wish to kiss or touch another affectionately.

nutaraqpaluktuq: to resemble a child. This is a derogatory term applied to individuals who evince a lack of reason *(ihuma*— see above).

pai: to be or to feel left behind; to miss a person who has gone.

piyuma: to want something, often with connotations of greed, jealousy, or envy.

pittiaq/pittau: to be good, likeable, or worthy. The term may refer to an object, a person, or an act.

qiquq: literally, to be clogged up with foreign matter; metaphorically, to be on the point of tears; to feel hostile.

quya: to be grateful or to arouse gratitude; to be kind, unfrightening, helpful.

quvia: to feel or to arouse happiness, pleasant emotions.

tiphi: to provoke laughter or to feel like laughing.

tuhuu: to want for oneself a possession or a skill belonging to someone else; to want to participate in another's activities or life situation; or to rouse such wishes.

tumak: to be silent and withdrawn in unhappiness, especially because of the absence of other people.

tupak: to wake from sleep; to startle or to be startled.

unga: to wish or to rouse the wish to be with another person.

ujjiq: to realize, fearfully; to worry.

urulu: to feel, express, or arouse hostility, annoyance; also used as an expression of sympathy at the misfortunes of others.

References

Back, George. *Narrative of the Arctic Land Expedition to the Mouth of the Great Fish River and Along the Shores of the Arctic Ocean, in the Years 1833, 1834, and 1835.* London: John Murray, 1836.

Balikci, Asen. *Development of Basic Socio-Economic Units in Two Eskimo Communities.* National Museum of Canada Bulletin No. 202. Ottawa, 1964.

Bergson, Henri. *Laughter.* Translated by Cloudesley Brereton and Fred Rothwell. London: Macmillan, 1911.

Birket-Smith, Kaj. *The Chugach Eskimo.* Nationalmuseets Skrifter, Etnografisk Raekke No. 6. Copenhagen, 1953.

Boas, Franz. *The Central Eskimo.* Annual Reports of the Bureau of American Ethnology No. 6. Washington, 1888.

Brower, Charles D. *Fifty Years Below Zero.* New York: Dodd, Mead, 1942.

Chance, Norman A. *The Eskimo of North Alaska.* New York: Holt, Rinehart and Winston, 1966.

Coccola, Raymond de, and Paul King. *Ayorama.* Toronto: Oxford University, 1955.

Coser, Rose Laub. "Some Social Functions of Laughter," *Human Relations,* 12:171–181, 1959.

———— "Laughter among Colleagues," *Psychiatry,* 23:81–95, 1960.

Damas, David. *Igluligmiut Kinship and Local Groupings: A Structural Approach.* National Museum of Canada Bulletin No. 196. Ottawa, 1963.

———— Personal communication, 1963.

Duncan, Hugh Dalziel. *Communication and Social Order.* New York: Bedminster, 1962.

Freeman, M. M. R. Personal communication, 1967.

Freuchen, Peter. *Book of the Eskimos.* New York: Bramhall House, 1961.

Freud, Sigmund. *Wit and its Relation to the Unconscious.* Translated by A. A. Brill. Vienna, 1922.

Gilder, William H. *Schwatka's Search.* New York: Scribner, 1881.

Gubser, Nicholas J. *The Nunamiut Eskimos: Hunters of Caribou.* New Haven: Yale University, 1965.

Guemple, D. L. "Saunik: Name Sharing as a Factor Governing Eskimo Kinship Terms," *Ethnology*, 4:323–335, 1965.

Hobart, Charles. *Eskimos in Residential Schools in the Mackenzie District.* Northern Co-ordination and Research Centre, Department of Northern Affairs and National Resources. Ottawa, 1965.

Holm, G. "Ethnological Sketch of the Angmagsalik Eskimo," *Meddelelser om Grønland*, 39:1–147, 1914.

Ingstad, Helge. *Nunamiut.* London: Allen and Unwin, 1954.

Jenness, Diamond. *The Life of the Copper Eskimos.* Report of the Canadian Arctic Expedition 1913–1918, vol. 12. Ottawa, 1922.

—— *The People of the Twilight.* New York: Macmillan, 1928.

Jenness, Jonathan. Personal communication, 1966.

Lantis, Margaret. *The Social Culture of the Nunivak Eskimo.* Transactions of the American Philosophical Society, n.s., vol. 35, pt. 3. Philadelphia, 1946.

—— *Eskimo Childhood and Interpersonal Relationships.* Seattle: University of Washington, 1960.

Marshall, Robert. *Arctic Village.* New York: Literary Guild, 1933.

Mauss, Marcel, and M. H. Beuchat. "Essai sur les variations saisonnières des sociétés Eskimos," *L'Année Sociologique*, 9:39–130, 1904–1905.

M'Clintock, F. L. *A Narrative of the Discovery of the Fate of Sir John Franklin and His Companions.* London: John Murray, 1859.

McGill, F. G. Personal communication, 1968.

Metayer, Maurice. *I, Nuligak.* Toronto: Peter Martin, 1966.

Monro, D. H. *Argument of Laughter.* Melbourne: Melbourne University, 1951.

Mowat, Farley. *People of the Deer.* Boston: Little, Brown, 1952.

—— *The Desperate People.* Boston: Little, Brown, 1959.

Olesen, Virginia L., and Elvi Waik Whittaker. "Adjudication of Student Awareness in Professional Socialization: The Language of Laughter and Silences," *Sociological Quarterly*, 7:381–396, 1966.

Pitchford, Henry Grady. "The Social Functions of Humor." Unpublished doctoral dissertation, Department of Sociology, Emory University, 1961.

Poncins, Gontran de. *Kabloona.* New York: Reynal and Hitchcock, 1941.

Rasmussen, Knud. *Intellectual Culture of the Iglulik Eskimos.* Report of the Fifth Thule Expedition 1921–1924, vol. 7, no. 1. Copenhagen, 1929.

――――― *The Netsilik Eskimos: Social Life and Spiritual Culture.* Report of the Fifth Thule Expedition 1921–1924, vol. 8, nos. 1–2. Copenhagen, 1931.

――――― *Intellectual Culture of the Copper Eskimos.* Report of the Fifth Thule Expedition 1921–1924, vol. 9. Copenhagen, 1932.

Smith, Derek. Personal communication, 1965.

Spencer, Robert F. *The North Alaskan Eskimo: A Study in Ecology and Society.* Bureau of American Ethnology Bulletin No. 171. Washington, 1959.

Stefansson, Vilhjalmur. *My Life With the Eskimo.* New York: Macmillan, 1951.

Thalbitzer, William. "The Ammassalik Eskimo," *Meddelelser om Grønland,* 40:569–739, 1941.

Thompson, Charles T. Personal communication, 1967.

Vallee, Frank G. *Kabloona and Eskimo in the Central Keewatin.* Northern Co-ordination and Research Centre, Department of Northern Affairs and National Resources. Ottawa, 1962.

Van de Velde, Frans. "Les règles du partage des phoques pris par la chasse aux aglus," *Anthropologica,* 3:5–14B, 1956.

Victoroff, David. *Le rire et le risible.* Paris: Presses Universitaires de France, 1953.

Washburne, Heluiz Chandler, and Anauta. *Land of the Good Shadows.* New York: John Day, 1940.

Wilkinson, Doug. *Land of the Long Day.* New York: Henry Holt, 1956.

Williamson, Robert. Personal communication, 1968.